Women, Death, and Literature in Post-R

Less ☑ 20% 60.00

48.00

Purchased by:_____

WOMEN, DEATH AND LITERATURE IN POST-REFORMATION ENGLAND

In *Women, Death and Literature in Post-Reformation England* Patricia Phillippy studies the crucial literal and figurative roles played by women in death and mourning during the early modern period. By examining early modern funerary, liturgical, and lamentational practices, as well as diaries, poems, and plays, she illustrates the consistent gendering of rival styles of grief in post-Reformation England. Phillippy emphasizes the period's textual and cultural constructions of male and female subjects as predicated upon gendered approaches to death. She argues that while feminine grief is condemned as immoderately emotional by male reformers, the same characteristics that open women's mourning to censure enable its use as a means of empowering women's speech. Phillippy calls on a wide range of published and archival material that dates from the Reformation to well into the seventeenth century, providing a study that will appeal to cultural as well as literary historians.

PATRICIA PHILLIPPY is Associate Professor of English at Texas A&M University. She is the author of *Love's Remedies: Recantation and Renaissance Lyric Poetry* (1995) and numerous articles on early modern women writers, literature, and culture.

WOMEN, DEATH AND LITERATURE IN POST-REFORMATION ENGLAND

PATRICIA PHILLIPPY

CAMBRIDGE
UNIVERSITY PRESS

PUBLISHED BY THE PRESS SYNDICATE OF THE UNIVERSITY OF CAMBRIDGE
The Pitt Building, Trumpington Street, Cambridge, United Kingdom

CAMBRIDGE UNIVERSITY PRESS
The Edinburgh Building, Cambridge CB2 2RU, UK
40 West 20th Street, New York, NY 10011-4211, USA
477 Williamstown Road, Port Melbourne, VIC 3207, Australia
Ruiz de Alarcón 13, 28014 Madrid, Spain
Dock House, The Waterfront, Cape Town 8001, South Africa

http://www.cambridge.org

First published 2002

Printed in the United Kingdom at the University Press, Cambridge

Typeface Baskerville Monotype 11 / 12.5 pt.   *System* LaTeX 2ε [TB]

A catalogue record for this book is available from the British Library

ISBN 0 521 81489 8 hardback

To my mother, Betty,
my sisters, Susie and Barbie,
and
my daughter, Iman

et à la mémoire de Khédidja, ma belle-mère

"it was a pretious child, a bundle of myrrhe, a bundle of sweetnes,
shee was a child of ten thousand . . ."

Contents

Illustrations

Acknowledgments

In many ways this is a communal work, and I am indebted to a number
of individuals and institutions who have contributed to the research and
writing of this book over the course of the past four years. I appreci-
ate and have profited from the comments of readers of both early and
later versions of these chapters, including Harriette Andreadis, Randall
A. Dodgen, Marian Eide, Margaret J. M. Ezell, Katharine Goodland,
Katherine E. Kelly, Howard Marchitello, and Naomi J. Miller. Much of
the material of this book was presented at conferences, where the input
of colleagues including Elaine V. Beilin, Elizabeth Hageman, Margaret
Hannay, Cristina Malcolmson, Kathryn McPherson, Susan Gushee
O'Malley, Elizabeth Harris Sagaser, Mihoko Suzuki, and Linda Vecchi
greatly improved the chapters as they were being conceived and written.
In England, I received helpful guidance from Robert Yorke, Archivist
of the College of Arms; Sue Irwin, Vicar of the Parish Church of All
Saints, Bisham; David Pascall; Patricia Burstall; Marian Hodgkinson;
Peter Davison; and J. B. Stevenson. The astute insights and friendly
contributions of Katharine Goodland throughout the completion of this
project have shaped the book and my thoughts on its subject significantly.

Two grants from the Program to Enhance Scholarly and Creative
Achievement at Texas A&M University enabled me to conduct crucial
research in Summer, 1997 and again in Summer, 1999. Faculty fellow-
ships from the Center for Humanities Research at Texas A&M University
in 1997–98 and 1999–2000 supported this research in its nascent and final stages, and the valuable insights of the faculty fellows and members
of the Center have aided me throughout. Women's Studies Faculty Fellowship support and a research bursary from Dean Woodrow Jones, Jr.,
of the College of Liberal Arts, Texas A&M University, allowed me to
complete my research in England in Summer, 1999. I am also indebted
to Hyonjin Kim, whose work as a graduate assistant greatly contributed
to compiling the research on which the first chapter is based.

Special thanks go to Lael Parish: our lively, month-long conversation on the subject of this book in Summer, 1997, thoroughly informs my treatment of it here. And as always, my greatest thanks go to my husband, Fouad Berrahou, and my daughter, Iman, who offer daily instruction in the art of living.

Portions of chapter 1 have appeared in *English Literary Renaissance* 31 (2001): 78–106. Reprinted by permission of the editors.

Portions of chapter 4 have appeared in Naomi J. Miller and Naomi Yavneh (eds.) *Maternal Measures: Figuring Caregiving in the Early Modern Period*, 319–32. Ashgate, 2000. © Naomi J. Miller and Naomi Yavneh.

A version of chapter 7 appears as 'The Mat(t)er of Death: The Defense of Eve and the Female *Ars Moriendi*' in *Debating Gender in Early Modern England, 1500–1700* edited by Cristina Malcolmson and Mihoko Suzuki, published by Palgrave Macmillan, a Division of St. Martin's Press.

Introduction

To mark the death of Falstaff, Shakespeare's *Henry V* pauses briefly for an elegiac scene in which Pistol both expresses his particularly masculine grief over the loss of the knight, and convenes a community of male mourners to lament him:

No; for my manly heart doth ern.
Bardolph, be blithe; Nym, rouse thy vaunting veins;
Boy, bristle thy courage up; for Falstaff he is dead,
And we must ern therefore.[1]

Pistol's view of mourning as a product of the manly heart and his catalogue of the unexpected characteristics required of male mourners to perform the rite to which he calls them (blitheness, vaunting veins, and courage) are typical of a consistently gendered treatment of mourning, its affects, and its emblems in post-Reformation England, in which feminine lament is devalued, redefined, and circumscribed in ways that "contribute to new definitions of manhood."[2] Sixteenth and seventeenth-century death manuals, representational forms, and cultural practices revised women's long association with ritualistic acts of mourning to portray feminine sorrow as excessive, violent, and immoderate, while representing men's grief – both stoic and short-lived – as correcting and improving upon "wivishe" mourning.[3] Abraham Darcie's memorable rhyme, "No sorrow, is a signe of brutish state, / But yet too much proves one effeminate,"[4] summarizes the gendering of grief frequently put forth by early modern writers. As Juliana Schiesari has argued, this censure of immoderate grief as effeminate is part of "the Renaissance assault on mourning, and particularly on mourning insofar as it took place as a collective women's ritual."[5] To counterbalance the long history of religious representations of the three Maries mourning for Christ (including their embodiment in medieval liturgical dramas),[6] Pistol gives us a secular, masculine group of mourners engaged in collective sorrow for the

I

incongruous passing of the Henriad's preternaturally robust ("Give me life!")[7] Falstaff.

If Pistol's staging of a male pietà rewrites the gendering of an ear-lier, popular tradition of women's collective ritual lament, however,[8] the scene goes on to offer *not* the masculine performance of mourning, but the feminine report of the deathbed itself. In doing so, it marks the move-ment from the public acknowledgment of death, enacted through male lament, to death's occurrence as a semi-private affair located within a do-mestic sphere over which women preside.[9] Mistress Quickly, the female attendant upon and witness to Falstaff's final illness and death, describes his demise as an *exemplum* of the Protestant "good death," complete with a deathbed recantation (of sack, if not of women):

'A made a finer end, and went away and it had been any christom child. 'A parted ev'n just between twelve and one, ev'n at the turning of the tide; for after I saw him fumble with the sheets, and play with flowers, and smile upon his finger's end, I knew there was but one way; for his nose was as sharp as a pen, and 'a [babbled] of green fields. 'How now, Sir John? quoth I, "what, man? be a' good cheer.' So 'a cried out, 'God, God, God!' three or four times. Now I, to comfort him, bid him 'a should not think of God; I hop'd there was no need to trouble himself with any such thoughts yet. So 'a bade me lay more clothes on his feet. I put my hand into the bed and felt them, and they were as cold as any stone; then I felt to his knees, and so up'ard and up'ard, and all was as cold as any stone.[10]

The specific nature of the Hostess's attendance on Falstaff is clearly subject to censure when read in light of the decorum governing the be-haviors of both dying Christians and those who comfort them, frequent topics of early modern treatises on the art of death. Miles Coverdale's 1555 translation of Otto Werdmuller's *ars moriendi*, for example, numbers among the works of mercy "to visit the sick, to have compassion upon them, to give them good counsaile, and to comfort them."[11] Deathbed attendants must exhort the dying Christian to "turne . . . for Goddes sake from all creatures, to [his] creator and maker," lead him to a confession of sins, and pray for the soul of the dying.[12] While the Hostess's attempt to comfort Falstaff by urging him *not* to turn to his creator displays a bittersweet disregard for the wisdom of post-Reformation advisers on death, the fact of her attendance on the body in death, like Pistol's "erning," responds to the gendering of early modern death ritual and lament which ascribed to women not only the task of attending the dy-ing, but also the "menial and gendered" work required to prepare the body for disposal.[13] Thus the wills of widowers and bachelors frequently leave sums to landladies or hostesses for assisting them during their final sickness and death: John Stayworthe of Pagelsham (d. 1562), for example, leaves 12d "to Fanner's wife my keeper," and John Wyncome of Saffron Walden (d. 1563) similarly bequeaths goods "to my hostess Agnes wife of Richard Prowe."[14]

Economic and literary evidence such as this points toward the unpaid work of attending and mourning the dying and the dead performed by women within households – work which placed them collectively, prior to the initiation of any public acts of mourning, in a uniquely intimate relationship with the body of death. This relationship, and the cultural currents informing, describing, and defining it, comprise the subject of this book. By examining early modern funerary, liturgical, and lamentational practices, diaries, poems, plays, and instructional and consolatory works on death and dying, I illustrate the consistent gendering of rival styles of grief in post-Reformation England and, conversely, the period's constructions of male and female subjects (both textual and cultural) as predicated upon gendered approaches to death. The chapters that follow argue that while feminine grief is condemned as immoderately emotional by male reformers, the same characteristic that opens women's mourning to censure enables its use as a means of authorizing and empowering women's speech.

By engaging both material and representational aspects of the topic, I mean, on the one hand, to ground images of women's grief in the work they performed in carrying out the rituals that attended the demise of the physical body. This recovery and documentation of the material practices of early modern women's mourning offer new and valuable insights into an aspect of post-Reformation culture that has been largely overlooked. On the other hand, I explore the ideological functions of images of women's mourning in early modern England to describe the cultural work performed by these characterizations of female grief. Based on archival research as well as textual reflections of the face of early modern death, this study reconstructs the variety and extent of women's lamentational practices in the period and explores the different inflections given to gendered grief within male and female-authored texts.[15] Since early modern women's intimacy with death's materiality characterizes them as empathetically *physical* mourners, I am concerned not only with images of feminine lamentation but also with the period's treatments of the female body in death; for example in discussions and deployments of the art of embalming, male-authored narratives of women's deathbed performances, and the active polemical afterlife of Elizabeth I's royal corpse.

My treatment of works by women including Aemilia Lanyer, Anne de Vere, Mary Carey, Katherine Philips, Elizabeth Russell, Rachel Speght, Alice Sutcliffe, and Isabella Whitney clearly illustrates the widespread interest of early modern women in the matter of death and suggests the material practices lying behind their encounters with it.

Despite an impressive number of recent historical, literary and cultural studies devoted to early modern death and mourning,[16] little attention has been paid to women's crucial roles, both literal and figurative, either in the period's changing lamentational practices or in its highly gendered formulations of the nature and meaning of grief. This oversight is unfortunate, since ample historical evidence shows that, prior to the appearance of professional undertakers in the late seventeenth century,[17] women were the most frequent and most immediate attendants on bodies in death, carrying out the tasks of caring for the dying, washing and winding the corpse, watching the body during its period of laying-out, conducting ritual lamentations within the home, serving as almsfolk and mourners for funerals, and donning mourning garments according to cultural rules of relation and class. Moreover, a surprisingly large number of texts written by early modern women concern themselves explicitly with the matter of death and bespeak not only women's widely-perceived intimacy with death's physical ravishments[18] but also the unusual license to write and publish afforded to women in proximity to death – from lamenting wives and mothers, to women who speak with the heightened authority granted by the deathbed.[19] Approaching early modern literary works with an eye to their participation in the period's gendered culture of grief permits suggestive contextualizations of canonical works by male authors and familiar texts by women, as well as introductory readings of relatively unknown authors and works.

Throughout this study of the early modern gendering of mourning and its rituals, I engage the pressing question of the means by which contemporary criticism should approach the history of emotion, and offer a model for this approach that takes its cue from the affective structures emergent in post-Reformation English culture itself. Recent criticism devoted to exploring and theorizing the period's emotions has increasingly sought to historicize affect in order to refine our understanding of early modern subjectivity. As this project has unfolded in contemporary criticism, it has itself been gendered in ways that parallel the early modern gendering of grief. As Sarah Tarlow observes, "to express a past which involves passion, fear, grief and love is to risk one's own credibility, to appear soppy, romantic and weak. The emotional in our society is consistently devalued. The associations of overt emotionality are with femininity, weakness. Emotional responses are held to be incompatible with proper rational thought and seriously out of place in an academic discipline."[20] As ideological resistance to the project of constructing historical genealogies of the emotions has begun to relax, the pragmatic problem of identifying reliable forms of evidence with which to support this undertaking remains. In my discussions of textual and cultural gestures of mourning, I assume that individual subjectivity is always both created and mediated by one's interactions with available generic forms of representation and self-representation. For example, Elizabeth Russell's affective epitaph on the death of her daughters, Anne and Elizabeth Hoby, in 1570 (discussed in detail in chapter 6) insists upon the depth of her maternal grief at the girls' loss – "eheu mea viscera," she complains, "o my visceral pangs"[21] – but does so through the conventional language of memorial poetry and in the difficult and technically restricted medium of the engraved inscription on monumental stone. If emotions are at once physiologically experienced and culturally conditioned, their expression is partially reflective of the individual's interiority and partially determined by the conventions, including linguistic and artistic conventions, in which they are cast.[22] The ceremonial practices and discourses attending early modern grief clearly mediate the direct expression of emotional subjectivity, while emotions are, at the same time, "shaped and evolved by the very process of expressing them."[23] As such, this study describes the pervasive, commonplace figures and gestures employed in post-Reformation England to express grief, and attends closely to the personal nuances and inflections given to these figures in the hands of individuals, particularly insofar as these inflections relate to the subject's gender and the period's gendering of affective states.

This book responds to two recent, influential studies by Lynn Enterline and Juliana Schiesari which discuss, in different ways, the gendering of early modern mourning and melancholia. Both firmly rooted in contemporary psychoanalytic theory, Schiesari sees melancholia as an elite male affliction that displaces and appropriates female mourning,[24] while Enterline asserts that melancholic narcissism in male-authored works "disturbs the representation of a stable, or empirically knowable, sexual difference."[25] Although both studies helpfully indicate that scenes of mourning enable self-conscious constructions of early modern masculinity, their assumptions of the congruity between early modern culture and psychoanalytic theory proceed, for the most part, without reference to the gendered culture of grief in the period itself, and fail to consider the cultural practices that suggest the period's discrimination between clearly gendered versions of mourning.[26] Contextualizing the matter of melancholia within early modern discourses on death and mourning indicates the overwhelming tendency of these works to describe insuperable grief as feminine and to feminize the male mourner who veers into immoderation. This book, therefore, supplements and corrects these studies of melancholic male subjectivity through a thorough reading of the vast literatures of early modern death and dying and, most significantly, through examinations of works by early modern *women* which not only deploy mourning in ways demonstrably different from those of male authors, but also begin to construct portraits of male and female subjectivity as rooted in the period's gendering of grief.

My insistence upon viewing constructions of gendered subjects in relation to the literary and cultural – that is, generic – discourses that enable them has significant implications for the project of recovering and reading early modern women writers as it occurs in my work and more generally in contemporary criticism. In interpreting men's and women's texts, whether intended for publication or not, I demonstrate that authorial presence is constructed and gendered according to the literary and cultural codes by which rival styles of mourning are also identified as masculine or feminine. Accordingly, I delineate the features of early modern formulations of gendered grief with which individuals, as readers and writers, interact, and seek intersections between textual and cultural performances of grief informing men's and women's voices within their works of mourning. Instead of assuming that the fact of a writer's sex has a necessary bearing on representation and self-representation within his or her work, I read broadly across a variety of discourses and genres in order to return the affective and gendered aspects of mourning persistently to the cultural practices from which they emerge. As such, my approach offers a corrective to critical discussions of women writers that assume the woman's voice simply as a by-product of an author's sex.

Moreover, I understand this historicization of gender as defining the features of both early modern authors within texts, and early modern bodies in death and mourning. To account for post-Reformation constructions of the gendered body of death, therefore, I accept Judith Butler's statement that "gender is not to culture as sex is to nature; gender is also the discursive/cultural means by which 'sexed nature,' or 'a natural sex' is produced and established as 'prediscursive,' prior to culture, a politically neutral surface *on which* culture acts."[27] This book traces similar aspects of early modern grief, which, both in written documents and cultural enactments, are assumed to be essentially linked to sex while they, in fact, work to construct through normative performances the sexes to which they refer. Thomas Laqueur's persuasive description of the "one-sex model" of gender identity expounded by early modern medicine, with its claim that "there was no true, deep essential sex that differentiated cultural man from woman,"[28] lends additional support to this view of the performative qualities of early modern lamentation and illuminates the quantitative gendering of grief in terms of moderation and excess, characteristics easily aligned with the period's constructions of sexed bodies. Butler's questions, "Does sex have a history? Does each sex have a different history or histories?"[29] are here answered in the affirmative, and reformulated to ask, "In what ways do the histories of (male and female) mourning also constitute the histories of the sexes themselves?" To provide an answer, the chapters that follow both assume and demonstrate the affinities between gender and mourning as performative acts that "constitute the identit[ies they] purport to be."[30] Construed in this way, cultural and textual performances of mourning offer points of contact between the gendering of authorial presence and of the body of mourning itself, while women's excessive grief, enacted as natural through the bodily gestures which constitute it, "become[s] the site of a dissonant and denaturalized performance that reveals the performative status of the natural itself."[31] This transgressive quality of women's mourning, which threatens to expose the structures upon which gendered discourses of grief and, by extension, gendered subjects are constructed, is a continual object of policing in male reformers' condemnations of feminine lamentational excesses, and a vital source of energy and empowerment in women's expressions of loss.

This book supports two complementary arguments presented in two main sections and anticipated by a summary chapter, on Mary Magdalene's post-Reformation career as scripture's quintessential mourner and her legacy in the culture of grief and in Lanyer's *Salve Deus Rex Judaeorum*. This anticipatory "map of Death" serves as a template for the discussions that follow.

Part I, "Disposing of the Body," examines men's textual manipulations of the figure of the mourning woman and of the female body in death to argue that a nascent definition of Protestant masculinity in post-Reformation England depends upon a gendering of grief that constructs the male subject through his opposition to stigmatized feminine lamentational practices. Readings of the Shakespearean histories *Richard III* and *Henry VIII*, plague literature, elegies for Elizabeth I, and Protestant

reports of the exemplary deaths of Christian women show how a variety
of early modern masculine cultural, spiritual, and political discourses
were supported by the casting of women's mourning (and the essential
nature on which it was said to rely) as excessive, physical, and resistant
to the will of God. Male reformers' rejection of Catholic spirituality involves a reassessment of mourning in which moderate, internal grief –
that is, stoicism[32] – is valued and construed as masculine while external
demonstrations of sorrow are devalued and associated simultaneously
with femininity and with Catholicism. While the Protestant approval of
internalized spiritual and sacramental forms over the outward show of
Catholic ceremonies has long been considered a distinguishing feature
of Reformation spirituality, the highly gendered character of this shift
has only recently been discussed,[33] and its implications for orthodox
or sanctioned expressions of emotion by men and women have rarely
been noted. This uniquely Protestant assault on wivish mourning conflates excessive feminine grief which unduly laments the body's demise
with Catholic mourning, consistently stressing the continuity between
women's mourning as an imperfect version of men's stoic sorrow and
Catholic liturgical excesses as imperfect (per)versions of reformed ceremonies. As a result, the Protestant male subject understands himself *as*
a moderate mourner.

During the Reformation, the relationship of the living to the dead un-
derwent radical changes that influenced not only liturgical and doctrinal
approaches to the afterlife but also affective responses to the fact of death.
Medieval piety emphasized the continuities between life and death built
upon the professed efficacy of intercessory prayers to influence the location of the dead in the immortal topography of hell, purgatory and
heaven.[34] Based upon this faith, liturgical practices developed, such as
the public recitation of the obits, masses for the dead performed at regular
intervals commemorating their passing, and the elaborate apparatus of
the chantries, which employed both clergy and poor men and women to
undertake continual prayer to improve the soul's station in the afterlife.[35]
In the wake of the Reformation, however, the outlawing of prayers and
masses for the dead and dissolution of the concept of purgatory virtually redefined the relationship of the living to the dead and resulted in a
widespread sense of powerlessness on the part of the bereaved to influence
the fate of their departed and anxiety about the prospect of facing the
suddenly final sentence of the deathbed. Werdmuller is careful to point
out, for instance, that all prayers for the dying must cease at the time of
death, since "the soule of the dead, as soone as it is departed from hence,

cometh into a state there as praiers (if one would make them for him afterward) have no place, and are either unprofitable or else vaine."[36] Isolated from the dead, the living sought new avenues for channeling their grief and new applications for the commemorative and liturgical practices now rendered useless to souls in the afterlife. Accordingly, funerary practices became increasingly didactic, encouraging auditors to daily remembrance of their last ends rather than seeking to aid the dead, while the post-Reformation collapse of the chantries led to new forms of monumental and commemorative art.

These chapters argue that the reformation of *affect* resulting from these doctrinal and ritual reforms occurs on clearly gendered terms. In the absence of corporate, active, external forms through which to mourn, post-Reformation grief is rendered individual, static, and internal by the acknowledged pointlessness of prolonged or repetitious commemorative acts and by the transgression implied by stubborn grief. As a result, male reformers stress the ineffectualness of Catholic lamentational practices by casting them as both excessive and feminine, while mourning in measure is the masculine expression of grief approved by reformed piety. The period's "masculinization of piety," which involves, as Carlos M. N. Eire argues, "a definite shift away from a gender-balanced, feminized piety to a more strictly masculine one" with the removal of feminine representations of the Virgin and the saints,[37] is here expanded to account for gendered approaches to death and mourning in post-Reformation England.

Part II, "Sisters of Magdalene," takes up feminine responses to the Protestant gendering of grief to show that while male reformers stigmatized women's mourning as excessive and violent, early modern women found in this acknowledged excess a rhetorical and emotional power to support their public and private expressions of loss. The demarcation of women's grief as a particularly volatile emotional site, in effect, licenses women's writing and publishing of textual works of mourning. The construction of a notional space in which the decorum governing grief might be temporarily suspended (despite men's efforts to limit that space and restrain women's behavior within it) authorizes female speech, itself often associated in the period with excess, incontinence, and lack of restraint.[38] Discussions of elegies and diaries by maternal mourners, of public funerary monuments commissioned and designed by women, and of female-authored examples of the *ars moriendi* demonstrate that early modern women consistently reinterpret and deploy unorthodox forms of immoderate mourning to support their textual expressions of grief.

In doing so, moreover, they challenge the teleology of death and resurrection on which early modern discourses of consolation were based.

While I am especially interested in these pages in early modern women's mourning and its representations, I do not wish to suggest that *only* women mourned in the period, to the exclusion of men, or that women only took part in death rituals and acts of mourning privately while men performed the more public duties attending death and burial. Neither of these suggestions would accurately describe the role of gender within early modern approaches to death and mourning. Rather, an examination of the subject unpredictably complicates our notions of public and private spaces and the gendered work appropriate to them. While the rite of watching the body was most often performed by women within the household, for instance, Anne Clifford's diary account of the death of Elizabeth I names women as the primary attendants upon the corpse, but notes, too, that men as well as women watched the body during its laying-out:

A little after this Queen Elizabeth's Corps came by night in a Barge from Richmond to Whitehall, my Mother & a great Company of Ladies attending it, where it continued a great while standing in the Drawing Chamber, where it was watched all night by several Lords & Ladies. My Mother sitting up with it two or three nights, but my Lady would not give me leave to watch by reason I was held too young.[39]

Certainly the death of a monarch – particularly of a female monarch – might be considered an exceptional case, one in which the household itself is a public forum, composed not only of the immediate members of court but also, more generally, of the nation of mourning subjects. It is, however, a case where the blurring of borders between public and private, always implicit in early modern mourning and funerary practices, is especially apparent. For the very concept of laying out invites into the domestic space housing the body neighbors and friends, members of the public beyond the household, who come to pay their respects.[40] Indeed, Philippe Ariès's description of early modern "tamed death" stresses the social orientation of the deathbed itself: death was a "public ceremony," he writes, "a ritual organized by the dying person himself, who presided over it and knew its protocol."[41] Once the corpse left the household, moreover, the public rites attending burial did not fall within the exclusive realm of men's activity: both men and women took part in the cortège accompanying the body to burial and attended the funeral service. Margaret Hoby, for example, reports in her diary entry for August 6, 1601, that she "went to the church to the sarmon, which was made att

Mr Proctors buriall, who died this morning about 4 a Clock."[42] Despite frequent portrayals in sixteenth and seventeenth-century *artes moriendi* and representational forms of women's grief as excessive, physically violent, immoderate, and sexualized (or, conversely, of excessive grief as feminine), women continued to participate in public death rituals as they did in the more properly domestic rites. Sharon T. Strocchia's account of the relegation of women's mourning to the private sphere of the household in Quattrocento Florence, therefore, is both a valuable template through which to assess the gendering of grief in post-Reformation England, and one which can be adopted only with qualification. Largely as a result of the rise of humanism, she explains, "mourning in the mid-Quattrocento was increasingly viewed as 'women's work.'"[43]

These new models of public behavior introduced deep cleavages between the disciplined actions of learned men, on the one hand, and the customary, 'disorderly' behavior of women on the other. Paradoxically, at the same time humanists denied themselves this traditional emotional outlet, they still anticipated that women, especially their female kin, would honor the dead in the usual ways, although preferably at home rather than in the streets . . . [making] the customary work of mourning a gendered task.[44]

The inroads of humanism into English treatments of death and mourning prompt a similar reconsideration of the gendering of grief, but two main areas of difference are evident between reformed England and Catholic Italy, as reflected in the book's two major arguments, described above.

First, for theorists of the Anglican art of dying, immoderate grief is commonly associated both with femininity and with Catholicism. The Protestant censure of effeminate mourning involves the frequent conflation of excessive feminine grief and its preoccupation with the material body of death with Catholic mourning, viewed as especially violent due to its uncertainty of the soul's predestination. Permeated by a humanist interest in the recovery of ancient cultural practices, and by a stoic emphasis on mourning in measure, death manuals and antiquarian texts (devoted to a comparative anthropology of ancient and modern funerary practices) record the excesses of classical, "heathen," and pre-Reformation women's mourning in order to distinguish them sharply from the contemporary, reformed practices of both men and women. Thus Radford Mavericke's consolatory treatise on Elizabeth I's death speaks for numerous reformed *artes moriendi* when it informs its specifically female readers that they must "mourne as Christians, and not as the Heathen and the Papists doe . . . as though they had no hope of their eternall salvation."[45]

An understanding of women as universally and transhistorically prone to hysterical grief underpins these discussions. At the same time, however, the argument that men who grieve immoderately are feminized prompts frequent chastisements of men's excessive mourning through shameful comparisons with women. The 1531 English translation of Erasmus' *De Morto Declamatio*, for instance, admits that death is a "ryght good cause to be hevy," but encourages men to moderate their sorrow, since even the "selye mother" is eventually able to overcome the extremes of maternal mourning:

And for what cause shulde ye nat clene forgette it? Seinge that the space of a fewe dayes wyll cause idiottes to do so/me thynketh reason shulde persuade an excellent wyse man. For what selye mother doth so extremely bewayle the deth of her childe but that in shorte space of tyme her sorrowe some what asslaketh, and at length is clene forgotten? To have always a stedfast mynde is a token of a perfecte wyse man.[46]

Erasmus' (slightly dismissive) allusion to maternal grief points toward the second area of difference in the ways in which the early modern gendering of grief is manifested in English, as opposed to Italian, cultural and textual practices. While the enforced confinement of women's mourning to the domestic sphere, which Strocchia has shown took place in Quattrocento Florence, is less evident in sixteenth-century England, the particularly feminine work of preparing the body for burial, performed within the household, informs the period's images of female grief. Women's physical intimacy with the body in death merges with the idea of women's association with the flesh and men's with the spirit often observed in the period's more general constructions of gender, from Gouge's explication of the domestic hierarchy's natural bases, to Milton's sexually stratified portrayal of Eve's creation.[47] As such, women's concern with the body of the departed, rather than the soul, characterizes their excessive grief in texts authored by both men and women. When Erasmus invokes the example of maternal grief to censure male immoderation, he also recognizes the "short space of tyme" in which a mother's excessive lamentation for a child's death can be expected. Women's textual works of mourning, accordingly, tend to focus on the physical death of the beloved body, at the expense of Christian confidence in the resurrection of the soul. Maternal elegies of the period, for example, frequently play on the merger of *womb* and *tomb* to articulate the unique physical link between the living–dead body of the mourner and the corpse of her offspring. Such brutal emphases on the body's physical demise, often accompanied by female speakers' graphic visualizations of the decaying corpse and empathetic longings for death, challenge not only the decorum of post-Reformation mourning but also the promise of salvation fundamental to Christian consolation.

Even as women's physical intimacy with the corpse expands, figuratively, beyond the privacy of the household to define appropriate forms of public mourning, women's written expressions of mourning reside at a complex intersection of publication and privacy. Kate Lilley's description of seventeenth-century women's elegies as "an unusually mobile genre, which upsets the putative divisions between high and low culture, literary and non-literary women, private and public, occasional and non-occasional writing,"[48] applies to other kinds of women's writing on death as well, comprised of works which often appear not to have been meant for publication (women's diaries, for instance), or which find an audience beyond the author's immediate family only after, and because of, her death (mothers' legacies), or which are sanctioned for public consumption because they celebrate the family and a woman's place within it (such as familial elegies recording the loss of male relatives, which account for the greatest number of women's elegies in the period).[49] Thus Elizabeth Russell is praised for her epitaphs which appear on the tombs of her family members – verses that straddle the border between public and private in the same way that the stones on which they appear attest to private loss in a monumental form.[50]

The variety of representations of women's involvement in death rituals and mourning in works by early modern men and women bespeaks both the rich culture of female grief in the period and the wealth of ideological uses to which the figure of the female mourner could be turned. I derive my first chapter's portrait of early modern women's mourning from a biblical mourner whose legacy persists into the post-Reformation. Mary Magdalene's complex and fruitful career in early modern "tears" of Magdalene, both Catholic and Protestant, her memorable role as chief mourner (replacing the Virgin in Protestant treatments) to Christian history's most illustrious corpse, and her penitential retreat to a hermitage where she imitates Christ's death and entombment, make her representations especially dense and profitable sources for castings of women's mourning in the world beyond her narrative. Magdalene's lamentational model, as it emerges from medieval piety, is redefined by Protestant spirituality in ways that concisely characterize the period's gendered approaches to mourning. My discussion of male writers' manipulations of Magdalene's lachrymose *exemplum* in support of various polemical and doctrinal approaches to grief, and the reversal of these discourses in Aemilia Lanyer's brilliant "map of Death," serves as a summary of and preface to the chapters that follow, plotting the course of my argument as it unfolds in the remainder of the book. The post-Reformation reassessment of Magdalene and her characteristic art, embalming, clearly displays the means by which masculine spiritual, theological, and political discourses are underwritten by the period's definition and construction of women's lamentational practices as excessive, obdurate, and violent. Lanyer's redemptive approach to women's mourning, though, demonstrates the affective and rhetorical power available to early modern women grounding their textual expressions of loss in the female mourner's immoderate form.

These pages show that the feminized excesses of mourning, so frequently condemned by early modern men, lay the groundwork for women's revitalized approaches to the matter of death in numerous written works, both public and private. While supporting this thesis, it is the work of this study to uncover the material body of early modern women's mourning that lies encrypted in its figurative manipulations, an occult and intractable body, but one whose indelible imprint can be traced on the texts that mark its remains.

A map of death

In the late fourth century, St. John Chrysostom condemned women's excessive mourning in terms that would be echoed twelve centuries later by writers of the Reformation, for whom the excesses of ancient ritual lamentation were easily aligned with those of Catholic superstition. He complains that women:

make a show of their mourning and lamentation: baring their arms, tearing their hair, making scratches down their cheeks. Moreover, some do this because of grief, others for show and vain display. Still others through depravity both bare their arms and do these other things to attract the gaze of men . . . I have heard that many women, forsooth, attract lovers by their mournful cries, gaining for themselves the reputation of loving their husbands because of the vehemence of their wailings. Oh, what a devilish scheme! Oh, what diabolic trickery![1]

Four interrelated points of interest to an assessment of women's literal and figurative roles as mourners in the early modern period emerge from Chrysostom's comments. First, female lamentation is depicted as a group activity in which a community of women (united by shared sorrow and often by bonds of kinship) joins together to mourn. As such, it is a unique forum for woman-to-woman address, a discursive community whose characteristic forms of speech[2] are specific to the sex of its members and to their task. Second, mourning is "women's work" whose casting as excessive in literary and cultural forms supports the post-Reformation construction of masculinity as manifested in measured sorrow. As Claudius advises Hamlet, his "obstinate condolement" amounts to "unmanly grief."[3] Third, the physical nature of women's mourning (frequently reflected in the period's literary and visual images)[4] stresses the body's centrality to lamentation and the figurative merger of the (collective) body of mourning with the (individual) body of death. Thus the mourner's self-mutilation arises from her intimacy with the flesh and mirrors, empathetically, the ravages of death on the corpse itself. The female speaker of Zachary Boyd's "The Queenes Lamentation for the Death of Her Son" (1629) graphically illustrates the empathy between the metaphorically entombed female body of the maternal mourner and (here, and most commonly) the male body being mourned: "My flesh and skinne hath he [God] made olde, hee hath broken my bones . . . Hee hath set mee in dark places, as they that bee dead of olde: Hee hath hedged mee about that I cannot get out."[5] Finally, Chrysostom's censure of women's amatory motives in excessive lament points toward the blending of mourning and sexuality, Thanatos and Eros, in the female mourner.[6] From this potent conflation, images such as Elisabetta Sirani's *Penitent Magdalene* (figure 1) emerge, where Magdalene's penance (enabled by her grief at Christ's tomb) is at once a feminized version of Christ's scourging and the incorruptible remains of her sexual body.[7]

This chapter traces the trajectories of these four characteristics of female mourning through a series of texts that reflect the material and cultural work performed by mourning women in post-Reformation England. The communal, excessive, physical, and sexual aspects of feminine mourning emerge clearly from a survey of women's lamentational and funerary activities in the period, offering points of focus for a discussion of the figurative uses to which the mourning woman was put. My goal is to read from the historical evidence of early modern women's various and intimate associations with the body in death, through a collection of works which adapt these themes to portray the period's most popular biblical mourner, Mary Magdalene, and, finally, into the post-ascensional poetics of Aemilia Lanyer's *Salve Deus Rex Judaeorum*. I contend that reformers stigmatize mourning as feminine – as associated with the body rather than the soul, earth rather than heaven – to support a new formulation of men's internal grief; the stoic acceptance of death which, as Protestant *artes moriendi* instruct us, is the sign and certainty of election. This emphatic association of women with death's materiality aestheticizes the female mourner and approximates the technique of embalming by offering a permanent, female memorial to displace the male body's corruption onto the sexualized icon of the woman who mourns him. The post-Reformation advocacy of moderate mourning rewrites Catholic approaches to death by locating the unacceptable or heretical within the figure of the mourning woman. While male polemicists encode female mourning with specific forms of ideological and affective power, women writers find in feminine lament an unusual license to write and publish. In her "map of Death,"[8] Lanyer transvalues and reinvents immoderate mourning as a means of authorizing her text.

1 Elisabetta Sirani, *Penitent Magdalene.*

A central metaphor employed in my discussion is embalming, a term referring in the early modern period to both the ritual anointing of bodies and the "balsamic art"[9] of their preservation. It is a practice of particular interest, since, as sixteenth and seventeenth-century historians and surgeons frequently report, it is authorized for use by Christians by Mary Magdalene's anointing of Christ's body.[10] As such, its conceptualization in the period and its figurative deployment are sites of conflict between

gendered treatments of the corpse, while the material aspects of "opening the body" (the common term for embalming in the period) stand in a
difficult relationship to the perceived sexual enclosure of female bodies.

Embalming's flexible meanings and implicit register of gender can
be glimpsed in this brief comparison. After arguing in his *Nekrokedeia, or
The Art of Embalming* (1705) that the art was "approved by Christ" when
he cast Magdalene's anointing of his head as proleptic ("She is come
aforehand to anoint my body to the burying," Mark 14:8),[11] the surgeon
Thomas Greenhill calls embalming "an Emblem of the Resurrection,"
a necessity for Christians who believe in the eventual reunion of body
and soul.[12] John Sweetnam's sorrowful Magdalene, on the other hand,
"not finding her deare Maisters dead body which she hoped to have
imbalmed," is herself, "imbalmed in woes . . . As with her Maister she
had byn intomb'd."[13] In the former instance, Mary's foundational gesture of mourning and attendance on the corpse are appropriated and
spiritualized in Greenhill's efforts to find a scriptural precedent for the
contemporary art of embalming – a procedure whose rightful practition-
ers (he argues vigorously) are male surgeons.[14] In the latter, the aesthetics
governing feminine mourning dictate Magdalene's dissolution in tears,
rendering her – just shy of knowledge of the Resurrection – a lachrymose emblem of the material, rather than spiritual, *corpus Christi*. Finally,
Lanyer revises these two masculine castings of the feminine art of embalming, when Christ's anointing by female mourners (that is, the female
Church) becomes not an emblem of, but a means to, resurrection:

> The *Maries* doe with pretious balmes attend,
> But beeing come, they find it to no end.

> For he is rize from Death t'Eternall Life,
> And now those pretious oyntments he desires
> Are brought unto him, by his faithfull Wife
> The Holy Church.

> (106)

Although she is indebted to the tradition of feminine lament, Lanyer
founds a new poetics of mourning, authorized by and composed of the
sanctified tears of female mourners.

I

Early modern embalming, and the period's discussions of the practice
in antiquity, suggest that issues of gender and class are intertwined with

the art and its cultural meanings. Alexander Read, in his *Chirurgorum Comes* (1686), invokes the question of class in describing the ancient Jewish method of embalming: "Then [the corpse] is anointed with Oyntements made of several sorts of Spices, and after the Head is shaved, the Body is wrapt in white Linen Shrouds made for this purpose, which are of no great value, that a mean may be kept between the rich and the poor." He adds, unbiblically, "After this manner, in all probability, was *Lazarus* embalmed before his burial, he being not of the meanest Jews; and yet *Martha* feared he would stink in four days time."[15] Death rituals in early modern England, embalming included, were less concerned with keeping "a mean . . . between the rich and the poor" than with articulating class distinctions even in the grips of the great leveler, death. For the most part, embalming occurred in accordance with rank, since the procedure was reserved for monarchs, the nobility, and high church officials whose protracted heraldic funerals necessitated the preservation of the corpse.[16] Philibert Guibert's *The Charitable Physitian* (1639) describes the process in detail. After "the Chyrurgeon make[s] a long incision from the necke to the lower belly," he removes the heart, lungs, stomach, bowels, bladder, and diaphragm, "and taken all out . . . put into a large basin or vessell." He continues:

The head or Cranium shall be sawed in two, as you doe in an Anatomie, and the braines and parts shall be put into the vessell with the bowells, together with the blood that hath been drawne out of the three bellies; that is, the head, the brest, and the belly infoerious, and put them altogether into the barrell, and hoope it round, to be buried . . . The head, brest, and belly inferiour being also emptied and cleansed, you shall begin to emblame them: beginning at the head being well washed within with the said vineger compounded, and then with pieces of Cotton soaked in the said vineger and filled with balme, the head shall be filled, and both the pieces of the skull shall bee bound together with thred.[17]

After draining the blood from the neck and extremities, the embalmer washes the corpse with vinegar, stuffs it with "cotton balmed," and anoints it with "Venice Turpentine, dissolved in oyle of Roses or oyle of Spike, and then it shall be covered over with Sear-cloth and put into a Coffin of Lead."[18]

Guibert's treatise offers a starting point for considering women's literal and figurative relationships to the increasingly professionalized technique of embalming. The text, while addressed to male surgeons, was printed in a volume with treatises which, as the title page announces, "shew the manner to make and prepare in the house with ease and little paines all those remedies which are proper to all sorts of diseases,

according to the advice of the best and ordinariest Physitians, serving as
well for the rich as the poor."[19] It appears, in other words, within a volume
addressed to female as well as male householders, but assumes (without
demanding, as Greenhill will sixty years later) a professional, male readership. Recipes for household balms (for treating wounds, burns, and
common medical conditions) appear alongside those for oils used in
embalming, neatly illustrating in fact the figurative cross-gendering of
embalming as it draws its authority from Mary Magdalene's practice.
The translator's prefatory advice that readers purchase "roots, Hearbes,
Seeds, Flowers, &c. at the Herborists or herbe women in Cheap-side,"[20]
casts these women as descendants of the three Maries and female counters to the London Company of Barber-Surgeons, under whose authority
embalming was placed.[21] While the structure of Guibert's text implies
that women understood the process of embalming, if only from a theo-
retical viewpoint, accounts describe their participation in the procedures
themselves, as assistants to male surgeons. Clare Gittings reports, for instance, that four women were employed to dress and trim the embalmed
body of Nicholas Bacon (d. 1578) before it was shrouded, and when
James Montegue, Bishop of Winchester, was embalmed, 10s was paid
to "a woman to attend the surgeons with water, mops, cloths and other
things."[22]

These activities are clearly an extension of women's time-honored domestic duties of preparing the corpses of family members and neighbors
for burial. In the absence of an undertaking profession, the ceremonial
washing of the corpse (which, like embalming, derived its biblical authority from Magdalene's anointing of Christ)[23] was commonly performed
by women within the household, often with the help of neighborhood
women and female servants.[24] Midwives were sometimes employed to
undertake this duty. Parochial and household accounts from the period,
as David Cressy reports, frequently note payments to poor women for
washing, watching, laying out, and winding – the mundane work of
preparing the corpse for disposal. Shrouding, too, was women's work:
sixteenth-century probate accounts mention payments to women who,
following the washing of the corpse, wrapped it in its shroud or winding
sheet.[25] In numerous affidavits dating from the late seventeenth century,
women who had shrouded corpses witness that they had used shrouds
made of wool, rather than linen, in compliance with the Act of 1678.[26]
Women not only shrouded the corpse but also provided shrouds. At her
death in 1514, for example, Alice Bumpsted left "2d to each of the two
women that shall sew my winding sheet."[27]

By tradition, the corpse was watched continually during its laying out from the moment of death to the moment of burial, a duty which, at all social ranks, most often fell to the women of the household. During the laying out, women grieved and prayed over the corpse, perhaps in the company of men who pursued the more worldly pastimes of drinking and playing cards.[28] Women's occupations as watchers reflect the pre-Reformation habit of hiring poor women as beadswomen to pray for the souls of the departed, a practice which was condemned by reformers as Popish superstition but persisted through the early years of Elizabeth's reign.[29] At the deaths of children, maidens, brides, or women dying in childbirth, women sometimes served not only as watchers but also as pallbearers.[30] Ralph Josselin records that on his infant son's death in 1647, "Mrs. King and Mrs. Church: 2 doctors of divinities widdowes: the gravest matrons in our towne layde his tombe into the earth: which I esteeme not onely testimonie of their love to mee, but of their respect to my babe. Mrs. King and Mr. Harlakenden of the priory closed up each of them one of his eyes when it dyed."[31] After his daughter's death in 1650, he notes, "Mrs. Margarett Harlakenden, and Mrs. Mabel Elliston layd her in her grave, those two and Mrs. Jane Clench and my sister carryed her in their hands to the grave."[32] Finally, women's wills often extend ties between female mourners into the afterlife through woman-to-woman bequests which, as J. S. W. Helt writes, "served as gendered markers which sustained and maintained a sense of spiritual and material affinity between the dead and the living community."[33]

Early modern women took part not only in death's domestic rites but also in public mourning. College of Arms regulations governing heraldic funerals required that chief mourners be of the same sex as decedents: "a man being deade hee [is] to have only men mourners at his Buriall, And at a woman's buriall to have only women moreners."[34] As such, spouses could not appear as chief mourners for their deceased partners, nor mothers for sons, sisters for brothers, and so on. When Mary Sidney Herbert opens "The Dolefull Lay of Clorinda" with the question, "Ay me, to whom shall I my case complaine, / That may compassion my impatient griefe?" (1–2), she indicts the gendering of public mourning ceremonies and the cultural foreclosure on women's expressions of grief. In the absence of a public place (both literal and figurative) to accommodate a sister's lament for her brother, Herbert resolves, "Then to my selfe will I my sorrow mourne, / Sith none alive like sorrowfull remaines" (19–20).[35] Her complaint reflects the social restraints imposed upon heraldic mourners which, in fact, prevented Herbert's

participation in her brother's funeral in 1587.[36] While spouses' roles
were limited in heraldic funerals (a limitation that led to the popularity
of private nocturnal funerals in the seventeenth century, whose accom-
modation of personal grief offered relief from College of Arms rules),[37]
they were not entirely excluded. At Sir Edward Coke-Lee's funeral in
1605, for example, the procession included fifty-six male mourners and,
following the chief mourner (Sir Henry Lee), "Mrs. Cecill, Mrs. Goore,
Ladye Lee, Mrs. Mary Lee, Mrs. Durning, Mrs. Ame Lee, Mrs. Wilford,
Mrs. Blackwell, Mrs. Masie, Mrs. Hopgill, Mrs. Tourner, and Aldermen
with out blacke."[38] Conversely, William Cecil's note on the order of
mourners for the funeral of his second wife, Mildred Cooke Cecil, in
1589 lists thirty women including the deceased's sister, Elizabeth Russell,
as chief mourner, followed in the procession by twenty-one men, among
them (one surmises) Burghley himself.[39]

   While the most intimate relatives of the deceased might be relegated
to the most marginal of roles at the funeral, provisions of mourning garments for almsfolk of both sexes ensured women's participation in public
mourning, distantly removed from emotional center stage.[40] Thomas
Becon's *Sicke Mannes Salve* (1561) objects to the custom "that, when a
man of honest reputation departeth, and is brought to be buried, there
should follow him certain in fine black gownes, and certain poor men
and women in coarser cloth," saying, "Let the infidels mourn for their
dead: the Christians ought to rejoice when any of the faithful be called
from this vale of misery unto the glorious kingdom of God." Although
Becon's protagonist insists, "if it were not for offending other, and that
it should also be some hindrance unto the poor, I would wish rather
to have none, than otherwise," he nonetheless provides "that 'thirty
poor men and women do accompany my body unto the burial, and
that each of them have a gown of some convenient colour . . . [and] that
thirty poor children be there also, and that every one of them have a
seemly gowne.'"[41] At Queen Elizabeth's funeral in April, 1603, 260
poor women, recipients of the crown's charity, led the cortège.[42] Henry
Machyn's diary records the details of numerous London funerals from
1550 to 1563, and often reports charitable bequests of mourning garments to poor men and women who marched in the procession. At the
burial of "my lade Mores, wyff of sir Crystoffer Mores, knyght" on May
22, 1551, Machyn reports, "she gayff . . . men and women vijxx mantylls,
fryse gownes, and o[ther] gownes and cotts iiijxx," and on February
20, 1554, "master G[e]orge Pargeter, Thomas Pargeter's sone late mare
of London," was buried "with mony mornars, and with armes, and

mony goewnes gyffyn to pore men and women."[43] Not all of Machyn's
records distinguish the sex of mourners, but of those that do, thirty-
one involve gifts to men only, fifteen to women only, and thirty-nine to
both male and female almsfolk. While bequests to female mourners are
slightly more frequent by women (in twenty-two of the thirty-nine cases
recorded by Machyn), men also include the female poor as almsfolk with
some regularity. These numbers imply women's extensive participation
in public mourning in the period, but with important qualifications of
their affective bonds with the deceased: while female almsfolk – mourners for hire, as it were – testify to the decedent's generosity and good
works, women with an emotional stake in the burial of a male relative are relegated to minor roles and marginal places in the ceremony
proper.

Post-Reformation almsfolk carry the traces of their Catholic ancestors,
beadsmen and beadswomen. When Becon's dying Christian makes out
his will, he provides for the poor but insists that "these purgatory-rakers
shall neither rake nor scrape for me with their masses and diriges, when
I am departed."[44] More remotely, almsfolk recall classical examples of
the *threnos*, hired female mourners whose expertise in ritualized gestures
of grief was a central feature of Greek and Roman burials.[45] Antiquarian
treatments of classical hired mourners in the period generally approach
them with a disapproval that suggests the easy conflation of Catholic
beadswomen with the classical *threnos*: Scottish clergyman William Birnie,
for example, condemns both the "hypocrysie" of Roman professional
mourners ("whom they styled Praeficae") and "the exorbitance of superstitious exiquies . . . (as in their bel-ringings, lamp-lighting, dirge-singing,
incense burning, holy watering, letanie praying, soule-massing, vigilles
keeping, and other such gear)" current in Catholic funerary rites.[46] John
Weever, similarly, describes the "counterfeit hired mourners" of antiquity ("which were women of the loudest voices, who . . . cried out mainly,
beating of their breasts, tearing their hair, their faces, and garments") and
the "Praefica" ("an old aged Beldam") who led them, adding disapprov-
ingly, "This is a custome observed at this day in some parts of Ireland, but
above all Nations the Jewes are best skilled in these lamentations."[47] The
provision of mourning garments to almsfolk (whose function, unlike that
of their classical and pre-Reformation predecessors, was to celebrate the
decedent's generosity rather than to amplify grief at his or her passing)
and the relative exile of close female kin from the funeral proper reflect
the post-Reformation rejection of both Catholic and feminine excesses in
mourning. The replacement of female kin by recipients of and witnesses

to the decedent's civic-minded charity diminishes the likelihood of public displays of affective excess.

These well-documented practices suggest the largely unacknowledged and unrecorded work of attending and mourning the dying and the dead undertaken by early modern women, activities whose traces can be gleaned in the textual remains of the period. The ubiquity of women's death rituals in post-Reformation England is indicated by allusions to the collective body of female mourners of all stations. In the domestic tragedy, *Arden of Faversham*, gentlewoman Alice Arden invites her maidservant to join her in a short-lived rite of mourning for the murdered Arden (whom moments before Alice has stabbed): "Come, Susan, help me lift the body forth. And let our salt tears be his obsequies."[48] Alice's desire, however ironic, to create a small community of mourners is symptomatic of the degree to which women were expected to engage in ritualized lamentation – so much so that the absence of these obsequies could signify (as it certainly does in the play) domestic disorder and cultural decline.[49] At the same time, female mourners frequently appear as a synecdoche of the chaos and instability surrounding them: William Muggins' *London's Mourning Garment* (1603) calls upon the "Dames of London Cittie" to mourn thousands of deaths during a five-month epidemic of bubonic plague and uses "weeping Mothers" to emblematize the city's general sorrow.[50] In the same year, Radford Mavericke's *The Mourning Weede* convenes "all the Ladies of honor, and others in this land" to mourn the passing of the queen on the model of the Old Testament lament for Jephthah's daughter:

When the virgin daughter of *Jepthah*, Judge of Israell was . . . put to death . . . the virgin daughters of Israell her fellowes *went foure times a year*; while they lived, out into the wildernesse, that there they might bewaile her Virginity. That Virgin doubtles, never loved *Israell* halfe so well, as our Virgin Queene hath loved England; therefore . . . let all the Virgins in this land, establish it for a law in their hearts, to mourne yearely in measure upon the day of the death of their fellow Virgin, (in respect of their virginity) though while she lived, far above them in authority.[51]

Similarly, the female speaker of "The Queenes Lamentation," Elizabeth Stuart, daughter of James I and Queen of Bohemia, invites her countrywomen to join her in mourning: "O yee Daughters of Britaine my native Soile: Conveene your selves together: Come all and joyne your sorrowes with mine: Come contribute teares in aboundance, that wee may deplore our domage: Come, come and helpe mee to mourne for my first Borne."[52]

When Mavericke advises England's virgins to mourn *in measure*, he echoes reformers who frequently accuse women of excessive grief and, conversely, censure immoderate mourning as feminine. The anonymous *Preparacyon to Deeth* articulates the scriptural basis of this Protestant assault on grief: "We muste not lamente and mourne of ungodlynesse and superstycion, as the unfaythefull heathen do whiche beleve not the resurrecyon of the dead."[53] As many texts of the period do, *The Preparacyon* cites as the biblical authority for moderate grief Christ's lamentation at Lazarus' tomb: "For the hope of Christen men is perfytelye assured, that the deade peryshe not, but slepe, as Chryste sayeth, Lazarus our frend slepeth."[54] Mavericke glosses the episode as showing that we must "mourne as Christians, and not as the Heathen and the Papists doe,"[55] while Greenhill makes explicit the gendering of grief implicit in early modern versions of the story which contrast the simplicity of Christ's mourning – "Jesus wept" – with the excesses of Magdalene's sorrow.[56] The ancients, he writes:

also on occasion sha'vd off their Hair, beat their breasts, cut their Flesh, and with their Nails tore holes in their Faces . . . These Frantick Actions, tho' practis'd sometimes by Men, were more frequent among Women, whose Passions were more violent and ungovernable . . . These cruel and ridiculous Ceremonies were restrain'd by Laws made on purpose, to restrain such Excesses in Funerals; nevertheless a moderate Sorrow and Mourning was never disallow'd, but on the contrary commended and promis'd as a Blessing to the Godly.

The proof of this promise is Christ's moderate mourning at Lazarus' grave.[57]

Protestant portraits of wivish grief attempt to devalue and circumscribe female mourners' practices and power. Far from disappearing from the currency of mourning, the female mourner is given a central role that reflects both the gendering of grief and a new fascination with the physical, female, body in and of mourning as a living extension of the body in death. "The Queenes Lamentation" typifies male writers' uses of women's physical grief: following the Queen's violent lament, in which her body is empathetically wracked with sorrow and entombed by grief, Boyd offers his "Balme of Comfortes," urging the queen to moderate, masculine mourning.[58] This interest in the female mourner as both a living–dead image of the corpse and a work of art is reflected in early modern embalmers' shift in focus from the pragmatic goal of par-boiling the body (to make it portable) toward an ideal of aesthetic preservation.[59] Claude Gaichard's 1581 description of ancient Egyptian embalming voices this awareness of the female body, and its sexuality,

in death: he reports, following Herodotus, that noblewomen and those
who were renowned for their beauty ("qui ont . . . reputation de beauté")
were kept three or four days at home before being delivered for embalming, so that "les embaumeurs ne s'accointent d'elle. Car, certain d'entre
eux, à ce q'on dit, fut une fois treuvé abusant du corps d'une femme
nouvellement mort"[60] (the embalmers would not have [sexual] contact
with them. Because, a certain one, they said, had one time been found
abusing the body of a newly dead woman). The same consciousness of
the body that prompts Gaichard to share this information accounts for
noblewomen's increasing reluctance to commend their bodies into the
hands of male embalmers (a phenomenon which will occupy us more
fully in chapter 2). This reluctance suggests not only women's modesty,
extending even to the insensible corpse, but also a willingness to forego
the presumed physical benefits of balsamic preservation to safeguard
their sexual integrity and the moral incorruptibility that chastity implies.

Not only the female corpse but also the body of feminine grief was
subject to scrutiny and regulation. In post-Reformation England, the
female mourner's unruly body was clothed according to culturally determined rules to ensure the transfer of property within a patriarchal
system of exchange. Following the death of Lodovic, Duke of Richmond
and Lennox in 1624, Abraham Darcie published a volume in praise of
his widow's tears designed to display her "mournfull life, and disconsolate estate . . . by which her most entire, matchlesse and sacred love is
evidently manifested."[61] Darcie clearly understands the widow's public
expressions of insuperable loss as evidence of her chastity and wifely devotion: "She lives in moane/ Single in bed; He lies in tombe alone."[62]
After describing the duchess's excessive grief, Darcie offers "A Most Consolatory Comfort," encouraging the duchess, and his readers, to forego
immoderate sorrow:

> Sorrowes excesse doth no lesse vicious seeme,
> Then we the overplus of mirth do deeme;
> For the excesse of griefe or exaltation,
> Is a disorder in our mind and passion.[63]

Although Darcie presents the duchess's immoderate grief in order to
correct it, his praise of her mournful widowhood argues that a widow's
public display of grief is essential to her self-representation as a chaste,
loving spouse. The duchess's excessive mourning is not only a *textual* necessity, supporting Darcie's orthodox moderation, but a *cultural* necessity
as well, guaranteeing her continued submission to her husband's will

(now literally manifested in a legal document), her agreement with its provisions for the transfer of property, and her willingness to restrain her unruly passions within the confines of culturally sanctioned mourning. The passion of excessive grief displaces, even as it refers to, the more threatening sexual passions assumed in the period to be especially uncontrolled in widowhood due to a woman's sexual experience in marriage.

Absent from her husband's funeral in fact, the textually present widow of Darcie's *Funerall Teares* adorns and supports the dynastic continuity assured by the burial rites themselves.[64] But an early modern widow would wear mourning for a period far exceeding the brief public performance of the funeral. On the model of Roman civil law, a year's mourning was generally observed by spouses, while shorter periods were, by the eighteenth century, recognized for other blood relations.[65] Some early modern widows, though, continued to wear mourning clothes or veils for years, and sometimes for the rest of their lives.[66] The widow's veil marked her empathetic death with her husband, her "participation . . . in the mortuary state."[67] This suspended animation also restricted widows to their homes for fixed periods, their rooms and beds hung in black.[68] After her husband's death in 1632, for example, Elizabeth of Bohemia "lay in a bedroom hung with black serge for eight days" before publicly donning her widow's weeds.[69]

While widows' mourning garments symbolized chastity and submission (to God's will and to the perpetually potent will of their husbands),[70] their reliability as indicators of widows' moral characters was uncertain. Concerns about grieving widows' potential hypocrisy stemmed from the perception that "donning mourning could also send out a signal of matrimonial availability."[71] As women became increasingly interested in fashionable mourning habits[72] – an interest reflected in Anne Clifford's note that after Queen Anne's funeral in 1619, "I went to my Sister Beauchamp to shew her my mourning attire"[73] – their male governors expressed growing fears about possible manipulations of grief's symbols toward less-than-submissive ends.[74] The anonymous *Englands Welcome to James* makes a slightly incongruous use of the common view of widows' weeds as symbols of sexual availability to praise the new sovereign. When the widowed England, "clos[ing] her mourning thoughts in sable hew," hears the news that she "shalt have a King," she resolves:

> Then as the widdow I rejoyc't a fresh,
> And quite forgot the sorrow I was in:
> When she is tempt with frailty of the flesh

To take new husband, new Joyes to begin,
And having taine him being trick and trim,
As she is gladsome on the wedding day
So I rejoyc't hearing them thus to say.[75]

The fear that women might exploit sexuality in mourning recognizes both the necessity of their public mourning to masculine exchanges of property and the impossibility of controlling feminine desire through imposed codes of dress or conduct. Pastor Robert Willan hints at this dilemma when, in a funeral sermon preached in 1630, he approves of the custom "barring noble widdowes from ceremoniall and solemne sorrow, confining them to closset mourning," concluding, "Tears shed in private as they fall lesse visible, so lesse forced."[76] John Weever's *Ancient Funeral Monuments* (1631) worries about the potentially fraudulent grief of both husbands and wives, who, like latter-day Wives of Bath, "with a few counterfeit teares and a sowre visage masked and painted over with dissimulation con[tract] second marriages before they have worne out their mourning garments, and sometimes before their cope mates be cold in their graves."[77] Although *widowers'* grief sometimes also veered toward immoderation (Robet Cecil and Kenelm Digby providing notable examples), their excessive mourning did not prompt suspicions of amorous or deceptive motives.[78] When John Dunton's *Mourning-Ring* (1682) cribs Weever's comments fifty years later, he portrays a self-conscious widow contemplating the difficult balance she must maintain to avoid unacceptable expressions of immoderate grief, on the one hand, and an inappropriate lack of emotion, on the other: "I cannot allow an intermission or forbearance of Tears, lest I should appear unnatural," she reasons, "If I do not weep I did not love."[79]

This memorable phrase of Dunton's grieving widow expresses a double-bind implicit in the "second widowhood"[80] of women's public mourning. While public expressions of grief affirm a widow's chastity and sincerity, over-expressive mourning promotes her sexual availability. Despite post-Reformation prescriptions for moderate mourning, *some* public sorrow on a widow's part was an expected tribute to her departed husband. Figures from the notebooks of physician Richard Napier reflect widows' willingness to admit (at least to their doctor) their difficult restraint of sorrow and, by implication, the cultural license afforded them: one-third of the episodes of illness, despair, or melancholy treated by Napier were triggered by the death of a spouse, and of these forty-two cases, thirty-three were widows.[81] The mean in mourning becomes particularly hard to negotiate in codes of conduct for grieving widows: if too little grief implies a lack of love, too much suggests an uncontrollable will that might as easily express itself in sexual promiscuity as in self-serving manipulations of mourning's habits. Rowland Whyte records just such a transgressive use of mourning in 1599: "My Lady of *Essex*," he writes, "is a most sorrowful Creature for her Husbands Captivity; she wears all blacke of the meanest Price, and receves no Comfort in any Thing."[82] Elsewhere, he notes that Essex's sisters also donned mourning with overtly political goals in mind: "The two ladies, *Northumberland* and *Rich*, all in black, were at Court before the remove; what success they had with her *Majesty* I do not know; they were humble suitors to have the *Earl* removed to a better air and to a more convenient place."[83] If the Essex women manipulate mourning to their own ends, the *absence* of mourning could also denote a perverse and powerful female will. Arguing Elizabeth I's guilt in the murder of Mary, Queen of Scots, Robert Persons asks:

What mourning garmentes were there seen throughout the whole Courte, for this facte? What signe of sorrow, and publick affliction? Of her Mother, it is written, that when she heard of Queen *Dowagers* death, she mourned in yellow sattin with gould lace: what apparell Queen *Elizabeth* did mourne in for Queen *Maryes* death by her selfe commanded, I read not: but that then as the cause was, somewhat like of both theyr joyes, both of Queene *Anne* and Queene *Elizabeth*, mother and daughter, by the fall of their adversaries, it is probable also that their mourning habits were not unlike.[84]

Elizabeth's political will, conflated with Anne Boleyn's sexuality, manifests itself in her imagined, sexualized transgression of the rules of mourning ("yellow sattin with gould lace"), her refusal to grieve at Mary's first, hurried burial in March, 1587, and her failure to appear as chief mourner (or otherwise) at the second.[85] A woman's public performances of mourning – necessary to attest to her submission, humility, and genuine grief – uncomfortably testify to the troublesome relationship between her hidden desires and passions and their outward show.

Jeremy Taylor's appropriation of a story from Petronius encapsulates this heightened awareness of the female body as a point of merger for death, mourning, and sexuality, and the female mourner's value in efforts to authorize moderate grief. An Ephesian widow "descended with the corpse into the vault, and there being attended with her maid resolved to weep to death, or dye of famine, or a distempered sorrow." A soldier who is guarding an execution nearby, struck by "the comely disorder of sorrow" and "sad prettiness" of the widow, promptly falls in love. She, in turn, "fell in love, and that very night in the morning of her passion, in the grave of her husband, in the pompes of mourning, and in her funeral garments, married a new and stranger Guest." The next morning, upon finding that one of the executed bodies has disappeared, the widow advises the soldier to "take the body of her first husband whose funeral she had so strangely mourned, and put it upon the gallows in the place of the stolne [*sic*] thief; he did so, and escaped the present danger to possess a love that might change as violently as her grief had done."[86] The striking elements of the story, among them the widow's violent mourning, living death, and self-entombment, the necrophilic wedding in the grave, and the tale's troubled relationship to the Crucifixion – all of which are taken up in the "tears" of Mary Magdalene – are both lingered over by Taylor in his lengthy narrative, and dismissed in his moralization of the tale as a call to mourn "gravely, decently, and charitably."[87]

II

Like Taylor's Ephesian widow, early modern Magdalene is both entombed and eroticized. Near the end of the pseudo-Chaucerian *Complaynte of the lover of Cryst saynt Mary Magdaleyn* (1520), she resigns herself to the grave: "My body also unto this monumente/I here bequyeth with boxe and oyntemente."[88] The poem closes with the standard *imitatio Christi* of the dying Christian, but stops woefully short of resurrection:

> My soule for anguysshe is now full thrysty
> I faynte ryght sore for hevynesse
> My lorde my spouse (Cut me derelinquisti)
> Syth I for the suffer all this dystresse
> What causeth the to se me thus mercylesse
> Syth the it pleaseth of me to make an ende
> (In manus tuas) My spyryte I commende.
>
> (B6v)

Sixteenth-century treatments of Mary Magdalene, both Catholic and Protestant, emphasize her mourning for the lost body of Christ, exploiting women's association with death's materiality. Gervase Markham's *Mary Magdalens Lamentations for the Losse of her Master Jesus* (1601) recalls Mary's proleptic anointing of the living Christ as she mourns his absent corpse:[89]

And to embaulme his breathlesse corps I came,
As once afore I did anoint his feet,
And to preserve the reliques of the same,
The only remnant that my blisse did meet:
    To weepe afresh for him in deapth of dole,
    That lately wept to him for mine owne soule.

J. C.'s *Saint Marie Magdalens Conversion*, which appeared during the plague
of 1603, emphasizes Magdalene's pre-Resurrection grief and offers its
subject "as most fitting this time of death... much like a mourning
garment, fitting both the time and the matter."[90] Of the period's two
most popular versions of the story, the pseudo-Chaucerian *Complaynte*
leaves the disconsolate Mary in Christ's empty tomb, oblivious to the
Resurrection, while Southwell's *Mary Magdalens Funerall Teares* (1591) devotes only ten of its sixty-eight pages to events following her expression of
recognition, "Rabboni."[91] In Markham's tears, moreover, Mary's story
is told through seven separate "lamentations," the sixth of which is performed at this famous moment of peripeteia (and the seventh following
Christ's "noli me tangere"). Even in her joy, Mary Magdalene figures
mourning. This paradox is reflected in Gian Girolamo Savoldo's painting of Mary at the tomb (figure 2): she appears with her jar of balm
before the empty tomb in the standard pose of classical female mourners (huddling within her hooded cloak, hands to her face), the emblem
of female lamentation. Yet she turns toward the source of light which
must, subtly, symbolize the Resurrection.

The emphasis of these images on the moment just before, on
Magdalene languishing in sorrow, portrays female mourning as at once
excessive, exemplary, and aestheticized. Mary's graphic memory of the
Crucifixion in the *Complaynte*, where Christ's "blood dystylled downe on
my visage / My clothes eke the droppes began to steyne" (A3v) as she
knelt at the foot of the cross, concludes by referring to traditional visual
motifs for representing violent grief:[92]

> Than gan I there myne armes to unbrace
> Uplyftynge my hande mournyngly
> I lyghed and sore sobbed in that place
> Bothe heven & erth myght have herde me crye
> Wepynge I sayde alas incessauntly
> O my sweete herte my goostly paramoure
> Alas I may not thy body socoure.
>
> (A4v)

2 Gian Girolamo Savoldo, *Saint Mary Magdalene Approaching the Sepulcher.*

In the empathy between Magdalene's mourning body and the male body being mourned, she rivals and usurps the Virgin's privileged claim to grief, a commonplace of the Catholic cult of the Virgin exemplified in the medieval genre of the *planctus Mariae.*[93] An example drawn from this genre displays the continuities between the Virgin's physical lament and Magdalene's: at the Crucifixion, the Virgin "uttered a great shout and said, 'My Lord, my Son. What has happened to the beauty of your body? How can I bear seeing you suffer so much?' And with these words she tore her face with her fingernails and beat her breast."[94] In the Catholic *ars moriendi*, the Virgin acted as an intercessor for the dying based on her empathetic Passion: "her sone cryst Jhesu hath dyed &

suffred so tourmentous a deth & in her owne syght to her grete socour
and motherly compassyon I hope she wolde be loth that theke precyous
passyon sholde be loste in ony creature that her blessyd sone suffred so
pacyently."[95] While Sweetnam portrays the Virgin's sorrows, affirming
that "the dolours of Childbirth (from which by particular priviledge she
was freed) were doubled at the foot of the Crosse," he also asks her leave,
"by the greatness of thy grief to take proportionable measure of the
sorrowful pangs of the weeping Magdalene" (95).[96] Similarly, the *Complaynte* claims for Mary Magdalene the heart-piercing grief traditionally
given to the Virgin: when Christ's side is pierced, she exclaims, "My
herte was perced with very compassyon / that in me remayned no lyfe
of nature / Strokes of dethe I felte withouten mesure" (A4).[97] This displacement of the mother of Christ by the "lover of Cryst" clearly reflects
a reformed view of mourning which rejects intercession and restrains
excessive grief with a stoic certainty of salvation. By the end of the sixteenth century, the Virgin's right to excessive mourning is devalued by
Protestants and Catholics alike. In Southwell's *Triumphs Over Death* (1595)
she is "the patterne of christian mourners [who] so tempered her anguish, that there was neither any thing undone that might be exacted
of a mother, or any thing yet done that might be disliked of so perfit
a matron."[98] While the Virgin thus becomes an example of moderate
mourning, it is left to Mary Magdalene to enact her excessive grief. The
loss of the Virgin's maternity as a justification for violent mourning, on
the one hand, casts the mourner's privileged relationship to Christ as
accessible to all Christians, since it is attained by Magdalene only by her
love. On the other hand, the mother's replacement by lover produces
a remainder which is aestheticized in Magdalene's textually embalmed
form.

Mary Magdalene's special status as the lover of Christ transforms her
grief from excess to *exemplum*. Thus Markham states:

> And Marie shewes to maids and matrones both,
> How they should wepe and decke their rose-like cheekes
> With showers of greefe, whereto hard hearts are loth,
> And who it is her matchlesse mourning seekes:
> > And when we ought to send our reeking sighs,
> > To thicke the passage of the purest lights.
>
> And Marie showes us when we ought to beat
> Our brasen breasts, and let our robes be rent,
> How prostrating, to creepe unto the feat

Of that sweet lambe, whose bloud for us was spent,
And that we should give way unto our woes,
When the excesse no fault or errour showes.

(A4v)

Although Mary's grief is excessive, Markham exhorts women to imitate her "matchlesse mourning" in commemorating not the physical death of loved ones, but the Crucifixion of Christ.[99] While Mary's unknowing grief actually constitutes an instance of excessive lamentation for the body's demise, for Markham and writers like him she figures spiritual sorrow (that is, penance). As Sweetnam's Magdalene advises the sinner, "View him upon the Crosse, and choose this part. / Then take him downe, and bury him in thy hart."[100] This internalization of grief – literally of Christ's sepulcher – is supported by Magdalene's overt, immoderate mourning, much as mourning in measure is supported by reformers' casting of women's collective tears as excessive.

Meanwhile, Mary mourns forever within works that aestheticize her sorrow, presenting it for readers' edification and pleasure – in the humanist formula, to teach and delight. This aestheticization is implied by the form that her tears usually take: three of the five texts under discussion are lyric poems, and a fourth, Sweetnam's, cannot resist breaking into verse at the maudlin moment when Mary, "not finding her deare Maisters dead body which she hoped to have imbalmed, she stood at the monument without, weeping."[101] To counter the reader's heart-as-sepulcher, the *Complaynte* gives us Mary's embalmed heart as a relic of her devotion to her "dere love" – not the body as emblem of the spirit, but the opposite: the spirit literalized in the permanently preserved, eternally material body:

And in token of love perpetuall
Whan I am buryed in this place present
Take out my herte the very rote and all
And close it within this boxe of oyntement
To my dere love make therof a presente
Knelynge downe with worde lamentable
Do your message speke fayre and tretable.

(B5v)

Guibert's description of the procedure for embalming the heart explains the practice lying behind Mary's apparently literary love token:[102]

The Heart being washed with the said Vineger compounded, shall bee put to infuse in the said Vineger in a pipkin being plaistered round the lidde, that the aire enters not the space of five or sixe dayes, then take it out and make an incision in it, and fill it with balme and pieces of Cotton balmed, and sowe it up againe, and sew it well into a little bag made of Searecloth, and put it into a case of Lead, Silver, or Pewter, fashioned in the forme of a Heart, and cary it whither you please.

The heart-shaped casket makes explicit the aesthetics governing the embalming of the heart itself: the crafting of a permanent memorial object from bodily remains within which the internal seat of affection is laid open, externalized, literalized. The spirit made flesh.

Mary's embalmed heart points toward an aestheticization of her metaphorically entombed form whose results, first, objectify her as the mummified body of grief, second, graphically depict the dead *corpus Christi,* and third, emphasize her sexuality. Complementing the *Complaynte*'s image of the embalmed heart, Sweetnam describes Mary's transformation by grief into myrrh, the bitter material of embalming: "No Mary more, but Mara be thy name, / Let bitterness in thee thy name expresse."[103] Mary is at once the embalmer of Christ, the embalmed, and the balm itself. The image of Mary as balm easily merges with that of the text as a balm. Thus Markham ends by recounting the disciples' "content, the balme of troubled mind" (HI) upon hearing Mary's report of Christ's Resurrection (supposing that his work will produce the same results in readers), while the *Complaynte* consigns Mary's body with her balm to the grave ("My body also unto this monumente / I here bequyeth with boxe and oyntement"), presenting her mournful self-embalming as a balm and model for empathetic readers.

Mary's petrified mourning reflects her obsession with the body of Christ. Since it is because she is unable to complete the rites of mourning that she mourns, the early modern Magdalene carries the trace of women's attendance upon the dying and the dead. Markham's pragmatic Magdalene displays her familiarity with the physical aspects of attending the corpse when she wonders, "Would any theefe have so religious beene, / To steale the bodie, and the clothes not take":

> I know that Mirrhe makes linnen cleave as fast
> As pitch or glue, well tempered or made;
> And could a theefes stolne leasure so long last,
> As to dissolve the Mirrhe, and bare the dead,

> Breake up the seales, open the Tombe and all?
> Where was the watch when these things did befall?

> If all this yet cannot persuade my mind,
> Yet might my owne experience make me see,
> When at the crosse they stripped him, unkind,
> I saw his garment would not parted bee
> > From goarie backe, but tare his tender skin,
> > Much more if it with Mirrhe had nointed bin.

> Ile looke into the sheet, if there remaine,
> Any one parcell of his mangled flesh,
> Or any haire pluckt from his heads soft maine,
> If none, that shall my wearie woe refresh:
> > Ile thinke a better chaunce betides my love,
> > Than my misdeeming feare will let me prove.

> > > (E4–E4v)

Mary's experiential knowledge of death's materiality informs her graphic portrait of the corpse's demise which, inscribed within the poem, embalms Christ's "mangled flesh" alongside her own entombed, benighted sorrow.

The female mourner's intimacy with the physical body of death, as we have seen in the period's conflations of mourning and marriage, implicates female sexuality in grief. As both embalmer and embalmed, Mary Magdalene engages the art's nominal pun by embodying the opening that is at once anatomical and sexual. Thus Sirani's Magdalene (figure 1, p. 17) continues in her penance the empathetic passion which characterizes her career as Christ's chief mourner. Her dishevelled garments mirror the dishevelled state of the wounded body she both mourns and imitates, carelessly revealing her breasts as Chrysostom's female mourners might bare their arms "to attract the gaze of men," or as Taylor's Ephesian widow unknowingly seduces the soldier with her "comely disorder of sorrow."

Textual manipulations of Magdalene's sexualized grief support the Protestant advocacy of internal, penitential tears. In Lewis Wager's dramatic interlude, *The Life of Marie Magdalene*, Mary's "life in sinne vile and vain" is characterized by her preoccupation, and that of the play's male personifications of the Vices, with her sexual body.[104] Mary enters the play, "triflyng with her garmentes," and complaining that the shoddy work of a tailor has inadequately framed her form as a work of art:

MARY I beshrew his heart naughtye folishe knave,
The most bungarliest tailers in this countrie,

That be in the world I thinke, so God me save,
Not a garment can they make for my degree.
Have you ever sene an overbody thus sytte?

. . .

What, I am ashamed to come in any mans sight,
Thinke you in the waste I am so great?
Nay by this twentie shillings I dare holde,
That there is no gentlewoman in this land,
More propre than I in the waste I dare be bolde.[105]

As the play progresses, Mary's seduction by the Vices proceeds entirely on the basis of her body. Infidelity flatters her with, "I warrant you with these clothes they wil be content, / They had leifer have you naked, be not afrayde, / Then with your best holy day garment,"[106] while Pride, Cupidity and Concupiscence give her a lesson in seductive dressing:

PRIDE   Your garments must be so worne alway,
         That your white pappes may be seen if you may.
CUP   If yong gentlemen may see your white skin,
         It will allure them to love, and soone bryng them in.
CON   Both damsels and wives use many such feates,
         I know them that will lay out their faire teates,
         Purposely men to allure unto their love,
         For it is a thyng that doth the heart greatly move.[107]

Finally, when Christ enters the play announcing that "For to salvation I have hir dressed" (F3v), Mary appears "sadly apparelled" to perform the "obsequie" toward which the play's action is directed, replacing her "carkas," entombed in vice, with the living–dead *corpus Christi*:

MARY   With this oyntment most pure and precious,
        I was want to make this carkas pleasant and swete
        Whereby I was mayd more wicked and viscious,
        And to all unthriftynesse very apt and mete.
        Now would I gladly this oyntment bestowe,
        About the innocent feete of my saviour,
        That by these penitent fruictes my lord may know
        That I am right sory for my sinfull behaviour.[108]

In Wager's interlude, Mary's conversion involves her body as completely as did her life of vice, and because it proceeds by point-by-point reversal (from suggestive to sad apparel, from concern for one's own body to the care of the Savior's), her sexual body is implied by and present within her saved one. Magdalene's sexualized mourning constitutes a marriage in the tomb. As Sirani's setting for Mary's self-flagellation reminds us (figure 1, p. 17), in Magdalene's subsequent career as a saint she is self-entombed in a hermitage where, dead to the world, she enacts an imitation not of Christ's life but of his death. And, as the painting also suggests, her sexual body is not swallowed by the grave, but remains vital, miraculously preserved by the painter herself.

In the *Complaynte*, this marriage is performed by Mary's self-willed death for love of Christ. She records in her own epitaph, "Here within restesth a gostely creature / Crystes true lover Mary Magdaleyn / Whose herte for love brast in peeces tweyn" (B5). Echoing the Song of Songs, Magdalene merges the languages of religion and eros ("Adieu my lorde my love so fayre of face / Adieu my turtyll dove frende of hewe," B6) and invites a community of female mourners to join her in lamentation, and to lament her death: "Ye vertuous women tender of nature / Full of pyte and of compassyon / Resorte I pray you unto my sepulture / To synge my dyinge with grete devocyon" (B5). This address reflects Mary's traditional role in collective mourning (as one of the three Maries), and points outward toward readers – in Markham's judgment ("And Marie shewes to maids and matrones both, / How they should wepe"), specifically female readers – to establish a community of mourners whose empathetic Passion, their excessive but acceptable grief, unites them spiritually with Christ. In J. C.'s portrait of the communal sorrow of Mary and the Virgin (who is "like the dead, or deathes palle wife"), mourning is a marriage consummated in the grave:

> Shall you and I (deare Ladie) plight our troth,
> And wed our selves to sorrowes restles bed;
> Our love and ioye is taken from us both,
> And we are lefte for to bewale the dead.[109]

If the embalmed figure of sorrowful Magdalene seems constructed for the sake of establishing internal, masculine mourning, she also embodies a physical intimacy with Christ which serves as a model for Christian fellowship, for a community based upon the rituals of collective female mourning. Sweetnam makes this clear in his handling of Christ's tears at Lazarus' grave. Rather than the episode's conventional deployment to correct excessive female mourning with moderation, Sweetnam offers it as an *exemplum* of the affective bond between Mary and the Savior, and of the persuasive power of women's tears:

But when the shining lame of Eternity cast his beautifull countenance upon that watry cloud [Mary], it did not turne the cloud into a bright and gladsome

hew, but rather (O Miracle!) was himselfe invested with a cloud of griefe, &
lacrymatus est Jesu, and Jesus wept. O beautiful teares of Blessed Magdalen
unto the which Christ Jesus joynes his tears! O strange Adamant of divine love
of our devout Pilgrime, who draweth water from the rocke, and teares from
Christ himselfe![110]

From this point of view, female mourning is not merely justified, but
sanctified and able not only to mourn, but also to raise, the dead.

III

Aemilia Lanyer's lyric retelling of Christ's passion, *Salve Deus Rex Judaeorum*, presents a "map of Death" to a community of mourning women
constructed by the text itself. The centrality of women's mourning to
the narrative is expressed on the title page: "*Salve Deus Rex Judaeorum,
Containing, 1 The Passion of Christ. 2 Eves Apologie in defence of Women. 3 The
Teares of the Daughters of Jerusalem. 4 The Salutation and Sorrow of the Virgine
Marie*" (1). Numerous dedicatory poems praising noblewomen from
whom Lanyer sought patronage[111] invite these women, like sisters of
mourning Magdalene, to anoint and embrace Christ's body, already
entombed in their hearts:

> Therefore (good Madame) in your heart I leave
> His perfect picture, where it shall stand,
> > Deeply engraved in that holy shrine,
> > Environed with Love and Thoughts divine.
>
> There may you see him as a God in glory,
> And as a man in miserable case;
> There may you reade his true and perfect storie,
> His bleeding body there you may embrace,
> And kisse his dying cheekes with teares of sorrow,
> With joyfull griefe, you may intreat for grace;
> > And all your prayers, and your almes-deeds
> > May bring to stop his cruell wounds that bleeds.
> > > (108)

Lanyer's poetics of mourning are deeply indebted to the discourses of
female lament current in her culture and to the aesthetics of female
lamentation, with its attendant strategy of embalming the female body
of mourning, governing the tears of Magdalene. But she revises these
commonplaces, rewriting Magdalene's metaphoric embalming and entombment in the image of women's restorative tears as a balm. "The
oyles of Mercie, Charitie, and Faith" (106) enact the body's healing and,

ultimately, its resurrection, no longer preserving the body *in* death, but freeing it *from* death: "These pretious balmes doe heale his grievous wounds" (107). Lanyer also reverses the devaluation of mourning as feminine when, incorporating Mary Magdalene's excessive but exemplary grief into her text, she represents female lament both as the basis of a privileged relationship between women mourners and Christ, and as sanctified by that communion. In her address "To all vertuous Ladies in generall," Lanyer recasts Magdalene's embalming of Christ as the ritual anointing of the faithful that consecrates these women as priests of Israel, and as gifts of the Magi now offered by grieving women: "Annoynt your haire with *Aarons* pretious oyle, / And bring your palmes of vict'ry in your hands . . . / Sweet odours, mirrhe, gum, aloes, frankincense, / Present that King who di'd for your offence" (14). United with the *corpus Christi* in death and in the afterlife, these sanctified mourners "flie from dull and sensuall earth, / Whereof at first your bodies formed were" (15). Thus Magdalene's marriage to Christ in the grave becomes the mystical marriage of the Church and Christ: "Take this faire Bridegroom," Lanyer advises the ladies, "in your soules pure bed" (20).

The erotic language of the Song of Songs infuses Lanyer's poem, as it does the tears of Magdalene, but adorns not the eroticized female church as lovers of Christ, but Christ as "dying lover" (33). Christ's crucified corpse expresses his love for the specifically female faithful: "Which I present (deare Ladie) to your view, / Upon the Crosse depriv'd of life or breath, / To judge if ever Lover were so true, / To yeeld himselfe unto such shamefull death" (105).[112] Indeed, the female witnesses to the Passion, whom Lanyer conducts to the foot of the cross, intimate with the mourning Maries and the maimed Christ, are asked both to mourn the brutalization of Christ's dying body and to learn desire for his restored corpse, anointed and attended by mourning angels:[113]

> No Dove, no Swan, nor Iv'rie could compare
> With this faire corps, when, 'twas by death imbrac'd;
> No rose, nor vermillion halfe so faire
> As was that pretious blood that interlac'd
> > His body, which bright Angels did attend,
> > Waiting on him that must to Heaven ascend.
>
> In whom is all that Ladies can desire;
> If Beauty, who hath bin more faire than he?
> If Wisedome, doth not all the world admire
> The depth of his, that cannot searched be?

If wealth, if honour, fame, or Kingdoms store,
Who ever liv'd that was possest of more?

(39–40)

Drawing on the aesthetics of Magdalene's opening in her tears, Lanyer performs a textual preservation of the *corpus Christi* which understands embalming not as the art of death, but as the art of life.

A pair of blazons further objectifies and eroticizes Christ's dualistic body in Lanyer's revision of the female mourner embalmed in grief.[114] In the first blazon, the ladies are asked to gaze upon the mournful image of the body in death:

His arms dis-joynted, and his legges hang downe,
His alabaster breast, his bloody side,
His members torne, and on his head a Crowne
Of sharpest Thorns, to satisfie for pride:
Anguish and Paine doe all his Sences drowne,
While they his holy garments do divide:
His bowells drie, his heart full fraught with griefe,
Crying to him that yeelds him no reliefe.

(101)

The second blazon, drawing heavily on the Song of Songs, supplements the first with the highly artful image of the resurrected Savior:

This is that Bridegroome that appeares so faire,
So sweet, so lovely in his Spouses sight,
That unto Snowe we may his face compare,
His cheekes like skarlet, and his eyes so bright.

. . .

His head is likened to the finest gold,
His curled lockes so beauteous to behold.

. . .

His cheekes are beds of spices, flowers sweet;
His lips, like Lillies, dropping downe pure mirrhe,
Whose love, before all worlds we doe preferre.

(107)

The figurative dismemberment of the body in the blazons and the transformation of the flesh into precious objects (alabaster, gold, spices, myrrh) recall Magdalene's embalmed heart and her transformation into balm. In Lanyer's handling, however, this spiritual embalming is not performed on the female mourner's body, but attends the male body being mourned.

She retains the empathy between female lament and its male object, but while male authors entomb and eroticize the female body of mourning as an external emblem of internal, masculine grief, Lanyer displays the textually embalmed body of Christ – to borrow Greenhill's phrase and return the art of embalming to women's hands – as "an Emblem of the Resurrection."

As for the female body in *Salve Deus Rex Judaeorum*, it is, like Wager's Magdalene, dressed for salvation, first by donning mourning garments and then, newly arrayed for the bridal, by casting them off. The poem begins with the image of the night sky as clothed in mourning, "Then will I tell of that sad blacke fac'd Night, / Whose mourning Mantle covered Heavenly Light" (65), an image that delivers readers to an inaugural echo of Christ's scriptural suffering in Gethsemane: "That very Night our Saviour was betrayed."[115] Similarly, the Countess of Cumberland's piety is figured in "the sack-cloth [she] do'st weare both night and day / ... Which [she] shak'st off when mourning time is past, / That royall roabes [she] may'st put on at last" (116). In the poem's opening moments, "vertuous Ladies" are arrayed in "wedding garments" of "purple scarlet white" (12), colors which "celebrate Christ's passion,"[116] while at its close, the Countess exchanges her mourning garments and appears, "Deckt in those colours which our Saviour chose: / The purest colours both of White and Red" – as a marginal note explains, "Colours of Confessors & Martirs" (129). Lanyer's post-ascensional view of the Passion with its certainty, so unlike Mary Magdalene's, of resurrection safeguards the purity and modesty of the poem's inscribed community of female mourners. She thus replaces the physical, sexual body of mourning with the emblazoned body of Christ as the poem's central metaphor, emblem, and work of art.

Lanyer's use of the embalmed male body expands ultimately to authorize her activities as writer. Her frequent images of Christ's body as the text itself suggest this: "Thy Soule," she explains to the Countess, "desires that he may be the Booke, / Whereon thine eyes continually may looke" (109), and elsewhere, "your soule may read / Salvation, while he (dying Lord) doth bleed" (32). As the *corpus Christi* is literalized in Lanyer's literary corpus, she gains authority from it, presenting her text as the embodiment of Christ, preserved in precious balms, and herself as a female Magus, bearing gifts:[117]

For having neither rich pearles of India, nor fine gold of Arabia ... Arramaticall Gums, incense, and sweet odours, which were presented by those Kingly Philosophers to the babe Jesus I present unto you even our Lord Jesus himselfe ... The sweet incense, balsums, odours, and gummes that flowes from that beautifull tree of Life, sprung from the root of *Jessie*, which is so super-excellent that it giveth grace to the meanest & most unworthy hand that will undertake to write thereof; neither can it receive any blemish thereby. (34–5)

Lanyer's "unworthy hand" is empowered by the balms distilled from Christ's body to present the "Lord Jesus himselfe." Her poem, like Markham's narrative of Mary Magdalene, becomes a "balme of troubled mind," enabled not by the embalmed body of female mourning but by the body of Christ, opened and objectified as the book itself.

Lanyer's validation of her authorial voice through its association with the transubstantiated *corpus Christi*, present in and as the book, is mirrored in her narrative of the Passion and women's roles within it. Her address "To the Vertuous Reader" famously condemns men who slander women as "such . . . that dishonoured Christ his Apostles and Prophets, putting them to shamefull deaths" (48). Women, on the other hand, enjoy a special place of privilege in relation to Christ:

it pleased our Lord and Saviour Jesus Christ, without the assistance of man . . . to be begotten of a woman, nourished of a woman, obedient to a woman; and that he healed women, comforted women: yea, even when he was in his greatest agonie and bloodie sweat, going to be crucified, and also in the last houre of his death, tooke care to dispose of a woman: after his resurrection, appeared first to a woman, sent a woman to declare his most glorious resurrection to the rest of his Disciples. (49–50)

This hierarchy of gender is apparent throughout the poem, reaching its most polemical moment in "Eves Apologie in defence of Women," which exonerates Eve for her part in the Fall and informs men that, "Her weaknesse did the Serpents words obay; / But you in malice Gods deare Sonne betray" (86):

> Whom, if unjustly you condemne to die,
> Her sinne was small, to what you doe commit;
> All mortall sinnes that doe for vengeance crie,
> Are not to be compared unto it:
>   . . .
> If one weake woman simply did offend,
> This sinne of yours, hath no excuse, nor end.
>   (86–7)

Lanyer not only censures the Passion's male villains but also criticizes the Disciples for their lack of constancy: "Those deare Disciples that he most did love," she complains, "were earth, / Which made them apt to flie, and fit to fall: / Though they protest they never will forsake him, / They do like men, when dangers overtake them" (78). While men, even the Apostles, are "earth," and thus "apt to flie," the women of the Passion, "flie from dull and sensuall earth." If men are Christ killers in Lanyer's poem, women, including the author and readers, are empathetic mourners:

> When spightfull men with torments did oppresse
> Th'afflicted body of this innocent Dove,
> Poore women seeing how much they did transgresse,
> By teares, by sighes, by cries intreat, may prove,
> What may be done among the thickest presse,
> They labor still these tyrants hearts to move;
> 　　　In pitie and compassion to forebeare
> 　　　Their whipping, spurning, tearing of his haire.
>
> 　　　　　　　　　　　　　　　　　　(94)

Lanyer's "Teares of the Daughters of Jerusalem" clearly recalls other textual communities of female mourners (Mavericke's comparison of the virgins of England to the Daughters of Israel, for instance, or Elizabeth Stuart's invocation of the Daughters of Britaine in "The Queenes Lamentation"). Moreover, the central place given to the Virgin's sorrows in Lanyer's poem repairs the maternal mourner's eroded status in post-Reformation religious works and arts of dying. Lanyer's Virgin appears in "griefes extreame" (94), in excessive but justified sorrow: "How canst thou choose (faire Virgin) then but mourne, / When this sweet offspring of thy body dies, / When thy faire eies beholds his bodie torne, / The peoples fury, heares the womens cries" (99–100). In the midst of reporting the Virgin's grief, she recalls the Annunciation to note that a woman is the agent by which Christ gave "his snow-white Weed for ours in change / Our mortall garment in a skarlet Die, / Too base a roabe for Immortalitie" (99). A similar conflation of the Virgin's sorrows and the Annunciation appears in Protestant *artes moriendi*, when the dying Christian is advised not to call upon the Virgin as mediatrix but to imitate her humility at the Annunciation: "saye with the good Virgine Marye, behold thy servant (O Lorde) be it unto me according to thy word."[118] Lanyer's quotation of Mary's song of thanksgiving, the Magnificat ("All people Blessed call, and spread thy fame," 95), also asserts this merger of the Annunciation and the Virgin's sorrows, implying that Mary's speech might validate Lanyer's. The poem affirms the Virgin's privileged status

and that the *women more wept* then the men. *More women: more weeping.*"[123]
He explains this immoderate weeping by, startlingly, attributing women's
tears not to their essential, bodily weakness but to the cultural and providential functions they served: "*More women* wept then men, partly by the
permission of men, who thought that the womens weeping came rather
from weaknes in themselves, then from kindness towards Christ. Partly
by the providence of God, who suffered *more women* to weepe then men,
that the women, which bewailed Christes death, might condemne the
men, which procured it."[124] Moreover, he defends the daughters' tears
in imagery that anticipates Lanyer's: "And had not these women then far
greater reason to lament the death of Christ who made every one of them
a wedding garment, wherein he did marrie them unto himselfe ... who
cloathed every one of them with Scarlet, and with the royall robe of his
righteousnesse, yea and gave his owne deare selfe unto them, that they
might put on the Lord Jesus?"[125] Playfere not only offers a precedent
for Lanyer's view that women's tears condemn men's wrong-doing at the
Crucifixion, but he also associates the episode with Eden, foreshadowing
her defense of Eve: "For the sinne of a woman, was the ruine of man.
Therefore the women willingly *wept the more*. That though a woman did
most in the second death of the first Adam; yet these might doe least in
the first death of the second Adam."[126]

While Playfere's sermon contains tantalizing points of contact with
Lanyer's poem, its gendering of mourning is vastly different: Playfere
uses the biblical episode to feminize and condemn immoderate grief and
to defend mourning in measure. "They to whom Christ here speaketh
offend in th'excesse," he explains, "And so here, Christ ... sayeth unto
them, *weepe not*. Forbidding thereby immoderate weeping, which is condemned *in nature; in reason; in religion*."[127] Further stigmatizing women's
mourning as excessive and, conversely, immoderate mourning as feminine, the sermon presents masculine wisdom as a balm and comfort
that counters Lanyer's presentation of women's tears as balm. Thus
he concludes, "if wee must not weep immoderately for the death of
Christ, then we must not greeve our selves greatly for the death of any
Christian."[128] Playfere surveys moderate biblical mourners, including
"Christ for Lazarus his friend," to correct the daughters' tears and to
prove that, "It is great folly and childishness to weepe immoderately
for the dead, and that it is on the other side a hie point of *wisdome* to
be moderate in this matter."[129] Rather than approving women's public
mourning, as Playfere's opening passage promises and as Lanyer's poem
enacts, *The Meane in Mourning* uses feminine tears to support an orthodox

gendering of grief that silences women's excesses and authorizes the moderate examples of their male governors.

Salve Deus Rex Judaeorum, however, illustrates both Lanyer's indebtedness to and reversal of the aesthetics of embalming current in the tears of Magdalene and early modern treatments of women's mourning. The post-Reformation censure of feminine grief as physical, immoderate, and sexual casts Magdalene's excessive but exemplary tears as external performances of grief that enable internal, moderate male mourning and the potency of the text as balm. For Lanyer, excessive mourning is both desirable and spiritual, since the anointing of Christ's body becomes an emblem of resurrection and a restorative tool in the hands of the chaste female Church. Thus the period's ideological demarcation of feminine grief as a uniquely volatile emotional site energizes Lanyer's textual work of mourning, allowing her to transvalue women's tears as tokens of the affective and spiritual bonds between themselves and Christ which sanctify women's speech. Her feminization of mourning responds to and releases the affective power of the mourning woman – a power embalmed within the static figure of feminized grief – by opening the *corpus Christi* within her map of Death. Released from self-entombment, feminine mourning supports Lanyer's convocation of a tearful but triumphant community of female saints.

PART I

Disposing of the body

A copy of Otto Werdmuller's *A Most frutefull, pithye and learned treatise, how a christen man ought to behave himself in the daunger of death*, now in the collection of the Folger Shakespeare Library, contains a preface by the publisher, William Blackwell, that names as the work's author Lady Jane Grey. "At last it was my good hap," he writes, "to light upon this most excellent, learned and godlye Treatise, which was written by a most vertuous and honourable personage, pure in life, and zealous in Religion: the Lady Jane Dudley. A worke so full of consolation and comfort, as in my poor opinion never better was printed."[1] Appended to Werdmuller's substantial *ars moriendi*, accordingly, is a copy of "An Exhortacion written by the Lady Jane, the night before she suffered, in the end of the newe Testament in Greeke which she sent to her Sister the Lady Katherine." While Werdmuller's treatise covers well over two hundred pages in the volume, Lady Jane's exhortation occupies only five. Blackwell's attribution of the volume to Grey suggests either that the value of the female-authored testimony outweighed that of the male-authored manual, in at least one reader's mind, or that in ignorance of the author's identity, the nomination of a woman as author was not only likely but (for novelty's sake) attractive. The same high estimation of Grey's last words is found in an early seventeenth-century reprinting of the exhortation, along with a report of her examination for heresy in the Tower and an affective record of her last words on the scaffold, which the editor describes as "comming, in an olde auncient Printed Copie unto my hands as it were halfe forgotten in the world, or like a curious monument whose well-carved figures, and rare architecture the dust and Cobwebs had injuriously defaced." He explains:

I could not out of Charitie and Christian love to a mirrour of such excellence, but with my best Art and industry pollish and clense a perfection so Noble, Holy and Worthy all good mens imitations, and as it were to awaken the sleepie world from her fantasticke Lethargie, to behold in that which we call the weaker sexe a strength matchlesse and invincible.[2]

Thomas Hoby's commonplace book also includes for the year 1554 a
handwritten transcription of the same three works copied, Hoby tells us,
from an account "written and penned with her own hand."[3]

The value of Grey's last words clearly depends not only on the
content of her exhortation, but on her status as a Protestant martyr, widely promulgated during Elizabeth's reign and rediscovered in
James's. The works' poignancy, too, and their incidental publication further heighten their appeal. While the account of her examination by
Bishop Feckenham[4] records Grey's staunch Anglican faith, even unto
death, in literate and well-reasoned terms, the moving description of her
very public death captured the imagination of her generation and many
to follow.[5] The "Exhortacion," finally, offers the perfect combination of
feminine modesty and masculine strength: as a personal meditation and
self-consolation, addressed in a private document to a close female relative and inscribed in Grey's own copy of the Greek New Testament, it
testifies to both her devotion and her erudition. Without seeking print,
Lady Jane created an *exemplum* of the early modern woman's good death
which resonated throughout the Reformation and beyond.

This section examines similar manipulations of feminine deaths and
mourning in the hands of male writers and reformers in order to show
how women's intimacy with death could be used to support a variety
of masculine polemics in post-Reformation England and, finally, to support a new definition of masculine subjectivity. The textual ravages and
adornments of Mary Magdalene's body practiced by the male authors of
her tears, undertaken to establish internal, spiritual mourning as the orthodox response to loss, finds its historical counterpart in the fortunes of
Queen Elizabeth I's corpse, whose treatments by Catholic polemicists
illustrate the lingering potency of the body-turned-object. In chapter 2,
embalming's concern with the female corpse informs a reading of
Shakespeare's *Henry VIII*, where the history of the Reformation is enacted and recorded through masculine approaches to the female body
in death.

Chapter 3 discusses male-authored representations of women's good
deaths, especially Phillip Stubbes's *A Chrystal Glasse for Christian Women*
(1591) and a volume dedicated to the memory of Katherine Brettergh,
Deaths Advantage (1602). In both works, inscriptions of women's dying
discourse within the political, theological, and cultural agendas of their
male authors recreate the literal corpse as an emblem of the causes
within which it is enlisted, sublimating physical death to spiritual ends.
These authors, moreover, approach the deathbed as a clearly gendered

site, where their subjects' feminine virtues in life both recommend their deaths as exemplary and are surrendered in death to a heroic, masculine fortitude.

Chapter 4 considers the intersection of mourning and maternity in texts published in the year of England's "general mortalitie," 1603, and examines the maternal mourner's complex role in plague literature and elegies for Elizabeth I as a prelude to a reading of maternity, mourning, and succession in Shakespeare's *Richard III*. I argue that for the plague authors and elegists, the figure of the maternal mourner symbolizes both the pathos of death and the stasis of feminine lamentation. These works, accordingly, trace the movement from feminine to masculine versions of grief and government, imitating the trajectory of the monarchy with Elizabeth's death and James's ascension. Shakespeare's history, finally, responds to the same gendering of grief evident in the plague texts and elegies, but interrogates the casting of feminine lament as merely static and ineffectual by employing an energetic nostalgia for lost Catholic forms of spirituality, embodied in the play's mourning mothers. While reformers ostracize women's mourning, depicting it as both excessive and incomplete, Shakespeare's maternal mourners deploy the lingering power of women's lamentation and the vitality of the bonds between the living and the dead severed by the Reformation.

The body of history: embalming and historiography in Shakespeare's Henry VIII

Elizabeth Southwell reports that, despite Queen Elizabeth I's directions that her corpse should not be embalmed, Robert Cecil ordered her surgeon to open her, with unexpected results:

Now, [the Queen's] bodie being seared up was brought to whit hall. where, being watched everie night by six several Ladies. my selfe that night there watching as one of them being all about the bodie which was fast nayled up in a bord cofin with leaves of lead covered with velvet, her bodie and head break with such a crack that spleated the wood lead and cer cloth. whereupon the next day she was faine to be new trimmed up.[1]

This reversal in death of the integrity and enclosure of the Virgin Queen's body offers a vexed case study in early modern notions of the physiological mirroring of interiority by the visible exterior; the sometimes contradictory ways in which the body – particularly the body in death – might reflect the soul.[2] This concern, if Southwell is to be believed, caused the story of Elizabeth's exploding corpse to be suppressed in the aftermath of her death: "no man durst speak of yt publicklie," she writes, "for displeasing *Secretarie Cecill*."[3] Until Catherine Loomis's recent reconsideration, Southwell's account of Elizabeth's death had been discounted by historians due to its singularity in describing the exploding corpse and, more significantly, on the basis of Southwell's Catholicism, which provided an all-too-ready motive for the unsavory details she conveys.[4] Robert Persons' use of the story in his *Discussion of the Answer of M. William Barlow* (1612) to "ghesse" Elizabeth's damnation on the evidence of her "disastrous death" attests to the presumed relationship between Elizabeth's crimes in life and the misfortune of her corpse, and to the narrative's appeal to Catholic polemicists, serving further to weaken its credibility.[5]

The story raises valuable questions, though, about early modern women's relationships to the body in death, and the cultural significance the female corpse – particularly the royal corpse – could convey.

Elizabeth's resistance to embalming was typical of the growing distaste among noblewomen for the practice in the late sixteenth and early seventeenth centuries, and the controversy over whether the procedure was undertaken in her case emphasizes the art's problematic gendering and the perceived vulnerability of the *female* body before its invasive scrutiny. Certainly men as well as women may have wished to avoid the *post mortem* disfigurement involved in embalming, but the culture's insistence on feminine chastity and corporeal enclosure marks women's interactions with the art in different, highly sexualized, terms. While Southwell tells us that "Cecill having given a secreat warrant to the surgions they opened her," Loomis suggests that the secretary may have honored Elizabeth's wishes to avoid being opened, prompted not by his distaste for bodily mutilation but by the desire to "avoid the difficult questions an inspection of Elizabeth's reproductive organs might have raised about possible heirs or about the Queen's moral character."[6] John Manningham's contemporary diary provides another interpretation. "It is certaine the Queene was not embowelled, but wrapt up in cere cloth, and that verry il to, through the covetousnes of them that defrauded hir of the allowance of clothe was given them for that purpose."[7]

Southwell's narrative, moreover, sheds light on the protracted moment of the body's transformation from living flesh to an iconic vessel containing only a residue of the spirit – and meaning – it contained in life. The body's existence as an object in its own right, both severed from and alluding to its animate meanings (among them, gender), lies at the heart of Southwell's report and accounts for its gruesome sensationalism and its eerie metaphysics. The story and its polemical afterlife point toward the various means by which cultural value could be assigned to the corpse, but also assumes that the material body in death responds to and reveals (perhaps ironically, perhaps with a truth unavailable in life) the departed soul: for Elizabeth's virginal modesty, death repays her with violent rupture; in place of her carefully maintained veneer of youth and beauty she finds in death a stench of decay that prompts Southwell to remark, "yf she had not ben opened the breath of her bodie would a ben much worse."[8] Depending upon the emphasis one places on the elements of Southwell's report, embalming appears at once as an intervention into the metamorphosis from life to death and from subject to object, or perhaps the means by which this transformation is accomplished, or perhaps, finally, a resistant symbol of one's uncontrollable physical, if not metaphysical, afterlife. Embalming is an operation performed upon the female corpse by male interpreters,[9] and a marker of female will extending beyond the grave. It is an expression of the desire to render the body in death permanent and unchanging, and a poignant and powerful comment on the impossibility of that desire. Meanwhile, Southwell's embalming of Elizabeth *in* her narrative, her complex presentation of the female body in death, suggests that the *functions* of the queen's corpse – ideological, political, or polemical – are the point. As R. C. Finucane states it, early modern death ritual "was not so much a question of dealing with a corpse as reaffirming the secular and spiritual order by means of corpse."[10]

The fortunes of Elizabeth's corpse within the factional discourses following her death prefigure this chapter's central interest in male writers' uses of the embalmed female body to support a metaphorics of embalming within their texts, particularly in Shakespeare's *Famous History of The Life of King Henry VIII*. The posthumous career of Queen Elizabeth's corpse reveals how the royal remains could inform or, indeed, script history. Nigel Llewellyn's comment that Elizabeth I's tomb in Westminster Abbey, commissioned by James I, "is a permanent memorial of the funeral" offers an example of a male interpreter reading the queen's body in a politically interested way and gaining political capital from his thoughtful manipulation of the corpse.[11] Southwell's account reminds us that historical meaning is constructed through the notional, and sometimes through the literal, embalming of bodies.

Accordingly, this chapter further opens Elizabeth's corpse to argue that the early modern genderings of grief and embalming inform Shakespeare's treatment of the gendered body of history in *Henry VIII*. I argue that embalming, like mourning, functions performatively to construct the sex that it purportedly reveals in the anatomical opening of the gendered body. Embalming mediates between the body's material exteriority and noumenal interiority. As a performative gesture constructing *masculine* interiority, the art relies on the *feminized* body in death to literalize interiority in aestheticized remains. Early modern views of embalming align women with the material aspects of the art, while men deploy its figurative aspects in the service of spiritualized consolatory discourses. The Reformation's reassessment of sacramental power – including the sacrament of embalming, extreme unction – associates women's material embalming, on the biblical model of Mary Magdalene, with Catholic ritual and men's spiritual embalming with reformed piety. In *Henry VIII*, embalming appears as a historiographical style, a marker of gender, and an operation performed upon the female body by male interpreters in the play's "construction of good women."[12] Through a selective survey of the preserved bodies of queens – Katherine of Aragon, Anne Bullen, and Princess Elizabeth – the play also constructs an authorizing genealogy for James I. Shakespeare nostalgically resurrects Elizabeth's corpse within the vicissitudes of "emballing" and "embalming" (2.3.47 and 4.2.170) that mark the borders of femininity in the play's mourning for the body of history. The corpse's power not only to *mark* but also to *make* history, to signal and emblematize the passage of time and to influence present and future events with its animated insistence on interpretation, enables Shakespeare's treatment of the Reformation's founding moment as a function of the shifting means by which value is assigned to the female body in death. Quite literally, the treatment of women's bodies in death charts the course of Reformation piety, while their figurative embalming and reinterment in Shakespeare's history supports its masculine narrative of dynastic continuity. The gendered struggle to define – literally and figuratively – the body in death informs Shakespeare's scripting of Reformation history as the struggle of competing queens, Catholic and Protestant, to control their historical afterlives.

I

Like early modern mourning rituals, the art of embalming in the period offers an arena wherein gender is both constructed and defined. In both cases, spiritualized approaches to death and its bodily effects are identified as masculine through an emphatic association of the feminine with the physical body in and of death.

Elizabeth I's reported wish to avoid embalming, perhaps prompted by a desire to protect her corpse from male penetration, is echoed by her countrywomen. Although some men and women alike certainly looked with dread toward the prospect of embalming, women's recorded desires to avoid opening seek to protect their chastity even in death, and thus attribute to the dead flesh the remnants of living morality and reputation. Death's materiality, in other words, is at the center of their interest. Mary, Countess of Northumberland (d. 1572), for example, requests in her will that she not be embalmed, reasoning, "I have not loved to be very bold afore women, much more would I be loath to come into the hands of any living man, be he physician or surgeon."[13] A seventeenth-century account of Sister Chiara of Montefalco's embalming three centuries earlier similarly reports that, because the nuns considered it improper for a man to touch the virginal corpse, "Sister Francesca, inexperienced though she was, opened [the body] as best she could with a razor."[14]

Cautionary tales, both fictional and historical, of male embalmers' sexual abuse of female corpses[15] may have augmented women's modesty, rendering the material disruptions of the corpse in embalming an especially horrifying future for them to contemplate. Fears of necrophilia and of being buried alive[16] help to explain both men's and women's requests that their corpses should remain undisturbed in the household for hours or days before preparation for burial. Thus Elizabeth Russell's will asks that, "after I shall depart this life I be suffered and permitted to lye . . . by the space of fowre and twentye howers after my breath shall seem to have leafte my bodye . . . before I be wrapt up."[17] Although the fear of premature burial might have enhanced the popularity of embalming, which guaranteed beyond doubt that death had actually occurred, the desire to avoid the hands of male embalmers seems to have outweighed in the minds of early modern *women* whatever benefits the procedure may have promised.[18]

Early modern Englishwomen's disdain for the invasive opening of their own bodies and those of loved ones bespeaks a clearly gendered relationship to the art. Anne Clifford's diary is remarkably specific about the *post mortem* treatment of family members and friends, including details of bodies' embalmments – or most often, the absence of the procedure – with a persistence that suggests her ongoing interest in the practice and its applications. She reports that on June 1, 1616, eight days after her mother's death, she directed "that the Body might be wrapp'd in Lead till they heard from me,"[19] a necessary measure since the corpse was not actually buried until July 11.[20] Clifford states that following the death of Miss Anne Seymour on January 29, 1619, "the child was opened, it having a Corrupt Body, and so it was put in Lead."[21] In her old age, she recalls, "how this day was 26 years [since] dyed my second Lord Philip Herbert, Earle of Pembroke & Montgomery . . . and my said Husband's dead Body being unopened was wrapt in Sear Cloth and lead and so carried down and buried in the Cathedral Church at Salisbury."[22] Again, "I remembered how this day was 72 years dyed in North hall in Harfordshire, in her owne chamber there, my worthy Aunt Anne Russell, Countesse Dowager of Warwick, & shee was buried awhile after, un-opened, in the vault of Chenies Church in Buckinghamshire."[23] Clifford's interest in whether the bodies of family members were opened and her impressive memory of these details indicate that she, like other early modern women, viewed the balsamic art as an unhappy practice imposed upon their loved ones and a prospect toward which they themselves looked with dread. Her references to the art and her desire concerning the treatment of her own corpse, "that [her] body may be unopened, wrapt onely in a sear cloth and led, with an inscription on the breast whose bodie it is,"[24] imply that the unopened body is greatly to be preferred over embalming, and that only royal status (Queen Anne) or physical corruption attending a violent final illness (Anne Seymour) might require the procedure to be undertaken. Collectively, these comments in Clifford's diary (which becomes as the years go on a quilt of memories of departed loved ones) argue that self-history, too, is constructed by memorializing one's dead through their figurative embalming within the pages of the book itself.

A mourner for Queen Anne's funeral in 1619, Clifford also notes that, on March 5, "About 9 o'clock the Queen's Bowels all saving her Heart were buried privately in the Abbey at Westminster in the place where the King's Mother's Tomb is. There was none came with it but three or four of her servants and Gentlemen Ushers which carried it, and a Herald before it." The remainder of the Queen's body was not interred until eight weeks later, on May 13.[25] The description offers another ex-ample, like Southwell's, of a noblewoman's response to royalty's female corpse that explores the function of a woman's body in death. The ac-count recalls the image of the embalmed heart (whose secular career in romance literature was spiritualized in the tears of Magdalene) and the cultural practices that converted this aesthetic embalming into re-ality in early modern England, rendering explicit in an object crafted of bodily remains the invisible soul within. In the entombment of the queen's organs, one witnesses the royal body's complex treatment in death, which substituted the embalmed body for the corpse ravaged by death, and further substituted a wax effigy, displayed above the coffin, for the embalmed corpse contained within.[26] With each substitution, one moves literally and notionally away from the physical body and closer to its conversion from living flesh to aestheticized object. Clifford's note, however, that "the Queen's Bowels *all saving her Heart*" received burial in Westminster points toward the *absent* heart, the missing organ which must also have been harvested from the body but is not interred here. This fact implies that the organ may have been otherwise and elsewhere preserved, perhaps fashioned into an object for private use and devotion. When Alexander Read notes that "the Heart may be embalmed apart, according to the Relations pleasure,"[27] he bows to survivors' wills in de-termining the treatment and ultimate use of the loved one's organs, and attests to their desire for memorial objects that permanently preserve the beloved-but-lost body.[28] The queen's aestheticized heart offers a literal parallel to Southwell's textually embalmed body of Elizabeth. While

3 David des Granges. *The Saltonstall Family.*

Southwell and her later redactors use Elizabeth's corpse to challenge the morality and legitimacy of her reign, Clifford reflects a desire to resolve whatever uncertainties may have attended Anne's body in life within a memorial object bespeaking the permanence in death of her literalized affections, the heart itself.

Objects such as Queen Anne's embalmed heart have affinities with a new genre of memorial painting which developed in the early seventeenth century representing the female corpse on her deathbed, examples of which construct masculine cultural and dynastic narratives on the basis of the embalmed female body. M. David Des Granges' *Saltonstall Family* (figure 3) provides a good example of the genre's social and cultural aspects. The painting shows Sir Richard Saltonstall drawing aside the curtains of his wife's deathbed to reveal her living–dead form forever gesturing toward her two surviving children. Also included in the portrait is Saltonstall's second wife, holding on her lap the child of his subsequent marriage. By condensing narrative time to include both wives, the painting illustrates the absent–presence of Saltonstall's first wife as a member of the family he establishes with his second, most clearly expressed in the bond between the dying mother and the children who survive her. The continuity of familial identity, of course, is affirmed by Richard Saltonstall's continuous presence despite the loss of one wife and her replacement by another. The painting articulates patriarchal presence as the foundational feature of the early modern family, [29] but does so by deploying the permanently fixed female body in death to underwrite Saltonstall's resilient domestic government.[30] Paintings such as this may have "helped protect . . . husband[s] from the shock of [wives'] death[s],"[31] but they also embody death *as* female, and permanently entomb the female subject on the canvas itself. Interested in preserving not the living wife's likeness but the image of her body in death, Des Granges aesthetically embalms the incorruptible corpse within the space of the frame. As Sir Kenelm Digby said of Anthony Van Dyck's deathbed portrait of his wife, Venetia, "Me thinkes I see her dead indeed."[32]

While early modern women retain their investment in death's materiality in their attitudes toward embalming, clergymen of the period utilize women's associations with the corpse to support spiritualized discourses of consolation. Throughout the period, women's intimacy with the material body's demise emphasizes the role of sexuality in death; that is, the troublesome relationship of the female body in death – with its living legacy of chastity apparently intact – to the invasive surgical procedures demanded by opening. At the same time, the aesthetics of embalming objectify the female corpse itself, locating and literalizing physical death within it to construct internal, masculine responses to death. This movement away from the actual practice of embalming toward its metaphoric or notional applications reflects the problematic places of the art within the funerary rituals of middle class culture, on the one hand, and of reformed theology, on the other.

Although embalming was almost exclusively reserved for members of the nobility, clergy, and royalty, middle-class families occasionally made use of the art. William Gouge, in his compendious handbook on the domestic duties of householders and their families, argues that one duty of children to is bury parents with the decorum, pomp, and celerity appropriate to their station. "It being a great deformity to have a mans corps lie above ground," he explains, "(for no carkase will be more loathsome then a mans if it lie unburied) children, who are most bound to cover their parents deformity, are in this respect bound to burie their corps." He continues:

Contrary is their practise whose mindes are so set on their parents goods, as they cleane neglect their bodies. So soone as their parents breath is out of their body, they busie themselves about the things which they have left behinde them, as their corps is ready to stinke before care be taken for the buriall of it. Yea, some will purposely keepe their parents corps above ground till they be exceeding noisome, for receiving some revenues, or debts, or other accounts, which must be paid before the corps be buried. If their corps must needes for sometime be kept above ground, let them be imbalmed, or so used as they may not savour. They who are carelesse hereof, shew that they respect their parents wealth more then his person.[33]

For Gouge, embalming is an unnatural practice that perverts acceptable funerary rites to satisfy children's greed. While embalming appears here as the respectful option to the filial neglect that would allow the corpse to savour, it nonetheless violates the parental body's right to decent and swift burial and implies children's pretensions toward a higher social rank mirrored in their desire to secure parents' wealth. Embalming measures filial duty or negligence. Children's unnatural greed is literalized in this unnatural use of the corpse.

Increasingly, embalming was a practice whose reassessment in post-Reformation polemical and didactic works could affirm or refute specific doctrinal positions. These figurative applications of the art revise the literal practices of the body's opening *after* death and its anointing *prior* to death, enacted in extreme unction. When Piero Camporesi describes embalming as belonging to "a world in which the dividing line between life and death, between presence and absence was not as well-defined as it is today," he implies that the collapse of intercessory practices in the Reformation, with the concomitant rupture of liturgical and imaginative links between the living and the dead, might precipitate a reinterpretation of embalming and its effects.[34] For instance, as Pierre Chaunu argues, French reformers' emphasis on the soul's immediate deliverance to its final resting place at the moment of death caused them to repudiate both cremation and embalming.[35] While Anglican reformers rejected extreme unction, they recast the sacrament within a metaphorics of embalming that objectifies dead Catholic rituals and associates them with the body in death and with excessive feminine mourning.

At the center of much debate in the period was the status of extreme unction, the ritual embalming of the body before death which hoped to preserve the spirit in the afterlife. Extreme unction, as Roberto Bellarmino's Counter-Reformation *Art of Dying* explains, was "instituted both for the recovery of perfect health, and to take away sinnes or relickes that remayned of them."[36] Bellarmino insists upon the sacrament's necessity to the forgiveness of sins, and also complains that its deferral often obscures its remedial character:

in our daye so few sicke men do recover their sicknes, notwithstanding that they receave this Sacrament . . . [because] this remedy is applyed to the sicke later them [sic] it should, for we must not expect miracles by this or any other Sacrament, and it were a miracle if one that is at the last gaspe should presently recover, but if this Sacrament were ministered to them when first of al they beginne to be daungerously sicke, we should then often see this effect of recovery.[37]

To support this claim, Bellarmino offers a story of "St. Malachy, a Bishop of Ireland," who is too late to administer extreme unction to a noblewoman so that she dies without benefit of the sacrament. The bishop, Bellarmino writes,

so farre forth repented himselfe, that with his priests in lay in the chamber of the dead woman all the night praying and lamenting & imputing it to his own fault, that the vertuous woman eyther had not recovered by the vertue of Extreme Unction, or had not receaved that ample pardon of her sins for the liberal mercy of our loving Lord: and because this holy Bishop was the friend of God, by his prayers and teares he obtayned of him that this sayd woman should come agayne to life, & receaved from the hands of the same Saint, both the effects of this holy Unction, for she recovered her health & lived many yeares after, & as we may piously conjecture gained also the pardon of her sins."[38]

Despite the disclaimer that "we must not expect miracles by this or any other Sacrament," the story depicts extreme unction as able to enact supernatural recoveries from the brink of death or failing that, at least to ensure (less spectacularly, but more efficaciously) the soul's smooth transition from life to death. Peter of Luca's Catholic *Dialogue of Dying Wel*, translated into English in 1603, promises that, "by vertue of this holie Sacrament of extreme unction he [God] will graunt thee plenarie remission in this life of all thy sinnes, that is to say, that when thy soule shalbe separated from thy bodie, immediately without touche of the paynes of purgatorie, thow mayest flie to the blisse of everlasting lyfe."[39]

Such beliefs were anathema to Protestant reformers and extreme unction became a focal point for reforming the liturgy of the deathbed. The body's literal anointing in the sacrament was discarded and replaced by a spiritualized metaphorics of embalming that informs post-Reformation consolatory texts and funeral sermons. When Martin Luther rejects extreme unction in *The Pagan Servitude of the Church*, he points to the sacrament's contradictory intentions (restored health, on the one hand, and salvation after death on the other) as evidence of its fraudulence, and traces the movement from outward sign to inward faith that Protestant arguments against transubstantiation also travel: "We cannot deny that forgiveness and peace are given through Extreme Unction. This, however, does not take place because it is a sacrament divinely instituted, but because he who receives it, receives it believing that forgiveness and peace are now his." Luther's nullification of sacramental power emphasizes "true spiritual eating and drinking" based not on "trumped-up" sacraments but on private meditation and prayer.[40] As an orthodox practice in England, extreme unction was included in a modified form in the 1549 *Book of Common Prayer*'s Order for the Visitation of the Sick, and disappeared altogether in 1552, part of the "abolishment of certain ceremonies that were so far abused, partly by the superstitious blindness of the rude and unlearned, and partly by the unsatiable avarice of such as sought more their own lucre than the glory of God."[41] In the same year that Peter of Luca's dialogue promised immediate entry into Paradise on the basis of extreme unction, James Balmford's *A Short Dialogue Concerning the Plagues Infection* condemned the "Papists . . . bastard Sacrament of Extreame unction"[42] as an unnecessary ritual derived from the false idea that a priest or clergyman must be present at the deathbed. He complains that in the absence of the sacrament, "the cursed people (which know not the law) neither care to know it (being ever addicted to superstitious vanities) must needes (forsooth) in stead thereof, have a Minister to visit their sicke, though they be more than halfe dead."[43]

In the post-Reformation absence, on the one hand, of extreme unction as a consolatory ritual of the deathbed and, on the other hand, of embalming after death as a doctrinally sound practice appropriate to all classes, Protestant preachers developed a metaphorics of embalming licensed by Mary Magdalene's anointing of Christ's body, in which rituals attending the body's demise were corrected and sublimated. George Hughes's *The Art of Embalming Dead Saints* (1642), for example, glosses Psalms 16:10, "For thou wilt not leave my Soule in Hell; neither wilt thou suffer thine Holy one to see Corruption," explaining, "the force whereof is to free the Soules from dereliction in the state of death, and to secure the bodies of Gods Saints from Corruption in the grave. It is the art which I desire to learne, and at this time, teach upon this sad occasion, even the preparings of this confection against our burialls."[44] Hughes's funeral sermon applies the metaphor of embalming throughout to describe the funerary rites themselves, offering a recipe for a "confection of Embalme" composed of holiness, God's mercy, and faith.[45] He concludes of his subject, "Let us Imbalme him, at least spread his own confection on him, his good name is a precious oyntment, Holinesse hath made it so."[46] Abraham Cheare's "Embalming of a Dead Cause," similarly glosses Magdalene's proleptic embalming of the *corpus Christi* in Mark 14.8, "She hath done what she could: she is come aforehand to anoint my Body to the Burying," as referring not to corporeal but to spiritual embalming in a gesture that parallels Luther's "spiritual eating" of the Eucharist: "Unto this his Body mystically and figuratively considered, there being such promises of Resurrection, there is also a spiritual embalming to be performed to it."[47] Since the human condition is corrupt, Cheare argues, Christians must preserve their bodies against putrefaction through a spiritual embalming of Christ that imitates Magdalene's anointing of his feet. In William Leigh's sermon on Katherine Brettergh's death in 1601, Magdalene's example is spiritualized in and as the language of the sermon itself: "For as the *Maries* could not bee satisfied with al [*sic*] that was done by *Joseph* and *Nichodemus* for their master *Christ,* unlesse their poore balme wente withal: so can I not content my selfe with all you have done (though most sufficient) unless I bring some sindon of mine own, and buy some balme to bestow upon this Saint."[48]

These metaphoric applications of embalming suggest not only the problematic status of the actual practice for Protestant clergymen and middle-class laypeople but also the gendering of the art within post-Reformation consolatory and funerary discourses. The art's concern with the body and its corruption prompts reformers to direct their figurative applications toward the spiritual rather than the material. Accordingly, Mary Magdalene no longer figures excessive grief, but consolation, and her insistently physical bond with Christ informs the corpse's metaphoric embalming with the confection of the sermon itself. The material rite of embalming is sublimated *as* the memorial language of the funeral sermon, performed not by a woman but by a man, interested no longer in the body in death but in the immortal soul.

A diptych of lachrymose poems by Gervase Markham – *Marie Magdalens Lamentations for the Losse of her Master Jesus*, published in 1601, and *The Teares of the Beloved: or, The Lamentation of Saint John*, which appeared only one year later – neatly illustrates the Reformation alignment of Catholic sacraments with excessive, external feminine mourning and of reformed spirituality with internal masculine piety. Of the seven lamentations that comprise Markham's *Marie Magdalens Lamentations*, the first five take place in the shadow of Christ's empty tomb and lament the loss of his body. The vast majority of the work depicts a weeping Magdalene whose tears are both excessive and exemplary. Turning toward his audience, however, Markham notes the Catholic history of the genre and signals its reformation for Protestant readers, which he himself undertakes. "*Maries* teares contemned, long have slept," he complains, "As jems unpriz'd, which corrupt age destroies" (A3v). His Mary manifests her Protestantism by rejecting the petrified Catholic rituals (with their mistaken emphasis on the body rather than the spirit) which she had been so frequently employed to emblematize. Her mourning for Christ's lost body, while rooted in early modern women's material practice of watching the corpse ("O had I watched, as I waile him now, / None could have taken him without me too," B2v), regrets her failure adequately to perform the duty in terms that, surprisingly, associate the feminine rite with the spirit rather than the body:

> But being too precise to keepe the Law,
> The lawes sweet maker I have thereby lost,
> And bearing to his ceremonies too much awe,
> I misse his sweetest selfe, of far more cost,
> > Sith rather with the Truth I should have beene,
> > Than working that, which by a Tipe was seene.
>
> > (B2v)

Luther's criticism of "Romanists" who, in their defense of transubstantiation, "fight for ceremonial but oppose love,"[49] resonates with Mary's claim that "the deepest passion of [her] true-burning love" (B2v) ought to have led her to violate the Sabbath in order to fulfill her duties of watching and embalming. Mary condemns the dead letter of the law as Markham revises her tears according to Protestantism's censure of "the merely outward signs" of Catholic ceremony.[50] Her equation of Catholicism's dead letter and Jewish law echoes the 1559 *Book of Common Prayer*, which explains the abolishment of Catholic ceremonies by affirming, "Christ's gospel is not a ceremonial law, as much of Moses' law was, but it is a religion to serve God, not in bondage of the figure or shadow, but in the freedom of spirit."[51]

Markham's Protestant Magdalene revises her own portrayal in Catholic antecedents, where she mourns the loss of the *corpus Christi* in terms that literalize the body in the Eucharist. Hers is a spiritual embalming after all, Markham insists. Thus his Mary rejects transubstantiation in the memorable imagery with which she describes the empty tomb of Christ: "Though I have lost the Saint of clearest shine," she complains, "I will at least have care to keepe the shrine":

> And to this shrine Ile sacrifice my heart,
> Though it be spoiled of the soveraigne host,
> It shall the altar be and sacred part,
> Where I my teares will offer with the most.
>
> (B4v)

The figure of the shrine devoid of the host offers a synecdoche of Protestantism's understanding of the host itself and Christ's absent–present relationship to it. Luther's censure of transubstantiation, for instance, conflates the feminine body, Christ's tomb, and the Eucharist in terms that prefigure Markham's imagery of the tomb as both the sign rather than the substance of the *corpus Christi* and the feminized site of death's dominion:

Christ is believed to have been born from his mother's virgin womb. Let [Catholics] aver, here also, that the flesh of the virgin was temporarily deprived of being, or, as they would more aptly have it put, "transubstantiated," in order that Christ, having been enfolded in the accidents, might come forth through the accidents. The same thing will have to be said of the shut door of the upper room and the closed mouth of the sepulcher, through which He went in and out without doing them injury.[52]

While Markham's Magdalene corrects her Catholic predecessors, though, the poem's spiritualized narratives – the Protestant story of sacramental reform, the typological rewriting of Old Testament letter with New Testament spirit, and the plot of internal masculine penance – are

written at her expense. Her lament and its penitential effects bespeak
a loss that is permanently mourned, a grief beyond remedy that leaves
Magdalene in tearful stasis and self-entombment.

Accordingly, the poem's sequel, *The Tears of the Beloved*, rejects Catholic
sacramental forms by replacing feminine mourning with masculine tears.
For Mary's stubborn emphasis on Christ's material body, St. John contemplates the resurrected Christ, a figure that promises the "broken
heart, pyning away with griefe, / Sorrowing for sinne, findeth in thee
reliefe."[53] John's masculine awareness of the spirit rather than the body,
the invisible rather than the manifest, refines and refocuses Magdalene's
lament:

> Fly foorth, my soule, for sure this Word divine,
> Hath power on thee, to call thee back againe;
> Unseene thou art, my body doth thee shrine,
> Bodilesse, and immortall, subject to joy or paine.
> > To none more like, then to that hidden grace,
> > The godhead hath, which Sathan would deface.
>
> > > (BI v)

While Mary mourns the lost body, John mourns the lost soul. While
Mary's mourning offers a self-mutilating, empathetic feminization of
Christ's Passion, John's tears internalize his suffering, rendering invisible
grief's ravages: "His inward griefe I moand, now is exprest," John insists,
"The outwarde anguish, that my Lord did finde" (c3). The poem never
dwells upon the crucified corpse, but spiritualizes mourning, turning
away from Mary's excessive grief toward productive, moderate lament.
In the place of Mary's self-entombment, John's account of the "exceeding griefe" (B2) of the Passion replaces sorrow with sorrow in a fluid series
of events that rewrites Magdalene's stasis:

> That griefe being past, another is in place,
> But may it be that thus thou shouldest faint?
> Ah, shew thy might, those hellish hags to chace,
> Who thee and us do force to sad complaint.
> > I say no more, that must my moane restraine:
> > This garden wils, I should a while refraine.
>
> > > (B2)

This quasi-heroic refusal of feminized mourning, appropriately figured
and stigmatized as "hellish hags," is the poem's goal. Thus John continues the story of Gethsemane by naming his specific cause for sorrow
(a masculine version of Mary Magdalene's failure to watch the corpse),

and by offering a portrait of the King of Kings experiencing the "griefe of griefes:"

> Refraine, said I? no, now began my moane,
> Seeing sluggish sloth, my eyes with sleepe opprest,
> I carelesse slept, but Lord of Life did groane,
> With griefe of griefes, that brought him such unrest.
> > Woe worth my sinne, the cause of his complaint,
> > Forcing my Lord indure such hard constraint.
>
> > > (B2)

Clearly Christ's suffering in Gethsemane is the model of masculine tears advocated by the poem. Heroic, temporal, and spiritual (Markham assures us that "from heaven an angel sent, / Did comfort him, whom we in griefe did leave," B3), Christ's mourning is a necessary means (submission to God's will) to a necessary end (salvation), and the pattern of all Christian tears: "These drops declare his inward sad lament; / For greater griefe no earthy tongue can tell" (B4).

In a poem dominated by this affective model, a series of minor lamentations also appear, of which John's sorrow for his lapse in the garden is one. Rather than focusing on the iconic figure of female mourning, the poem gives us a variety of male mourners (Judas and Peter as well as John), each of whom participates in Christ's sorrow but in imperfect, all-too-human ways. Far from the static enclosure of Christ's tomb where Magdalene's laments are staged, John's tears take place in a social and political world, a commonwealth governed by men whose productive grief is guaranteed by the heroism and stoicism with which sorrows are endured. Rather than offering an allegory of spiritual penance, John's tears portray the nascent Christian commonwealth, a brotherhood of Christian humanists, established on the model of Christ's exemplary grief.

Markham's diptych offers gendered performances of mourning that shift emphasis from body to spirit and from external sign to internal process with the movement from feminine to masculine voice. This shift parallels male reformers' use of embalming to figure spiritual health rather than bodily preservation, internal faith rather than sacramental power. The concerns of the material body become a matter of women's work. While reformers recast embalming to reflect their spiritual rather than physical interests, the embalmed remains of female corpses hold forth legacies of their own. Like Elizabeth's ruptured corpse, Queen Anne's heart – apparently removed and embalmed but absent and unaccounted for in the history of her demise – is a token of the aesthetics of embalming which seek to render permanent the mutable flesh, and also of the art's failure to preserve the too-perishable body. The embalmed heart is a literal parallel to the figurative *corpus Christi* in the tears of Magdalene. In both cases, the material body's death occasions obsequious efforts to reclaim and preserve the corpse and to literalize its loss in a memorial object.

Like Southwell's account of Elizabeth's exploding body, Markham's diptych assumes that the powerful corpse is not merely subject to historical events, but can be used to effect and record them. If feminine mourning embalms the mourner herself as an icon of permanence, masculine mourning looks toward the resurrected *corpus Christi* to articulate its faith in the spiritual balm that saves, grounding its progressive narrative of Christian salvation on the risen body of Christ, and on figurative remains of the mourning woman.

II

"Excessive was the sorrow of King Richard the Second," Thomas Fuller wrote in 1642, "beseeming him neither as a king, man, or Christian."[54] As a mourner who devotes his woeful pageants to static self-entombment, Shakespeare's Richard, like Catholic Mary Magdalene, mourns the body's loss, literalizing royal presence in the flesh as a parallel to transubstantiation. Richard's mournful self-deposition embalms the fallen body of kingship, anatomizes the corpse of divine right, and eulogizes the demise of Catholic ceremonial forms, their potency and presence. His faith in the performative power of ceremony to instill kingship reflects a pre-Reformation belief in an essential presence that guarantees the efficacy of ceremonial rites. "Not all the water in the rough, rude sea," he insists, "can wash the balm off from an anointed king."[55] For Richard, divine right is essentially present in and constructive of the body of kingship, even as the Catholic defense of transubstantiation argues Christ's real presence in the Eucharist.

The trajectory of mourning in *The Tragedy of King Richard II* parallels the movement from literal to figurative embalming enacted by reformers, while also moving from substance to figure (that is, from Richard to Bullingbroke) in its understandings of ceremonial presence and sacramental power. In its last moment, the play foregrounds the royal corpse to stage the darker side of masculine grief in the politically motivated period of court mourning inaugurated by Henry IV:

Lords, I protest, my soul is full of woe,
That blood should sprinkle me to make me grow.
Come, mourn with me for what I do lament,
And put on sullen black incontinent.
I'll make a voyage to the Holy Land,
To wash this blood off from my guilty hand.
March sadly after; grace my mournings here,
In weeping after this untimely bier.[56]

The mourning of Richard, a pragmatic tool to appease political factions, marks the play's final shift from Catholic to Protestant, feminine to masculine, tears. When Richard's feminized grief is corrected by Henry IV's stoic manipulation of affect, mourning in measure connotes the hollowing out of sacramental power and ceremonial presence. Mourning, like monarchy, is now a matter of wardrobe, and Henry's "sullen black" bears no direct relationship to the internal spiritual or emotional states it both signifies and veils.[57] Severed from a necessary, essential link to the soul within, the grieving body – like a grave robbed of its host – becomes a surface on which motives and meanings can and must be inscribed.

Lingering in the king's corpse at the play's close, however, is the remnant of Richard's Catholic faith in sacramental presence. Like Queen Elizabeth's potent corpse, whose putrefaction gives Catholic polemicists grounds on which to construct an argument for her moral corruption in life, Richard's career in the afterlife implies that royal power lives on in the body in death.[58] Richard's remains are the ultimate concern of his tragedy, and are also scattered through the rest of the second tetralogy where, like the prophecy he delivers to Northumberland in *Richard II*,[59] they exert an almost supernatural sway over events. The persistent animation and potency of the body in death also accounts for the fortunes of Cardinal Bellarmino's corpse in embalming, when as Edward Coffin's Catholic hagiography reports:

many were present with towells, handkerchiffs, sponges, and other linnen to save the bloud & preserve it for Reliques and so Religiously industrious and diligent they were, as nothing thereof was lost: the Phisitian himselfe in lieu of reward, cut away little piece of the hinder part of his scull, which he esteemeth as a peerles Jewel and inestimable treasure.[60]

When the cardinal's body "had bene exposed & layed open to be honoured," mourners "lifted beades being given to touch, and that so continually without any intermission all looked or rather feared that his face would have been disfigured therewith for it was touched, as most

conjecture by more then twenty thousand paire of beades."[61] While
Bellarmino's sacred body seems to have promised miraculous benefit
to those who came into contact with it, Richard's sacred corpse carries
with it the curse of regicide (as Richard states it, "Exton, thy fierce hand /
Hath with the King's blood stain'd the King's own land").[62] Accordingly,
Shakespeare's Henry V reinters Richard's troublesome remains in an effort to relieve his inherited guilt for the monarch's death:

> I Richard's body have interred new,
> And on it have bestowed more contrite tears
> Than from it issued forced drops of blood.
> Five hundred poor I have in yearly pay,
> Who twice a day their withered hands hold up
> Toward heaven, to pardon blood;
> And I have built two chantries,
> Where the sad and solemn priests sing still
> For Richard's soul. More will I do:
> Though all that I can do is nothing worth;
> Since that my penitence comes after all,
> Imploring pardon.[63]

Henry's penitential reinterment mobilizes the Catholic apparatus of the
chantry, albeit with an ambivalence toward the efficacy of intercessory
prayers. These rites are performed within a Catholic view of death and
its aftermath which, while historically accurate in the setting of the play,
may not be supported by the second tetralogy as a whole.[64] As a post-
Reformation history which glances nostalgically back to a moment when
the real presence of sacramental forms, and sacred corpses, could make
sense, *Richard II* both remembers and reinters pre-Reformation piety in
the body of Richard.

   Similar meditations on the lingering power of the corpse and its place
within Catholicism's and Protestantism's competing claims on the representation of historical events inform *Henry VIII*. In the play, the nascent
Reformation's historiography depends upon the aesthetically embalmed
figures of queens. Like Southwell, Shakespeare sees the royal corpse as a
table on which to inscribe rival versions of sacramental, historiographical
and theological realities. If, as I have argued, embalming is an operation
performed upon the female corpse by male interpreters, and a marker of
female will extending beyond the grave, *Henry VIII* employs the balsamic
art to anatomize and preserve the complex remains of Henry's troubled reign and those of his daughters. The play foretells the triumphant
return of "male issue" in James's ascension by notionally reinterring the
corpses of its queens.

In the Prologue, the powerful remains of lost monarchs are figured in effigies whose appearance on stage prompts not only a variety of interpretations of history's facts and meanings but also a collapse of emotional opposites – laughter and weeping, joy and mourning – that permeates the action to follow:

> Think ye see
> The very persons of our noble story
> As they were living. Think you see them great,
> And follow'd with the general throng and sweat
> Of thousand friends; then, in a moment, see
> How soon this mightiness meets misery;
> And if you can be merry then, I'll say
> A man may weep upon his wedding-day.
>
> (Pro. 25–32)

By presenting historical personages "as they were living," the play performs a metaphoric embalming of its dead, preserving them in the effigies of its actors. While this gesture serves the play's *de casibus* theme, promising to present matter for mourning ("Such noble scenes as draw the eye to flow," Pro. 4), the woeful pageants that follow frustrate distinctions between laughter and tears. Presumably mournful occasions such as Buckingham's execution, Wolsey's fall, and Queen Katherine's death are set in immediate and difficult relation to joyful ceremonies like Queen Anne's coronation and Princess Elizabeth's christening.[65] Buckingham's execution "offered sorrow," while Anne's coronation, following hard on the woeful display, promises "general joy" (4.1.6–7).

The effect of these fragile oppositions is not to qualify one emotional extreme with another, but to challenge the distinction between them, particularly as they are produced through the problematic means of historical report. In light of events occurring after the play's setting but before its first performance in 1613, joyful occasions take on an air of tragedy: Anne's coronation is also her death sentence, and Cranmer's optimistic prophecy remains ignorant of Mary's reign and his own martyrdom to it. This historical irony pervades Anne's empathetic lament for Katherine's fall, which proleptically mourns her own beheading:

> O, God's will! Much better
> She ne'er had known pomp; though't be temporal,
> Yet, if that quarrel, Fortune, do divorce
> It from the bearer, 'tis a sufferance panging
> As soul and body's severing.
>
> (2.3.12–16)

If death and divorce are equated in Anne's prophetic lament, birth and death merge in the play's final tableau, the christening of Elizabeth. The tiny princess appears at once as the infantile resuscitation of the monarchy's hopes for male issue (as the Old Lady assures Henry, Elizabeth is "a girl / Promises boys hereafter," 5.1.165–6)[66] and the already deceased predecessor of her heir, James I. Her death, in fact, is the condition of patriarchy's ultimate triumph:

> but as when
> The bird of wonder dies, the maiden phoenix,
> Her ashes new create another heir
> As great in admiration as herself,
> So she shall leave her blessedness to one
> (When heaven shall call her from this cloud of darkness)
> Who from the sacred ashes of her honor
> Shall star-like rise as great in fame as she was,
> And so stand fix'd.
>
> (5.4.39–47)

The infant Elizabeth is already dead and notionally embalmed to secure the legitimacy of James I, the boy promised by her instantaneous birth and death.

These mergers of birth, death, and divorce threaten to conflate the play's rival queens into a single female corpse. As a history of the Reformation, *Henry VIII* deploys this blending of emotive opposites, and a self-conscious historical relativism, to recall the expansive redefinitions of cognitive, emotional, and spiritual realities enacted by the split with Rome. Henry's divorce from Katherine also divorced his subjects from the familiar theological certainties of Catholicism. Shakespeare recognizes and emphasizes the fact that the most pervasive realignment of belief of his age was effected by Henry's manipulation of the bodies, living and dead, of his wives. Consequently, *Henry VIII* stages the replacement of one queen by another to investigate the rival claims of Catholic and Protestant versions of theological and existential fact. Anne's joyful coronation in Act 4, scene 1, accordingly, is qualified by Katherine's "celestial coronation" in her deathbed vision immediately following,[67] which is itself revised in Elizabeth's birth, where Anne's "suff'rance made / Almost each pang a death" (5.1.68–9). The birth, in turn, is eclipsed by Elizabeth's projected death in Cranmer's prophecy and the christening scene's exclusion of Anne in a "discursive caesarian section" of the princess from the difficult body of her fallen mother.[68] This survey of tragic queens, in which the death of one is trumped by that of the next, enables the play's unfolding narrative of patrilineal power. In *Henry VIII*, the death of male issue defines the female body as a tomb and necessitates the substitution of one female body (that is, one female corpse) for another in the effort to ensure dynastic continuity. Henry's complaint that Katherine's womb, "If it conceived a male child by me, should / Do no more office of life to't than / The grave does to th' dead" (2.4.188–90), locates death within womb to rationalize his divorce, as it will ultimately rationalize Anne's execution. Moreover, the gesture requires the Princess Elizabeth's complex gendering (as both "lovely boy" and girl, "As like [her father] / As cherry is to cherry," 5.1.164–9) and demands her simultaneous birth and death for the sake of the play's ongoing dream of male succession. The queens, like the "great-bellied" wives who throng to witness Anne's coronation, "all [are] woven / So strangely in one piece" (4.1.76–81). The subsequent proliferation of Henry VIII's wives following the play's action, moreover, continues in fact the endless replacement of imitation queens begun by Katherine's loss as an original, legitimate monarch. The movement is much like that traced by the second tetralogy's disastrous substitutions of kings following the loss of divine right in Richard, the downward spiral that he predicts will occupy both Shakespeare's histories and that of his country.

Throughout *Henry VIII*, these collapsed oppositions remind us that historiography is, above all, an act of interpretation. From the opening scene, where the description of the Field of Cloth of Gold dramatizes the remoteness and unreliability of historical record, events "turn on a series of antithetical perspectives, between which it is both necessary and impossible to choose."[69] The play's alternative title, *All is True*, seems to refer not to the historical veracity of its events, but to the contingency of all truth in the Reformation's wake. Two competing eulogies for Cardinal Wolsey vividly illustrate this historical relativism, significantly cast in terms of the cardinal's interpretive afterlife. To balance Katherine's low assessment ("Of his own body he was ill, and gave / The clergy ill example," 4.2.43–4), Griffith's positive appraisal of Wolsey's accomplishments causes the queen to insist:

> After my death I wish no other herald,
> No other speaker of my living actions,
> To keep mine honor from corruption
> But such an honest chronicler as Griffith.
>
> (4.1.69–72)

Katherine's comments figure the eulogy, the act of chronicling itself, as an embalming to preserve the reputation, if not the body, after death. The Epilogue, moreover, associates the interpretive embalming of his-toriography with "The merciful construction of good women" (10), not only turning to female audience members to provide the play's meaning but also suggesting that it constructs that meaning by embalming the bodies of its queens.

History's interpretive transformations occur between the two poles of "embalming" and "emballing," where femininity is constructed in *Henry VIII*. Anne submits to the ceremonial construction and embalming of her corpse by male interpreters, engaging in the traditional merger of sexuality and death in the feminine body of mourning. Katherine, how-ever, resists ceremonial fashioning and controls both the scene of her death and the fortunes of her corpse to establish embalming as a token of female will extending beyond the grave. In Anne's scene of dubious communal lamentation with her queen ("Our mistress' sorrows," she claims, "we were pitying," drawing the approving male interpretation, "It was a gentle business, and becoming / The action of good women," 2.3.53–5), her sexuality is displayed as a product of the play's aesthet-ics of embalming. In response to Anne's insistence that, "I would not be a queen / For all the world," the Old Lady states, "In faith, for a little England / You'd venture an emballing" (2.3.45–7). Shakespeare's usage of the word "emballing" is unique in early modern English texts. Derived from the French verb, *emballer*, to pack or wrap, the word im-plies "investing with a ball as an emblem of royalty," but certainly it also contains, as the *Oxford English Dictionary* puts it, an "indelicate sense."[70] Moreover, Shakespeare's usage carries the trace of the French noun, *em-balleur*, as Vanessa Harding explains, a man "deputed" in early modern Paris "to shroud the dead." *Emballeurs* join embalmers as men into whose hands women's corpses were delivered, sometimes with unsettling results. Harding's report that "in 1626, certain *emballeurs* were sacked for selling a corpse to a surgeon"[71] casts them as nefarious counterparts to "those who defrauded" Elizabeth I, as Manningham reports, "of the allowance of [cere] clothe" for her shrouding. Both stories hauntingly convey the haz-ards faced by women's bodies in an afterlife tended by tradesmen rather than female friends and neighbors. Anne's willingness to be emballed by Henry confirms her sexualized depiction in the play as both "queen" and "quean" and the ease with which her character is constructed by male interpreters (chiefly, but not exclusively, Henry) throughout.[72] Like the eroticized Magdalene, Anne's associations with the physical and sexual, underscored by her silent participation in ceremonial performance and the scarcity of scenes in which she actually speaks,[73] invite male interpreters to objectify and deploy her embalmed, emballed body within the masculine narrative of monarchical power. Anne is wrapped in an interpretive shroud that utterly veils and nullifies her subjectivity.

The figure of emballing merges with homonymic ease with Katherine's desire for embalming articulated in her deathbed scene. Speaking to a female attendant, appropriately named Patience (ubiquitously cited as the virtue of the deathbed throughout the period), she says:

> Call in more women. When I am dead, good wench,
> Let me be used with honor. Strew me over
> With maiden flowers, that all the world may know
> I was a chaste wife to my grave. Embalm me,
> Then lay me forth. Although unqueened, yet like
> A queen and daughter to a king, inter me.
> I can no more.
>
> (4.2.167–73)

To counter Anne's eroticism, Katherine imagines and wills the honorable use of her corpse to signify her well-guarded chastity. Assured of her sexual integrity and insisting upon her posthumous honor, she urges her women to protect her body from sexual violation after death, much as she asks Griffith to preserve her reputation in his eulogy. Katherine requests embalming as a symbol of both her chastity and her royalty: "like a queen . . . inter me." She feminizes and controls the art by replacing, rhetorically if not in fact, the male surgeon with the female community of co-mourners as guardians and interpreters of her corpse. She imagines a community like the convent of Montefalco into whose hands she may confidently commend her chaste body.

Katherine's control over the fortunes of her corpse is paralleled in her remarkable deathbed vision, where the prophetic image of her celestial coronation validates her as a queen in heaven if not on earth. Katherine's desire for embalming and her preservation within the vision itself use the feminized art to record and exert her will beyond death.[74] Her self-scripted opening manifests her will to persist in the narrative of historical events, as her vision marks her desire for heavenly bliss which, she insists, she "shall, assuredly" have (4.2.92). If Anne Bullen's acquiescent emballing emblematizes masculine control over the female body, Katherine's self-willed embalming offers an emblem of feminine control over the body, the good woman's self-construction by means of her exemplary death, and her resistance to the interpretive gaze of male embalmers or *emballeurs*, historians or husbands.

While Shakespeare's Katherine claims a control over her corpse which, in Southwell's report, the historical Elizabeth I could not command, the play is at pains to associate Katherine's will with Elizabeth's and, thereby, to return this potentially disruptive feminine force to the service of dynastic continuity. Anne Bullen's erasure by the figure of her infant daughter aligns Elizabeth not with her mother but with Katherine. While Katherine is described as "a jewel has hung twenty years / About [Henry's] neck" (2.2.31–2), Elizabeth is "a gem / To lighten all this isle" (2.3.78–9). As Katherine compares her death to that of "the lily, / That once was mistress of the field, and flourished, / I'll hang my head and perish" (3.1.151–3), Cranmer predicts of Elizabeth, "A most unspotted lily, shall she pass / To th' ground, and all the world shall mourn her" (5.5.61–2). The Old Lady says of Katherine, "Alas, poor lady! / She's a stranger now again" (2.3.16–17), and applies the same term to the newborn princess: "Sir, your Queen / Desires your visitation, and to be / Acquainted with this stranger" (5.1.166–8). As Katherine's "maiden flowers" merge with the "maiden phoenix," Elizabeth, the play replaces the queen's embalmed body with the hieratic image of James I, "star-like . . . stand[ing] fix'd" (5.5.46–7). Katherine's will indeed extends beyond the grave to script Elizabeth's redemptive reign, which effectively excises Anne Bullen's sexualized body by substituting one stranger for another, and to ensure the success of male issue through James's nomination as Henry's heir. This gesture erases not only Anne but Katherine as well. Henry's proud response to Cranmer's prophecy completes that erasure: "Thou hast made me now a man; never before / This happy child did I get anything" (5.5.64–5). But the gesture itself is underwritten by Katherine's will, embalmed and recast in the corpse of her figurative, if not actual, daughter, Elizabeth.

The ability of the complexly connected corpses of Henry's queens to figure the trajectory of the Reformation is reflected in the anecdote "that on the day that Anne [Boleyn] was beheaded the tapers round Queen Katherine's grave had spontaneously kindled themselves, and that 'this light contynuyng from day to daye' was a token of the restoration of the old order."[75] As a history of the Reformation, *Henry VIII* tells an ambivalent and contradictory story: thus some critics claim that "Shakespeare upholds a *Catholic* perspective" on Henry's divorce, while others see the play as "apparently designed as Protestant propaganda."[76]

Shakespeare's sympathetic treatment of Katherine, his comparative slight of Anne, and his comparisons of Elizabeth with the Catholic queen resuscitate Catholicism within the Elizabethan compromise to construct a good woman who is as much Katherine as Elizabeth. Cranmer's prophecy exorcizes not only Anne's ghost but also Mary's to provide a genealogy for Elizabeth that describes her as Catholic and Protestant, male and female, daughter and mother, infant and corpse. Although the play grounds the history of the Reformation in the embalmed bodies of its queens, it also *acknowledges* (in Katherine) a feminized art of embalming which would ensure the potency of the body and its legacy in the afterlife, and *uses* that art (in the masculine appropriation of Anne) to support the legitimate succession of kings. As the divorced Katherine is replaced by her imitation, Anne, Shakespeare stages the severing of sacramental power from its authenticating source: the virtues manifest in Katherine can only be guessed at or invested in Anne. With the sacraments' relocation within the individual conscience, the play asserts, all is true. The movement from Katherine to Anne imitates the shift from Catholicism's external ceremonial forms to Protestantism's internal, unseen sacraments, and genders that shift in the replacement of Katherine's self-authoring will by masculine constructions of Anne. While *Henry VIII* shares with *Richard II* a nostalgia for Catholicism's faith in the corpse's lingering power, embodied in the celestially embalmed Katherine, it also explores the mechanisms of that severance by locating Reformation history within the bodies of rival queens.

In its figurative embalming and reinterment of Katherine, Anne, and Elizabeth, *Henry VIII* mirrors James I's manipulations of female corpses and their implicit historiography. In the early years of James's reign, Elizabeth's memory challenged the new king's popularity. Thomas Fuller, for example, describes Elizabeth's afterlife in terms that echo Cranmer's prophecy:

as she lived and died an unspotted virgin, so her maiden memory is likely, in this respect, to remain sole and single . . . Her corpse was solemnly interred under a fair tomb in Westminster, the lively draught whereof is pictured in most London and many country churches, every parish being proud of the shadow of her tomb; and no wonder, when each loyal subject erected a mournful monument for her in his heart.[77]

James's reinterment of Elizabeth's corpse in 1606, much like Henry V's use of Richard's corpse in the second tetralogy, responds to the lingering

potency of the monarch's remains and gains political currency by deploying that power. Removed from its original burial site beneath the altar
in Westminster Abbey and reinterred in a joint tomb with her half-sister,
Mary, Elizabeth's body makes, in Julia M. Walker's words, "a powerful statement of James's intention to diminish Elizabeth by thus pairing
her with her childless, unpopular, and Catholic sister."[78] Meanwhile,
James's exhumation and reinterment of his mother's body in 1613 –
the year of Shakespeare's *Henry VIII* – in a tomb far more costly and
magnificent than that of Elizabeth and Mary completes the claim that
the reinterment of Elizabeth began. Situating the tomb in Henry VII's
Chapel adjacent to that of Margaret Beaufort, James "plac[es] his own
mother in a line of fruitful dynasty,"[79] exiling Elizabeth and Mary from
it. By burying the Queen of Scots near Henry VII's mother, Margaret
Beaufort, James retrospectively stakes his mother's claim to Elizabeth's
throne. In James's staging of dynastic continuity in the tombs of
Westminster, and in Shakespeare's treatment of the theme in *Henry VIII*,
male manipulations of the female body of death not only construct good
women but also deploy them within posthumous political currencies
that seem at once to be beyond their control and to react to their lingering insistence on reinterment and reinterpretation. Women's inscrutable
corpses thus enable and inform the cultural narratives predicted by and
predicated on their stubborn wills.

Humility and stoutness: the lives and deaths
of Christian women

Describing Phillip Stubbes's *A Chrystal Glasse for Christian Women*, which presents "the godly life and Christian death"[1] of Stubbes's twenty-year-old wife Katherine, Kate Aughterson states that the work – as if against its author's will – becomes "complexly dialogic" when it offers evidence not of "Katherine Stubbes's internalisation of the ideology of womanhood," but of her "resistance to dominant ideological discourses."[2] Apparently prompted by a desire to find in the early modern woman's voice a subversive chord that would signal the work's feminism and frustrate Stubbes's authorial and patriarchal monologism, Aughterson portrays Katherine as an autonomous speaker whose forays into extra-domestic theological debate and public deathbed confession of faith (that is, both performed before witnesses at her death and later published by Stubbes) run counter to her culture's – and her husband/author's – insistence on women's chastity, silence, and obedience. While Aughterson's motives may appeal to, and be shared by, many critics of early modern women's writing, her interpretation is troubled by Stubbes's own promotion of his subject as a "rare and wonderful example . . . who whilst shee lived, was a mirrour of woman-hood and now being dead, is a perfect patterne of true Christianity" (A2). A husband's pride in his wife's accomplishments (which bespeak his own exemplary government of household subordinates)[3] occasions Stubbes's memorial act and discounts the possibility that Katherine's speech or actions transgress the strictures placed upon her by his authority. Moreover, the text's popularity (it appeared in thirty-four editions between 1591 and 1700) attests not to Katherine's dialogic resistance to patriarchy, but to her effective exemplarity within it. More troubling, indeed, is the fact that Katherine Stubbes never truly *speaks* in *A Chrystal Glasse*: despite Stubbes's claim that her deathbed drama is "set downe word for word as shee spake" (A1), Katherine's voice is always represented for us by Phillip. Any dialogism contained in the text, therefore, would necessarily belong to Phillip Stubbes's voice – a polyvocality which might, in turn, suggest feminist tendencies *within* dominant patriarchal and theological discourses themselves. The binarism of women's monologic internalization of masculinity *versus* their dialogic resistance to patriarchal discourse must be refined to characterize more accurately the feminine voice in the work and in the period, and to ask how the *performance* of femininity within a culturally sanctioned (that is, masculine) genre might be given different inflections by the female writer than by the male. As such, *A Chrystal Glasse* might be read not as a primer on the restrictive masculine discourses against which early modern feminine (or feminist) speech continually struggled, but as an affirmation of more numerous, more productive generic and discursive options for early modern women than Aughterson's one-dimensional portrait of patriarchal monologism allows.

Such options, as Katherine Stubbes's deathbed performance implies, are clearly available to early modern women approaching the matter of death. This chapter focuses on the deathbed performances of early modern women as scripted by male authors – specifically, Katherine Stubbes's exemplary demise detailed in her husband's *A Chrystal Glasse*, and Katherine Brettergh's troubled but triumphant death, recorded in a pair of sermons preached at her funeral in June, 1601, by William Harrison and William Leigh and in an account of her deathbed agon by William Hinde appended to the two funeral sermons and published under the collective title, *Deaths Advantage*.[4] Like Stubbes's memorial, *Deaths Advantage* went through multiple printings (five before 1617 and eight by 1641), making it "one of the most popular volumes in the first two decades of the seventeenth century."[5] Both works promise to present reliable portraits of their subjects' virtues, but only under conditions that guarantee these subjects' erasure. Even as Stubbes's and Brettergh's deathbed acts are praised and valued as exemplary, they are mediated (possibly censored, possibly invented) by the male authors into whose hands these women, by necessity, commend their spirits.

The portraits that emerge from these works are marked by the paradoxical qualities of humility and stoutness, terms applied – significantly, after her death – to a woman's public theological debate in a seventeenth-century edition of "A Conference Dialogue-wise held between Lady Jane Dudley and M. Feckenham, foure dayes before her Death, touching her Faith and Religion." Throughout the "cathechising argument [that] was held in the tower publiquely," the editor tells us, Lady Jane "bore her selfe with such a modest humility, yet so honourably stout in all things, which either concerned her God and her religion, that she ravisht and stole

unto her all the hearts of her auditory."[6] Like their famous predecessor, Katherine Stubbes and Katherine Brettergh also exercise a tense
combination of modest humility and honorable stoutness during their
last acts that at once recommends them as models for imitation and
complicates our critical assumptions about women's acceptable domestic and extra-domestic functions, roles, and rights. This chapter traces
two aspects of the accounts of Stubbes's and Brettergh's godly lives and
deaths which, held in a constant tension, comment upon the gendering of grief in the period and the uses to which the female corpse,
and the feminine voice, could be put. On the one hand, these texts
contain and silence their subjects by representing them in the service
of the polemical and doctrinal aims of their male authors: by ideal-
izing their female subjects' humility in life and exemplary submission
in death, Phillip Stubbes and Brettergh's chroniclers support specific
political and theological positions with important resonances in the tumultuous post-Reformation debates surrounding them. Physical death
is thus allegorized and sublimated to spiritual and political ends. On
the other hand, though, licensed by male authors' treatments of their
bodies, these women are granted and assume surprising degrees of spiritual and cultural power, associated with the authority of the deathbed
itself. Death has the power to reconstruct gender relations within the
household and in the larger culture before which these women's last acts
are staged. Through sometimes contradictory gestures toward consolation and grief, gender is constructed in these works in relation to the
matter of death. Between rival impulses toward feminine humility and
stoutness, the faint echoes of actual women's voices may, perhaps, still
be heard.

I

"To praise the dead, is a thing lawfull in it self, and profitable unto the
living," insists William Harrison in his funeral sermon for Katherine
Brettergh, *Deaths Advantage, Little Regarded* (77). "God would not have the
vertuous deed, and holy examples of the righteous to be buried with
them, but to bee kept in remembrance, for the imitation of others" (78).
Harrison's opinion, one increasingly espoused by reformed clergymen in
the first decades of the seventeenth century, represents the resolution of a
lengthy dispute concerning the legitimacy and value of eulogies. As early
as 1561, Thomas Becon's *Sicke Mannes Salve* had recommended that the dying should provide a small amount (10 shillings) for a sermon "wherein the

people may be admonished of their mortality, and be taught how they ought to dispose themselves in this life, that, when the time come, they may yield up a good soul into the hands of the living God."[7] A half-century later, Lancashire clothier Anthony Mosley wills "that Mr. William Leigh parson of Standish" and author of the well-known funeral sermon for Katherine Brettergh, "shall make my funeral sermon and to have xxs. for his pains."[8] Critics of the practice, though, finding no scriptural support for it, feared that funeral sermons might be construed as reviving the Catholic faith in intercessory prayers. James Balmford, for instance, complains of parishioners "addicted to superstitious vanities" who "in stead of Diriges and Trentals, they must have funerall Sermons for fashion sake,"[9] and Harrison is careful to distinguish between lawful *praise of* the dead, whose didactic function to the living he approves, and unnecessary and unseemly *prayers for* the dead. Conscious of the eulogy's power to remind auditors of their last ends, Anglicans defended the practice: "Surely there is as much difference," Whitgift writes, "betwixt our funeral sermons and the papistical masses and trentals, as there is betwixt cold and hot, black and white, light and darkness, truth and lies, heaven and hell."[10] Performed in the presence of the corpse, a funeral sermon could offer a potent visual and verbal *memento mori* whose lingering effects on the audience justified the sometimes overblown praise in which preachers engaged. While "the sight of the body forced the bereaved to confront the finality of death and separation,"[11] the spectacle also drove home the advice that the good death is one for which the Christian prepares daily. Lancelot Langhorne's funeral sermon for Mary Swaine (1610) employs this physical emblem: "But leaving Allegories, let us fall upon literall sense, which is Christ's approbation of Maries choice, and . . . let us compare Mary with Mary; this Mary before our eyes, with Mary in the Text."[12] By the early seventeenth century, the funeral sermon had become an established Protestant genre.[13] The remarkable increase in number of funeral sermons published in the 1590s and 1600s hints at greater numbers of unpublished sermons delivered at burials of the faithful, both male and female. From 1600 to 1630, twenty-three funeral sermons for women appeared in print, and forty-five for men, while sermons for women generally were reprinted more often than those for men.[14]

A number of related types of memorial works emerge in the last decades of the sixteenth century which praise women's virtues and promulgate their memories. Poems or collections of poems published in praise of dead noblewomen – such as Edmund Spenser's *Daphnaida* (1591),

Thomas Powell's *Vertues Due* (1603), and Henry Peacham's *Thestylis astrata* (1634) – memorialize their subjects within overt bids for patronage to wealthy widowers. Poems and ballads by less illustrious authors also survive, including broadside epitaphs on the deaths of noteworthy women. These popular forms suggest the appeal of the reports of women's lives and deaths to a wide audience at all social levels, and the broadside's status as a source of news. Thus J. Phillips's epitaph on Lady Margaret Douglas (d. 1577) begins:

> Reporte run on, ringe forth thye doleful Bel,
>   That worldly wightes may wayle our great anoye:
> In Court and Towen, our cause of woe do tel,
>   That stand distrest bereft of al our joye.

The ballad goes on to describe in generous detail the countess's good death and her pious, albeit clearly invented, deathbed speeches.[15] Following Stubbes's influential work, a number of eulogistic biographies of women appeared in print. John Mayer's *A Patterne for Women* (1619), written in praise of Mrs. Lucy Thornton, is a good example. Dedicated to the widower, the work presents a monument, rather than a prayer, for the dead: "But to set forth the praises of the dead & to erect monuments to their memory, are (I know not how) though no . . . salves unto the dead, yet . . . comforts of friends surviving."[16] Most often, these pious biographies were appended to funeral sermons. For example, *The Christian life and godly death of the Lady Courtney* was published with Robert Wolcomb's funeral sermon in 1606,[17] and Humphrey Gunter's *A Profitable Memoriall of the Conversion, Life and Death of Mistris Mary Gunter, set up as a Monument to be looked upon, both by Protestants and Papists*, written, like *A Chrystal Glasse*, by the grieving but proud widower, appeared with Thomas Taylor's funeral sermon in 1622.[18] Finally, funeral sermons themselves often included accounts of their subjects' lives and deaths, although, as Frederic B. Tromly reports, the ongoing controversy as to what constituted permissible praise led pastors to limit these biographies. Since virtually all participants in the controversy agreed "that praising the dead should not be an end in itself," these gestures are invariably presented as models for imitation.[19] Langhorne, for example, concludes confidently and optimistically, "Let us all for our application learne of a woman of the weaker sexe: especially women, imitate her in her Piety, in her meeknesse of spirit, in her obedience to her husband, her modesty, her Gravity, mildnesse of Nature, in her charity: Imitate her in her Life, that you may be like her in her death."[20]

Although Langhorne presents Mary Swaine to inspire both men and women, he stops short of theorizing how her example might apply to men, while exhaustively describing the virtues that make her an appropriate model for feminine behavior. His title page advertises the work as "incouraging of all Christian Gentlewomen, and others to walke in the steps of this religious Gentlewoman."[21] Similar gestures attend accounts of Lucy Thornton's and Katherine Stubbes's exemplary deaths: both Mayer's title (*A Patterne for Women*) and Stubbes's (*A Chrystal Glasse for Christian Women*) emphasize their subjects' exemplarity for women in particular, although not to the exclusion of men. Hinde, too, insists of Katherine Brettergh that "by her Christian life and death she might teach many Gentlewomen, how vaine the pleasures and fashions of this world are, and how farre unable to bring that peace to a distressed heart, that the embracing of true Religion can" (1–2). While Henry Peacham calls the Countess of Warwick "so faire a President for Posteritie to imitatte" and offers her example to both men and women,[22] the Princess of Condes, at her death in 1563, presents herself as an *exemplum* for her female maids and servants: "Farewell my maydens," she tells them, "thynke me happy and contented, and learne you to dye wel."[23]

These eulogies bifurcate on gendered terms the relevance of their subjects' lives and deaths to women and men, respectively. The living virtues applauded by their authors construct idealized portraits of feminine piety and domestic management. Reflecting the increase in middle-class literacy in humanism's wake and the period's new emphasis on women's roles as spiritual educators within the home,[24] Stubbes tells us that "you could seldome or never have come unto her [Katherine's] house, and have found her without a Bible, or some other good book in her hand" (A2v). Hinde also commends Brettergh's practice of reading at least eight chapters of the Bible a day, as well as "some godly writer, or expositor of Scripture, or in the booke of Martyrs," the latter causing her to "weepe most bitterly" (8–9). Mary Gunter, too, "would every yeare read over the whole Bible . . . beginning her taske upon her birthday" and memorizing "any select Chapters and Speciall Psalmes; and of every Booke of the Scripture one choyse verse: all which she weekly repeated."[25] Beyond pious devotion, these women demonstrate a catalogue of feminine virtues. Thus Wolcomb writes that despite long and repeated trials – including "the captivitie of her husband by rebells in the Western Commotion in the raigne of king Edward the 6," "the change of the true religion into forged superstition in the dayes of Queen Mary," and the deaths of her husband, sons, sons-in-law, and several nephews, nieces and daughters – Lady Courtney's "patience . . . was shaken, but it stoode firmely."[26] She was humble, modest, and sober; she relieved the poor, particularly orphans and desolate widows, and nursed the sick and dying. "Her life being beawtified with these induements and qualityes," she died peacefully, free from Satan's temptations and confident of salvation.[27] The Princess of Condes, similarly, exercised exemplary modesty and patience in her life and during her final sickness, caused by "a Carcinoume, or eatyng canker, in the Matrice: whiche hyr shamefastnesse and chastitie woulde never suffer to be dressed as it was requisite and necessarye." This "floure of bloud" began on April 26 and continued until her death on July 23, and despite griefs "so dyvers and violent that they had bene undurable to any other . . . she never opened her mouthe to murmer, nor made any shewe or countenance of impacience."[28] Langhorne also notes Mary Swaine's long-suffering and "great wisedome in houshold government,"[29] and Mayer, finally, praises Lucy Thornton for displaying Abigail's wisdom, the Virgin's humility, and Sarah's "due subjection to her husband."[30]

While these exemplary women's lives construct an ideal femininity through their successful fulfillment of domestic, spiritual, and marital duties, their deaths move away from this gendering toward ostensibly ungendered models of godly dying. As Stubbes's description of Katherine as "a mirrour of woman-hoode" in life and a "perfect patterne of true Christianity" in death (A2) suggests, *A Chrystal Glasse* and its imitations place women on their deathbeds, "occupying," in Aughterson's words, "the literal space between a gendered and submissive present and an ungendered and equal future."[31] But, as Doebler and Warnicke note, early modern funerary rituals, like the texts that record them, aim "to uphold the fabric of the social order": eulogies, heraldic funerals, rules of mourning, and other cultural forms that distinguish between male and female decedents and mourners, display a tension between the social and political values they seek to affirm and the spiritual values toward which they refer. "Only in the afterlife," Doebler and Warnicke conclude, "did the Church of England and the scriptures promise full sexual equality."[32] This side of heaven, male authors of women's godly deaths deploy gender to subordinate women's actions and words to larger spiritual, political, and cultural goals. Accordingly, women on the deathbed defy the culture's more usual and pervasive alignment of femininity with immoderation and frequently articulate masculine words of consolation, urging witnesses to moderate mourning. Mary Gunter, despite her fears of Satan's assaults, is able "to comfort her mournfull husband & friends, saying; Mourne not for me, but for your selves, for I shall very shortly be more happy then the wishes of your hearts can make me, and therefore cease your mourning, and help me thither by your Prayers as fast as you can."[33] Katherine Stubbes addresses her husband in almost identical terms, supporting her consolatory words with scriptural authority: "And further she desired him that he would not mourne for her, alleaging the Apostle Paul, where he saith, Brethern I would not have you mourne, as men without hope, for them that die in the Lord: affirming that she was not in any case to be mourned for" (c3v). Despite the Princess of Condes' stoicism in the face of death, her husband, hearing of her demise, is afflicted with "sighing & sorowing . . . bitter complaints & lamentations," before finally resolving "that in very deede he had good reason to content him selfe, for the assurance he had of the good rest of hys deare wyfe & moitye, who had dyed the death of a saint."[34] Following his recovery, the prince resumes the role of spiritual head of household temporarily occupied by his dying wife by comforting his grieving children and advising them to moderate their sorrow as he has learned from his wife's heroic death to do.

By reversing the usual hierarchy of gender implicit in early modern constructions of men's and women's mourning, the women of the eulogies, in effect, die like men. Their exemplary victories are all the more remarkable precisely because of the frailty of their sex. Thus Stubbes writes of Katherine's heroic demise, "[it] is so much the more wonderfull in that she was but young and tender in yeares, not halfe a yeare above the number of twentie, when she departed this life." Then, turning to address an ungendered audience, he affirms the value of her godly death as a model for men and women alike: "The Lord give us grace to follow her example, that we may come to those unspeakable joyes, wherein she now resteth, through Jesus Christ our Lord" (c3v). Carefully constructed by her husband's memorializing prose, Katherine's feminine humility guarantees the efficacy of her equally exemplary stoutness in the face of death's terrors. Her license to escape the limitations of gender, a license both issued and revoked by death itself, transvalues the sexes to cast the domestic subordinate momentarily in the role of governor, and to recast cries of mourning, temporarily, in the voice of consolation.

II

Two years before his marriage, Phillip Stubbes published the work for which he is most often remembered, *The Anatomie of Abuses*. Like

A Chrystal Glasse, Stubbes's *Anatomie* provides "a Mirrour pure" where readers may view not exemplary female virtue but "the vices of the World displayed."³⁵ Also like the memorial, it is a work of mourning in which Philoponus, a thinly veiled Stubbes, is "moove[d] to such intestine sorrowe, and grief of minde" by the abuses of England's mirror-image, Ailgna, which he narrates in generous detail.³⁶ Part jeremiad and part utopian social satire, *The Anatomie* condemns a series of social ills, from gorgeous apparel to "playes, tragedies and enterluds," in Puritanical terms that imply Stubbes's firm management of his charges within the domestic sphere beyond the text.³⁷ He seems, in fact, a likely candidate to embody the patriarchal monologism that Aughterson assumes for him in her interpretation of *A Chrystal Glasse*. Certainly insofar as Katherine's virtues reflect Phillip's sound household government, the memorial extols its author's accomplishments more roundly and reliably than it does his wife's. At the same time, though, despite Stubbes's apparent drive to impose a normative morality in both works, *The Anatomie of Abuses* is remarkably even-handed in its gendering of vices. Women – so often singled out for attack in male-authored polemics of the period – fare no worse than men in Stubbes's anatomy. Even in his censure of pride in apparel, a favorite theme in men's published reproaches of femininity, Stubbes devotes only slightly more space to discussing women's vices as opposed to men's.³⁸ In his treatment of the other abuses, gender is rarely an issue.

My point is not to nominate Stubbes as the outstanding proto-feminist of his period, but to qualify the all-too-easy assumption of his overwhelming will to patriarchal power; to allow for the possibility that other forms of domestic, spiritual, or cultural power – equally orthodox and sanctioned – might manifest themselves in *A Chrystal Glasse* to override and realign, at least temporarily, the sexes' predictably stratified relationship in the early modern household. For example, the work's title page advertises Katherine's deathbed drama as "set downe word for word as shee spake, as neere as could be gathered, by Phillip Stubbes, Gent" (A1), vividly placing Phillip at his wife's bedside and reversing the genders of the dying and their attendants common in the medieval and early modern *artes moriendi*. The claim, moreover, authorizes Stubbes's account through the authenticity of his wife's speech, suggesting that the deathbed also reverses the usual hierarchies of gender in the household and the text. *Katherine*'s persuasive, genuine discourse rather than her husband's, we're told, bestows value on the work. Phillip relinquishes the role of domestic governor and assumes those of attendant and scribe,

faithfully recording his wife's final struggle. This reversal is supported by
Stubbes's guarantee of the purity and decorum of Katherine's speech
throughout her life. Unusually preoccupied with the topic, Stubbes tells
us that she "was never heard to give any Lye in all her life, nor so much
as (thou) in anger" (A2v); she never would "scou'd or brawle" (A2v) and
"there was never one filthy, uncleane, undecent, or unseemly word heard
to come forth of her mouth, nor ever once to curse or ban, to sweare,
or blaspheme God, any manner of way, but alwaies her speeches were
such, as both might glorifie God, and minister grace to the hearers"
(A3). Confirmed as a judicious speaker in life, Katherine's last words,
diligently recorded by her husband, gain dignity and weight by the fact
of her death. By investing his wife's speech with a value above his own
(although, of course, all of Katherine's words – rendered unverifiable by
her convenient death – are scripted by her husband),[39] Stubbes challenges a critical reading that sees him simply as a spokesperson for the
dominant ideology based upon an essentialist notion of his superiority as
male. If Stubbes's voice is parcelled out in those of Katherine and the narrator throughout *A Chrystal Glasse*, we are invited to believe that the *male*
voice here surrenders itself to the *female*, and not the other way around.

Stubbes's insistence on the veracity of his report touches on related concerns of his contemporaries and of current criticism: while
sixteenth-century opponents of the funeral sermon complained of its
"mercenary praisemongering,"[40] feminist critics in our own period
have hoped to find in eulogistic biographies "rare insights into the
lives of ordinary women."[41] Early modern eulogies tend to guarantee
their content as true by relying on the direct testimony of deathbed
attendants and presenting "infallible tokens" culled from eyewitnesses,
particularly from clergymen whose accounts were, presumably, above
question.[42] Thus Langhorne inscribes Mary Swaine's last words within
a web of corroborating testimony: "Let us heare her wordes, which she
offered unto two reverend Divines, and often repeated to us that were
present with her in time of her sicknesse." Marginally, he names as
witnesses, "Mr. Clarke and Mr. Paget."[43] Of modern efforts to read the
facts of early modern women's lives from these works, however, David
Cressy warns, "there are serious problems with these sources" since "the
form itself is rarely given to candor. No historical record is a faithful
reflection of reality; but commissioned sermons . . . and eulogies pitched
to mourners and admirers demand more than the usual caution." He
asks pointedly, "Are [women's] lives revealed, or are they veiled, by the
eulogies written about them after their deaths?"[44]

Admittedly, *A Chrystal Glasse* shares many features with other memorials and eulogies for women, so much so that it is impossible to know, finally, what percentage of the text is based in fact. Like Mary Swaine and Lady Courtney, for instance, Katherine Stubbes is praised as a model housewife who "would never suffer any disorder or abuses in her house to be unreproved, or unreformed" (A2v). She "was never knowne to fall out with her neighbours, nor with the least child that lived" (A2v). Always resisting the temptations of "dinner, or supper, or . . . playes or Enterludes," Katherine "would very seldome, or never, and then not neither, except her husband were in company, goe abroad with any, either to banquet or feast, gossip or make merry" (A2v–A3). Modest in her attire, humble in her carriage and her speech, she lived "circumspectly, . . . eschewing even the outward appearance or shew of evill" (A3). Because of his clear investment in Katherine's virtuous behavior, as both author and husband, Stubbes is implicated in the praises he bestows upon his wife. When he insists that Katherine, "would spend her time in conferring, talking and reasoning with her husband of the Word of God, and of Religion: asking him, what is the sense of this place, and what is the sense of that? how expound you this place, and how expound you that?" (A2v), Stubbes's own role as spiritual head of the household is established and affirmed by his wife's willing acceptance of his exegeses. Thus, he notes, "She obeyed the commandement of the Apostle, who biddeth women to be silent, and to learne of their husbands at home" (A2v). While *A Chrystal Glasse* and works of its kind cannot be read as reliable indicators of the material facts of early modern women's lives, they are valuable records of the period's constructions of masculinity and femininity in terms of the event of death, as it occurs within and comments upon the household.

Husbands' memorials undeniably serve as self-testimonials,[45] but they also reflect a heightened awareness of loss in the post-Reformation, an awareness supported by new genres to express that emotion. "Funeral monuments . . . and more intimate and revealing private records bear witness to the pain of personal loss," Ralph Houlbrooke writes, "But the increasing evidence of pain was due not to a change in emotional climate but to the development of new vehicles of expression."[46] Eulogistic biographies are such vehicles, profiting from their authors' intimacy with their departed subjects to turn mourning to consolation. In preface to his life of Mary Gunter, her husband voices the sentiment implicitly motivating *A Chrystal Glasse* by explaining his "true Narration of her assured Comforts and Conquests in her so Christian death and dissolution" is the result of productive mourning:

I could not better spend some part of the dayes of my mourning for the losse of my deare wife, then in setting downe briefly some Passages of her course and Pilgrimage, that the happie memory of her graces and vertuous life might ever live with mee, both for incitation, and imitation. And if my desires were strong to make them more publicke for the direction of some others, I hope it will rather be charitably ascribed to the working and stirring of my affection towardes her Ashes, then to any vanitie of mind, or ostentation in her.[47]

As intimate accounts of household stuff, husbands' eulogies for their wives play out on the public stage relationships and events most often performed behind closed doors and include details apparently derived from everyday life that escape the genre's generalized portraits of wifely virtue. Gunter, for example, tells us that, "for the space of five yeares before her death, she [Mary] kept a Catalogue of her daily slips, and set downe even the naughtie thoughts which she observed in her selfe, that one day in every weeke she might extraordinarily humble her self for all the faylings of that weeke." Haunted by guilt at having pilfered from her mistress' chamber as a child, "so that over the course of seven years she had accrued thirty or forty pounds," the adult Mary records in her catalogue everything of the Countess's that she uses.[48] Stubbes, too, recounts an episode during Katherine's final illness that smacks of truth:

she espied a little puppy, or Bitch (which in her health she loved well) lying upon her bed: she had no sooner espied her, but she beat her away, and calling her husband to her, said, good husband, you and I have offended God grievously, in receaving this Bitch many a time into our bed: we would have been loth to have received a Christian soule, purchased with the precious bloud of Jesus Christ, into our bed, and to have nourished him in our bosomes, and to have fed him at our Table, as we have done this filthy Curre many times; the Lord give me grace to repent it and all other vanities. And afterwards could she not abide to look upon the Bitch any more. (A4v)

While Mary Gunter's obsessive catalogue of slips and Katherine Stubbes's sudden disdain for her pet both appear to reflect the actual characters of their subjects, they are also contained within their male authors' itemizations of feminine virtues. Gunter uses the catalogue to illustrate Mary's "very tender Conscience,"[49] and Stubbes's anecdote provides a *seque* between Katherine's attachment to worldly goods and her "godly dispos[ition] of all things" (A4v) in preparation for death. Thus even these traces of fact are arranged and interpreted as examples of piety appropriate to Christian women.

Katherine Stubbes's conscientious rejection of her puppy is remark-able, too, in censuring both her own vanities and her husband's.

Throughout her final illness, she takes center stage to perform last acts in a manner that earns her the right to shame men's (including her husband's) shortcomings. Armed with a prophetic foreknowledge of her death, "which thing no doubt," Stubbes reports, "was revealed unto her by the Spirit of God: for according to her prophecie so it came to passe" (A3v), Katherine succumbs shortly after the birth of her first child to "a hot and burning quotidian ague, in which she languished for the space of six weekes or thereabouts" (A3v). A model of patience throughout her ordeal, Katherine "remained faithfull, and resolute in her God, and so desirous was she to be with the Lord, that these golden sentences were never out of her mouth: I desire to be dissolved & to be with Christ" (A3v–A4). A litany of "golden sentences" follows, recounting Katherine's "godly meditations" and "glorious visions" (A4), generously peppered with her accurate quotations of the scriptures. Resolved to "forsake her selfe, her husband, her child & all the world besides," Katherine movingly, if somewhat disconcertingly, commends her newborn son to his father's care:

And calling for her child, which the nurse brought unto her, she tooke it in her armes & kissed it, and said: God blesse thee my sweet babe, & make thee an heire of the kingdome of heaven: and kissing it againe, delivered it to the nurse, with these wordes to her husband standing by: Beloved husband, I bequeath this my childe unto you, he is no longer mine, he is the Lords, and yours, I forsake him, you and all the world; yea and mine owne selfe, and esteeme all things but dung, that I my winne Jesus Christ: and I pray you sweet husband, bring up this childe in good letters, in learning and discipline, and above all things, see that he be brought up and instructed in the exercise of true Religion. (A4v)

Knowing she will be unable to fulfill her educational responsibilities to the child, she deputizes her husband, incidentally informing him of the curriculum appropriate to a son. Katherine's disposal of her household concerns offers a feminine example of the deathbed practice advocated by medieval and early modern *artes moriendi*: Becon advises, for example, "they, whom the Lord hath endued with the goods of the world, should before their departure set a godly order and quiet stay in their temporal possessions."[50] As Houlbrooke notes, though, "the last requests of married women gained added poignancy from the fact that they could not legally make wills without their husbands' consent."[51] Katherine Stubbes has nothing but her newborn son and her power over his primary education, allowed by her culture, to bequeath.[52]

With her thoughts solely on heaven, Katherine performs a public confession of faith before "them that were present, as there were many (both worshipfull and others)" (A4v), that displays her mastery of the rites of the reformed deathbed. Her confession, while a time-honored component of the deathbed drama as scripted by the traditional *ars moriendi*,[53] is noteworthy in its degree of doctrinal intricacy – indeed, it is superhuman in light of the fact that throughout her six-week illness "she was never seene nor perceived to sleepe one houre together neither night nor day, and yet the Lord preserved her (which was miraculous) in her perfect understanding, sense, and memory to the last breath" (A3v). If the confession could be attributed with certainty to Katherine, it would demonstrate a middle-class laywoman's sophisticated and thorough-going understanding of the most difficult theological controversies of the Reformation. She affirms her belief that the "most glorious Trinitie is consubstantiall and coessentiall together" (B1v) and that salvation is available through Christ alone, "a Sacrifice propitiatory, satisfactory, and expiatory for the sinnes of the whole World" (B2). She rejects the faith of "the professed enemies of God, the Papists" in salvation through works and argues that since Christ's body "is circumspectible, and contained in one local place" the Papists err in denying "the body of Christ to be a true, and essentiall, and naturall body, by teaching it to be present in their so many and sundry Pixes at once" (B2v). She asserts her belief in the predestination of the elect (B2v), and that "the Soules of the Elect Children of God, immediately after their departure out of their bodies," enter heaven, "and not into Purgatory, Limbo Partum, or any other place whatsoever . . . And therefore is the opinion of Popish Purgatory, both blasphemous and Sacrilegious" (B3). She attests that the "Canonicall Scriptures are the infallible Word of God" (B3v), that there are only two sacraments rather than seven and that they are "Seales of his grace . . . & as conduits of his mercy . . . and therefore cannot be the things themselves. For it is against the nature of the Sacrament to be the thing signified thereby" (B4–B4v). Accordingly, neither the bread nor the wine of the Eucharist, "neither before nor after the words of consecration, as they term them, are changed, altered or transubstantiated into the reall, essentiall, or materiall body of Christ." If this were so, "Rats, Cats, and Mice might eat his body, which were blasphemous and sacrilegious once to imagine, though the Papists are not ashamed to teach it openly" (B4v–C1). Finally, insisting that Christ "is the onely to be called upon, invocated & prayed unto, and neither Saint, Angell, Patriarcke nor Father, Martyr nor Confessor, Peter nor Paul, Apostle nor Evangelist, James nor John, no nor Mary her selfe" (C1), she rejects intercession.

We cannot know what portion of Katherine's dignified and lucid deathbed confession actually reflects her own language, understanding, and belief, rather than those of her husband. Stubbes's energetic anti-Catholicism, though, and the popularity of *A Chrystal Glasse* with readers throughout the seventeenth century argue that mastery of doctrinal subtleties and Protestant zeal were considered acceptable for pious women who, in turn, were seen as capable of acquiring and deploying this knowledge. Far from subverting patriarchy's strictures, Katherine appears on her deathbed to display a culturally sanctioned wealth of scriptural erudition and spiritual fortitude. The dramatic climax of *A Chrystal Glasse*, "A most wonderfull conflict between Satan and her Soule, and of her valiant conquest in the same by the power of Christ" (c2v–c3), presents Katherine's struggle in heroic terms that augment the portrait of humility drawn elsewhere in the work. The thorough command of deathbed theatrics that Phillip Stubbes bestows upon his wife vividly illustrates the cultural expectation for women to attain this degree of scriptural knowledge and spiritual self-control as they approach the moment of death. Ostensibly ungendered, women's godly deaths underwrite their male authors' political and denominational polemics, gaining heroic status by demonstrating fortitude, patience, and wisdom beyond their sex.

Although in accordance with and in support of the social, cultural, and spiritual hierarchies which contained them, early modern women's deathbed dramas nonetheless present powerful episodes of self-creation and self-expression for their subjects. The events of the deathbed can reverse gender hierarchies in the household and in the culture beyond. Katherine's public confession of faith, in fact, continues the extra-domestic theological debates in which she engaged (again, to her husband's pride) in her health:

if she chanced at any time to be in place where either Papists or Atheists were, and heard them talke of Religion . . . she would not yield a jot, or give place to them at all, but would most mightily justifie the truth of God against their blasphemous untruths, and convince them, yea, and confound them by the testimonies of the word of God. (A2v)

As Patricia Crawford notes, "the apparently natural religiosity of women" such as Katherine Stubbes, "was a social construct. Women's piety was not so much a success story in social control, as a story of women gaining control over their own lives."[54] In life, Katherine's theological stoutness supports and enhances her role as co-governor of the household: thus Stubbes reports approvingly, "She would never contrary him

in any thing, but by wise counsell and sage advice, with all humilitie
and submission seeke to perswade him" (A3). At the moment of death,
however, Katherine gains a supremacy in the domestic sphere that temporarily surpasses her husband's. Thus her constancy and strength in the
face of death prompt her to chastise Phillip's selfish lapse in faith: "And
when her husband and other would desire her to pray for her health, if
it were the will of God: she would answer, I beseech you pray not that I
should live, for I thinke it long to be with my God: Christ is to me life,
and death is to me advantage" (A4).

A Chrystal Glasse urges us to reassess the idea that the male author
necessarily sees himself as essentially superior to his female subject and,
consequently, casts her as his natural inferior. Stubbes's account of the
scriptural rather than essential basis for his wife's subordination ("She
obeyed the commandement of the Apostle, who biddeth women to be
silent and to learne of their husbands at home"), his portraits of her
courageous acceptance of death and his own weakness, his praise of her
activities as counsellor within the home and as a witness to the true faith
beyond it, and his deployment of her authentic speech to authorize his
text – all of these suggest that the deathbed drama rewrites the gendering
of social relations within the household and within the culture to which
A Chrystal Glasse was addressed. The deathbed is not a gender-neutral
space, but a stage on which sex is constructed and performed.

III

Katherine Stubbes's miraculous lucidity throughout her protracted final
struggle points toward a concern that dying women (or, more correctly,
their biographers) frequently voice in early modern deathbed accounts.
Mary Gunter, for instance, reportedly prays:

that she might have her memory continued unto the last, that so by no idle, or
light speech she might dishonour God, or bring scandall to her profession; for
she said, If I through Payne, or want of sleepe (which she much wanted) should
have any foolish, or idle talke, I know what the speech of the world useth to be;
This is the end of all your precise folke, they die madde, or not themselves, &c.[55]

While Mary Gunter retained her sense (thereby avoiding "scandall") to
the end, Katherine Brettergh was not as fortunate. In May, 1601, after two
years of marriage to William Brettergh, she succumbed to "a hot burning
Ague, which made her according to the nature of such diseases, now and
then to talk somewhat idly" (Hinde 11). Her idle deathbed speeches

threatened to compromise her good death. As a result of her ravings, Hinde reports, "the Papists abiding in our countrey . . . since her death, have not ceased to give it out that she died despairing, and by her comfortles end, shewed that she professed a comfortles Religion" (M6–M6v).

The overriding aim of the three memorial works included in *Deaths Advantage*, in fact, is to stop "the mouth of the sclanderer" (Hinde N3v) by responding to local charges that Katherine Brettergh's troubled demise reveals Protestantism as a fraudulent faith. The volume also seeks to affirm on a national level, via publication, the truth of reformed (specifically Puritan) beliefs by repairing her tarnished deathbed performance and installing her as a Puritan martyr (figure 4).[56] All three authors treat directly the scandal of her disturbingly uncomfortable death to counter the rumors it provoked. Harrison, for example, provides a humoral explanation for her ravings:

> others beholding them which were reputed righteous, to die very strangely, to rave, to blaspheme, to utter many idle and impious speeches, to be unrulie and behave themselves very foolishlie; they begin to suspect their profession: but let them know, that these things may arise from the extremitie of their disease. For in hote fevers and burning agues, the choler ascending into the braine, will hinder the use of their understanding; and so cause them *to misbehave themselves rather like madmen then Christians.* (59–60)

Hinde prefaces his eulogistic biography with a five-page "Post-Script to Papists," in which he objects to Catholics' "false and slanderous reports," criticizing "the sottish people [who] say: *If a man dye like a lambe . . . he is certainly saved*, although neither holines were in his life, nor God in his mouth; grace in heart, nor yet repentance, faith, or feeling at his death" (N1–N1v). Accordingly, he offers the biography as evidence that "her death [was] more comfortable, then possible any of yours can be, so long as you continue *Papists*" (N2). Reflecting the immediacy and materiality of the controversy surrounding Brettergh's demise, Hinde also prints three poems which were affixed to her hearse at her funeral to ensure that "prejudice in all" might be "happilie suspended" (N3v). The first, spoken in Katherine's voice, emphasizes her heroic stoutness in confronting Satan's temptations:

> True it is I strove: But 'twas against mine enemie,
> Strongly I struggled; It was my strongest adversarie.
> Strongly, not in my selfe; but in my ever-helper strong:
> Strongly, alas weake woman weakely strong.
>
> (Hinde N3v).

C. BRETTERG

4 Portrait of Katherine Brettergh, frontispiece of *Deaths Advantage, Little Regarded* (1602).

William Leigh agrees that Brettergh's death, far from proving the false-hood of her religion, represents an exemplary *imitatio Christi* and a pow-erful conquest over Satan: in death, he tells us, "she walked, as Christ did to *Calvary*, with much care, and many agonies," thereby confirming her identity as one of the "Saints of God" who "have their firie trial in this world, by bickerings, buffetings, and winnowings of Satan" (71–2). Her endurance of this trial, the volume explains, should convince readers of her beatitude. Unlike the wicked who, as Harrison describes them, die "sottishly, like blocks & idiots, having neither penitent feeling of their sins, nor comfortable assurance of salvation" (48), Katherine Brettergh's deathbed struggle shows "that the divell doth most tempt the best" (57). Harrison offers an analogy to prove his point:

In any commotion, whom doe rebels kill and spoile? not those which submit themselves unto them, and joyne with them in their rebellion: but those which are faithfull to their Prince, & fight for their Prince against them, as hath ap-peared of late in the *rebell of Ireland*. Now the divell is as a rebell in the Lords kingdome: whome then will he most trouble and assault? not the wicked which submit themselves to him and joyne with him in rebellion against God, but the godlie which abide faithfull, and fight under the Lord's banners against him. (57–8)

Brettergh is just such a soldier in God's camp and her valiant conquest over Satan, rendered more remarkable because of the violence of his assaults and the common frailty of her sex, is praised throughout the volume.

Harrison's analogy, with its assumption that political and cultural struggles reflect spiritual warfare, bears upon the context of Brettergh's death and its subsequent deployment in the factional polemics of post-Reformation Lancashire. In the last years of Elizabeth's reign, Lancashire was a notorious bastion of Catholic recusancy, and *Deaths Advantage* bears the clear imprint of tensions between Catholics and Puritan clergy and laymen which escalated throughout the 1590s.[57] The timing of Brettergh's death, which followed a period of particularly intense hostility culminating in the so-called "Recusant Riots" on May 19, 1600, allowed Catholics to charge that it constituted divine punishment for her hus-band's persecution of them.[58] William Brettergh had assumed the office of High Constable of West Derby Hundred in April, 1600 and, a month later, was charged by the Ecclesiastical Commission with the arrest of recusants in Huyton and Childwall parishes, specifically of one Ralph Hitchmough.[59] Overly zealous in fulfilling his duty, Brettergh attempted the arrest just four days after the funeral of Hitchmough's wife on May 16, which was itself a ceremony marked by tensions between reformed ritual and persistent Catholic beliefs. At the burial, minister Edmund Hopwood noticed that, despite the rejection of the sign of the cross by the 1552 *Book of Common Prayer*, "a large cross of red cloth had been attached to the covering sheet over the breast whilst two other crosses were made upon the sheet with a burning iron." When the minister chastised Hitchmough for his "blindness and folly," the latter answered that "he would have a cross as long as he lived." Hitchmough and the other recusants, moreover, accompanied the corpse to the churchyard but refused to enter the church for the funeral service proper.[60] Their disdain for the reformed burial service reflects the "Manifolde popishe Superstition used in the Buriall of the dead" in Lancashire of which reformed clergymen had complained by petition to the High Commission Court in York in 1590. There, the ministers assert that, "when in this superstitiowse sorte they have brought the corse to the Church, some with hast prevent the minister, and burie the Corse them selves, becawse they will not be partakers of the service saide at the Buriall." When the service is about to begin, they complain, many take their leave: "ffor, Recusantes refuse not to bringe it to the Churche, thoughe they will not partake the Service of the Churche."[61]

Such a funeral, for the "notorious recusant" Katherine Chaloner, was in progress when, on May 19, 1600, Brettergh attempted to apprehend Hitchmough. When Hitchmough shrank back from his would-be captor, Brettergh struck him to the ground with his staff, an assault witnessed by an estimated eighty mourners in the passing cortège. As the procession approached Childwall, "the wife of Thomas Almond of Allerton called to the people, saying 'Help, help for the passion of God;' James Molyneux also heard the 'sudden cry of women.' John Poole claimed that only five people stayed with the corpse whilst the rest raced to the scene of the struggle."[62] The mourners restrained Brettergh, allowing Hitchmough to flee to his home with the constable in pursuit, and then returned to complete the funeral. "The vicar went to the church stile to meet the corpse and thence to the porch: hearing no sound of people following him, he looked back and saw that the corpse was being taken direct to its grave." Despite the minister's refusal to perform the burial unless the body was brought into the church, "the people put the corpse of the unfortunate Katherine Chaloner in its grave . . . [with] such haste that they broke the feet off the bier and were about to lay Katherine in her grave with her head to the East" until a bystander intervened and they turned her and "'decently buried the corpse without the minister.'"

Meanwhile, Hitchmough remained holed up in his house armed with a bow and arrow (and his maid, Margery Farrer, wielding a pitchfork) until the mourners arrived from the funeral. With their protection, he escaped to a neighbor's house, where he "drank for a short space of time, then returned to his own house."[63] Three days after the attempted arrest, cattle belonging to William Brettergh were maimed, an act repeated three months later, shortly after his indictment of several of Hitchmough's rescuers as well as "many other recusants dwelling near unto him."[64] Hinde reports, "It is not unknowne to *Lancashire*, what horses and cattell of her husbands were killed upon his grounds in the night, most barbarously at two or three severall times by Seminarie Priests (no question) and Recusants that lurked thereabouts" (5–6). The claim that the attackers were led by "Seminarie Priests" reflects the 1590 petition's general complaint of the "Continuall recourse of Jesuites and Seminarie Priestes unto these partes,"[65] and the specific suspicion cast upon a priest, Thurstan Hunt, arrested in September, 1600, and executed in Lancaster a month before Katherine Brettergh's death.[66]

In the events of the Recusant Riots, one observes a complex intersection of political and social resistance, gender, and mourning that is also present in the pious life and death of Katherine Brettergh. From the disorderly burial of Ralph Hitchmough's wife, to Katherine Chaloner's maimed rites, the Recusant Riots take place against a backdrop of religious and cultural resistance persistently associated in the post-Reformation with the unruly practices of Catholic – and women's – public mourning. Christopher Sutton's *Disce Mori*, published in the same year that the disturbances in Lancashire occurred, insists that "decent interring, exequies, and seemely mourning, is not unfitting the practice of these, amongst whome all thinges should bee done in order."[67] The "wailinge of the dead with more then Hethenishe owtcries" of which the Lancashire ministers complained,[68] bespeaks both the persistence of Catholic practices in the region and the gendering of those outlawed practices: it is *women's* excessive public mourning in particular that employs the disorderly and disruptive aspects of pre-Reformation ritual to which reformed ministers so vehemently object.[69] The Anglican call to measured mourning, of course, is intimately tied to this censure of feminized Catholicism: the energetic anti-papal polemics of *Deaths Advantage*, after all, support the stoic acceptance of death summarized in Harrison's rehearsal of the familiar moral, "we must learne not to mourne immoderately for the death of the righteous" (74). Katherine Brettergh – at first distressingly despondent and idle but ultimately

schooled to accept death with courage and fortitude – is not only enlisted in this cause but, in fact, guarantees it. Thus it is no surprise to find
Leigh's *Soules Solace*, which undertakes the most thorough-going critique
of Catholicism in the triptych, condemning the mistaken faith in intercessory prayers for the dead: "say no more eyther for your selves, or over
your dead. Heare heaven; help saints; send peace; give rest: they see you
not; they heare you not; nor have they feeling of your miseries. Your *ora
pro nobis* is out at doores, and your *Missa requeim*, is a pregnant idoll" (30).
The vast majority of Leigh's sermon, in fact, presents doctrinal grounds
on which to challenge Catholicism's basic tenets, clearly responding to
William Brettergh's local adversaries and Katherine Brettergh's detrac-
tors. Thus "that popish puddle," purgatory, he states, "heathenish in
devise, hellish in practice, and Romish for gaine," is condemned as "our
adversaries bath, to supple and ease their dead," and is corrected with
a reformed confidence in salvation through faith alone: "let onely the
price of the bloud of my Lord, availe me unto the perfection of my delivery" (31–45). With this confidence, he assures us, Katherine Brettergh
valiantly faced death.

Deaths Advantage, a volume collated and brought to press by Katherine
Brettergh's besieged husband, sublimates its subject's material demise
toward an aggressively anti-Catholic polemic, but also traces *her* history
of high-profile, public activism in support of her Puritan beliefs. Thus
Hinde tells us that, like Katherine Stubbes, Brettergh held Catholicism
in disdain and was compelled to challenge its proponents publicly: "For
Poperie, she saw it so grosse and foolishe, that shee would not once
name it, except it were to argue against it, but never for it" (9). Moreover,
Katherine appears to exert indirect pressure on public events and debates
through her husband. For Hinde, for instance, the maiming of William
Brettergh's cattle showcases Katherine's willingness to "[turn] it into a
matter of praising God, and submitting herself to his good providence."
Thus she was often heard to say, "It is good in respect of Gods Church,
that the weake may be confirmed in the trueth, and that Papistrie may
be disgraced when the world shall see such wickednesse flow from it"
(6). Not only did she forgive these transgressors, but she encouraged her
husband to do so as well: "And for feare least her husband should faile in
that poynt through infirmitie and weakenes . . . she never failed, but daily
prayed unto the Lord to sanctifie her husbands thoughts, and direct his
heart aright, only to seeke Gods glorie, without either desire of revenge,
or satisfying his owne affections" (Hinde 7). Katherine's attempts to repair, through prayer, William's presumed infirmity and weakness paints

a portrait of a woman who assumed power within the household based upon the strength of her religious convictions. In this respect, Katherine represents a Protestant equivalent to the politically active and culturally resistant women who took part in the Recusant Riots. From "the wife of Thomas Almond of Allerton" who breaks the ranks of mourners to call attention to Bretergh's attempted arrest, to Margery Farrer, a maid willing to defend her master with violence, the riots offer examples of women exercising remarkable political and ideological power in the public sphere. In each case, though, the performance of these acts within the suspended arena of death enables these exercises of feminine power. The "sudden cry of women" at the funeral of Katherine Chaloner, signaling women's disorderly mourning, blends easily with the cries that alert the crowd to Hitchmough's and Bretergh's violent encounter. Given that the legal position of women engaged in unrest in the period was uncertain, so that male rioters sometimes exploited this ambiguity by dressing as women,[70] the additional impetus to disorder implicit in volatile feminine mourning further fosters women's entry into the tumultuous public sphere. Katherine Bretergh, meanwhile, portrayed in her eulogies as a woman embroiled in religious controversy in her lifetime, is an even more powerful corpse: her death promotes her life story as one of vigorous anti-Catholic activism – a story, perhaps, too dangerous, in its challenge to gender restrictions, to be told in other circumstances. In death, moreover, she becomes a trump card in her Puritan authors' hand, able to appear before the virtually unlimited public established by print as an unassailable witness to the truth and success of the reformed rites of dying.

Katherine Bretergh's actual degree of influence over her husband's performance of his public duties is unknown. Certainly, as Dottie argues, the riots were a spontaneous reaction to William Bretergh's "aggressive hostility." He suggests, based on the coincidence of the Childwall disturbances with the two-year period of Bretergh's marriage, that his religious fervor was encouraged by that of his wife. By 1604, three years after Katherine's death, Dottie points out, William "had withdrawn from the extremist position which [he] had formerly occupied," possibly because her influence over him had relaxed.[71] Hinde's biography (based on materials and testimony provided by William Bretergh) reports that William "was farther builded up in Religion by her meanes, and his face daily more and more hardened against the divell, and all his plaguie agents; the *Popish Recusants, Church Papists, prophane Atheists, and carnall Protestants* which swarmed together like Hornets in those parts" (5).

Hinde's comments have led Warnicke and Doebler to conclude that Katherine Brettergh "was more than a religious deputy to her husband." Rather, they argue, she provides: [72]

yet another example of an early-modern woman whose faith, which was more deeply rooted and felt than that of her husband's, gave her the strength to take on the dominant religious role in the family. That the account of her life and death was, along with the funeral sermons and their eulogies, published, attested to the willingness of the clergy and gentry to encourage the almost ministerial actions of an extremely religious woman in the face of her husband's apparent weaknesses.

While there is no doubt some truth to this portrait, neither the funeral sermons nor Hinde's biography, nor indeed the historical accounts of the events surrounding the Recusant Riots, offers direct evidence of the depth of Katherine's religious convictions. These are scripted for us in her absence by male-authored polemics expressly aimed at discrediting William Brettergh's Catholic enemies. That this representation is sanctioned by her husband and the reformed clergymen enlisted in his cause attests not so much to their desire to foster similar behavior in women readers as to the accessibility and flexibility of Katherine's example, guaranteed by her timely death.

Moreover, Hinde's indebtedness to earlier eulogistic biographies, specifically Stubbes's, must qualify any reading of the work as an unmediated reflection of fact. The work's conventionality is apparent as early as the title page, which asserts its truth and advertises the "bitter conflict she had with Satan, and blessed conquest by Christ before her death" as the work's dramatic climax (Hinde M4), gestures that both imitate Stubbes. Elsewhere, Hinde echoes this commitment to historical truth – an issue of paramount importance in a work whose overarching argument is that its subject's death, contrary to all appearances, was blessed. Thus he assures readers:

that howsoever I may sometimes misse the forme of words which possibly the Gentlewoman used in her speech; yet have I faithfully set downe the substance of the matter, and for the most part also faithfully related the words themselves, and reported nothing but that which is most true, and testified by persons of good honest report, as they are named in the margent: out of whose fresh memories the substance of that which I publish was presentlie set downe. (M8–M8v)

Accordingly, Hinde carefully names the witnesses to Brettergh's last acts in the margins of his account: eight men, mostly relatives and clergymen (William Brettergh, John Brettergh, John Bruen, Edward Aspinwell,

William Harrison, William Fox, William Woodward, and John Holland) and three women (Maud Brettergh, Scholastica Fox, and – interestingly, in light of the notorious recusancy of Katherine Chaloner – one Elizabeth Challoner). At the moment of death, all three women are present along with five of the men "and divers moe" (Hinde 36).

The prominence of male attendants at Brettergh's death reflects not so much the common gendering of the event as Hinde's masculine casting of the deathbed and of Brettergh's final acts. Her temptations, unlike Katherine Stubbes's, are remarkable in their emphasis on gender and desire to replace feminine weakness with masculine fortitude. Thus in her despair, "she wished, that she had never been borne, or that shee had been made any other creature, rather then a woman. She cried out oftentimes, *Woe, woe, woe, &c. a weake, a woefull, a wretched, a forsaken woman*, and such like pitifull complaints against her selfe" (Hinde 13). In the throes of her temptation, she charges Satan, "*reason not with me, I am but a weake woman*" (Hinde 15). To help Brettergh to bear these assaults, male counselors "discharged the duties of . . . faithfull Christian[s]" by recalling the promise of salvation. While Katherine Stubbes performs an impressive confession of faith, doctrinal and consolatory discourses are relegated in Hinde's biography to male speakers: he records at length the comfortable words of both laymen and clergymen in attendance (16–20). When Brettergh's temptations "vanished away" several days before her death, Hinde reports, "she would then very cheerfully joyne with the company in prayer, and singing Psalms, as occasion offered, and performed all such duties, as was meete for her in that estate" (22). Her reported speech from this point forward is comprised almost exclusively of quotations from the Psalms: the biography subsumes the feminine voice entirely within the masculine voice of scriptural authority. As death approaches, William Harrison "praied twice with her" and "she sent for him, to pray once more with her before he went, which he did" (35). The next morning, "Another faithfull man or two came presently in that morning, and divers more well affected, who were with her at the time of her death, and often prayed with her that forenoone, she still abounding in spiritual consolations" (36). Katherine Brettergh's pious stoutness in life enables her *masculine* courage, wisdom, and confidence in the face of death. So remarkable is this "weakly strong" woman's performance of masculinity that, forty years after her death, Hinde's life of Brettergh's brother, John Bruen, promotes its subject on the basis of his relationship to this now-famous *exemplum* of good death: he is, Hinde writes, "Brother to that Mirror of Piety, Mistris Katherin Brettergh."[73]

Despite Hinde's assertion that his account is "faithfully collected out of the fresh memories of those that were present, and eye-witnesses as wel as my selfe" (M7), its similarities to Stubbes's memorial are extensive. All three works of *Deaths Advantage*, in fact, highlight Brettergh's idealized feminine virtues in life: Harrison calls her "by nature very humble and lowly" (79) and Hinde assures us that "she used not to gad abroad with wandering *Dinah*, to dancing greenes, markets or publike assemblies" and "never used to sweare oth [*sic*] great nor small; nor yet to abuse her tongue with vaine or unseemly speeches" (2). She provides "a glasse before [women's] eyes, that so her life, and death, may be an example" (Hinde 4). Rather than offering a true report of Katherine Brettergh's life and death, Hinde's biography idealizes and contains its subject within cultural and theological polemics that are supported by and profit from her volatile, but ultimately cooperative, model. The thrust of these polemics, of course, is found in the volume's vigorous anti-Catholicism. While Phillip Stubbes conducts his campaign against Papists through the sophisticated confession of faith scripted for the dying Katherine, *Deaths Advantage* denies its heroine that power. Katherine Brettergh's final words are comprised of praises of God delivered in a "voyce as most heavenly musicke and melodie of peace, sounding praise, and honour, and glorie to God in a wonderfull manner" (Hinde 25). Following her temptation, her ecstasy is extreme. "For now I perceive Christ my redeemer is turned towards me," she assures witnesses, "*O happy am I, that ever I was borne, to see this blessed day!*" (27). As death overcomes her, she announces, "*My warfarre is accomplished, and my iniquities are pardoned.*" "And with that," Hinde concludes, "she presently fell asleepe in the Lord, passing away in peace, without any motion of body at all; and so yeelded up the Ghost, a sweet Sabboaths sacrifice" (37). From war to peace, from debate to silence, the trajectory of Katherine Brettergh's death invites her incorporation into the energetic polemics of her authors who, authorized by her powerful *exemplum*, speak for her.

But the echoes of women's voices may yet resonate in the male-authored mirrors that contain their austere images. Katherine Brettergh, like Katherine Stubbes, is represented as both chastising and counseling her husband. "One time," Hinde reports, "as her husband and she were riding toward the Church, he was angry with his man: *Alas husband* (quoth she) *I feare your heart is not right towards God, that can be thus angry for a trifle.* And weeping she said further, *you must pray against this your affliction*" (9). "Another time," he tells us, "a tenant of her husbands was behinde with his rent, she desired him to beare yet with him a quarter of a yeere, which he did: and when the man brought his money, with teares she said to her husband: *I feare you doe not well to take it of him, though it be your right, for . . . then you oppresse the poore*"(Hinde 10). On her deathbed she warns him, "*O Husband, beware of Papistry, keepe your selfe holy before the Lord: Yeelde not to the abominations of the wicked, least they rejoyce and so you dishonour God*" (24). Women's eulogies and biographies, authorized by their husbands, willingly include episodes of wifely censure that require us to expand our sometimes limited vision of early modern domestic and political hierarchies in which gender relations are firmly fixed and immutable. Langhorne describes a similar episode in Mary Swaine's life in terms that indicate both her husband's approval of her reproof and her minister's as well: "if at any time she used ordinary recreation, to beare her husband and his friends company, her affections were so wholly set upon heavenly things, as she often used this gracious and sanctified speech: *This is a passing away of the time, but no redeeming of the time.*"[74] When reported posthumously, a wife's censure of her husband, far from being subversive, is "sanctified." Licensed by death, these women engage in final acts that rewrite gender in the household and in the larger culture beyond it as intimate with their approaches to death. Far from being an ungendered space, the early modern deathbed is a point at which gender is both fluid and defined.

Katherine Brettergh's disposition of her worldly goods eloquently articulates the persistence of femininity even into the highly masculine scene of her demise, and beyond. Although Galatians 3:28, "There is neither Jew nor Greek, there is neither bond nor free, there is neither male nor female for ye are all one in Christ Jesus," promised early modern women a gender equality in death unavailable to them in life, both Katherine Stubbes and Katherine Brettergh suggest their undying faith in a *gendered* afterlife where their female bodies, whose frailty had failed them in life, would be perfected rather than eradicated. Katherine Stubbes confesses that "when God cast Adam in to a dead sleep, and made Woman of a rib of his side, he brought her unto him, and he knew her straightway and called her by her name" to support her belief that "we shall know one another in the life to come, talk with one another, love one another, and praise God one with another, and all together world without end" (CIV). While she returns to the femininity's founding moment, the creation of Eve, to imagine a paradise in which "we shall know one another" in gendered but equal terms, Brettergh commends her child, a daughter, to her husband's care – but only temporarily. With none of the concern for her daughter's training in letters that Katherine

Stubbes appropriately expresses for a son, she prays, "*Let my little child be brought up among the children of God, and in the true feare and knowledge of his Majesty so shall I meete there in heaven, whom now I must leave behinde me on earth*" (24). In this affective and wholly gendered image of a mother's and daughter's reunion in the afterlife, Brettergh's femininity – although challenged by death and her by chroniclers – is performed.

4

London's mourning garment: maternity, mourning and succession in Shakespeare's Richard III

Unlike the numerous elegies and memorials issued by London publishers following Queen Elizabeth's death in March, 1603, William Muggins' *Londons Mourning Garment*, published in the same year, mourns the loss to the plague of nearly 38,000 citizens between July and November.[1] Muggins' eighty-seven-stanza lament for London's dead, however, shares the elegies' preoccupation with the figure of the mother as the central image through which death, its pathos, and its implications – spiritual, social, and political – are negotiated and represented. Elizabeth's frequent casting as the maternal object *of* lament, "the aged mother of these orphane lands,"[2] is complemented by Muggins' grieving mothers. The narrator, seeking mourners to accompany London in her complaint, dismisses male citizens (as "stronger, sorrowes to begyle") and calls upon the "Dames of London Cittie" (B3), particularly its mothers:

> Oh, mothers sigh, sit and shed teares a while,
> Expell your idle pleasures, thinke on woes:
> Make not so much as countenance of a smile,
> But with downe lookes, which inward sorrow showes,
> And now a fresh, remember all your throwes,
> > Your gripes your panges, your bodies pinch with paine,
> > As if this instant, you did them sustaine.
>
> > (B3v)

As this physiology of mourning suggests, Muggins' poem constructs the maternal body as a synecdoche for the city's suffering from the perceived continuity between the "paine yet willing" of "breeding, bearing, and delivery" (B3v) and the unwilling sorrow of child-loss. Maternal mourning, predicated on women's physical abilities to bear and breast feed children, is figured in the poem and more generally in early modern discourses of death and consolation as especially violent due to the affective bond between mother and child – as Muggins puts it, "Mothers love, to Child . . . fixte so fast" (B4v). Muggins is not alone in seeing maternal grief as a powerful image of the general suffering of plague-time. Thomas Dekker embodies the horrors of 1603 in London's "wofully distracted mothers that with disheveld haire falne into swounds . . . lye kissing the insensible cold lips of [their] breathlesse infants,"[3] while Thomas Brewer's *Weeping Lady* casts plague-ridden London as a mourning Rachel who, seeing death "gorg'd with [her] Sonnes and Daughters" appears "with nothing but grones, Sighs, teares, shreaks, folding of armes; beating of brests, wringing of hands, pale looks, dejected eies, bleeding heart, & most heavy and bitter condolements."[4]

This chapter examines the complex figure of the maternal mourner in early modern England as an ideologically charged icon of feminized, immoderate mourning whose troubling presence compromises the political and spiritual teleologies of Muggins' text, of providential theories of the plague, and of post-Reformation discourses of consolation. Taking Muggins' poem as a starting point, I examine representations of maternal mourning in male-authored texts, including plague literature and elegies on Elizabeth's death, to argue that the works construct maternal grief as a unique site of affective and emotional license whose suspension of orthodox responses to loss is useful to male authors approaching difficult social phenomena – a female monarch's (long-anticipated) death and her male heir's accession, or the city's descent into the unfathomable darkness of the plague. The juncture of maternity and mourning supports a notional shift from static to active responses to death, from unproductive excess to profitable moderation – that is, from female to male – that follows the trajectory of royal succession with Elizabeth's death and James's accession. If male writers use maternal mourning's transgressive potential, suitably contained by masculine orthodoxy, to enact the conceptual shift from feminine to masculine styles of mourning and government, the lamenting mothers of Shakespeare's *Richard III* memorialize history's casualties to challenge the masculinist values implicit in recording the rise and fall of kings. Shakespeare's grieving queens script an alternative history in their memorial acts of maternal mourning. As excessive grief is both feminized and eulogized in *Richard III*, maternal mourning becomes a repository of communal, corporate memory and identity in the face of Richard's Machiavellian rule. Through a gendered construction of alternative versions of mourning, Shakespeare engages and anticipates the troublesome question of royal succession that dominated the last years of Elizabeth's reign and charted the course of the nation's grief in the "wonderfull yeare," 1603.

I

Early modern representations of maternal mourning reflect women's intimacy with bodies in birth and death. In his portrait of maternal grief, Muggins encourages London's mothers to recall their experiences of childbirth as liminal moments at which, poised with their children in the threshold between life and death, they glimpse a prolepsis of child-loss:

> Againe bethinke you, at that instant hower,
> The little difference, was twixt life and death:
> When as the infant, with his naked power,
> Laboured for life, to have his rightfull birth,
> And with the sickly, Mother gaspt for breath,
>   The one nere death, as nigh to death the other,
>   Sore to the babe, worse Travell for the Mother.
>
> (B3v)

Muggins' merger of childbirth and child-loss reflects the social histories of early modern birth and death and women's unique roles within them. While the practice of midwifery ensured that, "up to the mid-seventeenth century, the presence of any man at a childbirth was unusual,"[5] the gendering of death and its rituals placed women in especially intimate relationships to the dying and the dead, as nurses for the sick before death and caretakers of the body afterward. Sometimes these duties merged: Thomas Bentley's *Monument of Matrones* includes among fifty pages of prayers for the childbed those for use at mothers' deaths.[6] Certainly birth and death often merged in fact as well as figuratively for early modern women who survived their children's deaths, recording these losses in a variety of works which will occupy our attention in the next chapter. As Lucinda Beier puts it, "Infants, young children, child-bearing women, and the elderly inhabited a kind of no-man's-land between life and death."[7] With the chance of death in the first year of life at about twenty percent, and with another one in five children likely to die before their fifth birthday, child-loss was a pervasive and painful fact of life for most parents.[8] Thomas R. Forbes's study of mortality in early modern London concludes that "in Shakespeare's day, of every hundred babies born in St. Botolph's parish about seventy survived to their first birthday, forty-eight to their fifth, and twenty-seven to thirty to their fifteenth."[9]

Rooted in the physical bond between mother and child forged, according to early modern views, during gestation and nursing, mothers' stubborn concern with the body of the departed rather than the soul – with insuperable loss rather than spiritual comfort – characterizes maternal mourning in both its male and female-authored representations. In the voice of London's mothers, "with lamentations and with Tears good store" (C2), Muggins graphically recalls the maternal bonds now severed by death:

> Ah my sweet Babes, what woulde noe [*sic*] I have done?
> To yeelde you comfort, & maintaine you heere:
> Early and late, no labour would I shun,
> To feede your mouthes, though hunger pincht me neere;
> All three at once, I woulde your bodies cheere.
> > Twaine in my lappe, should sucke their tender Mother,
> > And with my foot, I would have rockt the other.
>
> Me thinkes I see them still, and heare their cryes
> Chiefly a nights when I on bed am layde,
> Which make fresh teares goe from my watry eyes,
> When I awake and finde I am deceived;
> Sweet pretie Babes, Christ hath your souls received;
> > Faire Babes to me, you nere shall come againe,
> > But where you are, I trust ay to remaine.
>
> (C2–C2v)

Despite her acknowledgment that her children are now in heaven, Muggins' maternal mourner refuses consolation, "byd[ing] more sorrowes in this wretched earth" (C2v). The materiality of maternal grief leads Muggins to a labored description of breast feeding, in which the mother's pain and tears explain and prefigure her mourning in child-loss:

> And when the Babe doth gather strength amaine,
> Most strongly labouring at his mothers dugge.
> She patiently endureth all the paine,
> Suffering his lippes her nipple still to lugge.
> And with her armes most closely doth it hugge,
> > As she should say, draw childe and spare not mee,
> > My brests are thine, I feele no paine with thee.
>
> Though that poore heart her brest doth ake full sore,
> And inwardly fell prickings she indures,
> Till eyes gush teares, and lippes reach kisses store;
> Which in true mothers gladsome joyes procures,
> And to more ardent love them still allures.
> > That teates and kisses greet the Babe together,
> > Like to sunne-shine when it is dropping weather.
>
> (C1)

As William Gouge notes, urging mothers to nurse their own children, "Together with the milke passeth some smacke of the affection and disposition of the mother: which maketh mothers to love such children best as they have given sucke unto."[10] This affective bond, unfortunately, made child-loss difficult for mothers to bear.[11]

The idea that the violence of maternal mourning results from mothers' physical and emotional intimacy with children reflects the period's naturalization of maternal mourning, its casting of maternal grief as essentially linked to the reproductive functions of women's bodies.[12] Although this construction of maternal mourning as a natural category of affective and discursive expression depends upon the body, it extends notionally to feminize all excessive mourning and, conversely, to stigmatize immoderate grief as effeminate. Thus mothers who did not nurse their children (as was frequently the case in upper-class and noble families) could be considered to suffer as deeply at children's deaths as those who had, while nurses might mourn as profoundly as breast feeding mothers at the death of children whom they had nursed, though not their offspring.[13] Richard Niccols' *Three Sister Teares at the Most Solemne Death of Henry Prince of Wales* (1613) illustrates this merger of grieving nurses and mothers. "How can the Nurse but wayle her infant lost / Tooke from her breast, who she shall never see," the poem asks, and goes on to figure England as mother lamenting her failure to attend her son's death:

> But that which grieves a tender Mother most
> And heapes huge Sorrowes on her mournfull breast
> When she her deare beloved Sonne hath lost,
> Is now the cause of my mindes most unrest.
> I was not by to close dead Henries eyes.[14]

Similarly, Jeremy Leech's funeral sermon for James I's daughter, Mary, who died in 1607 at the age of two years, five months and eight days, as her tomb in Westminster Abbey (figure 5) records, is dedicated not to Queen Anne, but to Lady Elizabeth Knyvet, the toddler-princess' "tutor." Leech attributes to Knyvet the excessive sorrow usually reserved for mothers, hinting that malicious interpretations have been placed upon her immoderate grief:

if you might have begged but her life of God, it would have been the greatest gaine you desired; and . . . God having taken her way, the want of her self is the greatest losse you have lamented. If there be any that will speak evill of those things which they know not, they be such whose tongues doe burne with malice: and let them blyster with the fire that kindles them: you may make a garland, for yourself, of their reports.[15]

5 Maximilian Colt, Tomb of Mary Stuart. Westminster Abbey.

Based on her intimacy with Mary, which, given the division of labor within the royal household in the period, may well have been greater than the queen's, Knyvet is imagined as a surrogate mother whose excessive sorrow is explained by her affective bond with the child.

While Leech exonerates Knyvet's immoderation, he also uses her authenticating grief to support his sermon, which rationalizes the toddler's death by arguing, in Lear-like terms, that "the infant that is newly brought into the world, hee prophecies of himselfe that he is borne the heire of misery, when he salutes the light of his nativitie with crying & complaining."[16] Leech gains currency from Knyvet's maternal sorrow to advocate Christian mourning in measure. Similar gestures are found in other male-authored consolatory and devotional works, where the excesses of maternal grief are used to correct both male and female mourners. Andreas Hyperius' *Practice of Preaching* (1577) typifies this gendering of grief in condemning "wommanish kinde[s] of wayling and shricking" and insisting that, "All that be of sound judgement, do thincke it very uncomly and womannishe to lament without measure, & to take so impaciently the chaunce that happeneth."[17] Immoderate mourning, as Werdmuller argues, rebels against God's providential design:

When thou givest forth thy childe to a nource, and shee hath kept it long enough, thou takest it home again, the nource having no reasonable cause to complaine upon thee, for taking again thine own, yet much less have we to grudge against God our creditor when he by death taketh his own again. For as for father and mother, brother & sister, wife and child, freend and lover, yea and all other thinges that wee have, what are they els but lent goods, and free giftes of God which he hath committed to us.[18]

The argument that men who mourn immoderately are effeminate controls masculine grief through shameful comparisons with women. Erasmus' *De Morto Declamatio*, for example, states that "were it a right shamefull thyng, if menne should not bee found as stedfast and as stoutly minded as women have been" in suffering the death of their children. As an example, he cites the Roman mother Cornelia, who, "behelde hir two sonnes [Titus Graccus and Caius Graccus] slaine and unburied: and whan hir freendes comforted hir and saied, she had a wretched chaunce: I will never saie (quoth she) that I am unluckie or unfortunate, that have borne suche two children."[19] Werdmuller also rehearses the story to assert that "to wayte still till heavines forget it selfe is a wivishe thing: and againe, to bridle it betimes beseemeth the naturall reason and sobernes of a man."[20] Christian men, he concludes, confident of God's providential

plan, should show at least the forbearance of this "heathenish" virago:
"This woman now overcame her owne naturall feeblenes and motherly
heart: should not then a man (which woord noteth the stronger kinde
and more valiant stomack) declare himselfe even as stout?"[21]

Maternal mourning, understood as a site of unusual affective and
expressive license, provides male writers like Muggins a unique stage on
which to theorize political and cultural transformations. As an image of
debilitating pathos, the maternal mourner frozen in grief and dedicated
to the dead rather than the living (in Henry Peacham's words, the mother
bereft of her daughter "would faine / Even with her fingers dig her up
againe"[22]) powerfully represents cultural, political, and artistic forms at
a dead end and in need of resuscitation, correction, or abandonment.
Although *Londons Mourning Garment* lingers over the figure of the maternal
mourner, milking it (as it were) of its pathetic power, the poem cannot
permanently fix its telos of plague and salvation in that static image.
Rather, Muggins begins and ends his poem with gestures of welcome
to the new monarch, poising the text chronologically between James's
entry into London in May, when crowds were "so greedy . . . to behold
the countenance of the King that, with much unruliness, they injured
one another," and his much-delayed triumphal progress through the
city, intended to accompany his coronation on July 25 but postponed
due to the virulence of the plague until March of the following year.[23]
Nostalgically recalling James's May entry and optimistically anticipating
his progress, Muggins closes his poem:

> My crowned Cesar and his Peerlesse Queene,
> Comes now tryumphing with their princely sonne,
> Deck't with rich robes the like was never seene,
> Nor never none more welcome to London,
> Me thinkes I see the people how they runne,
>> To get them roome this happy sight to see,
>> That this may come say all Amen, with mee.
>
> (D2v)

The condition of this triumph – figured not only as a political arrival
but also as a resurrection, a triumph over death – is the cessation of
the plague. This, in turn, would signal a triumph over sin, since *Londons
Mourning Garment* shares with other examples of plague literature from the
period an understanding of the epidemic as a scourge of God.[24] Thomas
Cogan, for example, explains that the 1584 visitation of the plague in

Oxford had "one principall or generall cause, that is the wrath of God for sinne."[25] Lady Margaret Hoby records in her diary for October 23, 1603, "it was reported that, [at] London, the number was taken of the Livinge and not of the deed: Lord graunt that these Judgmentes may cause England with speed to tourne to the Lord."[26] Wednesdays were designated days of fasting "appointed by the Kinge to be heald thorowe the wholl Realme in regard of the generall mortalitie," and were occasions for repentance, charity, and prayer.[27] Brewer's *Weeping Lady* portrays London as a mourning mother explicitly to recall God's punishment and to call citizens to virtue:

My intent in erecting this poore Monument of Misery, was, to make this Ladies Teares out-live her Teares: that, when by the infinite Mercies of God they shall bee wip'd off, and all her Sores made whole; we may . . . re-view them; in them those infinite Mercies; and in both, be made mindfull of them, and eternally thankfull of them: which God grant.[28]

These plague treatises hope to reform citizens' behavior by publicly condemning their sins. Roger Fenton's *A Perfume Against the Noysome Pestilence* (1603) speculates as to how Londoners have incurred God's wrath, locating among their general "profaneness and neglect of God's service" women's behavior as a likely cause for the calamity. He wonders whether "those wanton attyres and unseemelie fashions wherein our women disguise themselves" and "the toleration of such uncleane and notorious harlots as keepe about this place have infected the Citie."[29] The appropriate atonement for these sins, for Fenton, is penitential weeping: "and duly considered how their sinnes had offended the Almightie, *they should lament for them, as one mourneth for his onely sonne.*"[30]

In their programs of reform, Muggins' poem and the plague treatises it resembles show clear affinities with the early modern jeremiad, which, imitating the Old Testament Books of Jeremiah and Lamentations and their New Testament recasting in Christ's tears for Jerusalem, bemoans the nation's sins and foretells its well-deserved doom. Nathaniel Cannon's *Lachrimae* (1616) summarizes the basic tenet of the genre: "Good Christians . . . mourne and melt into teares, to heare, to see, to understand how God is provoked, his holy name blasphemed, his word neglected, his Sacraments contemned."[31] Perhaps the most remarkable of these lamentational texts is Thomas Nashe's *Christs Teares Over Jerusalem* (1593), which shares with Fenton a concern about the moral culpability of London's women, and with Muggins the deployment of maternal mourning to emblematize the sorrows, and abuses, of the stricken city.[32]

Nashe's work opens with Christ's lament for Jerusalem, where the Savior himself veers dangerously close to excessive grief: "Having no sinne before, thou hast almost made me commit sin, in sorrowing for thy sinnes . . . I have not cleane Teare left more, to wash or embalme any sinner that comes to me."[33] Nashe then surveys Jerusalem's turbulent history, admonishing London as its latter-day twin and pleading for the city's relief from the pestilence that grips it: "With so many Funerals are wee oppressed, that wee have no leysure to weep for our sinnes for howling our Sonnes and Daughters. O heare the voice of our howling, withdraw thy hand from us, & we will draw neere unto thee."[34] In describing Jerusalem's suffering under famine, Nashe presents a memorable figure of maternal grief, Miriam, "a Matron of great port, and of a high lynage discended" who "was constrained (for her lives supportance), having but one onely sonne, to kill him and rost him."[35] "Mothers of London," Nashe exclaims, "(each one of you to your selves) do but imagine that you were *Miriam*, wyth what hart (suppose you) could ye go about the cooquerie of your own chyldren?"[36] Although his task is difficult, not only to exonerate but actually to praise the maternal care of this cannibalistic mother, Nashe accomplishes it. "It is better to make a Sepulchre of him in mine own body," Miriam reasons, "than to leave him to be lickt up by over-goers feete in the streets. The wrath of God is kindled in every corner of the Citty." In a parody of both immaculate conception and transubstantiation, she vows, "Ile bind thee to me againe, in my wombe Ile beare thee againe, and there bury thee ere Famine shall confound thee . . . Returne into me, and see the Mould wherein thou wert cast."[37] From this grotesque portrait of maternal lament, in which the mother's body literally becomes the son's tomb, the religious and political implications of Miriam's sacrifice emerge: as she is constrained to kill and eat her only son, "yet [God's] onely chyld, *Christ Jesus*, (as deere to him as thou to mee, my sonne) he sent into the World to be crucified." She continues, "O sorrowe-conceiving Mothers, looke to have all your children crucified, to have none of them remitted, since our Husbands have beene so hardy to lay harmfull hands on the Lord of lyfe."[38] Miriam, like one of Lanyer's mournful daughters of Jerusalem, genders the Crucifixion to indict male misgovernment as the cause of female lament. This casting of Miriam's roasted son as a second sacrificial lamb is clear when Jerusalem's citizens discover her gruesome feast:

Eate, I pray you, heere is good meate, be not afrayde, it is flesh of my flesh, I bare it, I nurst it, I suckled it . . . Beholde his pale perboyld visage, how pretie-pitteous it lookes. His pure snow-moulded soft fleshe will melt of itselfe in your mouthes . . . Eate of my sonne one morsel yet, that it may memorize against you, ye are accessary to his dismembering. Let that morsell be his hart if you will, that the greater may be your convictment.[39]

Miriam's "convictment" of the city's male governors blames their "crueltie" for having "robd [her] of all [her] food, & so consequently robd [her] of [her] onely son." She uses the child's body to literalize the physical ravages of both famine and empathetic maternal mourning. "For sauce to thy flesh I have infused my teares," she mourns, "who so dippeth in them shall taste of my sorrow." In fact, the result of Miriam's spectacle of maternal sacrifice is "mellancholie": Nashe tells us, "the Chiefe-taines of them were over-clowded in conceite."[40]

Miriam, "the Monarch-monster of Mothers,"[41] is an extreme version of Muggins' mournful plague mothers, whose excessive sorrow for her son's starvation prompts a euthanasian reincorporation of his flesh into her own. Her story conflates the womb and the tomb to reflect a naturalization of maternity that interprets her actions as sacrifice rather than murder, indicting male misgovernment rather than revealing her selfish desire to survive at her son's expense. The maternal mourner's violent self-mutilation informs Miriam's sacrifice while her actions, in turn, suggest the frighteningly uncontrollable depths of maternal suffering, certainly associated in the period with the mysteries of reproduction itself.[42] Her mournful incorporation of her son's body into her own literalizes maternal mourning with its obsessive concern for the body of the dead and its empathetic self-consumption. As her son's sepulcher, Miriam marks Jerusalem's interment as well.

Literal counterparts to Miriam's threatening maternity are the female watchers and searchers charged by the crown with attending the dying and witnessing the cause of death in plague-ridden London. The Plague Orders "appoint certain persons dwelling within the townes infected, to provide and deliver all necessaries of victuals, or any matter of watching or other attendance,"[43] and although women are not specified to fill these offices, their traditional duties ensured that watchers were female, "for the most part single or childless."[44] While the office was established to ensure "that according to Christian charity, no persons of the meanest degree shal be left without succour and reliefe,"[45] the women who filled these roles were often seen as far from charitable. Living embodiments of Nashe's "Monarch-monster of Mothers," they appear in

plague texts as terrifying perversions of maternal care givers, as likely
to cause their charge's death as to prevent it. Dekker writes of the
abuses of these "Keepers, Nurses, or Chare-women," "in the last and
late great sicknesse many of that Nursery were as she wolves . . . and in
outward shape were tender-hearted, (almost weeping to see a sicke man,
or sicke woman in their beds) but the aymes of a number of them, (as it
proved afterward) were to wrappe such Bodies in their winding sheets."[46]
Notorious pilferers of property from the dying, watchers are likely to steal
"Wast-coats, Night-capps, Sheets, Pillow-beers, Bands, Hand-kerchers,
any thing." While Dekker excuses some nurses, claiming that "a number of them are motherly, skillful, carefull, vigilent, and compassionate
women," many, he charges, are "Dry-Nurses, and starve so farre as they
dare, all that come under their fingers."[47]

Close relatives to nefarious watchers were the "honest and discreet
matrons" appointed by the Plague Orders to serve as searchers or viewers of bodies after death.[48] Although searchers were threatened with
pillory or corporal punishment should they be found guilty of giving
false report,[49] the women in these offices were infamous for profiting
from their positions by accepting bribes for misrepresenting the cause of
death or by otherwise taking advantage of the infirm. Ursula Barrett, for
instance, a searcher in Salisbury, was accused of burying people alive in
order to pilfer their goods. As Paul Slack reports, a neighborhood child
whom Barrett was accused of having abducted "cried out in horror at
the sight of her winding sheet: 'You shall not put me into a bag as you did
my sister.'"[50] Like Dekker's dry-nurses, female searchers appear as anti-
maternal figures whose frightening power over life and death contrasts
sharply with Muggins' affectively mourning mothers, but emerges from
the same intimacy of women with bodies in death. Moreover, watchers'
and searchers' abuses were themselves considered likely causes for the
plague's visitation: Nathaniel Hodges' *Loimologia* prays that "the wicked
Practices of Nurses . . . will not be a Means of bringing on us again the
like Judgement."[51] Suspended with maternal mourners in a connection
based upon good and evil nursing, these women are scapegoats, blamed
for the city's suffering, while maternal mourners are pitiable symbols
of it.

Miriam's political cannibalism, with its indictment of male misgovernment and its power to instill remorseful "mellancholie," casts its shadow
over the remainder of Nashe's admonition to the city of London. When
Nashe condemns London's Pride, he anatomizes this foundational sin
and offers a gendered portrait of the city's misdeeds. Accordingly, lengthy

condemnations of women's vainglorious display in clothing, of their painting, and of the city's "stewes" and their "veneriall machiavelisme" showcase the problematic behavior of London's women as a probable cause for God's wrath. Like Miriam, however, Nashe sees the solution to these ills as lying not with London's women, but with its (that is, *their*) male governors: he calls upon "Provident Justices, to whom these abuses redresse apperttaineth," to control the misdeeds of citizens, both male and female, and thereby to end the city's suffering.[52]

For Muggins, as for Nashe, the agent of reform within and for the plague-ridden city is not the maternal mourner, whose tears Muggins calls "the onely Physicke, women can bestow" (B4v). Rather, London's male magistrates are responsible for relieving the strokes of God's "heavie rod" (C4) by enforcing citizens' moral behavior:

> Reforme these things, you heads of London Citie,
> Punish lewd vice, let vertue spring and grow:
> Then Gods just wrath, now hot will turne to pittie,
> And for his children, you again doe know:
> Your former health, on you he will bestow,
> 　　The Plague and Pestilence, wherewith he visites still,
> 　　To end or send, are in his holy will.
>
> 　　　　　　　　　　　　　　　　　　　　(D2)

Recalling them to their duties (often necessary during plague-time since many city officials fled their posts for fear of infection),[53] Muggins encourages the magistrates to "Remember likewise, God hath plac't you heere, / To be as nursing fathers to the poore" (D1v). The movement in *Londons Mourning Garment* from nursing-mothers-turned-mourners, petrified in sorrow, to this masculinist appropriation of nursing (by way of Isaiah 49:23, "And kings shall be thy nursing fathers; and their queens thy nursing mothers") converts breast feeding from an emblem of maternal sacrifice to a figure for male government.[54] It replaces maternal tears, "the onely Physicke, women can bestow," with active paternal "rulers, of each publycke charge" (D1v) in whose hands the city finds not sterile complaint but productive remedy for its losses. This shift from static mourning to active government presents a gendered politics of the plague that parallels the gendering of early modern mourning, in which the unproductive excesses of maternal grief – a living–death distracting the mourner from God's providential design – are corrected by wise masculine mourning in moderation. The essentialist location of maternal mourning's stubborn stasis in the physiology of birth and breast feeding constructs the nursing father, or moderate male mourner, as a sublimation of natural maternal instincts. The body of Miriam's son, literally devoured by the maternal mourner, is figuratively resurrected in male governors' melancholic management.

The nursing father of plague-ridden London, moreover, is constructed on the literal bodies of female watchers and searchers, women who emblematize the fearful dependence of sick and dying men on women's charitable nursery. James Balmford adopts the image of the nursing father to describe male government in plague-time, particularly with regard to the policies put forth in the Plague Orders. Urging his parishioners to suspend visits to the sick in accordance with the 1603 Plague Orders, Balmford reminds them that since "Kings and Queenes ought to be nursing fathers and nursing mothers to the Church," James seeks "(out of fatherly care) [to] preserve [his] subjects from destruction."[55] Since, as Werdmuller states it, "among the greatest workes of mercy, this is reckoned to visite the sick, to have compassion upon them, to give them good counsaile, and to comforte them,"[56] the Plague Orders' pragmatic efforts to stem infection by limiting contact with the sick were, of course, considered morally reprehensible by some.[57] Moreover, since women traditionally attended the sick and dying,[58] these prohibitions sought to curtail women's charitable works, replacing these "motherly" care givers with frightening female watchers and searchers.

While the maternal mourner supports the movement from unproductive to productive grief in *Londons Mourning Garment*, from domestic sorrow to public policy, and from maternal to paternal nourishment, she is nonetheless a resistant, transgressive presence in the poem and in early modern literatures of death and consolation more generally. Mothers' and nurses' sovereignty over the body's physical demise challenges not only the decorum of post-Reformation mourning but also the teleology of death and resurrection fundamental to Christian consolation. Muggins' maternal mourners – striking in their powerful, passionate suffering – are the figures that remain in the reader's mind when the text is over: like Nashe's Miriam and Brewer's "Monument of Misery," their "Ladies Teares out-live [their] Teares," but with a transgressive pathos that cannot easily be accommodated by their authors' views of the plague as providential. Mourning mothers' refusal to be consoled is symptomatic of both the deferred closure of Muggins' text – able only to hope for rather than guarantee the city's political and spiritual triumph over death – and the uncertainties attending death itself, where men's frightening dependence on women's care imagines extremes of maternal compassion and cruelty.

II

Muggins' replacement of futile female mourning with productive male government takes place in the shadow of Queen Elizabeth's death and imitates her replacement by a male successor. Dekker describes this transfer of power as a shift from barrenness to fertility: "The losse of a Queene, was paid with the double interest of a King and Queene. The Cedar of her government which stood alone and bare no fruit, is changed now to an Olive, upon whose spreading branches grow both Kings and Queenes."[59] Muggins never mentions Elizabeth in his poem, eliding her death in the pithy phrase, "With springing March, the tidings of a king" (B1). Mourning for Elizabeth is quickly overtaken by more pressing events, both preempted by James's triumphant image and displaced into the poem's maternal laments for London's fallen children. This elision reflects the ambivalence that attended the queen's death and the king's ascension. Lady Anne Clifford's report that "King James was proclaimed in Cheapside by all the Council with great joy and triumph" since "this peacable coming of a king was unexpected of all parts of the people,"[60] bespeaks the anxiety over succession in the latter part of Elizabeth's reign and the general relief at a peaceful transfer of power.[61] But John Manningham's note that "the proclamacion was heard with greate expectacion and silent joye, noe great shouting," glances mournfully toward the lost mother even as it anticipates the coming father: "I thinke the sorrowe for hir Majesties departure was soe deep in many heartes they could not soe suddenly shewe anie great joy, though it could not be lesse then exceeding greate for the succession of soe worthy a King."[62]

Exhorting the Ladies of England to "mourne as Christians" (that is, moderately), Radford Mavericke's *Mourning Weede* sees the queen's maternal nurturing of the nation as accounting for her subjects' excessive grief. "And forasmuch as the Scripture calleth kings *nursing fathers, and Queenes nursing mothers* of the church and common wealth," he reasons, her subjects' grief is justified, they "being not lately weaned for any longer sucking the sweete and tender paps of our late most dearest beloved Queene, who living, loved us as dearely (doubtles) if not more dearly, then ever any nurse or mother loved her beloved babe."[63] Mavericke literalizes the biblical image to emphasize Elizabeth's maternal essence, but disturbingly casts her death as causing the nation's abrupt weaning, revising a natural process of maturation with an unnatural severance of the mother–child bond. He continues:

How then should wee not weepe and mourne for the lacke & losse of such a mother? *Rahell* the mother of some of the children of Israell, by a fine figurative speech is brought in, in the scriptures, *mourning for her children* after shee is dead: we therefore, the living children of this land, may well mourne for our dearest mother, not because shee is dead for therein she hath but yeelded unto nature, but because shee is no longer living to care for us, and to comfort us, and dayly pray for us, as heretofore she hath done.[64]

Elizabeth is a second Rachel, the mother of her people whose affective bond with her children extends beyond the grave. Even in felicity, she shares her subjects' sorrow and, in turn, authorizes their grief. As a mother frozen in the posture of inconsolable grief (and, significantly, a mother who dies in childbirth, making the ultimate sacrifice for her children),[65] Rachel interjects into the discourses surrounding Elizabeth's death the specter of immoderate mourning, rife with political implications. As a response to royal succession, excessive mourning – both mourning *of* and *for* the mother – threatens to disable the smooth transfer of power, valorizing past over future, Tudor over Stuart, and female monarch over male. Moreover, Jeremiah's figurative invocation of Rachel's tears ("A voice was heard in Ramah, lamentation, and bitter weeping; Rahel weeping for her children refused to be comforted for her children, because they were not," Jer. 31:15) connotes political defeat and exile.[66] Elizabeth I as a second Rachel, whose mourning authorizes that of her subjects, implicitly figures political instability and loss.[67]

Mavericke exploits the affective bond utilized in Muggins' teleology of the plague to assert the providential succession of a male monarch. Weaned by death from Elizabeth's "Pelicanlike" body,[68] the infantile body politic turns to its nursing father, James. As Richard Mulcaster's *Comforting Complaynt* concludes, "though [God] tooke our Queene, a King he gave / To play the fathers part in mothers losse."[69] Mavericke's point, like that of virtually all of the 1603 elegies for the queen, is that this shift – from mother to father, from literal to metaphoric nursing, from sex to gender – is necessary and beneficial. The nation must mourn moderately, avoiding excess, for political rather than spiritual reasons: expanding on Psalm 30:5, "Weeping may abide at Evening, but Joy cometh in the morning," Mavericke exchanges the dark night of Elizabeth's demise for the joyful ascension of James. As Dekker puts it, "In the morning no voice heard but murmures and lamentation, at noone nothing but shoutes of gladnes & triumph."[70]

While the "nation almost begotten and borne under her"[71] mourned Elizabeth's death like that of a mother, her elegies invariably translate sorrow to joy by celebrating James's ascension, often at far greater length than they devote to eulogizing the queen. The oxymoronic titles of many of these works – *Sorrowes Joy*, *Queen Elizabeths Losse and King James his Welcome*, *The King's Prophecie*, or *Weeping Joy* – convey their double purpose to mourn Elizabeth while, more importantly, praising James.[72] They commonly imagine a seasonal, moderate grief that turns lamentation toward "attempt[s] to establish in the popular mind the new king's legitimacy."[73] Thus Henry Petowe, with a nod toward the pretensions of protracted mourning (especially in literary form), restricts the appropriate period of mourning for Elizabeth to a single day: "Of Aprils month the eight and twentieth day, / M. Sixe hundred three by computation, / Is the prefixed time for sorowes stay. / That past: my mourning weedes grow out of fashion."[74] The anonymous broadside ballad, *A Mournefull Dittie, entitled Elizabeths losse, together with a welcome for King James*, similarly encourages its audience, disconcertingly, "Now is the time that we must all forget / The sacred name of Sweet Elizabeth / . . . Praying for King James as earst we prayed for thee, / In all submissive love and loyaltie."[75]

Elizabeth's elegies argue that in royal succession, as in *Londons Mourning Garment*, feminine sterility must give way to masculine productivity; the feminine reification of the body in death must surrender to the masculine metaphorics of the body politic. While elegies for Elizabeth work to season mourning with joy, however, maternal mourning's tenacity would eventually resurrect the queen in the nation's heart and imagination. Although the number of elegies written for the queen in 1603 is impressive, it falls well short of the number commemorating Sir Philip Sidney's death in 1586, or Prince Henry's in 1612.[76] Noticeably absent from the ranks of her elegists are the major poets of the era, an absence suggesting ambivalence about Elizabeth's successor.[77] Drayton's complaint that in the wake of Elizabeth's death, "cowardyse had tyed up every tongue, / And all stood silent"[78] voices a curious reluctance to advance the Stuart claim to power by aligning the speechless poet with the mourning woman – both silent, static, unable to leave behind the corpse of Elizabethan monarchy. So indefatigable is that resilient, resistant corpse that thirty years after her death, amid growing dissatisfaction with James's heir, Diana Primrose would publish an idealized elegy to "Queene Elizabeth, of Glorious Memory" in which the nursing mother no longer figures static mourning but, like Nashe's Miriam, a threatening maternal power over life and death. In the stream emitted by her "Nectar-flowing Veine," Elizabeth "able was to drowne a World of men, / And drown'd, with sweetnes to revive agen."[79] Although delayed, the elegy presents a woman writer exploiting the provocative, productive merger of maternity and mourning to embalm the powerful female body as the emblem of women's political, and textual, authority.

III

Shakespeare's *Richard III*, like the other plays of the first and second tetralogies, are products of Elizabeth's final years and inscribe the anxiety surrounding her imminent death and the uncertain succession it implied.[80] Like *Londons Mourning Garment* and the queen's elegies, Shakespeare's history constructs a dichotomy between female lament and male government, associating the former with antiquated customs, oral culture, and pre-Reformation ritual and the latter with Machiavellian statecraft, manipulations of textual forms, and modern *realpolitik*. The world of *Richard III* is simultaneously one of ruthlessly pragmatic politics and remarkably potent supernatural elements – Margaret's powerful curses, prophetic dreams, and ghostly visitations by the play's long list of casualties. Like plague-ridden London, it is a world in which the etiology of physical corruption is linked to moral decay since "Richard's physical deformity and moral depravity [serve] as a synecdoche for the state,"[81] and where appeals to providential design – the city's redemption through penitential tears or a Tudor monarch's divinely sanctioned ascension – proceed by appropriating and supplanting women's lament. While Richard's aggressive politics argue that the power to script historical events belongs to the person most fearless in attempting to control Fortune, the play's supernatural elements pose the problem of how they ought to be read as a method of historiography. If we agree with Buckingham that, "curses never pass / The lips of those that breathe them in the air,"[82] what do we make of the apparent potency of Margaret's curses, noted by each character in turn as he or she succumbs to their power? As Richard's chief adversaries, the play's maternal mourners craft a rival version of history that rereads the genre not (only) as a vehicle for disseminating an interested view of royal succession but (also) as the repository of women's grief. Women's communal, ritualized lament assumes a central role in *Richard III*, where it memorializes history's losses to challenge Richard's pragmatic politics with the promise of more authentic, ceremonial forms of power, kingship included. While the play's maternal mourners aid and abet the providential plot of Tudor dynastic triumph that signals Richard's demise, Shakespeare uses maternal mourning to interrogate the teleological narrative of sterile female mourning's replacement by productive male government. Maternal mourning becomes a resistant force that outlives the political outcomes that it enables and within which it resides.

In its memorial function, maternal mourning challenges Richard's political amnesia by insisting on the continued relevance of history's losses. When Margaret describes her own and her co-mourners' lamentational task as "repetition of what [Richard] hast marr'd" (1.3.164), she names the play's gendered conflict between past and future, recollection and forgetfulness. Richard rises to power through a strategy of willful forgetfulness, a revisionist history that obscures his culpability in the play's numerous crimes.[83] He admits that he has murdered both Anne's husband and father-in-law, but claims, "Your beauty was the cause of that effect" (1.2.121). He gains the crown by implying "the bastardy of Edward's children" (3.7.4; cf. 3.5.73–94) and "rumor[s] it abroad / That Anne my wife is very grievous sick" (4.2.50) in preparation for her murder. To oppose this corrupt historiography, the weeping queens reiterate Richard's misdeeds, lamenting his victims and insisting on a factual historical record and an accountability that Richard seeks to avoid. Their "accurate political vision where Richard is concerned"[84] parallels Miriam's mournful condemnation of masculine misgovernment in *Christs Teares Over Jerusalem*. Accordingly, when the maternal mourners confront Richard in Act 4, scene 4 with a commemorative and accusatory recitation of the dead ("Tell me, thou villain-slave, where are my children?" 4.4.144), he attempts to drown their "telltale" voices out: "A flourish, trumpets! Strike alarum, drums! / Let not the heavens hear these telltale women / Rail on the Lord's anointed. Strike, I say!" (4.4.149–51). The play's gendering of rival models of historical record depends upon its deployment of the early modern gendering of grief. If Richard embodies the "excessive and unruly masculinity" that characterized the later years of Elizabeth's reign,[85] the attendant dichotomy between masculine action and feminine stasis also marks the sexes' different uses of mourning. Their gendered styles of grief explore and anticipate the argument that will be made by the plague texts and elegies of 1603.

If, as Jean Howard and Phyllis Rackin argue, "performative masculinity is demonic"[86] in *Richard III*, tears are a crucial tool in its construction.

Richard's manipulations of weeping engender not only of his character but also the political style that he represents. Time and again, he feigns tears on occasions when moderate mourning is sanctioned. Clarence, for instance, misreads Richard's contempt for commiseration when he recalls the latter's tears at his imprisonment: "he bewept my fortune, / And hugg'd me in his arms, and swore with sobs / That he would labor my delivery" (1.4.244–6). Clarence's son, likewise, reports Richard's tears on relating his father's death: "And when my uncle told me so, he wept / And pitied me, and kindly kiss'd my cheek, / And bade me rely on him as on my father, / And he would love me dearly as a child" (2.2.23–6). He weeps in the presence of Hastings' severed head, after, of course, ensuring his dispatch: "So dear I lov'd the man that I must weep" (3.5.24). By exploiting tears within his construction of masculinity, Richard engages in the early modern gendering of grief which reads moderate mourning as the reasonable, appropriate and essentially male response to loss. Thus he creates the appearance of conscience, pity, and compassion by performing grief. At the same time, though, Richard's tears (like Henry IV's strategic mourning at the close of *Richard II*) complicate the Protestant formulation of masculine mourning by associating it with deceptive theatricality and demonic performance.

Richard's lachrymose improvisations interrogate the post-Reformation gendering of grief, with its censure of feminine excess and advocacy of masculine mourning in measure. He reduces mourning to mere theatricality by admitting duplicity in his calculated deployment of tears (for example, in his confession that "Tear-falling pity dwells not in this eye," 4.2.6). In his wooing of Anne, he performs a stoic rejection of tears that further troubles the Protestant ideal of the mean in mourning by enlisting it in the service of, in Nashe's words, "veneriall machiavelisme." Thus Richard tells Anne:

> Those eyes of thine from mine have drawn salt tears,
> Sham'd their aspect with store of childish drops:
> These eyes, which never shed remorseful tear –
> No, when my father York and Edward wept
> To hear the piteous moan that Rutland made
> When black-fac'd Clifford shook his sword at him;
> Nor when thy warlike father, like a child,
> Told the sad story of my father's death,
> And twenty times made pause to sob and weep,
> That all the standers-by had wet their cheeks
> Like trees bedash'd with rain – in that sad time
> My manly eyes did scorn an humble tear.
>
> (1.2.153–64)

Richard's manly refusal of tears, here cast in the guise of Petrarchan flattery, represents a perversion of mourning in measure that reflects Richard's moral and physical deformities.[87] Repeatedly, post-Reformation *artes moriendi* insist that the failure to mourn bespeaks an unnatural lack of human emotion. Werdmuller, for example, states, "Naturally we mourn, weep & lament when our kinfolkes and freends depart . . . Such heavinesse, pittie, and compassion, dooth God allowe. For he hath not created us to bee stones and blockes, but . . . made us an heart of fleshe, that we might have feeling and love our freends, beyng sorrye when they suffer trouble."[88] Robert Southwell's claim that "as not to feele sorrow in sorrowfull chances, is to want sence, so not to beare it with moderation, is to want understanding, the one brutish, the other effeminate,"[89] defines Richard's misrepresentation of masculine stoicism as an utter lack of grief, emphasizing not only his inhumanity but also the vulnerability of post-Reformation prescriptions for mourning to misappropriation and abuse.

Moreover, the gendering of tears in *Richard III* has implications for the play's genre as tragedy. Phyllis Rackin has argued that, while early modern history was gendered as masculine due to its promise to provide heroic models for imitation, "tragedy . . . was likely to inspire womanly emotions in its spectators." She quotes Stephen Gosson's censure of tragedy's power to "drive us to immoderate sorrow, heavines, womanish weeping and mourning, whereby we become lovers of dumpes, and lamentation, both enemies of fortitude."[90] While Gosson's antitheatricality employs the misogynistic language of immoderation to condemn tragedy's effects, the Aristotelian idea of catharsis (rediscovered in Renaissance works like Sidney's *Defence of Poetry*) bases the genre's efficacy and value on its ability to elicit pity, whose emblem, as Werdmuller suggests, is moderate grief. Measured tears are the appropriate response to tragic action, while both immoderation and the obdurate refusal to mourn are gendered perversions of this mean. Sidney, following Plutarch, enlists the pitiless tyrant Alexander Pheraeus from whom "the sweet violence of tragedy" "drew abundance of tears"[91] to illustrate tragedy's positive effects. Like the masculine tears advocated by Markham's *Tears of the Beloved*, pity enhances political action within the humanist commonwealth. The melancholy that befalls Jerusalem's governors at the sight of Miriam's mournful feast and the pity elicited by Muggins' maternal mourners are appropriate responses to these tragic spectacles.

While Richard's perversions of the cultural meanings and gendering of early modern tears challenge tragedy's benefits toward one extreme, maternal mourners' immoderation threatens to undermine the genre's efficacy toward the other. The mean in mourning is necessarily vulnerable to corruption in either direction, toward the excesses of feminine mourning or the apathy of masculine stoicism.[92] With Richard and his female adversaries suspended in a tense relationship based upon their violations of moderate mourning, Shakespeare scripts Richard's successful (if transient) appropriation of women's lamentational power in his wooing of Anne. The play's providential resolution suggests, meanwhile, that the queens' lamentations are contained and tamed by the Tudor propaganda that they ultimately serve. Thus Rackin argues that the shift from chronicle history to tragedy in *Richard III* depends upon male characters' (not only Richard's but also Richmond's) appropriations of feminine power, while the women of the first tetralogy surrender their "subversive, theatrical energy" in the last play to assume "tragic roles as pitiable victims," particularly as bereaved mothers.[93] Richard's modernity and Richmond's divinely sanctioned victory are both supported by maternal mourning, much as Muggins' invocation of beneficial male government is rooted in mothers' material grief. In both cases, however, the play questions the deployment of gendered mourning within these masculine narratives of productive government, demonizing Richard's will to power and stressing Richmond's conventionality as a token of providential design so clearly that the play's conclusion, in Charnes' words, "becomes monstrous in its own right."[94] The queens' laments, considered in light of early modern women's material practices of mourning, display maternal mourning's affective, resistant power that challenges both the teleology of Tudor providential history and Richard's demonic politics.

Women's mourning in *Richard III*, as in the pre-Reformation culture to which the play alludes, fulfills a number of functions.[95] Anne's ritualized lamentation over the corpse of Henry VI in Act 1, scene 2 introduces feminine mourning into the play and indicates its culturally and historically difficult position in Shakespeare's treatment of pre-Reformation events. Promising that her tears will embalm the body of the king ("Lo, in these windows that let forth thy life / I pour the helpless balm of my poor eyes," 1.2.11–12), Anne's lament initiates the memorializing process undertaken by women's mourning throughout the play. Her formal address to Henry VI articulates the hereditary relationships on which masculine identity and political power are based:

> Poor key-cold figure of a holy king,
> Pale ashes of the house of Lancaster,
> Thou bloodless remnant of that royal blood,

> Be it lawful that I invocate thy ghost
> To hear the lamentations of poor Anne,
> Wife to thy Edward, to thy slaught'red son,
> Stabb'd by the self-same hand that made these wounds!
>
> (1.2.5–11)

She describes the lines of patrilineal inheritance determining Henry's and Edward's identities in the unfolding narrative of chronicle history, and explains her investment in lamenting their loss. Her lament both records the names of the dead and identifies the agents of their demise. The curses that follow ("O, cursed be the hand that made these holes!" 1.2.13), like those of Margaret and the Duchess of York, rely upon a confidence in retributive justice that is reiterated in the play's turn to providential design in Henry VII's ascent.

Anne's address to the murdered king and her formal lament suggest a Catholic belief in the affective power of mourning and prayer to influence the soul's fate in the afterlife. The king's ritualized funeral procession carries the trace of the Catholic practice in which the cortège made frequent stops at public crosses, shrines, and taverns where "family members were obliged to provide drink for the pall bearers. Sometimes," as Richard Davey reports, "very disorderly scenes ensued . . . The hired mourners and more unruly member of the guilds got drunk, and it is on record that on more than one occasion the body was pulled out of its coffin by these rascals and outraged, to the horror and indignation of honest people."[96] Although Richard's charge, "Stay you that bear the corse, and set it down" (1.2.33), recalls this practice, the ritual's threatened disorder was ostracized by reformed clergymen in the period, who associated it with Catholicism, on the one hand, and femininity, on the other. "All thinge being accomplished in right Popishe order at home," the ministers of Lancashire lamented in their 1590 complaint to the High Commission Court in York, "[recusants] carie the Corse towardse the Churche . . . which they sett downe by the way at everie Crosse, and there all of them devowtly on theire knees make prayers for the dead."[97] These popish assemblies involved:

Crossinge and knockinge them selves . . . wailinge the dead with more then Hethenishe owtcries; others, with open Invocations for the dead; and an other sorte with Janglinge the Belles, so disturbe the whole action, that the minister is ofte compelled to lett passe that parte of the Service appointed for the Buriall of the dead and to withdrawe him selfe from theire tumultuowse Assembly.[98]

Here the pre-Christian native (that is, "Hethenishe") tradition of
women's wailing the dead merges with Catholic superstition, and both
are condemned in the post-Reformation revision of funerary liturgy and
practice.

Anne's lament is invigorated by the lingering memory of Catholic
lamentational rituals within which women took a prominent role. It
restages the "ocular communion" enabled by the communal contem-
plation of Christ's mortified body in Catholic ritual performances such
as the Corpus Christi plays or the Easter Sepulcher (in which the faithful
gathered around a symbolic coffin of Christ in imitation of the three
Maries).[99] The liturgy of the Easter Sepulcher, for example, fostered empathy and identification between worshipers and the mourning Maries.
John Longland's 1535 Easter sermon underscores the associations of the
corpus Christi with Henry VI's wounded body as he exhorts the faithful,
"Lett us goo thidre, lett us wepe with thee Maryes, lett us turn and wynde
thys bodye of Christe . . . We shall fynde a bloody bodye, a body full of
plages and woundes."[100] As the experience of presence in the liturgy of
the Easter Sepulcher depends upon the ritualized act of mourning, so
women's lament in *Richard III* energizes this Catholic notion of mourners' intimate, effective communion with the dead as the queens name the
casualties of Richard's ruthless rise to power.[101] Accordingly, the body's
mystical ability to contain and convey its living affects, symptomatic of
a pre-Reformation intimacy between the living and the dead,[102] is affirmed when Henry VI's corpse bleeds in the presence of his murderer:
"O gentlemen, see, see dead Henry's wounds / Open their congeal'd
mouths and bleed afresh!" (1.2.55–6).[103]

Anne's ambivalent gesture toward intercessory prayer, however
("Be it lawful that I invocate thy ghost / To hear the lamentations of poor
Anne"), questions the validity of pre-Reformation models of mourners'
relationships with the dead, displaying the play's self-conscious deployment and scrutiny of ritual lamentation throughout. Elizabeth, similarly,
calls upon the lingering ghosts of her murdered sons with uncertainty as
to the possibility of their presence and the lawfulness of her plea: "If your
gentle souls fly in the air / And be not fix'd in doom perpetual, / Hover
about me with your aery wings / And hear your mother's lamentation!"
(4.4.11–14). Women's lamentations in *Richard III* long for and recall the
Catholic faith in intercessory prayers whose abandonment in the Reformation left mourners powerless to convert grief into action which could
benefit the departed. Both Anne's ritualized mourning for Henry VI and
the queens' "copious . . . exclaims" (4.4.135) assume the power of ritual

lamentation to bridge the gap between the living and the dead even as they acknowledge the eroded doctrinal foundations on which that power was based.

If Anne's lament stages the lingering potency of Catholic ritual lament, her appearance as chief mourner for the king approaches the ambiguities of mourning ritual on the level of cultural practice. Her service as chief mourner violates College of Arms rules for noble funerals, which require an agreement in sex of the decedent and chief mourner: a male relative, in other words, should fulfill this role. Accordingly, Richard replaces Anne, encouraging her to, "leave these sad designs / To him that hath most cause to be a mourner" (1.2.210–11). By posing as a communal mourner with Anne and manipulating the conventions of grief (for example, the customary bestowing of mourning rings at funerals, here recast as an erotic token),[104] Richard usurps the power of feminine lament. One inappropriate mourner, traditionally barred by her sex from fulfilling the role, is replaced by another, the king's murderer himself.[105] Anne's roles as Henry's mourner and as Richard's vocal accuser depend upon the subversive power of women's mourning in the play. Her appearance suggests the possibility of social resistance implicit in funerary ritual – a threat to which Buckingham refers later in the play when he worries that the mourning of Hastings might provoke civil unrest ("the citizens . . . haply may / Misconster us in him and wail his death," 3.5.60–1). Anne's transgressive lament for Henry VI, in Charnes' words, "seems less grief-laden . . . than warrior-like."[106] Like Muggins' maternal mourners, Anne's concern with the body of death challenges the teleological pattern of death and resurrection that supports the post-Reformation advocacy of mourning in measure.

The specter of the Catholic lamentational tradition infuses the women's laments of *Richard III* with the richness of the cultural tensions surrounding the outlawing of these practices in the Reformation and their persistence well into the period of the play's composition and performance. The queens' repetitions of history's losses share with Catholic practice the communal memorialization of the dead. The repeated masses for the dead, performed on the third, ninth, and thirtieth days after death and annually thereafter,[107] and the practice of reading the obits contain the "potential for endless accumulation and repetition."[108] They are the formal equivalents of the queens' ritualized laments in *Richard III* and imply a similar faith in the oral transmission of historical fact and the corporate construction of collective memory.[109] Set against the oral culture of women's lament are Richard's manipulations of texts.

He appears, for instance, in the engineered scene of his recruitment with a prayer book in his hands (3.7.96). He claims that he "made [Hastings] my book, wherein my soul recorded / The history of all her secret thoughts" (3.5.26–7). And he controls the play's overt consideration of the virtues of "record" and "report" ("Is it upon record, or else reported / Successively from age to age, he built it?" 3.1.72–3), to display his linguistic duplicity: "Thus, like the formal Vice, Iniquity, / I moralize two meanings in one word" (3.1.82–3).

While Anne's lament stages a potential threat to the political order that Richard seeks to establish, the scene also scripts her seduction by masculine tears and anticipates the means by which male characters claim the right to govern based upon their control of mourning. This is quite literally the case, of course, in Richard's subsequent marriage to Anne, which installs him as her male governor through his successful manipulation of manly tears. Elsewhere, however, *maternal* grief becomes a privileged space within which women retain lamentational power and practice a potent mourning that successfully resists appropriation by the play's male governors. The Duchess's competitive mourning in Act 2, scene 2 valorizes maternal grief and prefigures its violent performance in the powerful scene of mothers' lamentation, Act 4, scene 4:

> Was never other had so dear a loss.
> Alas! I am the mother of these griefs:
> Their woes are parcell'd, mine is general.
> She for an Edward weeps, and so do I:
> I for a Clarence [weep], so doth not she;
> These babes for Clarence weep, [and so do I;
> I for an Edward weep,] so do not they.
> Alas! you three on me, threefold distress'd,
> Pour all your tear. I am our sorrow's nurse,
> And I will pamper it with lamentation.
>
> (2.2.79–88)

Accordingly, the Duchess weeps and beats her breast (2.2.3) while Elizabeth and Anne tear their hair or threaten to disfigure themselves with their nails (2.2.33, s.d. and 1.2.125–6), classic gestures of immoderate mourning that display the empathy between the mourner's physical mutilation and the body's corruption in death. Elizabeth's graphic imagination of her sons' violent demise illustrates the empathetic violence of maternal grief:

No doubt the murderous knife was dull and blunt
Till it was whetted on thy stone-hard heart
To revel in the entrails of my lambs.
But that still use of grief makes wild grief tame,
My tongue should to thy ears not name my boys
Till that my nails were anchor'd in thine eyes;
And I, in such a desp'rate bay of death,
Like a poor bark of sails and tackling reft,
Rush all to pieces on thy rocky bosom.

(4.4.227–35)

In Act 4, scene 4, the scene of mothers,[110] the communal, ritualized voice of maternal lamentation receives its most sustained and powerful hearing in the play. The familial bonds between the maternal mourners and their dead are prefigured in Act 4, scene 1, where the queens assert maternity as the basis of their rival authority to Richard's:

Q. ELIZ. I am their mother, who shall bar me from them?
DUCH. I am their father's mother, I will see them.
ANNE. Their aunt I am in law, in love their mother;
Then bring me to their sights.

(4.1.21–4)

Unable to prevail against Richard's will, Elizabeth ends the scene by addressing the Tower, "Rude ragged nurse, old sullen playfellow / For tender princes – use my babies well! / So foolish sorrow bids your stones farewell" (4.1.101–3). In Act 4, scene 4, Elizabeth, Margaret, and the Duchess join in communal lament to exercise the power of telltale maternal mourning. The antiphonal, stichomythic form of the lament accentuates its ritualized character and echoes the form of classical women's mourning,[111] while the display of three disconsolate women mourners seated on the ground, as if around a grave, recalls the traditional imagery of the three Maries:[112]

Q. MAR. If sorrow can admit society [*Sitting down with them*]
[Tell over your woes again by viewing mine.]
I had an Edward, till a Richard kill'd him.
I had a [Harry], till a Richard kill'd him.
Thou hadst an Edward, till a Richard kill'd him.
Thou hadst a Richard, till a Richard kill'd him.
DUCH. I had a Richard too, and thou didst kill him.
I had a Rutland too, thou [holp'st] to kill him.
Q. MAR. Thou hadst a Clarence too, and a Richard kill'd him.

(4.4.38–46)

While Elizabeth mourns the slaughter of her "gentle lambs" (4.4.22) and Margaret recalls the death of her "sweet son" (4.4.25), the Duchess laments not only her sons' deaths but also that "from the kennel of [her] womb hath crept / A hell-hound that doth hunt us all to death" (4.4.47–8). As a result, maternal mourning and maternal curses merge in the scene, and the threatening aspects of devouring maternity illustrated in Nashe's cannibalistic Miriam emerge in the Duchess's violent curses of her son. In response to Richard's question, "Who intercepts me in my expedition?" the Duchess names maternal control over life and death as her distinguishing feature: "O, she that might have intercepted thee / By strangling thee in her accursed womb / From all the slaughters, wretch, that thou hast done" (4.4.136–9). The violence of maternal mourning itself replaces the mother's physical smothering of her son: "go with me," the Duchess invites her co-mourners, "And in the breath of bitter words let's smother / My damned son" (4.4.132–4). In damning her "accursed womb, the bed of death" (4.1.53) and its offspring, the Duchess assigns to maternal mourning a threatening power over life and death – a deadly nursery – that is not wholly contained either by Richard's machinations or by Richmond's providential victory.

While the portrait of maternal mourning in the scene of mothers is violently immoderate, the scene concludes with a gesture toward moderation and measure. At various moments in the play, the mean in mourning is advocated by Richard (who conflates it with unnatural obduracy and fraud) and by other male characters as well. Dorset echoes the conventional image of life as a loan from God in encouraging his mother to moderate her sorrow:

> Comfort, dear mother, God is much displeas'd
> That you take with unthankfulness his doing.
> In common wordly things 'tis call'd ungrateful
> With dull unwillingness to repay a debt,
> Which with a bounteous hand was kindly lent;
> Much more to be thus opposite with heaven,
> For it requires the royal debt it lent you.
>
> (2.2.89–95)

Similarly, Rivers urges Elizabeth to moderation by emphasizing the seasonal quality of succession, much as the 1603 elegies for Queen Elizabeth moderate sorrow for her death with joy for James's ascension: "Drown desperate sorrow in dead Edward's grave, / And play your joys in living Edward's throne" (2.2.99–100). Accordingly, the scene immediately following, Act 2, scene 3, showcases citizens' anxieties about succession in the wake of the king's death. In terms similar to Rivers', but with far more sinister implications, Richard responds to Elizabeth's charge that "thou didst kill my children" with the seasonal promise, "But in your daughter's womb I bury them; / Where in that nest of spicery they will breed / Selves of themselves, to your recomforture" (4.4.422–5). The view of succession as a cure for immoderate mourning, prominent in elegies for Elizabeth I, prompts Richard to suggest:

> Your children were vexation to your youth,
> But mine shall be a comfort to your age.
> The loss you have is but a son being king,
> And by that loss your daughter is made queen.
>
> (4.4.305–8)

The question of succession is central to the play's maternal laments, since the system of patrilineal inheritance, within which women play a central role, is the older order that they both emblematize and eulogize, while the modern construction of masculine identity is embodied in Richard's self-authored will to power.[113] The strategy of moderating grief by appealing to the seasonal nature of succession, though, is cast in demonic terms in Richard's second, unsuccessful, attempt to overwhelm feminine mourning with masculine tears. This failure, in turn, undermines Richard's politics of the self-made man.

As in Muggins' and Nashe's etiologies of the plague in London, the body of the maternal mourner in *Richard III* is a synecdoche for the suffering of the body politic in the throes of political and moral disorder. Moreover, as the elegies for Elizabeth I illustrate, the maternal mourner is a potent figure within which to focus the anxieties attending the death and succession of monarchs. Shakespeare's maternal mourners serve both of these functions. In the same way that Muggins, the plague authors, and elegists attempt to contain and profit from feminine immoderation by exchanging debilitating maternal pathos for the metaphoric nursing of benevolent male governors, so Richmond arrives at the end of *Richard III* like one of Nashe's "Provident Justices," like the nursing father of the commonwealth, to save the country from the political uncertainties of succession and the moral corruption of Richard's reign: "O now let Richmond and Elizabeth, / The true succeeders of each royal house, / By God's fair ordinance conjoin together!" (5.5.29–31). The wounded body of Henry VI is feminized in "poor England weep[ing] in streams of blood" (5.5.37) and repaired with the promise that "Now civil wounds are stopp'd" (5.5.40). Maternal mourning's profitable contribution to Tudor providence results in the gendered bifurcation of Henry VI's corpse into the lacerated body of the female mourner, on the one hand, and the resurrected body of masculine government in Henry VII's reign, on the other. While maternal mourners, petrified in grief, support Henry VII's productive government, their rituals of presence both predict and invoke the return of the dead in the ghostly visitations of the play's last act.

Rather than containing the resistant power of mothers' lamentations within male-authored notions of providential design, however, Shakespeare affirms maternal mourning as an authentic form of ritual power and challenges the Protestant ideal of seasonal grief in both its affective and political aspects. By emphasizing the body in death, literalizing death's ravages in empathetic grief, and prizing the costs of the past over the promise of the future, death over resurrection, maternal mourning threatens to disable the smooth transfer of power from one ruler to another, and from feminine forms of ritual power to masculine. In their stubborn sorrow for history's fallen bodies, mourning mothers argue that the memory preserved and conveyed by women's tell-tale laments presents an alternative but equally valid narrative of historical change whose power can recall, if not repair, the corruptions of the beloved body, so easily forgotten, sublimated, and obscured by the metaphorics of the nursing father. In constructing the maternal body as the tomb of its lamented offspring, mothers' mourning gains a discursive authority rooted in the physical that speaks with a disruptive, resistant voice to indict the ills of masculine government and to commemorate the price of that misrule. It is a voice that resonates in the words of actual mourning mothers in the period, whose works anatomize the body of death and the maternal mourner's unique relationship to it.

PART II

Sisters of Magdalene

Mourning the death of her "Deare Girle Kate" at the age of "a yeare and Ten Months," Elizabeth Egerton, Countess of Bridgewater, writes in her meditations:

To that end I know we bring them, to God, not to our selves . . . that we may live with our Saviour for ever; and he saith of such is the Kingdome of Heaven, that is of sweet Children, so innocent; thus do I not doubt her happynesse, but yet greeve for my owne losse, and know it was gods punishment for my sinnes, to separate so soone that deare body and soule of my sweet Babe, though her soule is singing Allelujahs, yet is her sweet body here, seized on by wormes, and turned to dust.[1]

Although the countess begins her self-consolation by acknowledging God's providential determination of her child's too-brief life, maternal grief threatens to derail consolation by dwelling on the dead flesh rather than the resurrected spirit, by emphasizing the body "seized on by wormes" rather than the "soule . . . singing Allelujahs." The downward glance of maternal mourning, which values the material rather than the spiritual, quietly challenges the post-Reformation's orthodox approaches to grief, which advocate moderation in mourning to prove the mourner's faith in the salvation of the departed. This tension between the material concerns of maternal loss and the normative discourses of Christian consolation renders Egerton's meditation both poignant and powerful. For every sweet child now occupying the kingdom of heaven, we are urged to imagine an inconsolably bereft parent. In this light, the Savior's *dictum*, "such is the Kingdome of Heaven," seems suddenly less a blessing than a curse; an ironic slaughter of the innocents before which grief-stricken mothers can only howl.

This section gives voice to early modern women suffering the loss of loved ones and defines the characteristics of women's textual and material rites of mourning in the period. Chapter 5 studies women's expressions of maternal mourning in published and unpublished works and shows how early modern women negotiated admonishments of both excessive mourning and public writing to reinvent the elegy according to the gendering of grief. The chapter reads maternal elegies and diaries in relation to similar expressions of paternal grief in order to locate the unique features of maternal mourning within the works' common performances of maternity as a matter of the body. Mothers' refusal to mourn in measure, moreover, marks their writings as especially transgressive of the period's orthodox approaches to grief.

Chapter 6 concentrates on the works of only one woman, Lady Elizabeth Russell, and examines the Hoby and Russell family tombs at Bisham and Westminster Abbey which she designed and commissioned. The chapter illuminates a sphere of activity in which early modern noblewomen exercised considerable economic and creative license: the use of the public rites of mourning to memorialize family members in funerary monuments and to script the epitaphs which adorn them. The chapter shows how Russell used the conventions of women's mourning available in her culture to fashion her public performances as devoted wife, chaste widow, grieving mother, and capable matriarch.

Finally, chapter 7 reads the only two *artes moriendi* written by female writers in the period, Rachel Speght's *Mortalities Memorandum, with A Dreame Prefixed* (1621) and Alice Sutcliffe's *Meditations of Mans Mortalitie* (1634), as women's unique entries into the typically masculine discourses of consolation. The chapter argues that both Speght and Sutcliffe capitalize on women's perceived intimacy with the mat(t)er of death – as embodied in the figure of Eve – to bring their texts to print. Both authors draw upon the early modern culture of female grief to energize their texts and to position themselves both within the community of female mourners and in the company of male counselors.

While the last section illustrated a variety of purposes to which representations of women's mourning could be put in the polemics of male reformers, this section allows early modern women to speak for themselves, in registers as poignant and powerful as Elizabeth Egerton's, in terms that often threaten to undo prescriptions for moderation and insist upon continued, empathetic communion between the living corpse of the female mourner and the beloved object of her grief.

5

"I might againe have been the Sepulcure": maternal mourning and the encrypted corpse

Writing on Lavinia Fontana's *Portrait of a Newborn in a Cradle*, dated *c.* 1583 (figure 6), Vera Fortunati states that the painting may "depict a deceased newborn." She explains, "At a time when European infant mortality was high, the artist may have sought to retain the memory of a young child for the family's history, which otherwise would inevitably have been lost."[1] From the elaborately decorated cradle, the infant's gaze calmly fixes upon viewers with a surprising maturity. While the rich adornments of the cradle, the delicate lace of the bedding and garment, and the pearls encircling the child's neck assert its aristocratic status, the form of the canopied cradle recalls funerary sculpture of the period whose English examples borrow from Continental models the living–dead postures of their reclining inhabitants. For instance, the tomb of Princess Mary Stuart in Westminster Abbey (figure 5, p. 114 and figure 8, p. 146), similarly offers a portrait of the toddler-princess *en vivant* while the tomb of John Russell (figure 12, p. 197), also in Westminster, and his widow's monument in the Parish Church of All Saints, Bisham (figure 10, p. 182), cover their dead with canopies below which, in both monuments, effigies of Francis Russell (figure 7), who died in infancy, rest. Fontana's newborn is thus displayed in a cradle that is also a tomb. Beyond the cradle, in a domestic scene, dimly lit and barely discernible, a female figure gestures with both arms toward a closed chest. Although she is almost inscrutable, her outstretched arms recall a standard gesture of mourning in the period,[2] while the grim enclosure of the small chest, which may figure the child's coffin, stands in sharp contrast to the open, well-lit, and opulent cradle in the foreground. Buried in the dark background of the portrait's memorial function is its recollection of maternal mourning – an obscure, but still visible figure whose violent reaction to loss, only partially contained within the domestic space, belies the calm surface of the portrait's semi-public face. A similar tension between public memorial and private

6 Lavinia Fontana, *Portrait of a Newborn in a Cradle.*

grief is displayed in Maximilian Colt's tomb for King James's daughter Sophia (d. 1606) in Westminster Abbey: tucked in a corner near the tomb of Elizabeth I, her cradle stands beside her sister Mary's monument with its head turned toward the viewer, at once creating a tombstone and protecting from public view the infant that lies within (figure 8). Her face can now be seen in reflection only, in a mirror provided specifically for this purpose. Without this aid, the princess is hidden from the invasive public gaze (figure 9), an insistent object and embodiment of private grief.[3]

While there is no way of knowing whether the newborn represented in Fontana's portrait is a son or a daughter, the death of a male heir (particularly in a noble family) and the failure of succession that his death entailed was more likely to prompt the memorial canvas than the relatively less meaningful death of a daughter. The portrait suggests,

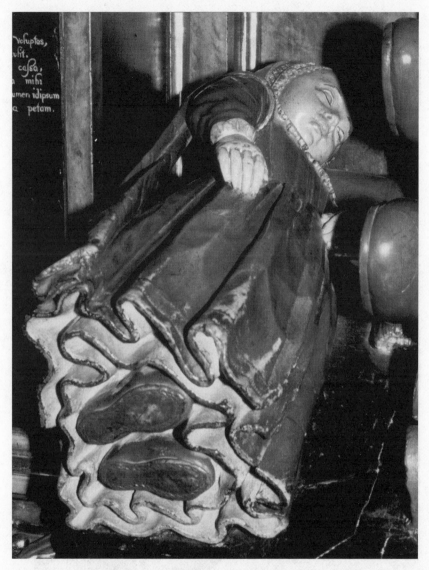

7 Cornelius Cure and William Cure II, Tomb of John Russell,
Westminster Abbey (detail).

however, that the post-Reformation experience of child-loss was gendered to cast the public sphere as that of paternal mourning where, in
the painting's visual language, stoic sorrow and living memory record
the socio-cultural loss exacted by the infant's death while consigning

8 Maximilian Colt. Tombs of Sophia and Mary Stuart, Westminster Abbey.

9 Maximilian Colt. Tomb of Sophia Stuart, Westminster Abbey.

maternal lament to the dimly lit reaches of the household. Similarly, early modern Englishwomen's private writings record and mourn the losses of daughters and of sons in terms that reveal not only the meanings of those deaths to the body politic but also their emotional toll on mothers. Retha M. Warnicke's comment that, "even a dying female child, who otherwise counted for very little in the social hierarchy, could win public laudation for demonstrating her preparation for death"[4] is illustrated – albeit in an private work – by Alice Thornton's description of her daughter Betty's good death at the age of "one yeare six months and twenty-one daies" in 1656:

That deare, sweet angell grew worse, and indured it with infinitt patience, and when Mr. Thornton and I came to pray for her, she held up those sweete eyes and hands to her deare Father in heaven, looked up, and cryed in her language, 'Dad, dad, dad,' with such vemency [*sic*] as if inspired by her holy Father in heaven to deliver her sweet soule into her heavenly Father's hands, and at which time we allso did with great zeale deliver up my deare infant's soule into the hands of my heavenly Father, and then she sweetly fell asleepe and went out of this miserable world like a lamb.[5]

In a work intended for circulation among family members and their descendants,[6] the report serves, much as Fontana's portrait does, to memorialize a lost family member and to suggest the contours of the obscure body of maternal grief from which the story emerges.

This chapter examines maternal mourning as it is recorded and represented by early modern women. In elegies for lost children by Anne de Vere, Katherine Philips, and Mary Carey, private writings by Lady Anne Clifford, Alice Thornton, and Lady Elizabeth Egerton, and the mother's legacy of Elizabeth Jocelin, I explore the cultural construction of maternity as a site at which female authorial presence is staged, and investigate the implications of that gendering as it informs, or rather complicates, the publicity and privacy of women's works. The productive tension between publication and privacy – that is, between the public performance of rites of mourning (either physical or textual) and the self-canceling insistence on privacy so often put forth by women mourners, is a defining feature of early modern maternal laments.[7] To understand fully women's uses of maternal mourning, I survey noteworthy works of *paternal* mourners in the period – particularly Philippe de Mornay's *Teares for the Death of his Sonne* – to describe the gendering of parental grief and the degree to which women manipulate, transgress, or resist male-authored prescriptions for acceptable mourning. While male writers of the period, as the previous chapter has shown, support a notional shift from static to active modes of grief and government by exploiting maternal mourning's transgressive power, women employ the mother's lament to empower and authorize their textual performances by rooting them within the resistant form of the maternal mourner herself.

One goal of this chapter is to challenge the assumption that the authority of these female-authored texts rests exclusively on their authors' sex
(with maternity as its prominent feature and emblem), and alternatively,
to wonder whether an essentialist notion of sex is deployed or performed
in the construction of the woman's voice in these works. My reading of
"maternal affection" – "the first cause of writing" according to Dorothy
Leigh's *The Mother's Blessing* – [8] sees this emotion, and the maternal body
to which it refers, "as an effect or consequence of a system of sexuality in
which the female body is required to assume maternity as the essence of
its self and the law of its desire."[9] I ask, in other words, what cultural work
is done by the performative concept of maternity as it is deployed by men
and women in the period? This question both informs and involves those
attending the publication of maternal mourner's texts – particularly vex-
ing questions since these works tend to ground authorial presence on
absence (that is, on their authors' assertions of private rather than public
performance). Works of maternal mourning are particularly valuable in
this respect, however, since they suggest that assertions of privacy may,
in fact, help to *construct* the view of mothers as domestic even as it seems
to *describe* them as such. Moreover, these works underscore the degree to
which the performance of gender is always in play, even in moments of
self-representation intended only for one's most intimate audience and,
ultimately, for oneself alone. If maternity is naturalized in the early modern period insofar as it masks the origins that produce it, women use this
essentialized notion to cast their textual performances of mourning as
uniquely feminine. An understanding of maternal grief as a matter of the
body sanctions mothers' extreme sorrow in child-loss. Unrestrained by
male authors' ventriloquism, maternal mourning becomes "melancholic
mourning"[10] which seeks, like Nashe's "Monarch-monster of mothers,"
to encrypt the corpse within the maternal body itself; in Anne de Vere's
words, within the living "Sepulcure, / Of him that I bare in mee, so long
ago."[11]

I

To explain the "meane in mourning," Thomas Playfere calls upon the
affective biblical emblem of maternal grief, Rachel: "When Rachel wept,
and would not be comforted, seeing neither her sonne Benjamin, or
almost any true Benjamite left alive; God sayd unto her, *weepe not . . .*
Forbidding thereby immoderate weeping, which is condemned *in nature;
in reason; in religion.*"[12] As an *exemplum* of the devastating physical effects

of immoderate grief, Playfere offers Niobe, who, "by overmuch weeping was turnde into a stone . . . So even blind reason, such as the heathen have had, doth yet plainely see this, That we must not weepe too much."[13] He returns to the origin of grief itself, the Fall of Eden, to argue that despite man's death sentence, "yet it pleased God to asswage and sweeten these our sorrowes with divers singular comforts" – specifically, with the knowledge that "the death of Christ is the death of Death." "Christes life," he concludes, "when hee lay in that new wombe, in which never any other was conceived, is nothing to his life, when hee laye in that new tombe, in which never any other was buried."[14]

Playfere's orthodox account of moderate mourning depends upon maternity: from Rachel, to Niobe, Eve, and finally the Virgin (implied by the "new wombe" housing Christ), maternal mourners not only adorn Playfere's argument but also enable it by illustrating unnatural and unreasonable grief (Rachel and Niobe) or by discovering death (Eve) through a fortunate fall that predicts the sanctified (albeit, from the Protestant point of view, excessive) tears of the Virgin.[15] Playfere capitalizes on maternity's notoriously excessive sorrow by deploying its exemplary figures in defense of moderation. Elsewhere, too, in male-authored *artes moriendi*, condemnations of maternal mourning support their writers' projects. For instance, Edward Bury's *Death Improved* (1693) addresses Lady Wilbraham in order to reprove her excessive grief:

Or that I could imagine your Sorrows were moderate, and no more than your Duty, I should not put you to the trouble of Reading, nor my self of Writing these following lines. But I not only fear, but also hear that you are a Woman of sorrowful Spirit, drench'd in Sorrow, overpower'd with Grief, and like *Rachel*, weeping for your Daughter, and will not be comforted, because she is not.[16]

Bury's attempt to restrain maternal mourning views this affective power as a challenge to Christian duty, a transgressive excess threatening to drown patience in despair. It is not only when treating the matter of death directly that male authors underwrite their advice by calling on immoderate maternal grief: William Herbert's 1648 *Herberts Child-Bearing Woman* adopts the grieving mother's voice, ventriloquizing her lament to argue for her submission to God's will:

What pitiful object is this? Since a few days my Child did looke so prettily and lovelie, that both my eyes and heart were much delighted at her sight: but death hath already so much altered her favor, and made her look wan, and feele cold; that though I will still love her ashes, yet I am loath or afraid, to looke upon her. Must I shortly be so?[17]

While male authors both assume and chastise the excesses of maternal grief, and utilize this figurative and rhetorical excess to support their calls to orthodoxy, women's diaries and autobiographies, in Patricia Crawford's words, "frequently reveal that their authors' adult lives were structured around the rhythms of their pregnancies, childbearing, and child rearing"[18] – and, often, child-loss. Women's accounts of child-loss are both more intimate and routine, articulating the actual bonds severed by the deaths of children and the material and affective losses they entail. Much of Lady Anne Clifford's diary for the years 1617–19 records events in the young life of her daughter, Margaret (b. 1614), that attest to her joy in motherhood and her fears for her daughter's health and life. These intimate details offer a collation of attributes defining and constructing femininity in the period, here recorded not only in Clifford's self-represented maternity but also in her daughter's acculturation. In January, and again in October, 1617, Margaret suffers illnesses which provoke considerable maternal anxiety, as Clifford's entries disclose: "The 30th [October] fell the Child to be something ill and out of Temper like a grudging of an Ague, which continued with him [*sic*] about a month or 6 weeks after."[19] So memorable are these life-threatening illnesses that nearly sixty years later, prompted by her earlier records, Clifford reiterates her gratitude for her child's preservation:

The 21st day [of January, 1676]. I remember how this day was 59 years since I went out of Great Dorset in London towne from my First Lord down to my first childe the Lady Margaret to lye there in Knowl house in Kent for a good while. I thank God I found her alive though extreamly weak & ill with her long Ague, of which shee had been in great danger those 4 nights I was from her.[20]

The depth of maternal affection apparent in Clifford's account of Lady Margaret's childhood is implicit in her records of the deaths of children and grandchildren as well. Her editor tells us that the loss of three infant sons between 1620 and 1622 led Clifford into depression, "not only for obvious maternal reasons, but also because it became painfully clear that her brother-in-law, Sir Edward Sackville, who she heartily disliked, still remained her husband's heir."[21] Clifford's "Kendal Diary," written late in her life between 1650 and 1676, recalls the first of these traumatic deaths: "The 2nd day [of February, 1676]. I remembered how this day was 56 years, about 12 o'clock in the day time, I was delivered of my little Son Thomas, Lord Buckhurst, in my owne chamber in Knowl house in Kent . . . who dyed in that house the 26th of July following."[22]

Similar comments attend the deaths of numerous descendants in the year 1659, where Clifford's disappointment over the loss of male children in particular pervades her report of her family's misfortunes: "So this yeare," she writes, "I had the Blessing of two male children borne into the world of the generation of my Bodie . . . [but] they both dyed in infancy."[23] While Clifford's chronicle of family history, especially in tracing the fates of male heirs, suggests the semi-public function of her diary as a record for posterity, intimations of a more personal grief emerge when she recounts her granddaughter's death in 1665:

The 22 November in this year, about 1 a clock in the afternoon, to my unspeakable grief, dyed my dear grandchild, the Lady Frances Drax . . . She dyed in labour of her first child (to my griefe) at Buckwell in Kent the 22nd of November following, the Child dying a little before, and she and it were buried together in Rainham Church in Kent the 15th of December after.

Clifford goes on to memorialize Frances in a lengthy account of her life, death, and burial.[24]

Anne Clifford's diary offers both a quasi-official dynastic history and a mother's more personal, affective responses to child-loss. While Clifford only subtly alludes to her grief, other women's diaries and autobiographies express maternal sorrow more overtly, revealing their authors' awareness of, and troubled relationship to, orthodox prescriptions for moderate mourning. The death of Alice Thornton's son, William, for example, is an occasion for the censure of maternal excess from an unexpected source:

After the death of my deare Willy Thornton I tooke the crosse very sadly . . . and one day was weeping much about it. My deare Naly came to me, then beeing about four years old, and looked very seriously on me, and said, 'My deare mother, why doe you mourne and weepe soe much for my brother Willy? doe you not thinke he is gon to heaven?' . . . Att which the child's speech I did much condemne myselfe, beeing instructed by the mouth of one of my owne children, and beged that the Lord would give me patience and satisfaction in His gracious goodnesse, which had putt such words into the mouth of soe young a child to reprove my immoderate sorrow for him, and beged her life might be spared to me in mercy.[25]

Ashamed of her rebuke by a child, Thornton remains silent on the subject of Willy's death throughout the rest of her autobiography – though her silence may imply hopeless submission rather than willing obedience to God's will. She is vocal on the deaths of other family members, however:

indeed, Thornton's autobiography is structured around the recorded deaths of five of her nine children, her parents, brother, sister, and husband. As Graham, et al., state, "Thornton's self emerges most strongly out of the greatest and most intensely experienced threats to self through loss and suffering. Paradoxically, it is an apparently identity-depriving loss which drives her to self-articulation."[26]

If the experience of personal loss prompts Thornton's self-fashioning, the autobiography is remarkable in its pervasive representations of her struggle with the early modern gendering of grief, a struggle at the heart of her construction of authorial presence. Thornton's reluctant acceptance of God's will in mourning her numerous losses is, in effect, the story of her life, and attests to the fact that maternal responses to child-loss represent a defining characteristic of early modern femininity. Even in a work intended for private readership, the dichotomy of masculine moderation and feminine excess informs and empowers Thornton's performance of maternity and its particular grief. Mothers' meditations on child-loss, such as Thornton's, involve complex exchanges between private loss and public mourning, and a tension between the expected censure of immoderate sorrow and personal expressions of an insuperable pain. Claims by Lawrence Stone and Philippe Ariès of parental indifference to child-loss in the period (in Stone's now-infamous words, "parents were obliged to limit the degree of their psychological involvement with their infant children")[27] have been effectively challenged by social historians and literary and cultural critics engaged in reassessing the evidence provided by female-authored sources such as these.[28] Women's complaints of child-loss in diaries and other semi-private forms deploy the affective bond between mothers and children to record their deep sorrow at and resistance to the severing of that bond. In doing so, they construct maternity on the basis of excessive mourning, using the gendering of grief not only to authorize their writing but also to articulate and define their functions within the families and cultures in which they lived.

Similar struggles between private grief and public acquiescence, between excess and moderation, occur in Lady Elizabeth Egerton, Countess of Bridgewater's meditations. Describing the death of her son, Henry, in 1656, Egerton serves as her own counselor, attempting to internalize the admonitions of excessive sorrow current in her culture. Recalling the common *dictum* that nature, reason, and religion require a mean in mourning, Egerton admits her vulnerability to a passionate grief that challenges the tenets of Christian consolation. "[W]hy should I wish my Babe had not beene, rather then to dye?" she asks, "I must not let passion overflowe so much, as not to let Religion come into my memory."[29] Her epitaph "On my boy Henry" affirms her resolve not to mourn the child's *birth*, despite the implicit charge that his life was meaninglessly cut short, but cannot conquer sorrow at his *death*:

> Her lyes a Boye the finest Child from me
> Which makes my Heart & Soule sigh for to say,
> Nor can I think of any thought, but greeve,
> For joy or pleasure could not me releeve,
> It lived dayes as many as my years,
> No more, whiche caused my greeved teares;
> Twenty and Nine was the number;
> And death hath parted us asunder.
> But thou art happy, Sweetest, on High.
> I mourne not for thy Birth, nor Cry.[30]

Egerton's equation of the infant's days with her own years stresses the physical bond between mother and child, severed by death, and reasserts maternal grief even as she attempts to calm that passion with Christian comfort.

Egerton's grief is more intractable when she recounts in three separate entries the death of her daughter Kate. "My sorrow is great I confesse," she admits, "I am much greeved for the losse of my deare Girle Keatty." Egerton's first entry concludes, "She now is not in this world, which greeves my heart, even my soule, but I must submit, & give God my thankes, that he once was pleased to bestowe so great a blessing as that sweet Child upon me."[31] Her submission is incomplete, however, and two more meditations follow in which Egerton tries to school her soul to acceptance as she morbidly imagines Kate's "sweet body . . . seized on by wormes, and turned to dust": "[L]et none wonder that I should lament for my losse, & knowe 'tis God which hath afflicted me, & let me aske pardon, & beg of the Lord to stay his hand, & to preserve my deare Husband, & those :5: Deare Babes I have."[32] The maternal mourner's emphasis on the body of the dead rather than its spiritual afterlife delays her submission to God's will. Egerton's reading of Kate's death as a punishment for her own sins is consistent with orthodox views in the period and is a form of productive mourning, insofar as the child's death prompts the mother's self-examination and correction. This productivity, however, is curtailed in Egerton's account by an admittedly extreme grief and anger at this unjust affliction. Whereas, in *Herberts Child-Bearing Woman*, maternal lament moves from physical corruption to spiritual transcendence in its predictable *memento mori* ("Must I shortly be so?"), Egerton's meditation affirms her right to mourn ("let none wonder that I should lament my losse") and overshadows spiritual salvation with empathetic sorrow for the body now consumed by death. Considering the decay of the child's corpse leads Egerton not to spiritual comfort in the certainty of her resurrection, but to a prayer, much like Thornton's, that her remaining children be spared – a prayer which is, implicitly, an indictment. The material basis of this plea becomes more poignant when Egerton reveals that she is carrying another child even as she experiences this overwhelming loss: "let us pray unto him, & beg his blessing to us and our deare ones, and to blesse the Child I am now with, all infusing his spirit of grace into it, that when our Change is come, he may call us all to his blessed Kingdome to live with him for ever."[33] The episode of mourning ends by returning to the moment of physical demise as Egerton carefully records Kate's good death:

my deare Jewell to shew she was going to happinesse, when her eyes were sett (Death having seised upon her) the last word she spooke was to me, when in passion I asked her if I should kisse her, she sayd yeas, Lengthening the word as if she was in high blisse, and lay so sweetly, desiring nothing but her Lord Jesus. Thus her life and death was nothing but sweetnesse, shewing us what we should performe at our last day; And God found her worthy of himself; So must my sorrow submitt.[34]

Maternal mourning seeks to retain the memory of the lost child as a matter of the body: that is, mothers' emphases on the physical bonds between themselves and their offspring and on the material rather than spiritual aspects of death result in images of the corpse's figurative rein-corporation within the maternal body itself. In this respect, and in its resistance to consolation, maternal mourning is melancholic, refusing the productive processes of normal mourning and seeking, rather, to en-crypt loss permanently within and as the mourner's identity.[35] Mourning is a distinct site at which gender is performed and constructed in early modern texts and culture, and maternal mourning's melancholic re-sistance to consolation offers women a means to establish their unique positions as subjects in works that record their losses. In tensions between excess and moderation, resistance and submission, the writings of early modern women challenge the representation of maternity and its grief as natural. Publicly and privately, in works that straddle that nebulous line, mourning mothers exploit this affective site to interrogate orthodox approaches to grief and its expression.

To describe maternal mourning as melancholic, however, is to invite inquiry into the relevance of the term's *psychoanalytic* legacy to the gendered culture of mourning in early modern England, with its pressure to subdue sorrow within moderation and to surrender private grief to corporate comfort grounded in the Christian teleology of death and resurrection.[36] A helpful model for the union of the psychoanalytic language of mourning and melancholia and early modern constructions of men's and women's different sorrows is offered by Julia Reinhard Lupton and Kenneth Reinhard in their brilliant reading of Freud's deployment of Shakespeare in his early representations of the Oedipus complex. There, they persuasively show that "*Hamlet*'s excessive mourning both resists and enables the Oedipal reading as such," insofar as its "scenes of imperfect mourning, which prevent Aristotelian closure and preclude reductive Oedipal readings, are precisely what render it a 'problem play' demanding interpretation."[37] At the same time, Lupton and Reinhard tease out the affinities between Freud's associations of *Hamlet* and *Oedipus Rex* and his slippage from pre-Oedipal mourning for the absent mother to the Oedipal law of the father: "Freud's presentation of *Hamlet* as a secondary, inhibited *Oedipus* resemble his lapsed attention to mourning in the process of inflecting the Oedipal, and to the accompanying displacement from the lost mother to the hostile father. Freud's early enunciations of the Oedipus complex bear within them the ellipses of objects emptied by loss."[38] Although grounded in the study of cultural commentaries on gendered grief in the early modern period rather than in contemporary psychoanalytic theory, these pages share with Lupton and Reinhard the notion that excessive mourning (coded as feminine in the period – as Hamlet's "obstinate condolement" and "unmanly grief" suggest) both resists and enables formulations of paternal law – specifically, the masculine faith in moderate sorrow as a marker of male subjectivity.

It is to the law of the father, as rendered through and within paternal mourning, that we must now turn.

II

In his seventeenth-century life of Martin Luther, Samuel Clarke describes a father's grief at the death of his daughter:

When he saw his daughter Magdalen ready to dye, he read to her Isay 26:19. Thy dead men shall live; together with my dead body shall they arise, &c. Adding, My daughter enter thou into thy chamber in peace: I shall ere long be with thee. For God will not permit me to see the punishment which hangs over the head of Germany, whereupon he wept plentifully; but when he followed the Corps, he so restrained his affection that he shed not a tear.[39]

The image of Luther's plentiful tears shed in private, while in public "he shed not a tear" implies that men as well as women participated in a culture of grief which mandated that public demonstrations of sorrow be suitably stoic while immoderation, if permitted at all, was confined to the household. The narrative recalls the early humanist complaint that women's excessive mourning constitutes a public nuisance: "If some lamentation is necessary to the grieved," Petrarch writes in a letter of 1373, "let them do it at home" and "do not let them disturb the public thoroughfares."[40] While Clarke's hagiography uses Luther's copious private tears to illustrate that "[h]e was full of affections toward his children"[41] and clearly posits paternal affection as a Christian virtue, the episode asserts the decorum governing public mourning and interjects into the moment of private child-loss the memory of civic government: thus Magdalen's death is an occasion for Luther to predict "the punishment that hangs over Germany." Luther's mourning for his lost daughter is painfully conflated with his sorrow for the nation. Moreover, Clarke's dissemination of this portrait of private paternal grief appropriates the moment within the politico-religious project advanced by his text. Paternal mourning – copious in private, stoic in public – is, in the end, neither fully private nor solely commemorative of the lost child, but also grieves the political and social losses figured in her death.

Early modern men's private writings display a paternal affection that parallels the maternal feeling apparent in women's self-representations, leaving no doubt that men were subject to grief as profound as their wives' at child-loss. Ralph Josselin, for example, lovingly records landmarks in the lives of his children, much as Anne Clifford had done. He writes affectively of the death of his adult son in 1673: "about one a clocke in the morning my eldest sonne Thomas and my most deare child ascended early hence to keepe his everlasting Sabbath with his heavenly father, and Saviour with the church above, his end was comfortable and his death calme . . . [A] wett morning, the heavens for some time have mourned over us."[42] While the profundity of paternal mourning cannot be questioned, men's grief and its role in constructing masculine subjects within the diaries display illuminating differences from female-authored examples. Josselin's emphasis on his son's spiritual transcendence despite his own sorrow is typical of paternal mourning as recorded in men's private writings. Josselin's moving account of his first experience of child-loss at the death of his infant son, Ralph, voices both his desire for moderation and his confidence in a "seasond" sadness:

This day my deare babe Ralph, quietly fell a sleepe, and is at rest with the lord, the Lord in mercy sanctifie his hand unto mee, and doe mee good by it and teach mee how to walke more closely with him: I blesse god for any measure of patience, and submission to his will. oh Lord spare the rest of us that are living for thy name sake wee entreate thee; this correction though sad was seasond with present goodnes.[43]

Like Elizabeth Egerton, Josselin responds to his child's death with a prayer for his remaining family members, but unlike the female-authored account, he emphasizes not his reluctance to submit to God's will (as Egerton puts it, "So *must* my sorrow submitt;" my italics), but his eagerness to do so. Josselin's gesture is toward, rather than against, submission, obedience, and consolation. As vicar of Earls Colne, Essex, from 1641 until his death in 1683, Josselin's personal losses are opportunities to reiterate privately the consolatory message of salvation whose public affirmation was his duty. In spite of himself, though, the diary indicates that Josselin, like his female counterparts, struggled with submission. His entry for the day following Ralph's death bespeaks his sorrow but also his faith in the teleology of death and resurrection on which Christian comfort rests:

Thes 2 dayes were such as I never knewe before; the former for the death, and this for the burial of my deare sonne . . . thy bones rest out of my sight, but thy soule liveth in thy and my gods sight, and soule and body shall assuredly arise to injoy god, and thes eyes of mine shall see it: yea and my god shall make mee see this dealing of his to bee for the best.[44]

Confident in the fact of resurrection, Josselin successfully moderates his grief: thus only one further entry, the following day, considers his loss. "[G]od hath taken away a sonne," he writes, "I hope the lord will keepe my feete in uprightness . . . and also that I should bee more carefull of my family to instruct them in the theory of god, that they may live in his sight and bee servicable to his glory."[45] Meditating upon his son's death results, finally, in a turn toward domestic government: as the spiritual head of his household, Josselin sees the loss as a call to diligence in the religious instruction of his family.

Josselin's most profound grief is expressed at the death of his eight-year-old daughter, Mary, in 1650, whom he eulogizes in terms that recall Mary Magdalene's figurative embalming in the consolatory sermons of Protestant reformers:

it was a pretious child, a bundle of myrrhe, a bundle of sweetnes, shee was a child of ten thousand . . . it was to us a box of sweet ointment, which now its broken smells more deliciously than it did before. Lord, I rejoyce I had such a present for thee . . . it lived desired and dyed lamented, thy memory is and will bee sweete unto mee.[46]

The lasting memory of his beloved child causes Josselin to recall, following the death of his daughter, Ann, in 1673: "twenty three yeares before god opened the grave and Mary my eldest of that brood . . . lay in the . . . grave. god hath taken 5 of 10. lord lett it be enough."[47] Even in the depth of his sorrow, however, Josselin seasons his grief with the knowledge that "the lord was wonderfull good to mee and my deare wife in this correction" since "he bore witnesse to my spirit that it was not in anger towards mee or my babe, but in love to both that he did what he did." He concludes, "the lord gave mee strength of heart to eye him, and quiettnes of heart to submitt to him, for which I blesse his name."[48]

The commencement of Josselin's diary with that of his religious career suggests,[49] as do his responses to child-loss, that his private meditations reaffirm his calling: throughout his undeniable experiences of grief, the orthodox, consolatory message of mourning in measure dominates his sorrow and creates the private subject as an extension of his public role. For mothers, whose cultural identity was intimately related to their reproductive functions and whose spiritual salvation, according to the familiar *dictum*, depended upon their successful bearing and nurturing of children (as the anonymous *Preparacyon to Deeth* states it, "The woman shal be saved throughe bearynge of chyldren, yf she contynue in faythe, love, and sanctificacyon, wyth sobernes"),[50] expressions of grief at child-loss are less measured and more prone to resistance, anger, and transgression. Based on the physical bond between mother and child, naturalized in early modern culture as essentially feminine, the maternal mourner contemplates the complete dissolution of identity in inconsolable grief.

The dichotomy of public and private mourning and its gendering are given a distinctive handling by Edward Vaughn in his *Divine Discoverie of Death* (1612), when he discusses the appropriate styles of mourning for "part[ies] private or publicke," counting among private losses the deaths of children. Vaughn "call[s] to minde out of my owne tormented heart and fatherly afflicted soule, my sorrow for many sonnes, specially for one," and concludes, "Parents [must] . . . truly be reckoned amongst those who mourne too much and overlong, being drawne thereunto as out of their unanswerable affections, derived no man knowes whence, nor how, saving that which is in respect of children begotten in mariage, to which the exceeding divine affection of God the Father in Christ Jesus hath relation and perfect reference."[51] This confession and defense of private immoderation, allegorized and thereby authorized as reflecting God's paternal love, is unusual in published works of the period. Few examples of paternal mourning appear in print in early modern England, and those that do tend to support the gendering of grief which casts the stoic acceptance of death as manly and excessive mourning as effeminate. Thomas Dekker, for example, balances his portrait of plague-ridden London's "wofully distracted mothers" with that of the mourning father who "behold[s] that darling of [his] eye ([his] sonne) turnd suddeinly into a lumpe of clay" and responds with effeminate immoderation: "Now doest thou rent thine hair, blaspheme thy Creator, cursest thy creation, and basely descendest into brutish & unmanly passions, threatning despite of death & his Plague, to maintain the memory of thy childe, in the everlasting brest of Marble."[52] Prevented from memorializing his son by the conditions of the plague, though, he must "with [his] owne hands . . . dig his grave."[53] Unlike the synecdochic maternal mourner, who reflects the city's grief in her own, Dekker's "most miserable father"[54] struggles and fails to assert the value and meaning of his personal loss to the commonwealth. The failure signals the collapse of social order and cultural continuity in the chaos of the plague.

A similar bifurcation of public and private responses to child-loss, advanced along gendered lines, appears in Ben Jonson's elegies for his daughter, Mary, and his son, Benjamin. In the former, Jonson deploys the gendering of grief to assert masculine moderation through the conventional imagery of life as a loan:

> Here lyes to each parents ruth,
> MARY, the daughter of their youth:
> Yet, all heavens gifts, being heavens due,
> It makes the father, less, to rue.[55]

The poem displaces Jonson's paternal mourning onto the sorrow of his wife, where the distinction between reasonable moderation and passionate excess is cast in gendered terms:[56] thus it makes the father less to rue *than* the mother. As Pigman argues, "Jonson makes himself more reasonable than his wife, since both mourn but only he is consoled."[57] In his elegy for Benjamin, Jonson's grief is less easily controlled and also less private, since it concerns a failure of succession (the disruption of Jonson's poetic legacy) marked in the social and cultural realms by the death of a son:

> Farewell, thou child of my right hand, and joy;
>> My sinne was too much hope of thee, lov'd boy.
> Seven yeeres tho' wert lent to me, and I thee pay,
>> Exacted by thy fate, on the just day.
> O, could I loose all father, now. For why
>> Will man lament the state he should envie?
> To have so soone scap'd worlds, and fleshes rage,
>> And, if no other miserie, yet age?
> Rest in soft peace, and, ask'd, say here doth ye
>> BEN. JONSON his best piece of *poetrie*.
> For whose sake, hence-forth, all his vowes be such.
> As what he loves may never like too much.[58]

From the social currency of patrilineal inheritance, maternal presence and lament are entirely excised: the child is the son of Jonson's right hand, the offspring of his pen alone. He is Jonson's "best piece of *poetrie*," the embodiment of his art.[59] While Jonson's equivocation, "O, could I loose all father, now" voices his twin desires to free himself from the grief accompanying child-loss and to loosen the constraints placed upon paternal sorrow,[60] the poem's stoic conclusion announces the sin for which Benjamin's death is the punishment (that is, "too much hope of thee") and its correction in the speaker's resolve – much in support of Stone's claims of parental indifference – to curtail emotional attachment in the future and thereby avoid the pain of separation. In mourning his daughter, then, Jonson invokes and contains maternal immoderation in support of consolatory measure. The death of his son, however, threatens his social and cultural legacies, and his mourning bears the mark of the masculine commonwealth in which the failed passage of (poetic) property from father to son is the subject of public lament. In the semi-private world of the household, maternal mourning, an excessive violation of paternal stoicism, lays claim to the lost daughter. In the world beyond, the lost son belongs solely to his father.

Perhaps the most coherent and programmatic work of paternal mourning in the period is Philippe de Mornay's *Teares for the Death of his Sonne*, translated into English by John Healey in 1609. Healey's dedicatory letter to John Coventry casts both translator and dedicatee as co-mourners with De Mornay and emphasizes the "pacient humility, and . . . humble patience" required to navigate the "darke sea of misfortunes" constituted by child-loss.⁶¹ The text displays, he concludes, "both the passions of a loving parent, and that restraint of them, that befitteth a religious Christian" (A3v). The description is accurate, since De Mornay's treatise, addressed throughout to his grieving wife, Charlotte d'Arbaleste, uses the voice of maternal mourning to embody excessive sorrow and to subdue it within stoic moderation. In doing so, it not only appropriates the power of maternal mourning that energizes so many male-authored works of the period, but also illustrates the passage from private tears to public restraint that marks the cultural performance of mourning as it moves from the household to the commonwealth.

Mourning the death of his adult son in October, 1605, De Mornay begins by stressing the mutuality of his own and his wife's "aboundant sorrow" (A4) and by confirming, like Playfere, that nature, reason and piety must all "weepe their partes" (A6). By associating his tears with his wife's, De Mornay participates in the excesses of mourning commonly figured as maternal in the early modern period: thus he complains that neither speech nor silence is adequate to express the depth of his sorrow (A7v), and voices his wish for death, since child-loss signals the loss of one-self (B3). Like the maternal mourners of *Richard III* or Boyd's "Queenes Lamentations," he casts excessive grief as an empathetic disfigurement: "Nay thou hast shot me thorow, & that through the sides of mine onely sonne: striking Father and child starke dead both at one stroke" (B5v). De Mornay's immoderate mourning is not undertaken innocently within his tears. On the contrary, these excesses are presented, we discover, to instruct De Mornay's wife and, incidentally, the reader in their appropriate restraint. Throughout the text, the speaker continually returns to the question of whether he ought to give voice to his sorrow: "What," he asks, "shall I speake out my woes, or shall I entombe them in silence?" (A6). Repeatedly, he displays his awareness that his unmeasured grief constitutes a rebellion against God and, like Jonson's paternal mourner, worries about the "looseness" of his lament: "Oh my LORD! I feele a rebellious battell within me! keepe downe my tongue, let it loose to no language, but those sounds of the Psalmist . . . that my redoubling dolour burst not out into outragious murmure" (A8–A8v). De Mornay self-consciously stages his dangerous swerves into blasphemous immoderation and, at moments of most "outragious murmure," his prayers for forgiveness and self-restraint, invoking the gendering of grief to censure his rebellious speech as a token of effeminacy: "Therefore thou talkest like a foolish Woman: go and learne better language of the wise" (B8).

This wavering between the venting of excessive sorrow and its attempted restraint continues until the speaker is able definitively to bridle his blasphemous speech: "I will now take the bitte out of my mouth my selfe, and plead the case of the all-sufficient Creator, even against mine owne soule" (C3). At this moment the speaker, no longer a feminized co-mourner but a stoic male governor, turns once again to his wife to encourage her to "Wipe away those tears once more that gush out in such aboundance (seeming as if hee wer [*sic*] not dead already, to drowne him in his grave)" (C7v). He explains that unruly sorrow is built upon "unreasonable passion" (C6), and points out that "rebellious affects . . . flye beyond the pitche of our obedience to our maker" (D2v–D3). Finally, the speaker transforms his mouth into a "trumpet" (D4) to announce his recognition and acceptance of God's providential plan. The treatise ends by offering the text as a school of sorrow, teaching De Mornay's wife and the reader how to weep lawful tears of penance, obedience, and acceptance: "In these teares (beloved wife) and in this manner of sorrow, it is no sinne to take our orders and proceed graduates: Wee may weepe lawfully thus, as long as the streames that raine from our eyes, do not make the river of our griefes over flowe their bankes" (E2v).

De Mornay's treatise tames maternal excess with paternal moderation, gaining affective and rhetorical power by exploiting maternal lament to stage a definitive turn toward masculine measure in the voice of the father which substitutes for, and articulates the will of, God the Father. De Mornay's self-conscious concern with the problematics of speech are figured in his opening image, which compares "aboundant sorrow" to a "deepe wound" and seeks a mean between extremes in its treatment: "stoppe it too soone," he claims, "it spoiles us: stay it too long, it kills us" (A4). At the treatise's close, the image returns, when De Mornay quotes Psalm 147 to affirm that God "*makest the wounde, and . . . bindest it up . . .* [H]e anointeth all their sores with his precious Balsam" (D8v). Like Anne Neville's description of Henry VI's wounds as "congeal'd mouths" which recount the history of his demise, De Mornay's imagery of the wound of child-loss conflates grief and its articulation, opposing the potentially toxic language of excessive mourning to the restorative embalming of submissive tears. Certainly the orthodox language of paternal measure is the balm offered by De Mornay's text to cure the wound of child-loss, but it is a cure enacted through the exercise and exorcism of maternal excess.

Charlotte d'Arbaleste de Mornay is given no voice in her husband's text, where her silence may as easily denote her submission to his lessons as her refusal of them. An assiduous chronicler of her husband's career, however, she comments elsewhere on her son's death in terms that imply her difficulty in accepting the treatise's consolatory message:

Happy end for him [our son] . . . But for us the beginning of a sorrow which can only end in death, with no other consolation but what the feare and the grace of God can give us while we chew the bitter cud of our grief . . .

And here it is fitting that my book should end. It was written for him, to describe the pilgrimage of our lives, and now God has willed that his life should end so soon and so sweetly. And truly did I not feare M. du Plessis' grief, whose love for me grows as my sorrow grows, I would fain not survive him.[62]

When her son's death signals the end of her career as biographer, Madam de Mornay leaves the stage by hinting at an unutterable maternal grief that can resolve itself only in the silence of death. Later biographers confirm her struggle to recover from this devastating loss: "Mde du Plessis depuis la nouvelle de la mort de son fils estoient en continuelle amertume," they write (from the time she received news of her son's death, Madam du Plessis was in continual grief). Although she hid her sorrow from her husband, "cependent entre ses femmes elle ne parloit plus que la mort, se la rendoit familier de jour à autre" (nonetheless among her ladies she spoke of nothing but death, making herself familiar with it daily). Only three weeks after her son's funeral, "la douleur se rengrageant, se met au lict" (the pain took hold of her again, forcing her to take to her bed). She died shortly thereafter, as a lengthy report of her good death describes. Her biographers conclude, "La cause de sa mort au Rapport des Medecins qui en firent l'ouverture fut; Que l'humeur melancholique se respandant dans les Intestins y avoit fair erosion, mesme au Colon, cause des insupportables tranchées qui la tourmentoient" (The cause of her death according to the doctors who opened her was that the melancholic humor spreading in the intestines eroded the colon, causing the insupportable colic that tormented her).[63] Madam de Mornay, in effect, dies of grief.[64]

In the elegies of mourning mothers, to which we now turn, Philippe de Mornay's consolatory conflation of the wound and the mouth bespeaks an injury as difficult to cure as the fatal melancholy of his wife. In these poems, "the complex of melancholia behaves like an open wound,"[65] and the transgressive language of maternal mourning – more a "rebellious affect" than a "precious Balsam" – seeks words to articulate its unspeakable loss.

III

In 1584, John Soowthern included in his collection of poems, *Pandora*, a series of sonnets written by Anne de Vere, Countess of Oxford, on the death of her infant son the year before.[66] Her clear disappointment at the child's death, the dynastic aspects of which are subsumed within a more personal maternal lament, resonates throughout the four complete sonnets and two fragments printed by Soowthern. In brutal, complex imagery completely devoid of allusions to Christian consolation, the poems reveal their author's engagement in, as Ellen Moody writes, "an impious, rebellious violence against her fate and that of her child." Their subject matter, quite simply, is "a mother's depression when her newborn baby dies."[67]

The depth of this despair can be gauged by the poems' images of self-consuming grief and melancholic gestures toward self-cancellation, dissolution, and death. In expressing their speaker's desire to join the lost child in death, De Vere's sonnets are characteristic of female-authored elegies, which tend to concentrate on the physical fact of death and on the corruption, rather than the resurrection, of the beloved body.[68] De Vere, for example, complains in her third sonnet:

> The heavens, death, and life: have conjured my yll:
> For death hath take away the breath of my sonne:
> The hevens receve, and consent, that he hath donne:
> And my life dooth keep mee heere against my will.
>
> (C4v; 1–4)

Again in the fragmentary sixth poem, she laments, "My sonne is gone: and with it, death end my sorrow," and displays her empathetic self-negation in mourning for the lost child as Death informs the speaker, "that [body] of yours, is no more now, but a shadow" (C4v; 4). Rather than devoting themselves to consolatory thoughts of the child's resurrection, De Vere's poems are filled with images of burial and entombment: "the Marble, of my Childe" (C3v; sonnet 1, 8) and the inarticulate "stone . . . that doth it inclose" (C3v; sonnet 2, 8) merge with the sequence's final image of the maternal body as tomb in De Vere's identification with Niobe:[69]

> Amphion's wife was turned to a rocke. O
> How well I had been, had I had such adventure,
> For then I might againe have been the Sepulcure,
> Of him that I bare in mee, so long ago.
>
> (C4v; sonnet 6, 1–4)

This emphasis on the physical body of mourning and on the material connection between the living–dead body of the maternal mourner and the corpse of her offspring poses an overt challenge to the consolatory poetics of transcendence. In the fourth poem, for instance, De Vere stages a parodic resurrection enacted by the mourning mother, in which the physical reincorporation of the lost child within maternal mourning's regenerative body revises the patriarchal idea of spiritual rebirth in the afterlife:

> But if our life be caus'de with moisture and heate,
>> I care neither for the death, the life, nor skyes:
>> For I'll sigh him warmth, and weat him with my eies:
>> (And thus I shall be thought a second Promet).
>>> (c4, 5–8)

De Vere engages the period's humoral theory of reproduction, which understands the female body as primarily moist and cold and the male as warm and dry,[70] to locate reproductive power exclusively in the female body of maternal mourning. Like a second, female, Prometheus, she will resurrect the dead child through the recreative sighs and tears of maternal lament.[71] De Vere's self-casting as Prometheus recreates the child within the offspring poems themselves, enacting not so much his immortality within the text as his perpetual entombment. Permanently encrypted in the poems – which are simultaneously the womb and the tomb constructed of the living–dead maternal body – the infant resides forever as an indelible marker of irreparable loss.

Elsewhere in the sequence, De Vere reflects the material practices of the early modern female culture of mourning. In both the first and fourth sonnets, for instance, she energizes the tradition of women's communal mourning by calling upon Venus as co-mourner for her lost son. In the first poem, the tears of Venus merge with those of the speaker, offering an affective, monumental portrait of the maternal mourner petrified in grief:

> Whose brest Venus, with a face dolefull and milde,
>> Doth washe with golden teares, inveying the skies:
>> And when the water of the Goddesses eyes,
>> Makes almost alive, the Marble, of my Childe,
>>> One byds her leave styll, her dollor so extreme,
>>> Telling her it is not, her young sonne Papheme,
>> To which she make aunswer with a voice inflamed,
>> (Feeling therewith her venime, to be more bitter)
>> As I was of Cupid, even so of it mother:
>> And a womans last chylde, is the most beloved.
>>> (c3v; 5–14)

By granting to Venus the tokens of immoderate mourning ("dollor so extreme," "a voice inflamed," "venime"), De Vere also claims these extremes for herself. Her revision of the three Maries' communal mourning, in which the Virgin gives way to the grief-stricken Venus, remarkably imports into the sequence the affective power of the Christian tradition but without its consolatory implications. This classicized Virgin is free to indulge in passionate excess. Thus she reappears in the fourth sonnet as well, where the Virgin's empathetic passion – the traditional subject matter of the *planctus Mariae* – is rewritten to reflect the speaker's desire for death:

> At the brute of it, the Aphroditan Queene,
> Caused more silver to distyll fro her eyes:
> Then when the droppes of her cheekes raysed Daisyes:
> And to die with him, mortall, she would have beene.
>
> (c4; 5–8)

De Vere's imagery of consumption and self-consumption shares De Mornay's merger of the wound of child-loss and its articulation, but, in doing so, clears a discursive space for a transgressive language of maternal mourning. The first sonnet complains of her son's arbitrary and meaningless death, employing, as Kim Walker notes, negative syntax and rough metrics to underscore the jarring, rebellious tone of the lament:[72]

> Had with moorning the Gods, left their willes undon,
> They had not so soone herited such a soule:
> Or if the mouth, tyme dyd not glooton up all.
> Nor I, nor the world, were depriv'd of my Sonne.
>
> (c3v; 1–4)

The image of Time as a gluttonous mouth suggests the emptying of meaning that Freud describes as the experience of the melancholic: "In mourning it is the world which has become poor and empty; in melancholia it is the ego itself."[73] The wound of child-loss – that is, the empty womb – is figured as the empty mouth, and De Vere's maternal laments are the effusions of that difficult rupture, attempting to fill the void left by the child's death with language that reincorporates the lost object into the maternal body itself.[74] The maternal mourner's fantasy of incorporation not only provokes De Vere's imagery of feeding but also prompts her own transgressive language of maternal grief. Like the mournful cannibalism of Nashe's Miriam, De Vere's maternal mourning seeks to articulate unspeakable loss by reincorporating the lost body into and as the empty mouth and empty womb. Thus to parallel the figure of Time as an empty mouth, De Vere's second sonnet turns to the image of the eaten heart to represent her own perpetual self-consumption: "In dolefull wayes I spend the wealth of my time: / Feeding on my heart, that ever comes agen" (c3v, 1–2). The merger of the bodies of mother and child constructs empathetic mourning as a self-consumption that simultaneously devours the lost child and gives voice to this unprofitable feeding. In its insistence upon the literal, material conditions of childbirth and child-loss as authorizing these feeding and self-feeding metaphors, De Vere's maternal mourning values excess as a symptom of the unfilled and irreparable void left by the empty womb.

As a symptom of her own wounded womb, Mary Carey's poem, "Upon the Sight of my abortive Birth the 31th: of December 1657," illustrates not only the poet's difficult acceptance of masculine calls to moderate sorrow but also, as Jonathan Sawday points out, the degree to which the view of flawed femininity grounded on scriptural texts "acted as a means of fashioning an internalized system of suppression and domination."[75] Certainly Carey's poem, unlike the sonnets of Anne de Vere, is thoroughly rooted in scriptural authority, as her copious marginal citations of Old and New Testament loci (thirty in a poem of ninety-two lines) reveal. Much of the poem recites not only conventional metaphors for female fertility but also commonplaces of Christian consolation. Thus we hear that despite the deaths of five children prior to this miscarriage, God still loans two surviving offspring to Carey: "My living pretty payre; Nat: & Bethia; / the Childrene deare, (God yett lends to Maria)."[76] She prays, "Lett not my hart, (as doth my wombe) miscarrie" (74), echoing the language with which Ralph Josselin records his wife's near-miscarriage a year before Carey's: "This morning my wife thought shee miscarried, lord a miscarrying womb is a sad affliction, keepe us from a miscarrying heart."[77] While Carey's unpublished poem and Josselin's diary share the allegory of miscarriage as symptomatic of spiritual health, only Carey, as a female, can fully experience the sad affliction of the miscarrying womb. As such, her deployment of the scriptural metaphors of reproduction, or more correctly, her representation of birth as a matter of the soul rather than the body, cannot forget the physical womb and bears the imprint of the material female body throughout. For a female speaker, whether literally or only figuratively connected to a female body, the issue of the womb is not *only* metaphoric. Rather, the female voice insists upon the material facts of the body and its issue, particularly as it mourns the loss of that issue. This naturalization of maternity as a matter of the womb, then, enables Carey's poem to negotiate doctrinal calls to moderate sorrow in order to transvalue the faulty womb and its all-too-perishable fruit. Carey's struggle to assert the experience of the female body as a grounds on which to validate maternal mourning constitutes female subjectivity in the poem.

This insistence on the material facts of birth and child-loss begins in the poem's title, where the *sight* of the abortive birth and its date both serve to underscore the materiality of the miscarriage as a real event – a death – to which the speaker reacts and which she seeks to commemorate.[78] The physical presence of the corpse in women's laments reflects the feminine culture of early modern mourning, which placed women in a unique intimacy with bodies in death: thus Gertrude Thimelby's elegy for her father, "Upon a Command to Write on my Father," positions the speaker before the body itself en route to burial: "Teares I could soone have brought unto this hearse, / And thoughts, and sighs, but you command a verse."[79] Grace, Lady Mildmay's "Meditation upon her [that is, her husband's] Corpse," similarly, takes place in the presence of the departed: "Let me behold my corpse which lieth folden in cerecloths, leaded and coffined here before me yet unburied, and consider: he was a man, and as he is, I shall be."[80] Carey's gesture toward presence continues in the poem's opening lines, where the speaker imagines herself to be with the fetus, looking upon its material reality as she begins the meditative process of allegorizing and spiritualizing the loss: "What birth is this; a poore despissed creature? / A little Embrio; voyd of life, and feature" (1–2). Carey's description of the fetus as a "poore despissed creature" implicitly questions the benevolence of a God who would despise, or render despicable, his own (innocent) creation and reflects her struggle with the idea of original sin as an orthodox explanation of the death of newborns. Thomas Tuke's *A Discourse of Death* (1613), for instance, reveals the resistance of some parishioners to this doctrine as he reiterates the rationale that "death is not the condition of Nature, but the Daughter and desert of sinne." He explains, "But you will say, How is it that Infants of a day olde doe dye, seeing that they commit no sinne? I answere, Sinne is either the corruption of nature, or any evill which proceedes as the fruits thereof; or thus, sinne is either originall, or actuall: the former is in Infants, though not the latter."[81] Katherine Stubbes shares the resistance of Tuke's congregation when she claims, as her husband relates, that "neither is the grace of God tied to the materiall Elements, that he cannot save without them. And therefore are the Papists more than cruell, that teach all children to bee damned that die before baptisme" (CI). While it is tempting to see in this position a feminist transgression of orthodoxy,

Stubbes is, in fact, wholly aligned with the Anglican belief (espoused, for instance, by Richard Hooker) that "grace is not absolutely tied unto the [sacrament] of baptism."[82] Will Coster has shown that changes in the meaning of the term "chrisom child" in sixteenth-century England reflect both the uncertain spiritual status of infants before baptism and the growing desire to assume their innocence. When Carey asserts her faith in the predestination of her unborn child that translates this "poore despissed creature" to a soule in bliss – "And that this babe (as well as all the rest,) / since 't had a soule, shalbe for ever blest" (18–19) – she similarly exploits this slippage in the doctrine of original sin to accommodate a maternal desire for her child's salvation as a remedy for her grief.

If Carey's expressions of moderate mourning emerge from her resistance to it, that resistance reasserts itself throughout the poem in her relentless imagery of female reproduction, already tainted by the indelible imprint of the poem's opening sight. When she searches for "the reason why [God] tooke in hand his rodd" (35), God himself enters the poem as Carey's co-mourner, locating the cause of his grief in the mother rather than her lost child:

> Methinkes I heare Gods voyce, this is thy sinne;
>   And Conscience justifies ye same within:
>
> Thou often dost present me with dead frute;
>   Why should not my returns, thy presents sute:
>
> Dead dutys; prayers; praises thou doest bring,
>   affections dead; dead hart in every thinge:
>   . . .
> Whose taught or better'd by ye no Relation;
>   thou'rt Cause of Mourning, not of Imitation:
>   (38–43, 46–7)

Carey's God attributes to the female mourner the "dead frute" literalized in the aborted embryo, thereby indicating the retributive nature of her affliction ("Why should not my returns, thy presents sute") and the spiritual lesson to be taken from this graphic embodiment of her sin: "Mend now, my Child," God advises her, "& lively frute bring me" (50). The exchange is characteristic of Carey's meditative stance in other maternal elegies, where her deal-making and claims of "equivalent parenthood" with God display, as Helen Wilcox puts it, "the ability to hold her own with God" as Carey's "outstanding quality."[83] In her elegy, "On the death of my 4th & only Child, Robert Payler," for instance, she proposes to trade her son for God's with the audacious statement, "Change with me; doe, as I have done / give me thy all; Even thy deare sonne."[84] Revising De Mornay's consolatory reminder that, "[God] hath spared our sonne, that spared not his owne onely begotten for us" (A5), Carey reverses the relationship between believer and God by insisting that the model of maternal sacrifice – *her* willingness to surrender all in sacrificing her child – should prompt God to offer his son in recompense for her loss. Her blending of the languages of physical reproduction and spiritual salvation, based on her willing surrender of the child – "a lovely bonne" – continues as the poem closes with a prayer for the speaker's "quikning":

> In my whole Life; lively doe thou make me:
>> for thy praise. And name's sake, O quicken mee:
>
> Lord I begg quickning grace; that grace aford;
>> quicken me lord according to they word.
>
> It is a lovely bonne I make to thee.
>> after thy loving Kindnesse quicken mee:
>
> Thy quickning Spirit unto me convey;
>> And thereby Quicken me; in thine owne way:
>
> And lett the Presence of thy spirit deare,
>> be witnessd by his fruts; lett them appeare.
>
> (76–85)

As a prayer for both spiritual quickening and pregnancy which will result in the delivery of "lively frute," the poem concludes on the material grounds on which it began, rooting its reciprocal vision of what is due to the obedient speaker firmly in the body of maternal mourning.

Both De Vere's and Carey's maternal elegies stand in difficult relationships to publication. The means by which De Vere's sonnets found their way into print remain unclear, as do her intentions regarding publication,[85] while Carey's elegies appear within her *Meditation*, written at the age of forty-five, probably with the private readership of her family and descendants in mind and not published until the twentieth century. The relative privacy of these works attests to the degree to which the gendering of grief and women's struggles to articulate the experience of child-loss in their own terms construct feminine subjectivity, even before an audience of one. The dynamics of resistance apparent in these private

works, however, are also employed in works of maternal mourning clearly
intended for public readership in the poems of Katherine Philips. The
public performance of maternal mourning in Philips's poems, as Kate
Lilley suggests, illustrates the degree to which "elegy provided a frame-
work for figuring the unstable relations and shifting boundaries of inside
and outside, self and other, family and nation, the private body and the
body politic."[86]

Katherine Philips's two poems on the death of her son, Hector, in 1655
question the boundaries between the public and private performances
of grief, the first in its form and the second in its theme. Her "Epitaph.
On her Son H.P. at St. Syth's Church where her body also lies Interred"
adorns a monument set within the public space of the church where the
deceased infant and his mother are interred in close proximity to each
other. Philips ironically employs the imagery of the small room in which
the child is confined to refer not to the grave but to the body:

> Too promising, too great a Mind
> In so small room to be confin'd:
> Therefore, fit in Heav'n to dwell,
> He quickly broke the Prison shell.[87]

The small room, of course, is also the brief stanza of the poem, which
seeks both to memorialize the child and to mourn him, to invoke the
literal presence of his corpse and to bemoan his absence. The poem's
concluding image suggests the overpowering of consolatory poetics by
the unsatisfied pathos of maternal grief in the burial of the "Sun"
(at once Philips's infant son and the Son of God) in the cloud of
mourning:

> And so the Sun, if it arise
> Half so glorious as his eyes,
> Like this Infant, takes a shroud,
> Buried in a morning cloud.[88]

As the epitaph straddles the line between private lament and public
memorial, Philips's "Orinda upon little Hector Philips," like Jonson's
elegy for his son, takes the occasion of child-loss to consider the poetics of
mourning as manifested in the elegy itself. Like Carey, Philips surveys
her maternal history in the poem's opening stanza ("Twice Forty months
of wedlock I did stay, / Then had my vows crown'd with a lovely boy")
before invoking the physical presence of the child and the material fact
of his loss: "I did but see him, and he disappear'd, / I did but pluck the

rosebud, and it fell."[89] The lines following both articulate the maternal mourner's inconsolable grief – "So piercing groans must by thy Elogy," Philips writes – [90] and paradoxically assert the privacy of her laments in public verse:

> Thus whilst no eye is witness of my moan,
> I grieve thy loss (Ah, Boy too dear to live!)
> And let the unconcerned World alone,
> Who neither will nor can refreshment give.
>
> An off'ring to for thy sad tomb I have,
> Too just a tribute to thy early hearse,
> Receive these gasping numbers to thy grave,
> The last of thy unhappy mothers verse.[91]

Like De Vere's melancholic mourning, Philips dismisses the "unconcerned World," suggesting its hollowness in her child's absence and its apathy to maternal loss, and envisions her own dissolution – here the dissolved poetic voice – in empathetic sorrow for her lost son. She refuses consolatory notions of the child's resurrection and dedicates the poem to expressing her self-consuming grief. The merger of the lost child, the poetic offspring, and the maternal mourner's voice emphasizes the flexible borders between self and other imagined as uniquely available in the experiences of pregnancy, childbirth, and child-loss. As such, Philips establishes a public space within which maternal mourning gives voice to its unique, private sorrow.

Philips's elegy for her step-daughter, Frances, whom she raised from the age of one, extends maternal grief beyond the body and revises its physiological bases to mourn the loss of the mother–daughter relationship established "through dearest ties and highest trust / Continued from thy cradle to thy dust."[92] The poem, "In Memory of F. P. who died at Acton on the 24 of May, 1660, at Twelve and an Half of Age," again, insists upon the physical loss of the child by memorializing the date of her death and presenting the poem as an adornment for the pall: "If I could ever write a lasting verse, / It should be laid, dear Saint, upon thy hearse."[93] Philips equates the body of the poem with the mourning maternal body, figured here not as an empty womb but as an overflowing mouth:

> But Sorrow is not Muse, and does confess,
> That it least can, what it would most express.
> Yet that I may some bounds to Grief allow,
> I'll try if I can weep in numbers now.[94]

In an elegy based not upon the natural bonds of childbirth but on affection established through the legal bonds of marriage, Philips understands the verse form itself as a metaphor for and means of obtaining the emotional restraint – the "bounds of Grief" – required to eulogize her step-daughter. As such, the poem's imagery is shot through with references to social and economic, rather than biological, versions of loss: the mourner, for example, is compared to a "bankrupt sitting on the brim, / Of those fierce billows which had ruin'd him," and later to "the poor swain [who] beholds his ripen'd corn / By some rough wind without a sickle torn."[95] Philips's rehearsal of the commonplace, "Alas! we were secure of our content; / But find too late that it was only lent,"[96] takes on special meaning when incorporated into the poem's affective economy of maternal loss, represented as a matter not of the body but of the law.

Like the maternal laments based on the body, though, "In Memory of F. P." exploits the gendering of grief to give voice to the excessive mourning proper to mothers, natural or otherwise. Thus the poem turns from its transcendental imagery of Frances' soul in bliss, which occupies its central portion, to consider the mourning mother's disconsolate state:

> But if to thy blest soul my grief appears,
> Forgive and pity these injurious tears:
> Inpute them to Affection's sad excess,
> Which will not yield to Nature's tenderness.[97]

Despite this admission that her sad excess is both physically damaging and unnatural, the speaker stops short of acknowledging any spiritual error or disobedience in immoderate mourning. Rather, she ends the poem by reasserting the depth of her maternal bond, and thus of her sorrow, and by refusing the consolation promised by her awareness of Frances' salvation in favor of endless mourning for her irreparable loss:

> But I'll resign, to follow thee as fast
> As my unhappy minutes will make me haste.
> Till when the fresh remembrances of thee
> Shall be my Emblems of Mortality.
> For such as loss as this (bright Soul!) is not
> Ever to be repaired, or forgot.[98]

As a public articulation of Philips's maternal loss, "In Memory of F. P." at once acknowledges the constructed bonds between the speaker and her step-daughter and implies the constructed nature of all gendered bonds, including the natural (that is, biological) ties between mothers and their children. Like Philippe de Mornay, Philips conflates the wound of child-loss and its articulation since her ability to weep in numbers accommodates and constrains the affective excess which she, as a mother by law if not by nature, nonetheless feels. The poem stages the impossibility of restraining maternal mourning's excesses within the culturally constructed body of grief, symbolized by the rigid form of the poem itself. As a result, Philips interrogates the period's naturalized understanding of motherhood even as she exploits it to authorize her resistant expressions of loss and to establish herself as a subject defined not by accepting the limited cultural roles assigned to her but by manipulating and resisting those bonds.

IV

In preface to Elizabeth Jocelin's *The Mothers Legacie to her Unborne Childe* (1624), Thomas Goad – who brought the treatise to press after the death of its author in childbirth two years earlier – inserts an "Approbation" which commends the book to the reader on the basis of its author's "piety and humility."[99] As simultaneously a confirmation or sanction, and a trial, the approbation elaborates the metaphor of the text as the author's will, describing Jocelin, first and foremost, as a subject before the law: "Our lawes disable those that are under *Covert-baron*, from disposing by Will and Testament any temporall estate. But no law prohibiteth any professor of morall and spiritual riches, to impart them unto others, either in life or in death by bequeathing."[100] While Jocelin, like any *femme covert* in the period, is prohibited from owning or disposing of property without her husband's consent, Goad puts forth a second, more compelling law to justify printing Jocelin's legacy. Under this moral law, Jocelin's sex (while, admittedly a "debility") actually recommends this exceptional work, since it is, Goad assures us, "the rather worthy, because proceeding from the weaker sex."[101] As such, he explains, "I willingly not only subscribed my *Approbat* for the registering of this *Will*, among the most publike Monuments . . . but also, as bound to doe right unto knowne vertue, undertooke the care of the publication thereof my selfe."[102] While Goad's intervention renders Jocelin's text a "most publike Monument," her own dedicatory epistle to her husband predicates the work on its self-avowed and intended privacy. In fear of "the danger that might prevent me from executing that care I so exceedingly desired, I mean in the religious training of our child," Jocelin explains:

I thought of writing, but then mine owne weaknesse appeared so manifestly, that I was ashamed, and durst not undertake it. But when I could finde no other meanes to expresse my Motherly zeale, I encouraged my selfe with these reasons.

First, that I wrote to a Childe, and though I were but a Woman, yet to a Childs judgment, what I understand, might serve for a foundation to a better learning.

Againe, I considered it was to my owne, and not to the world, and my love to my owne might excuse my errors.[103]

"I send it," she concludes, "only to the eyes of a most loving husband, and a child exceedingly beloved, to whom I hope it will not be altogether unprofitable."[104]

For Jocelin, privacy guarantees her self-representation as a dutiful mother and obedient wife. It is only after her death that the private document can become a public monument, a translation enabled by the maternal corpse itself. The enormous popularity of Jocelin's text (which went through eleven editions by 1674) and of the other mothers' legacies published between 1604 and 1624 by Dorothy Leigh, Elizabeth Lincoln, Elizabeth Grymeston, and M. R. and repeatedly reissued thereafter,[105] suggest that the genre interjects into the public forum of the printed text the privately entombed body of maternal mourning, a commonly recognized source of affective power. The dissolution and self-consumption figured by maternal mourners as their appropriate, if unorthodox, responses to child-loss are literalized as the conditions under which the mother's legacy appears in print. The public monuments of these texts, in effect, memorialize the private work of mourning performed in the household by mothers – in Jocelin's case by a woman whose pregnancy had been "as then traveling with death itself."[106] Like a Rachel who mourns her child's death even in the afterlife, Jocelin's work – written during her pregnancy, her child literally incorporated within her flesh – interrogates and troubles the boundaries between self and other, public and private, in terms that echo maternal elegies' preoccupations with the body of death. Goad's report that Jocelin, in a prophetic moment early in her pregnancy, "secretly tooke order for the buying of a new winding sheet" and, following the birth of her daughter, "instantly called for her winding-sheet to bee brought forth and laid upon her"[107] illustrates the translation from private fear to public performance implicit in the narrative of maternal death in childbearing. The winding sheet, secretly procured, becomes the main prop with which Jocelin stages her memorable good death. Significantly, Goad locates the unfolding of this

drama in a strangely crowded privacy where Jocelin communes with
God, with the inscrutable "bowels" of the maternal mourner herself,
and ultimately (in Goad's quotation of the text's opening sentence), with
the reader:

And about that time undauntedly looking death in the face, privately in her
Closet between God and her, she wrote these pious Meditations: whereof her
selfe strangely speaketh to her own bowels in this manner, *It may seeme strange to
thee to receive these lines from a Mother, that dyed when thou wert borne.*[108]

Jocelin's Closet – at once public and private, self-enclosed and reproductive, singular and plural, living and dead – is an apt figure for the
period's complex representations of the body of maternal mourning.[109]

Celeste Schenck has argued that the "coherence of a female funeral
aesthetic across centuries suggests that women poets have clearly en-
joyed an elegiac mode of their own, an intertextually verifiable tradition
of mourning their dead in a poetic form that calls the genre, as pa-
triarchally codified, into question."[110] While grieving mothers clearly
employ similar strategies for establishing the female subject as a function
of maternity and its proper grief, the transgressive discourse of maternal mourning is not purely or simply a matter of the body. The early
modern gendering of grief permits women as well as men, as we have
seen, to posit an affective bond between mother and child which, in
turn, contributes to constructing femininity by means of gestures that
describe and attend maternal mourning. Rather than insisting upon an
essentialist inscription of gender within the works of maternal mourners,
which would assign authorship (and authorial motives) to women who
are, or have been, mothers, this chapter has attempted to flesh out the
characteristics ascribed to maternal grief by early modern English men
and women and to trace the means by which these characteristics are
naturalized and made available for performance, adoption, and manipulation by men and women with a variety of motives, in a variety of
works.

The case of maternal mourning vividly illustrates the essentialist interpretation of women's grief more generally in the early modern period,
which sees feminine excess as naturally attending the weak, immoderate bodies of women themselves. In the hands of early modern women,
though, this naturalized grief was used to license women's emotions and
their public or textual expressions. The performance of mothers' extreme
sorrow at the loss of loved ones comprises and describes the woman's
voice in early modern maternal lament. Supported by an essentialist

reading of women's mourning as a matter of the body, it nonetheless remains a resistant, self-conscious, constructed voice that interrogates the gendering of grief from which it evolves by exposing the cultural needs and desires that cast feminine immoderation as the exiled but necessary means of defining the social body of mourning and its stable, unarguable sex. Represented as a matter of the body, maternal mourning is an index of the gendering of grief in the early modern period and an example of one of the strategies available to women to express a female subjectivity which might otherwise have remained forever entombed in silence.

6

"Quod licuit feci": Elizabeth Russell
and the power of public mourning

The visitor to Britannia.com's website for Bisham Abbey, a former monastic property given by Henry VIII to Sir Philip Hoby in 1538, finds under the distressing title, "Beaten 'til the Blood Ran," the unlikely story of "the most haunted house in Berkshire." The site rehearses the legend that the ghost of Elizabeth Russell,[1] the property's owner from 1566 until her death in 1609, haunts the abbey to atone for the death of her son, William Hoby. "She was very proud and ambitious," the story goes, "some might say even cold and hard":

Being one of the most learned ladies of the age, Lady Hoby was eager to ensure that her children received the same rigorous education that both she and her husband had had. She therefore oversaw all her children's tuition herself, going so far as to actually teach them certain subjects, such as Greek and Latin. Dame Hoby expected perfection from her pupils, and wielded a heavy ruler to make sure she got it.

Unfortunately "poor little William" was a less-than-apt pupil and his incompetence infuriated his mother. "One gossip even related, over a pint of beer, how he . . . clearly saw her Ladyship beating little William about the head with her ruler until he collapsed and fell to the ground. Blood streamed from his eyes, nose and mouth and saturated the grass." Following another episode in which William accidentally blots his copy-books, we're told, Russell ties him to a chair, ordering him to rewrite the lesson or bear the brunt of her anger. Soon after, Russell departs for Windsor at the invitation of Queen Elizabeth. On her return several days later, she realizes with horror that William has been left locked in the Tower Room, where, of course, he has expired. Shortly after her death, the account concludes, her repentant ghost is first seen wandering the abbey. "A miraculous fountain floats before her and, not unlike the evil Lady Macbeth, she tries constantly to wash the accusing blood stains from her hands." Although history provides no evidence of the birth or death of a William Hoby (while the births and deaths of Russell's seven children are well documented), "'proof' of William's existence is provided," the website assures us, by the discovery of blotted copybooks under the abbey's floorboards during alterations in 1840. Immediately after the discovery, however, the copybooks disappeared.[2]

Clearly a story as fantastic as this scarcely requires rebuttal. Its value (if any) lies in the light it sheds upon the tenacity of the early modern prejudice against the educated woman. The ghost story, after all, responds to – and distorts – the facts of Elizabeth Russell's life. Fourth-born of the five daughters of Sir Anthony Cooke and Anne Fitzwilliam, Russell's erudition and that of her sisters was widely noted by their contemporaries.[3] Her reputation as the author of epitaphs in three languages was spread in her lifetime by William Camden's publication of her verses on the Russell family tombs in Westminster Abbey in 1600[4] and augmented several generations later by Edward Phillips's praise of her work in his *Theatrum Poetarum* (1675).[5] In her first widowhood, following Thomas Hoby's death in 1566, and her second, after John Russell's demise in 1584, Russell was an active guardian to her children, protecting their rights and property in their minority, arranging appropriate career opportunities for her sons, and negotiating advantageous marriages for both sons and daughters.[6] She retained guardianship of the Hoby children (and, therefore, control of their inheritances) even after her second marriage, despite Lord Russell's protests.[7] She successfully managed the career and marriage (to Margaret Dakins Sidney, in 1596) of her youngest Hoby son, Thomas Posthumus; she fought relentlessly – but unsuccessfully in the end – to secure the inheritance of the Russell girls, Anne and Elizabeth, following their father's early death; and she arranged Anne Russell's marriage to Henry Somerset, Lord Herbert, in 1600, staging an opulent ceremony attended by Queen Elizabeth herself.[8] As indefatigable as she was in working to better her children's situations in their lifetimes, she was equally dedicated to promulgating the memories of the Hoby and Russell dead, herself included, for posterity. Russell is the designer of an unprecedented series of funerary monuments and the author of the epitaphs that adorn them, built to honor both of her husbands, four children who predeceased her, and, finally, herself and the legacy embodied in her three surviving children.[9] Her careful creation of the tombs not only attests to Russell's pride in her accomplishments as a wife, mother, and scholar but also constructs a public space within which her grief could be articulated. "The tombs," as Louise Schleiner puts it, "became her metier."[10]

Obviously the Bisham Abbey ghost story improvises on the details of Russell's life and character – perhaps unknowingly, given the distortions of oral history from which the tale certainly evolves (and which it inscribes in its mythical gossip and his requisite pint of beer).[11] Thus the autonomy of her widowhood is rewritten as maternal tyranny unrestrained by the absent paternal hand, her impressive education is recast as unintelligible vanity, her ambitions for her children become pride and perfectionism, and her robust interest in things funereal makes her a likely candidate for spectral revisitations. It is both ironic and poignant that a woman so dedicated to controlling her afterlife should fall victim to a legend constructed point by point on the demonized corpse of the early modern period's noteworthy exception to gender restrictions, the "learned lady."

This chapter reads more accurately the legacy that Elizabeth Russell crafted with such care through her manipulations of women's access to public rites of mourning in post-Reformation England – from her construction of funerary monuments, to her composition of epitaphs that adorn them, to her orchestrations of heraldic funerals for family members and for herself. Russell self-consciously treats public mourning rituals as cultural forms with the power to assert her household's honor to a contemporary audience and to convey her memory and that of her dead to future generations. Through mourning and its ceremonies, she created her self-image in her lifetime and attempted to control her reputation in the afterlife. In the monuments, she performs women's various domestic roles in the period – wife, mother, sister, and daughter – and translates them into the extra-domestic space established by culturally sanctioned rites of public mourning. As Helen C. Gladstone notes, Russell's monument to her own memory in the Parish Church of All Saints in Bisham (figure 10), "represents her and her seven children without either husband in effigy," and thereby "claims the family as her creation and celebrates the family as her achievement."[12] If funerary monuments enact, in Nigel Llewellyn's words, "a ritual of continuity,"[13] replacing the corruptible flesh with immortal stone, the Hoby and Russell tombs announce that the family's creation and continued memory rest firmly in the hands of its matriarch. Russell's exercises in the arts of mourning construct both the early modern family and the powerful and capable woman under whose care its members thrive and its memory lives on. They also indicate the potential of early modern mourning rituals to enable powerful performances of subjectivity for the women who engaged in them.

At the close of a consolatory poem to her nephew, Robert Cecil, following his wife's death in 1597, Russell writes, "Quod licuit feci vellem

10 William Cure II, Tomb of Elizabeth Russell, Parish Church of All Saints, Bisham.

mihi plura licere,"[14] "I have done what was allowed, I wish more were allowed me." The tag appears here in a private letter to affirm Russell's Protestant sense that only moderate mourning is allowed by God, a sentiment also expressed in a letter to Cecil six months later in which she encourages him, "not to offend God with sorrow without cause and to no end to overwhelm yourself with discontent for what is God's will."[15] While Russell here acknowledges the orthodox mean in mourning, she uses the phrase elsewhere to indict the cultural limitations placed upon mourning and to voice her desire to go beyond those bounds. This meaning is clear in her inscription on Thomas and Philip Hoby's tomb in Bisham All Saints (figure 11): "Quod licuit feci, vellum michi plura licere, / Sed tamen officiis quaeo faveto piis" ("I have done what was allowed, I wish more were allowed me, / But still in holy rites I pray that it [the tomb] be blessed").[16] Finally, the sequence of epitaphs adorning John Russell's tomb in Westminster Abbey (figure 12, p. 197) concludes, "Quod licuit feci, vellem michi plura licere."[17] As a statement on the tomb's elaborate, richly realized memorial program, the phrase becomes a gesture of *sprezzatura* – a concept with which Russell must have been well acquainted through her first husband's English translation of Castiglione's *Il Cortegiano* in the early years of their marriage.[18] With the tag, Russell simultaneously points toward the cultural restrictions on her laments, toward the spiritual borders beyond which grief becomes disobedience to God's will, and toward the considerable material limitations of the medium in which she chose to publish her sorrow.[19] The interplay of boundaries and their transgressions in Russell's memorial projects characterizes her treatments of the matter of death, her own immortal image, and the living memory of her family.

I

"The essential function of a memorial," Llewellyn writes, is "to replace the individual in order to repair the damage to the social fabric caused by the loss of the deceased."[20] When Sir Thomas Hoby, Elizabeth I's newly appointed ambassador to France, died suddenly of the plague that struck Paris in 1566, his wife planned to repair that damage in a style that would, at the same time, attest to her own erudition and virtue. Elizabeth Cooke had married Hoby in 1558, following a courtship arranged by her brother-in-law, William Cecil, and Hoby's half-brother, Philip.[21] At Thomas's death, she was appointed his sole executor[22] and was left in Paris with three small children (ages six, four, and three) and

11 William Cure I, Tomb of Philip and Thomas Hoby, Parish Church of All Saints, Bisham.

pregnant with her fourth child, born three days after his father's funeral and named Thomas Posthumus, as Gladstone puts it, thus "dramatising her situation."[23] Undaunted, she transported the body home in a carriage hung in black, presenting a bill for travel expenses to Queen Elizabeth.[24] For her pains, the queen wrote to Russell:

And for yourself, we cannot but let you now that we hear out of France such singular good reports of your duty well accomplished towards your Husband both living and dead, with other your sober, wise, & discreete behaviour in that Court & Country, that we find it a part of great contention to us, & a commendation of our Country, that such a Gentlewoman hath given so manifest a testimony of virtue in such hard times of adversity.

She signed the letter, "Your loving Friend, Elizabeth R."[25]

Upon her return to Bisham, Russell set out to memorialize Hoby in a tomb that would announce her exemplary fulfilment of wifely duties.[26] She oversaw the building of a chapel in Bisham All Saints and had Philip's (d. 1558) body reinterred in a joint vault with his half-brother Thomas (figure 11). On September 2, 1566, the church and chapel were "hanged to the ground with black clothe" and the Hoby brothers were buried in a heraldic funeral arranged by Russell.[27]

On the memorial, the material practices of early modern women's mourning become a rich source of gestures and attitudes that present Russell as the author of the reputations and characters she commemorates, and as the guarantor of her family's survival. Inscriptions on the tomb describe her crucial role in promoting Hoby's lineage in his lifetime and his honorable reputation after death:

Sir Thomas Hobye, married with Dame Elizabeth, Daughter to Sir Anthony Cooke, Knight, / by whome he had Issewe fower Children, Edward, Elizabeth, Anne, and Thomas Posthumus, / and being Embassador for Queen Elizabeth in France, died at Paris the 13th of July 1566, of the Age of 36, / leaving his Wife greate with Child in a strange Country, who brought him honourably home, and built this chapell, and layd him and his Brother in one Tomb together. Vivit post funera Virtus.[28]

The fact that the inscription is more about the widow than her deceased husband suggests the tenor of the memorial program generally, geared toward praising Russell as its chief architect and author while celebrating the tomb's twin inhabitants. On the base of the monument, an English epitaph describes the tomb's purpose and the character of its subjects: "Two worthye Knightes, and Hobies both by name / Enclosed within this marble stone do rest."[29] The poem praises Philip's civic virtues ("A deepe discoursing Head, a noble brest, / A Courtier passing, and a curteis Knight," 5–6) before eulogizing Russell's husband:

> Thomas in Fraunce possest the legates place
> And with such wisdome grew to guide the same,
> As had increast great honour to his race,
> Yf sodein fate had not envied his fame.
> Firme in Gods truth, gentle & faythful friend,
> Well learned and languaged, nature besyde
> Gave comely shape which made ruful his end.
>
> (11–17)

Finally, the poem records its author's grief and publicizes her performance of the duties of widowhood:

> Sins in his floure in Paris towne he died
> Leaving with child behind his woful wife
> In forrein land opprest with heapes of grief.
> From part of which when she discharged was
> By fall of tears that faithful wiefes do shead
> The corps with honour brought she to this place
> Performing here all due unto the dead.
> That doon this noble tombe she cawsd to make
> And both these brethren closed within the same
> A memory left here for vertues sake
> In spite of death to honour them with fame.
> Thus live they dead and we lerne wel therby
> That ye and we and all the world must dye.
>
> (18–30)

For the second time, the tomb recalls Russell's actions following her husband's death and advances her reputation as a loving wife and virtuous widow. Hoby's misfortune in dying far from home may inform Russell's emphasis on her dedicated efforts to bring his body home: one component of the good death in the period was, after all, that it should occur in one's own bed.[30] Russell's diligent attention to her husband's unfortunate corpse partially repairs the damage to his reputation that a bad death might wreak.

It is not only transporting the body that constitutes "all due to the dead," however. Russell offers the evidence of her tears, such as "faithful wiefes do shead," to support her claim to chaste widowhood and to imply that despite the partial reparation of her loss through moderate mourning, a lingering sorrow (the subject of the tomb's Latin verse to her husband) persists. Ultimately, the memorial itself is presented as proof of

Russell's eagerness to honor her dead and to perpetuate their fame to future generations. In doing so, she enhances her own reputation as a wife, fearlessly dedicated – despite her abandonment "in forrein land," despite her oppression by "heapes of grief" – to performing her duties to the dead. Because of her tenacity, and only because of it, Russell tells us, "[t]hus live they dead." She alone scripts the tomb's memorial lesson: "That ye and we and all the world must dye."

On the triumphal arch above the recumbent knights, two plaques contain Latin poems by Russell commemorating first Thomas and then Philip. These epitaphs employ the commonplaces of women's mourning to justify Russell's right to assume the responsibilities of governing her household. In "Elizabetha Hobaea, soror ad Philippum Hobaeum, Equitem fratrem" ("Elizabeth Hoby, sister, to Philip Hoby, Knight, brother"), Russell presents her brother-in-law as an *exemplum* of Hoby honor and elaborates her debt to his sound domestic government in negotiating her marriage to Thomas: "Judicioque tuo sum tibi facta soror. / Sic ego conjugium, sic omnem debea prolem" ("Through your judgement I have been to you a sister. / Thus to you I owe my husband, thus I owe each child," 8–9).[31] As payment for these familial debts, Russell dedicates herself to providing the knights an honorable burial while she hints at her willingness to surrender to death: "Et soror et conjux vobis commune sepulchrum, / Et michi composui, cum mea fata ferent" ("Both sister and wife, I have planned one tomb for you / In common – and for me, when my fates strike," 15–16). This desire for death, an acceptable sentiment when expressed in support of chaste widowhood, reappears at the poem's close, where personal sorrow also figures domestic and dynastic emptiness: "Sic, o sic junctos melius nos busta tenebunt, / Quem mea me solum tristia tecta tenent" ("Thus, O better thus the tomb will hold us joined / Than my sad house will hold me now alone," 23–4). By addressing Philip as patriarch of the Hoby family, by literally placing his heir in the tomb with him, and by figuratively projecting her own joint occupation of the tomb – at some future moment of death but also currently, in the equation of the empty house and the too-replete grave – Russell stresses her newly acquired role as head of household following the brothers' deaths and in her sons' minority. She deploys figures of wifely and sisterly grief to assure witnesses that her assumption of household duties is a necessary but unwilling undertaking. This assurance effectively guarantees her right to wield domestic power.

Russell's epitaph to Thomas, "Elizabetha Hobaea conjux, ad Thomam Hobaeum, Equitem Maritum" ("Elizabeth Hoby, wife, to Thomas Hoby, Knight, Husband"), more overtly expresses her grief in widowhood but, likewise, presents sorrow to authorize her inheritance of her husband's abandoned domestic post. She once again relives – in the present tense – his death and its traumatic aftermath:

> Dum patriae servis, dum publica commoda tractas,
>> Occidis, ignota triste cadaver humo.
> Et miseri nati flammis febrilibus ardent.
>> Quid facerem tantis, heu mihi mersa malis!
> Infaelix conjux, infaelix mater oberro,
>> Te vir adempte fleo, vos mea membra fleo.
> Exeo funestis terris, hic rapta cadaver
>> Conjugis, hinc prolis languida membra traho.
> Sic uterum gestans, redeo terraque Marique
>> In patriam luctu perdita, mortis amans.
>
> $(11-20)$

> (While you serve your country, public affairs in hand,
>> You have died, sad corpse in an unknown land.
> And the piteous children burn with feverish flames.
>> What shall I do, ay me, immersed in such misfortune!
> I wander about a hapless wife, a hapless mother,
>> I weep for you, my own body, husband seized from me.
> Plundered as here I've been, I leave these funereal lands,
>> I take my husband's corpse and children's feeble limbs,
> And so with filling womb I return by land and sea
>> To our homeland, lost in sorrow, loving death.)[32]

Russell's use of the present tense emphasizes her grief and implies that the widow perpetually, painfully re-experiences her husband's death. This sense of irreparable loss is augmented by images of unity and severance, equivalents of the mutual tomb envisioned in the epitaph to Philip. Thus the poem opens:

> O dulcis conjux, animae pars maxima nostrae,
>> Cujus erat vitae, vita medulla meae.
> Cur ita conjunctos divellunt invida fata?
>> Cur ego sum viduo sola relicta thoro?
>
> $(1-4)$

> (Sweet husband, greatest part of one soul,
>> The life of whom was the marrow of my life,
> Why do envious fates divide those once united?
>> Why am I left alone to a widow's bed?)

Russell's vision of the couple as united in one soul and now divided by death ("Corpus erat duplex, spiritus unus erat," "The body was twofold, the spirit one," 8) and her reference to Thomas as (the feminine) "mea membra" connote the widow's living–death in mourning. At the same time, this imagery allows Russell to undertake her husband's domestic privileges. The figure of the united spirit confers upon her Thomas's power to govern the family, since she is imagined as an almost equal partner in the union (although Thomas remains, admittedly, "animae pars maxima nostrae," the greatest part of the united soul).

Russell's preoccupation with the physical body of death in her epitaph for Thomas not only reflects the material circumstances of his demise – that is, his wife's responsibility for conveying the "sad corpse" home – but also enlists the period's common associations of women with the body in death (in Russell's Latin, the feminine "mortua membra," imagining husband and wife as united in the beloved corpse) to memorialize her husband and her own virtuous enactment of the rites due to the dead. Thus the poem laments and promises, "Non potui prohibere mori, sed mortua membra, / Quo potero, faciam semper honore coli" ("I could not keep off death, but this body of death / So well as I can, I'll always hold in honor," 25–6). Russell closes with a qualified gesture toward self-entombment that exploits her culture's common assignation of marital motives to overly-mournful widows: "Te Deus, aut similem Thomae mihi redde maritum, / Aut reddant Thomae me mea fata viro" ("O Lord, grant me a husband much like Thomas / Or let my fates return me to my Thomas," 27–8).

Russell's epitaphs imitate the empathetic sorrow of classical widows, transforming their literal self-sacrifice into the figurative means by which both her husband's honor and her own reputation as a devoted wife live on to posterity. In his translation of *Orlando Furioso*, John Harington praises Russell in terms that comment upon the living–death of widowhood and the function of widows' epitaphs as substitutes for self-slaughter: Ariosto "preferreth" Vittoria Colonna, he explains, "before *Porcia*, wife of *Brutus*, and divers others that dyed voluntarie soon after their husbandes ... because she wrate some verses in manner of an Epitaph upon her husband after his deceasse. In which kynde that honorable Ladie (widow of the Lord *John Russell*) deserveth no lesse commendation, having done as much for two husbands."[33] Throughout the poems to the knights, Russell employs the common figures and expressions of early modern women's mourning. She describes her empathetic desire for death and self-entombment, and devotes most of the space on the tomb to recording her sense of irreparable loss, her subjects' earthly accomplishments, and the material aspects of their demise and interment supervised by the widow into whose hands the body of death was routinely commended. Absent from the epitaphs is any mention of the knights' spiritual afterlife: consolatory gestures are thoroughly neglected in the interest of adorning the corpses and promulgating their living fame (and that of the woman who buried them) to contemporary and future audiences. When Russell writes, "Thus live they dead," she refers strictly to the brothers' immortality in effigies that she herself designed, not to the resurrection of their souls. Concerned with the physical body of death, the tomb articulates a woman's inconsolable grief and argues that her right to assume the domestic responsibilities left behind by her male governors is based upon her honorable ministrations to their remains. While Kim Walker claims that women's familial epitaphs, "act as guarantees of domesticity and embed their writer's learning in a reassuring private context that can be represented as the spontaneous and feminine expression of personal grief rather than as literary ambition,"[34] the knights' tomb at Bisham expresses its author's various ambitions more overtly than this notion of domestic privacy allows. Russell self-consciously deploys gestures of domesticity and the commonplaces of women's mourning to recreate her immediate public reality in her own image. She exploits her familial bonds and her grief at their severance to enable a *public* statement of her literary accomplishment, personal honor, linguistic erudition, and well-earned right to domestic government.

Another kind of statement is made by the knights' tomb as well, in its aesthetic treatment of the corpse. Although the recumbent pose had been commonly employed in medieval funerary sculpture in Britain, it was current in Russell's day only in France and Italy: the Hoby brothers' pose of "the armoured male, cross-legged" was to become a recognized "signifier of venerability" in the sculptural vocabulary of sixteenth and seventeenth-century England.[35] The drama and poignancy of the effigies, too, reflect French examples which Russell must have seen during her residence in Paris.[36] Gladstone argues persuasively that Russell herself had a hand in characterizing the effigies and thus "was responsible for importing the French idiom to Bisham and for introducing it to a London workshop sympathetic to that style in the presentation of the figures."[37] The workshop she identifies is that of William Cure I (1515–79), who had been employed by Russell's brothers-in-law, William Cecil and Anthony Bacon, and possibly by Thomas Hoby for a project at Bisham Abbey, and whose workshop Russell was to patronize "through its three generations of masters."[38] An innovative and influential work of art, the knights' tomb is a monument to Russell's sophistication and awareness of the latest artistic styles with which to adorn and immortalize the body of death.

Russell performed to the fullest what was allowed in commemorating Thomas and Philip Hoby and, despite her stated awareness of the limitations placed upon her memorial act, much was allowed. When her daughters, Elizabeth and Anne Hoby, died within days of each other in 1570 at the ages of nine and seven, the material restrictions on their monument were more stringent. John Weever, explaining that "sepulchres should bee made according to the qualitie and degree of the person deceased, that by the Tombe every one might bee discerned of what ranke hee was living," insists that "persons of the meaner sort of Gentrie" should be "interred with a flat gravestone."[39] Despite these constraints, or perhaps because of them, the emotion with which the girls are buried exceeds that expressed on the more opulent knights' tomb. Announcing her lament with the interjection, "eheu," Russell's epicedium memorializes her sorrow in terms that suggest her self-conscious literary imitation of classical mourning rituals:

> ELIZABETHA jacet, (eheu mea viscera) fato
> Vix dum maturo, vigo tenella jaces.
> Chara michi quondam vixisti filia matri,
> Chara Deo posthac filia vive patri,
> Mors tua crudelis, multo crudelius illud,
> Quod cecidit tecum junior ANNA soror.
> ANNA patris matrisque decus, post fata sororis,
> Post matris luctus, aurea virgo jaces!
> Una parens, pater unus erat, mors una duabus,
> Et lapis hic unus corpora bina tegit.
> Sic volui mater tumulo sociarier uno,
> Una quas utero laeta genensque tuli.[40]

> (ELIZABETH lies here [oh my visceral pangs], by fate
> You lie here, delicate maiden, scarcely grown.
> Dear to me you lived once, a daughter of your mother,
> Now live dear to God, a daughter of your father.
> Your death was cruel, a crueler one
> Because your younger sister ANNE died with you.
> ANNE, glory of your father and mother, after your sister's fate,
> After your mother's tears, golden maiden, here you lie.
> There was one mother, one father, one death for two,
> And here a single stone conceals two bodies.
> Together in one tomb, thus I your mother wanted you,
> Whom I, with joy and crying, carried in one womb.)

Like the maternal elegies studied in the previous chapter, Russell's epitaph focuses almost exclusively on the mother's physical experiences of childbirth and child-loss: thus she equates the tomb containing the girls with the womb that bore them, figuring the maternal body as the sepulcher of its lost offspring.[41] This materiality provides the rationale for the joint grave: since the sisters were born of the same parents and partake in the same death, "Together in one tomb," Russell states, "thus I your mother wanted you." As in her epitaphs for the Hoby knights, Russell stresses her instrumentality in creating and commissioning the monument in accordance with the rites due to the dead but also according to her own desires. Originally placed in front of the knights' tomb, the gravestone literalizes the epitaph's sense in transferring ownership of the children from the bereaved mother to the dead father, delivering them from living hope to living memory.[42] But Russell insists that this transfer takes place wholly under the mourning mother's control, enabled by her devotion in performing her duties to the dead. As her reproductive power initially helped to create the Hoby family, Russell recreates the family's reputation in death as the highly gendered product of her feminine grief, fearlessly materialized in the monuments that express it.

II

In 1631, John Weever complained that funeral monuments, "are (to the shame of our time) broken downe, and utterly almost all ruinated, their brazen Inscriptions erazed, torne away, and pilfered, by which inhumane, deformidable act, the honourable memory of many vertuous and noble persons deceased, is extinguished, and . . . so darkened, as the true course of their inheritance is thereby partly interrupted."[43] From the period of post-Reformation iconoclasm, funerary monuments survive as "the most important kind of church art."[44] Despite the Protestant suspicion that funeral monuments "taste somewhat of Poperie,"[45] they were protected by a 1560 proclamation which forbade "the breaking or defacing of Monuments of Antiquitie" erected "not to nourish any kinde of superstition" but to retain "the honourable and good memory of sundry virtuous and noble persons deceased [and] also the true understanding of divers Families in this Realme."[46] Important repositories of hereditary records, tombs also served the didactic function of providing exemplary lives for commendation and imitation.[47] Monuments like that of Thomas and Philip Hoby provided both *memento moris* ("we lerne wel therby / That ye and we and all the world must dye") and *exempla* to current and future audiences for whom they preserved the noble characters of the dead. Moreover, patrons advanced their own reputations based upon the material evidence of the tombs: because Russell has carried out the rites of death in so grand a style, the monuments argue, she is an exemplary wife, mother, and sister.

Although reformers such as Otto Werdmuller argued that "gorgeous graves & sepulcers . . . bestow vaine cost upon dead bodies" and amount to "a frensie, as to use pride after death,"[48] funerary monuments grew increasingly numerous and opulent in the Elizabethan period. With a family's honorable memory at stake, patrons took an active part in designing monuments and were responsible for procuring and providing inscriptions and heraldry.[49] Resources which in the pre-Reformation had been invested in constructing and embellishing chantries were now used to produce memorials to the dead which, like their Catholic antecedents, stood as monuments to their patrons' wealth.[50] In the sought-after sites of Old St. Paul's and Westminster Abbey, competition between patrons to erect the most spectacular tombs fueled creativity and increased expenditures throughout the period. In the face of the great leveler, funerary monuments reaffirmed the social distinctions lost in death.[51] As a result of this drive toward opulence, tourism in Westminster Abbey began to thrive at the turn of the seventeenth century, a trend to which Camden's guide to the monuments responds. Margaret Hoby, Russell's daughter-in-law, notes in her diary that she "went to the minster to see the monementes" in December, 1600, as did Anne Clifford in February, 1616 and again in May, 1619.[52] In this most public forum, the bereaved played out ambitious and erudite tributes to their dead. "Patrons sought to express their individual tastes as never before," Adam White notes, "and a few of them who had scholarly interests introduced the element of classical learning vital to Renaissance culture."[53] Due to "the diffusion of humanist culture among the educated elite and the growth of literacy in the middling ranks of society," and rationalized on the basis of memorial didacticism, inscriptions gained greater prominence on monuments, and post-Reformation epitaphs increasingly testified to affective bonds between family members and grief at their loss.[54] It is on Westminster Abbey's prominent stage that Elizabeth Russell, well prepared by her innovative memorial program at Bisham, was next to perform her rituals of mourning and commemoration for her dead.

By 1570, at the age of thirty-one, Russell had lost two brothers, a sister, a husband, and two children to death.[55] She retained guardianship of her ten-year-old son, Edward Hoby, and Thomas Posthumus, now four years old. Perhaps due to loneliness following her daughters' deaths, or because their considerable dowries were now available for her own use,[56] Russell embarked upon her second marriage, to John Russell, eldest son and heir to the second Earl of Bedford, in 1574.[57] Three children were born to the couple. Elizabeth (or Bess), born in 1575 and christened in Westminster Abbey, died in early adulthood and was buried in the Abbey in 1600. Anne (or Nan), born in 1577, married Henry Somerset in 1600 and became the Countess of Worcester before her death in 1639. The only son and heir, Francis, was born in 1579 and died the following year.

With her second marriage, Russell raised her social status, assuming the rank of baroness at the time of the marriage and facing the prospect of becoming a countess with the death of her father-in-law and John Russell's succession as Earl of Bedford. Unfortunately, this never came to pass: John Russell died in 1584, pre-deceasing his father by a year and severely reducing his legacy to his surviving wife and daughters. Although Russell received her jointure, which (along with her jointure from the Hoby estate) supported her throughout her lifetime and financed most of her memorial projects, her children were disinherited.[58] It was not until six years after her husband's death that Russell gained wardship of her daughters, who, as noble "orphans," had become wards of the crown. For eight years, she waged a heated legal battle with the earl's surviving children who claimed that at John Russell's death his inheritance reverted to the estate and thus should pass, by the rule of primogeniture, to the earl's grandson. In 1593, she wrote to William Cecil from her home in Blackfriars, where she had relocated to pursue the case, "I have done fully the part of a wife and of a mother in bringing [the case] thus far. Her Majesty is my last refuge for justice."[59] Despite the queen's favor, the case was finally decided against Russell, who complained bitterly to Burghley of her inability to provide for the girls' "preferment in marriage": "I have brought them up hitherto with mine own charge; I have righted their wrongs with mine own purse," she writes, "My house, being a private widow . . . is no longer fit place for them, unless I should make them no-ones."[60] A year later, Russell managed to place both daughters as Maids of Honor to Queen Elizabeth, thus providing them opportunities to meet likely prospects for marriage despite their relative poverty. It is from the queen's service that Nan was married and that Bess, just two weeks later, was buried.

Russell's tenacity in her fight for her daughters' inheritance forms part of a more general campaign of promotion and self-promotion conducted through her careful manipulation of cultural and ceremonial forms, including but not limited to those attending death. Bess Russell's christening, for example, elaborately staged at Westminster Abbey, was calculated to denote her parents' future, rather than current, ranks: "In the Chamber within the house where the Lady Russell lay was set up – a rich bed of Estate for a Countess . . . In the second Chamber was a cloth of estate for an Earl coming down to the Pomel of the Chair or somewhat higher."[61] Conducted by the College of Arms, the ceremony is marked by the same formality that we recognize in heraldic funerals of the period:

All things being ready for Thursday 28 October aforesaid at ten of the Clock, the Witnesses and the rest being all assembled they proceeded out of the Dean's Lodging through the Cloyster into the Church in the manner following:
First, the Gentlewomen that accompanied the Lords and Ladies went on before – then
Knights in their places – Barons – and Earls in their degrees – then
The Earl of Leicester – Godfather.
Then the Child in a Mantle of Crimson Velvet girded with two wrought laces of gold, having also over the face a Lawn striped with bonelace of gold [overthwart] and powdered with gold flowers and white wrought thereon, born by the Midwife, Mrs. Bradshaw
Then the Countess of Sussex – Godmother
A Gentleman Usher
The Countess of Warwick deputy for the Queen, her train born by
The Lady Burghley   and   The Lady Bacon
sister to Lady Russell   sister to Lady Russell
Other Ladies and Gentleman many.[62]

A similar manipulation of ceremonial forms marks Nan Russell's wedding on June 16, 1600.[63] Anticipating the event, Rowland Whyte wrote to Sir Robert Sidney that the marriage "wilbe honorably solemnized, and many take care to doe her all the possible Honor they can devise. The feast wilbe in Blackefriers, my Lady Russell making exceeding Preparacion for yt."[64] Russell invited Robert Cecil to serve "as my husband to command as the master of my house" during the festivities, characteristically adding that although she is but "a poor widow," she has nonetheless managed to arrange for "six mess[es] of meat for the bride's table, and one in my withdrawing chamber for M. Secretary and myself."[65] After the marriage, Whyte reports:

Her Majestie was at Blackfriars, to grace the Marriage of the Lord Harbert and his Wiffe. The Bride mett the Queen at the Waterside, where my Lord Cobham had provided a Lectica, made like half a Litter, wherein she was carried to my

Lady Russels by 6 Knights. Her Majestie dined there, and, at night, went . . . to my Lord Cobhams, where she supt. After Supper the Maske came in, as I writ in my last, and delicate was it to see 8 Ladies soe prettily and richly attired.

"The Entertainment," which lasted for three days, Whyte concludes, "was great and plentifull, and my Lady Rusell much comended for it."[66]

Bess's christening and Nan's wedding exemplify their mother's many forays into the theatrical world of polite society, engineered to assert her rank (prematurely, in her self-fashioning as a countess at the baptism) and to promote her children's interests. Russell's entertainment for Queen Elizabeth during a progress to Bisham on August 29, 1592, for instance, showcased her daughters as "two Virgins keeping sheepe, and sowing in their samplers" and was instrumental in acquiring their positions as Maids of Honor.[67] Following John Russell's death and throughout the legal battle that ensued, Russell made extensive use of death and mourning rituals not only to commemorate her absent lord but also – perhaps, more importantly – to proclaim publicly the rights and value of his children. Her husband's monument in Westminster Abbey comments on her daughters' plight and asserts their claims to their father's property and his nobility.

John Russell died on July 23, 1584, demonstrating his "great and singular wisdom" in death as in life, and was buried four days later in a heraldic funeral performed "at the cost of the Lady Elizabeth his wyffe."[68] The funeral was especially noteworthy in one detail: "Unusually," Gladstone reports, "his two daughters walked in the funeral procession."[69] In this mild transgression of funerary protocol, Russell displayed her daughters as orphans, utilizing the public rites of mourning to announce the emotional loss of the girls' father and, more urgently, the material costs of his death. This emphasis on the public mourning of the baron's daughters continues throughout the memorial program of John Russell's tomb (figure 12), erected in the prestigious St. Edmund's Chapel of Westminster Abbey. In the tomb, as in the funeral itself, Russell manipulates the customs governing women's public mourning to further her own and especially her daughters' material prospects, using the matter of death to cast their public lives according to her ambitious design.

Russell's program for her second husband's tomb affirms his virtues and announces the magnitude of his loss to his wife and daughters. Lord Russell's reclining figure appears in the traditional "toothache" posture,[70] "costumed," as Gladstone notes each of the Hoby and Russell effigies is,

12 Cornelius Cure and William Cure II, Tomb of John Russell, Westminster Abbey.

"at its permitted richest."[71] His baron's robes trimmed with fur encase his body as if he were standing, indicating his readiness for resurrection.[72] At his feet, the living–dead figure of his son and heir, Francis (figure 7, p. 145), rests awkwardly. Above the bodies, a triumphal arch symbolizes salvation, as confirmed by the inscription, "IN ALTO REQUIES," "REST ON HIGH." Within the arch, two female figures dressed in sixteenth-century mourning support the Russell coat of arms. Occupying a place traditionally reserved for the figures of fame, these female mourners are the sculptural reflections of Bess and Nan Russell as they appeared in their father's funeral procession.[73] Beyond the triumphal arch, two graces extend laurel crowns, emblems of immortality intended not only for the tomb's subjects but also, as is suggested by their position just above the two girls' heads, for Lord Russell's lamenting daughters. The identity of these female mourners as Bess and Nan is affirmed by a prominently placed inscription surmounting the coat of arms, bearing Russell's "Carmina aerumnosae matris in superstites filias" ("Verses of the devastated mother on her surviving daughters"), dedicated *not* to proclaiming the virtues of the dead, but to displaying the grief of his surviving heirs:

> Plangite nunc natae, nunc flebile fundite carmen,
> Occidit heu vestrae gloria sola domus.
> Mors rapit immitis florentem stemmate claro,
> Praesignem literis, tum pietate patrem.
> Haeredi Comitis quin vos succrescite, tali
> Ortu qui nituit sed bonitate magis.

> (Weep now, daughters, now chant out a mourning poem,
> Alas, he has died, the only glory of our home.
> Bitter death has ravished that flower in bright nobility,
> Distinguished in letters as in piety, your father.
> Heirs of an earl, grow up indeed – from such a springing
> Start you have thrived – but grow mainly in goodness.)[74]

This "proxy elegy"[75] begins by convening a community of women to perform ritualized mourning for the fallen patriarch, but ends by arguing the validity of Lady Russell's legal efforts to obtain her daughters' inheritance. Since John Russell's premature death prevented his succession to the rank of earl (as his description elsewhere on the monument as "haeres Comitis," heir of an earl, recalls),[76] the *comes* to whom the poem insists the girls are heirs must be their grandfather, Francis Russell, second Earl of Bedford – or rather, he is both John Russell *and* his father, conflated as joint progenitors in defense of the girls' rights to their combined property. The image of the Russell women joined together in lamentation thus is infused with legal and social implications that resonate in the culture beyond the Abbey. The monument's design, with its remarkable visual emphasis on the female mourners and communal lament surmounting the structure, converts women's grief into a public defense of their legal rights as heirs.

The sequence of poems adorning John Russell's monument shows a sophistication beyond that displayed on the Hoby tombs. The inscriptions go beyond the didactic, informational, and memorial functions of the Bisham epitaphs with striking imagery and textual interconnections that work in concert to pay tribute to their subject and to articulate their author's grief. Moreover, their placement on the monument contributes to the meaning of the poems individually and as a group, and directs interpretation of the tomb's various messages. Immediately below the female mourners, two epitaphs continue the theme of women's communal mourning announced in the upper register. On the viewer's left, "Εἰς θάνατον φιλτάτου καὶ λαμπρωτάτου αὐτῆς ἀνδρὸς Κυρίου Ρυσσελλίου τὸ παρὰ τῆς Ἐλιζαβήτης Ρυσσελλίας γράφεν ἐπιτάφιον" ("On the death of her most beloved and most illustrious Lord Russell, the epitaph written by Elizabeth Russell") mourns the loss of the family's "delight," elaborating especially on the traumatic effects of that loss on "the shorn ones, the widow and maidens his daughters" ("φεῦ μὴν οἱ ξυραὶ χήρη κοῦραι τε θύγατρες," 3).[77] Russell's image of the mourners as shorn works with the poem's language to energize the classical Greek tradition of women's ritual lament. While the Greek poem ends with a consolatory vision of Lord Russell enjoying a heavenly feast in the afterlife, "εὐσεβίης ἕνεκα πλὴν ὄλβου σεμνὸς ἐπαυρεῖ/οὐρανίου μετόχους συγγενέας καλεῶν" ("Through his piety, the blessed man partakes of joy, / Calling the dwellers in heaven his spirit-kindred," 7–8), the Latin poem that immediately follows (just to the right, below the second female mourner) overturns that comfort. It opens with the graphic image of death's feeding not only on the corpse but also, in a sympathetic disfigurement, on the mourning widow: "Mens mea crudeli laniatur saucia morsu, / Cum subit oblatae mortis imago tuae" ("My wounded mind is torn by death's pitiless feeding, / When the figure of your death, now soleminized, approaches," 1–2).[78] The Latin epitaph, like the Greek, focuses on the desolation of Russell's house and survivors in the aftermath of his death: "Usque cadens miseras, meque measque facis" ("In falling you leave both me and mine wretched," 4), Russell complains, reiterating the theme of women's communal sorrow as she eulogizes the object of their grief.

The top half of the monument gives visual and verbal form to the early modern culture of women's collective mourning to defend Bess and Nan Russell's rights to inherit their father's virtues and property. The bottom half, however, expresses Russell's dismay as a bereaved wife and mother and focuses on disruptions in the passage of property from father to son. The effigies of Francis and John Russell are framed by two poems which present their deaths as personal and dynastic disasters. Beside the infant's effigy, Russell's "Carmina aerumnosae matris Dominae Elizabethae Russ in obitum filii" ("Verses of the devastated mother Lady Elizabeth Russell on the death of her son") delves into the depths of maternal loss as rooted in the body – she calls the child "ipsa medulla mihi," "my very marrow" – and longs to exchange the mother's life for her child's. It predicates that essentialized sorrow, however, on his symbolic value as heir to both father and grandfather:

> En solamen avi, patri pergrata voluptas,
>   Ipsa medulla mihi, tristia fata tulit:
> O utinam mater jacuissem lumine cassa,
>   Solvissetque prior justa suprema mihi!
> Conqueror ac frustra, statuit quia numen id ipsum,
>   Orba ut terrenis sola superna petam.
>
> (O comfort of a grandfather, a father's happiest desire,
>   The very marrow of me, sad fate has taken you.
> O that I, the mother, lay dead, the light denied me,
>   And he had first fulfilled my final rites!
> I weep but in vain, for divine will itself has decreed that
>   Alone, bereft of earthly things, I seek the spheres above.)[79]

The importance of the male heir (especially one who would be guaranteed his grandfather's inheritance even in light of his father's premature death, as female children were not) is underscored by Russell's assertion – not wholly emotional, but also quite pragmatic – that his death has left her bereft of earthly things. A similar note of pragmatism marks the poem framing the effigies to the viewer's right, the only text on the monument not composed by Russell. "In obitum honaratissimi viri Domini Johannis Russelli, soceri sui charissimi Ed. Hobii Militis Epicedium" ("An Epicedium by Ed. Hoby, Knight, on the death of the most honorable man Lord John Russell, his most dear stepfather") incorporates into monumental form the memory of the heraldic funeral, since Edward Hoby originally wrote it to adorn the pall.[80] Like the heraldic funeral, the poem is devoted to publishing Lord Russell's reputation and establishing the meaning of his death to male survivors:

Quis, qualis, quantus fueris tua stemmata monstrant,
    Integra vita docet, morsque dolenda probat:
Sat sit privigno, posuisse haec carmina pauca,
    Tu sibi mente parens, filius ille tibi.
               (7–10)

(Who you were, what sort, and how much, your heraldry shows,
    Your unstained life teaches, and your woeful death proves.
May it suffice for a step-son to have offered these few verses,
    You in spirit a father to him, he a son to you.)[81]

The poem, a formal offering at the nobleman's funeral, uses the language, imagery, and assumptions of heraldic ceremony to transform the object of that ritual from property relations to the payment of an emotional debt. Together, Hoby's poem to his step-father and his mother's to his half-brother, Francis, count the economic and emotional losses exacted by the unexpected deaths of male heirs.

The final inscription of the sequence appears on the tomb's pedestal. As if Russell employed a linguistic hierarchy from top to bottom, the poem is written in English. Also reflecting a notional hierarchy which moves from the monument's celestial imagery of the resurrection to its earthbound, sepulchral base, the poem offers the tomb's most direct expression of the widow's insuperable grief and her dedication to preserving her husband's memory:

> My husband deare more than this worlds light
> Death hath my reft: but I from death will take
> His memory to whom this tomb I make.
> John was his name, (ah, was) wretch must I say
> Lord Russell once, now my tear-thirstie clay.
>   Quod licuit feci, vellem mihi plura licere.[82]

As in the knights' tomb at Bisham, Russell takes the occasion of public lament to affirm her creative control over her husband's reputation and her willing enactment of the expected rites of mourning and commemoration. The more complex and demanding artistic and literary programs of John Russell's monument reflect Russell's ambitions beyond the tomb itself. What was, in effect, the *raison d'être* of the Bisham tombs – the public articulation of Russell's uniquely feminine (re)productive power to create the family and ensure its immortality – is now subsumed by more pressing concerns and relegated to the lowest register of the tomb, figuratively associated with the feminine earth of the mourner's body: "Lord Russell once, now my tear-thirstie clay."

While Russell literalizes and memorializes women's communal mourning on Lord Russell's tomb to bolster her daughters' legal claims, she would be engaged thirteen years later in mourning one of the mourners. Two weeks after Nan Russell's wedding, John Chamberlain reports that, "Mistress Elizabeth Russell lies at the last cast, and is either dienge or dead. The Lady Warwick and [Lady of] Cumberland have watched with her by turnes, and gave her over as past hope."[83] On July 5, 1600, Whyte confirms that, "Mrs. Elizabeth Russell died 4 Daies agoe, and great Lamentacion is made by my Lady her Mother, my Lady Warwicke, and my Lady Harbert, who are in London."[84] Although Gladstone argues persuasively that Bess's fatal illness may have been obvious before marriage negotiations for her younger sister were undertaken,[85] Bess's death nonetheless had a profound impact on her mother. Five months after her death, Russell writes to her nephew that "my heart will not yet serve me to come to Court, to fill every place I there shall come in with tears by remembrance of her that is gone."[86] A full year later, she complains to Cecil that Bess "die[d] in her Majesty's service, worn with untolerable pains and yet not thought worthy of honorable burial as other her meaner maids had."[87]

The monument erected to Bess in 1602–3, probably the work of Cornelius Cure[88] (figure 13), casts in stone the female culture of mourning and the communal lament performed by the Russell women in the wake of Bess's death. While an inscription on the base announces, "Faelicissimae memoriae sacrum, Elizabethae Russelliae, posuit Anna Soror moerens" (Sacred to the most happy memory of Elizabeth Russell, her mourning sister Anne has erected this monument),[89] critics from the early eighteenth century forward have agreed that the monument, as Dart puts it, "was no doubt the curious Design of that ingenious Family, Sir *Antony Cook's.*"[90] The tomb was indeed curious, since it represented the first seated effigy in Britain. Its influences are continental and classical, compellingly arguing for Russell's participation in the innovative design.[91] The effigy was enormously influential, spawning at least seven imitations in the next decade, all but two of which adorn monuments for women.[92] Russell's responsibility for the monument's design is further supported by its location: she must have approved the placement of Bess's tomb at the foot of her father's monument – once again the daughter mourning her father – since the column required the removal of part of the metal railing around the earlier tomb.[93]

The effigy's melancholy pose, leaning on one arm, eyes closed, certainly reflects her mother's and sister's dismay at Bess's death, but also

13 Cornelius Cure. Tomb of Elizabeth (Bess) Russell, Westminster Abbey.

contributes to the monument's subtle assertion of its author's faith in the resurrection. Bess's right foot rests on a skull, indicating her triumph over death, while the inscription, "Dormit non mortua est," appropriately culled from the New Testament raising of Jairus' daughter (Matthew 9:24), reiterates this idea. So subtle is the tomb's narrative of resurrection that a legend evolved of Bess's sudden death from a needle prick (as Crull relates it, "the Fore-Finger of her Left only extend[s] downwards, direct-ing us to behold the Death's Head underneath her Feet, and to intimate the Disaster that brought her to her End") which has survived in some criticism to this day.[94] If the monument's ascensional program is subtle, however, its allusions to earthly power are richly detailed. Bess enacts a spiritual triumph over death, but also figures secular power in her eternal enthronement: she appears in court dress, the sculptural representation of Queen Elizabeth's annual gift of gowns to her Maids of Honor.[95] "The force of the costume on the monument," Gladstone concludes, "was that it enshrined the Queen's favor, and underlined Elizabeth's proximity to the sovereign, in a society in which access to the Queen implied power."[96]

Bess's burial in Westminster Abbey not only reflected her family's long association with the church and her own christening there twenty-five years earlier but also the growing sense that the Abbey was a particu-larly appropriate site to commemorate noblewomen. The monuments of Westminster from the Elizabethan period emphasize "that an hon-ourable reputation was legitimately an ambition for noble women, as it was incontestably in the domain of noble men."[97] John Weever ex-plains that women as well as men deserve commemoration, based upon the different histories of the sexes' interment: "Man was borne upon mens shoulders to signifie his dignitie and superioritie over his wife; and woman at the armes end, to signifie, that being inferiour to man, in her life time, she should not be equalled with him at her death." This prac-tice continued, he argues, "untill women, by renouncing the world, and living monasticall religious lives, got such an honourable esteeme in the world, that they were thought no lesse worthie of honour, in that kinde, then men."[98] Bess Russell's monument positions her permanently in a place of highest honor and asserts the inherent value of an unmarried woman, particularly to her female relatives, as few other monuments of the period do. As the last act in Russell's performance of familial honor on the public stage of London court society, Bess's tomb commemorates not only her mother's successful management of both daughters' for-tunes against almost insurmountable odds but also the devastation of female relations at her death. Simultaneously a mournful attendant on her deceased father and brother, a melancholy marker of her own loss, and a hopeful watcher for the resurrection, Bess's effigy recalls the power of early modern women's communal mourning and the unpredictable economics of birth, marriage, and death which ensured this "child of the Abbey" at least an opulent tomb if not a resplendent wedding.[99]

III

By 1600, as she approached the age of sixty, Lady Russell's thoughts had turned to her own mortality. In the midst of a dispute over her daughters' intentions to sell their lease to Russell House in London (which she opposed, explaining, "I cannot bring my heart to be content to dishonor the dead or not to give all due to my dead darling while I breathe"), Russell wrote in September, 1599, "I think that I go upon my last year. Some will kill me and therefore my kingdom is not of this world."[100] Within a year, with Bess dead, Nan married, and her duties to both daughters discharged, she turned her attention to planning her own monument to be erected alongside that of her first husband in Bisham All Saints. Her preoccupation with her death and its memorialization is reflected in her daughter-in-law's report that, following Queen Elizabeth's funeral in April, 1603, "I dined with Lady Russill, who after required the names of such as I would trust to passe some Livinge, after hirr death, unto me."[101]

Russell's monument is not the only means by which she intended to impress her lasting image on the world around her. In 1605, she published her youthful translation of John Ponet's treatise on the Eucharist, *A Way of Reconciliation in the Sacrament*, which she dedicated to her daughter Nan with the words, "I have left to you, as my last Legacie this Booke."[102] Russell conceived of her translation not only as a mother's legacy but also as a monument to her dead father: in a letter to Cecil accompanying her gift of the volume, she explains, "in token your grandfather and mother's father doth thank your Lordship for so much honoring his Cooke's blood, he hath sent you by me, his daughter, your Lordship's old aunt, a book of his own making in Germany in the time of his pilgrimage."[103] Her decision to publish the work so late in life is prompted, she explains, by the fear that "after my death, it should be printed according to the humors of other and wrong of the dead, who in his life approved my Translation with his own allowance."[104] An unauthorized edition, in other words, might mar her father's and her own reputation, which her publication seeks to control. The care with which Russell approaches posterity in the volume parallels her concern on the tombs: thus the title page announces that the text is, "Translated out of Latin into English by the Right Honorable Lady Elizabeth Russell, Dowager to the Right Honorable the Lord John Russell, Baron, and sonne and heire to Francis Earle of Bedford."[105]

Russell uses both textual means and cultural rites of mourning and commemoration to craft her legacy. In 1603, she writes to William Dethick, Garter King of Arms, in preparation for a heraldic funeral "aimed at ensuring that her identity was published at her death."[106] In the letter, she claims, as she had done prematurely in Bess's christening, a rank higher than that to which she was entitled: "Good Mr. Garter, I pray you as your lessur doth best suit you set down advisedly and exactly in sundry particuler by it selfe, the number of mourners, due for my calling, being a Viscountess by Birth."[107] Dethick's response, outlining "The order for mourners at the funerall of a Viscountesse of Estate, or an Earles eldest sonnes wife," indicates that she, in fact, was granted that courtesy rank (and, accordingly, the effigy on her monument wears a countess' coronet).[108] Her will, dated April 23, 1609, reflects precisely Dethick's advice: while she had asked him about provisions for "sixty-three women widows," corresponding to her age in 1603, her will provides for "Three score and tenn poore widdowes or soe many as I shalbe yeares old at the tyme of my deathe to everie of them a black gowne of twentye shillinge being three yards to each gowne and a kercher every kercher being of the price of sixe shillinge and eight pence." Despite her charge that her burial be "performed orderly and decently, and without any vaine ostentacion or pomp," her will provides that the impressive "some of sixe and twenty hundred poundes shallbe geven in and about my ffunerall."[109] Russell died on June 2, 1609, at Bisham and was buried there according to the terms of her will.

Since Russell's will makes no provision for her monument, it must have been completed and paid in full before her death in 1609. Once again, Russell patronized the Cure brothers' studio in Southwark.[110] At an estimated cost of £220 to £250, Russell's gesture of self-commemoration must have exhausted much of her wealth.[111] The practice of erecting one's funeral monument within one's lifetime was relatively common: at least thirty percent of early modern monuments were finished prior to their subjects' deaths.[112] In such cases, the effigy cogently depicts the subject's self-image. "The patron's own statue set himself or herself for ever in the very midst of life," Llewellyn writes, "For this reason we must always treat the effigial sculpture of this period . . . as fictions in stone."[113]

14 William Cure II, Tomb of Elizabeth Russell, Parish Church of All Saints, Bisham (detail).

Russell certainly had a hand in creating her fiction in stone. Her effigy on her monument in Bisham All Saints (figure 10, p. 182 and figure 14) idealizes its subject in the Elizabethan fashion, depicting her as eternally youthful in death's immortality. She appears in full mourning, the costume which she adopted after John Russell's death and wore for the rest of her life: a pleated white mourning hood covers a ruffled cap, widows' bands of pleated linen fall from her shoulders, and a white ruff and stomacher are worn above a black gown.[114] A viscountess's coronet surmounts her headdress.[115] Russell kneels before an open Bible, and lying in front of her, like the Christ child before the Virgin in a nativity scene, is the infant-heir, Francis. She places herself in the midst of her children, insisting firmly on her central role as matriarch.[116] Under a coffered canopy are the images of the dead: behind Russell and Francis kneel the three children who predeceased her, Anne and Elizabeth Hoby and Bess Russell, the latter wearing the same dress in which she appears as a melancholy Maid of Honor on her Westminster monument. Beyond the canopy, Russell's living sons, Edward and Thomas Posthumus Hoby, look on. And before Russell, dressed in fur-trimmed robes of a countess and wearing the coronet of her rank, Nan Russell kneels, the focus of her mother's attention in death as in life.

As does Bess's monument, Russell's tomb subtly conveys a consolatory message. Its single visible inscription announces "Nemo me lachrymis decoret, neque funera fletu faxit cut? vado per astra Deo" ("Let no one honor me with tears, nor should a funeral be held with mourning – why? I go through the stars to God").[117] Sequestered on the page of the open book, available almost exclusively to the effigy's eyes, is a passage from Job 19:25–7 that forms part of the Anglican Order for the Burial of the Dead: "Scio quod redemptor / meus vivit et in novissimo die de terra surrectorus sum; et / rursum circumdabor pelle mea et in carne mea videbo deum. / Quem visurus sum et ipse et oculi mei conspecturi sunt / et non allis, reposita et haec spes mea in sinu mea" ("I know that my redeemer liveth, and that I shall rise out of the earth in the last day; and shall be covered again with my skin, and shall see God in my flesh; yea, and I myself shall behold him not with other, but with these same eyes").[118] The passage, while obviously announcing Russell's confidence in resurrection, justifies the creation of a monument on which appear free-standing figures-in-the-round representing Russell and her children. These stone figures record the images of the Russells and Hobies in life, and predict their material reincorporation at the second coming. The effigies offer gendered portraits of both the past and the future.

While these consolatory markers of Russell's faith are undeniably present, the monument's theme is overwhelmingly secular. In addition to the effigies that permanently display the fruits of Russell's labors as mother and head of two households, a metal railing surrounding the monument is elaborately decorated with heraldry that commemorates the spectacular marriages of Russell's children and the genealogy of the Cooke family. Thirteen separate shields depict the coats of arms of Russell's parents (Cooke, Fitzwilliam, and Cooke impaling Fitzwilliam), her two marriages (Russell impaling Cooke, Hoby impaling Cooke, Russell, and Hoby), those of her children (Somerset impaling Russell and Hoby impaling Carey), and the marriages of her sisters (Cecil impaling Cooke, Bacon impaling Cooke, Cooke impaling Fitzwilliam, Rowlett impaling Cooke, and Killigrew impaling Cooke).[119] The symbolic vocabulary of the heraldic images articulates Russell's inclusive self-history and calls attention to the lasting importance of her relationships with her sisters throughout her lifetime.[120] By means of the language of heraldry, Russell is joined in communal mourning by the sisters whom she invokes to attend her grave. In her self-memorialization at Bisham, Russell establishes her honorable reputation for posterity and records the accomplishments of the Cooke sisters. She acknowledges the limitations of moderate mourning and, consequently, enhances the tomb's didactic function in affirming life after death. Her monument is one of triumph, not of tragedy, in which the heroic undertakings of an early modern wife, mother, sister, and scholar are recorded and celebrated.

Repeatedly in her commemorative programs, Russell approaches the limits of permissible self-expression and self-fashioning – in the transgressive grief of the Hoby tombs, the political program of the Russell monuments, and her daring self-promotion in her own monument – and manipulates culturally sanctioned forms of public mourning toward performances of her impressive and memorable presence. In the design of her monument, Russell reaches the limits of textual expression. Like Bess's tomb, Russell's monument at Bisham, textually speaking, is virtually silent. When read in light of her memorializations of the Hoby and Russell men in copious epitaphs, this relative neglect of written expression may suggest that there was simply less to be said about the deaths of early modern women than of men. But Russell's monument to Elizabeth and Anne Hoby, with its heart-wrenching epicedium, argues that familial bonds conferred value upon these otherwise "unimportant" female members of Elizabethan society. In memorializing her second Elizabeth, though, Russell boldly eschewed the floor slab required for gentry maidens and buried her daughter in a manner befitting the first-born child and heir (albeit female) of an earl's son. She was able, moreover, to let the visual language of the melancholy tomb speak for itself. The paucity of text on Bess's monument eloquently bespeaks her mother's devastation at her death and her resigned hope in salvation as a cure for sorrow – one remedy of two. The monument itself, of course, confers its own immortality, firmly in the control of the maternal hands which could not prevent her daughter's death.

If the silence of Bess's tomb witnesses both her mother's profound grief and growing confidence in the power of visual forms, a different explanation lies behind the textual vacuity of Russell's own monument. While its effigies offer visual evidence of her successful navigation of her children's lives through difficult straits, two inscriptions (one virtually invisible to the viewer) advocating the consolatory and celebratory rejection of mourning are the monument's only texts. No other inscriptions appear on the tomb of so prolific an author of epitaphs. Unable or unwilling to script her own epitaph or to record the details of her own life story, Russell provided blank inscription panels behind her kneeling effigy on which her children could record her achievements for posterity. Despite John Weever's advice that such ceremonies "should . . . not be neglected by us children, or nearest of kindred, upon [our parents'] interments,"[121] the panels remain blank today.[122] For the visitor to Lady Russell's monument, cradled in the chapel which she built, in the heart of a world she designed according to her own desire, the panels contain the ghost-written story, easily overlooked, of an early modern woman's bold and often misunderstood performance of self-expression and self-authorship on the suggestive stage of public mourning.

7

The mat(t)er of death: the defense of Eve and the female ars moriendi

"Thou dire death, but stately Sergeant," Radford Mavericke writes in the wake of Queen Elizabeth's death, "herein thou hast but done thy dutie." That duty, he explains, is:

to arrest Kinges as well as Clownes . . . and to take Princes and Potentates, as well as people and Subjectes, down from the Stage of this life, to rest a while in the atiring house of their graves, till others that succeede in the next scene of this earthly Tragedy, have plaied their Pageants, and so discend downe under the cloth of mortality, to accompany their fellowes that went before them.[1]

Mavericke's emphasis on death's theatricality comments on the public, didactic, and testimonial qualities of the early modern deathbed which rendered the exemplary narratives of men's and women's good deaths valuable tools to prepare readers and witnesses for their own inevitable demise. As the deathbed accounts of women such as Katherine Stubbes and Katherine Brettergh illustrate, the scene of early modern death – that theatrical exit to the tiring house of the grave – is one in which gender is performed and constructed. Given death's performativity, it should be no surprise to see Mavericke's (and Hamlet's) image of Sergeant Death[2] echoed in Phillip Stubbes's report of his wife's dying words: "send thy Sergeant to arrest me, thy Pursevant to attach mee" (A4v). The figure has a long history. It appears a century earlier in the opening words of Wynkyn de Worde's publication of *The Lamentacyon of the dyenge creature* (1507), when Moriens complains of "a sergeaunt of armes whose name is crewelte . . . lyenge on me his mace of his offyce."[3] In the late-medieval *ars moriendi*, the dying creature performs his good death before crowds comprised not only of readers but also of deathbed attendants, counselors, clergymen, saints, angels, demons, the Virgin, and the Trinity itself. In a drama based on "the assumption of an ongoing struggle between good and evil,"[4] Moriens pleads with his "good aungell" to defend him from his "bad aungell . . . one of my chefe accusers with legions of

fendes with hym."[5] The vivid figure of Sergeant Death joins the bur-
geoning cast of characters surrounding the pre-Reformation deathbed
(figure 15)[6] in a traditional art of dying that changed little in the century
preceding the English Reformation and was vigorously molded to reflect
liturgical, doctrinal, and cultural developments from the 1530s forward.
Much like a stage on which the dying creature "act[s] out the last role of
her life,"[7] the post-Reformation deathbed offered partially improvised
performances by the dying, but also was extensively scripted in healthy
numbers of *artes moriendi* published in the period to aid both the dying
and their attendants in the decorous and efficacious enactment of these
final scenes. Protestant arts of dying, like their Catholic predecessors,
sought to curb the fear of death by staging dress rehearsals of the event:
thus Richard Whitford's *Dayly Exercyse and Experyence of Death*, published
in 1537 but written twenty years before, explains that:

Lack ... of exercyse, use, and experyence / causeth these persons to feare and
drede dethe. As by example, chyldren and some women, or such persones never
had experyence ne knowledge of a bugge that is a personage, that in a playe dothe
represent the devyll at [the] first syght / ben moche affrayde thereof: in so moche
that some persones have ben in jeopardye to lose theyr wytte & reson thereby.[8]

As Whitford's title suggests, he seeks to remedy fear by offering experience
of death and, consequently, the awareness that Satan's deathbed assaults
on the dying Christian are merely the empty gestures of a theatrical
fraud. Only "chyldren and some women" would be foolish enough to
mistake the demonic actors on the stage of death for real threats.

Whitford's devaluation of the spiritual agon of the deathbed and his
derogatory gendering of audience response to this performance prefigure the masculine portrayal of the art of dying undertaken by post-
Reformation counselors who describe *mourning* as the duty of women
while claiming *consolation* as the property of men. While reports of early
modern scenes of death clearly depict the presence of women, the value of
their attendance was generally deflated in favor of the consolatory words
of clergy or laymen: thus Jeremy Taylor complains of the crowded stage
of early modern death, particularly of "the women and the weepers,
the swoonings and the shriekings" that only exacerbate, in his view, the
difficult task of dying.[9] At the same time, Protestant arts of dying revise
the Catholic belief in intercession not only by denying family and friends
of the dying creature the power to improve the state of the soul after
death but also by removing the Virgin and saints as powerful and reliable representatives of Moriens in the higher courts of heaven. Even as

15 "The Temptation of Faith." From *Ars Moriendi*.

post-Reformation iconoclasm exiled images of Mary and the saints – as Eire argues, largely feminine images whose removal "marks a definite shift away from a gender-balanced, feminized piety to a more strictly masculine one" – this "masculinization of piety" extends to re-engender the scene of death as well.[10]

In the face of women's increasingly marginal role in representations of the deathbed, and the doctrinal exile of the Virgin and female saints, two early modern women composed and published *artes moriendi* nonetheless, encroaching upon and appropriating the consolatory discourses usually claimed only by men.[11] Not surprisingly, Rachel Speght's *Mortalities Memorandum, with A Dreame Prefix'd* (1621) and Alice Sutcliffe's *Meditations of Mans Mortalitie* (1634) employ most of the commonplaces of the masculine tradition from which they emerge. Speght assumes the nearly dead metaphor of Sergeant Death, for example, to encourage readers to anticipate their last end: "So that if *Death* arrest them unawares, / Yet can it not them unprepared finde."[12] Sutcliffe also marshals the image as she warns, "when Gods Serjeant Death, shall arrest them, and they shall bee summon'd to appeare before the Tribunall of the Almighty, with what terrible feare will that Soule be shaken and smitten."[13] Despite their conventionality, though, both Speght's and Sutcliffe's works self-consciously undertake a productive, feminine redemption of mourning that supports their experiments in the art of consolation.

This chapter reads these two female-authored *artes moriendi* against the backdrop of the genre's development within pre- and post-Reformation understandings of the deathbed. My goal is to characterize the feminine voice within the genre and to ask in what ways these women redirect generic conventions toward constructions of their gendered presence as authors. Like many male writers in the period, both Sutcliffe and Speght dedicate their death manuals to women, but in the case of these female-authored *artes*, their dedications establish intimate connections between women joined in mourning that constitute textual reflections of the communal character of early modern women's grief. Both texts, moreover, are unusually concerned with questions of women's writing, education, and publication, and use the genre to theorize the possibility of women's public speech and to realize that possibility. Because of their relatively conventional entries into the masculine consolatory discourse, the female-authored *artes moriendi* of Speght and Sutcliffe invite the question (as do Stubbes's *A Chrystal Glasse* and Katherine Brettergh's deathbed performance in *Deaths Advantage*), "Is there a woman's voice in this text?" Rather than marrying the gendered speaker to the sexual identity of a text's author, I suggest that the woman's voice resides in discernible sites and gestures within the works at which gender is understood as a cultural act or social construction not uniformly or directly linked to the biological sex of the body. In Speght's and Sutcliffe's performative exercises in the art of dying, the figure of Eve proves to be such a site at which rival versions of femininity are staged. For these authors, the legacy of the defense of Eve staged in the seventeenth-century pamphlet debate, in which Speght participated, offers a potent figure within which to focus not only a gendered narrative of Christian salvation but also a gendered anatomy of Christian consolation; a *raison d'(ê)tre* for the *ars moriendi* itself that engages the commonplace, "Men live and learn to *die*, and *die* to live" (Speght, *MM* 84), through the unique merger of life, death, and knowledge in the female figure of Eve.

I

"The Art of dying well is easier learned by examples then by directions," writes Samuel Ward in his *Life of Faith in Death* (1622).[14] Accordingly, he records the last words of martyrs ancient and modern, some more poignant than others: "The Lady *Jane Grey*," he tells readers, "requested by the Lieutenant of the Towre to write her Symbole in his book before her beheading, wrot this, *Let the glassie condition of this life never deceive thee, There is a time to bee borne, a time to dye, But the day of death is better then the day of Birth*." Elsewhere, Ward reports, "*Marion* the wife of *Adrian*, seeing the Coffin hooped with Iron, wherein she was to bee buried alive: *Have you provided this pasty-crust to bake my flesh in*."[15] Ward's faith in the power of exemplarity to teach the art of death is a feature of the *ars moriendi* from its earliest embodiments, where Moriens is displayed in both visual and textual extremities for the benefit of onlookers. The same reliance on *exempla* prompts counselors to recommend visiting the deathbeds of friends and neighbors in life as in texts: *A Dialogue of Dying Wel* by Peter of Luca advises readers to "willinglie and oftentimes go to see men when they be in the agonie of death" so that they may remain in continual remembrance of their last end.[16] While Ward's gallery of martyrs responds to the exemplarity of the medieval art of dying and illustrates one of many stands of continuity tying the Catholic genre to its post-Reformation counterpart, he also reinterprets the *ars moriendi* as an *ars vivendi*, a daily preparation for Death's inevitable arrest. Thus the work concludes with the commonplace, "He that meanes and desires to dye well, must dye daily."[17]

In the wake of the Reformation, Philippe Ariès argues, interest in the deathbed drama *per se* as the climactic scene of the Christian life gradually gave way to an increased emphasis on the life of the dying creature prior to the moment of death.[18] Protestant arts of dying commonly affirm the need for daily recollection of death, seeing in exemplary last acts useful models of courage, fortitude, and faith for Christian readers in everyday life. At the same time, however, as Ralph Houlbrooke points out, "in England, recorded interest in deathbed performance was never greater than it was during the 150 years following the Reformation" – an interest prompted by the loss of a unified, authorized version of the deathbed, encapsulated in the medieval *Ars Moriendi*, and its replacement by improvisations of the maimed rites of dying.[19] Despite a heightened emphasis on the moral quality of one's life prior to its end, post-Reformation *artes* are prolific and thorough in their attention to the deathbed drama itself and reflect doctrinal reassessments of the status of the sacraments and roles of bedside attendants, both divine and human.

While pre- and post-Reformation arts of dying share similar gestures, language, and ideas, the overall tenor of their approaches to the crucial moment of death differs significantly. Erasmus' *Preparation to Deathe*, for example, updates and revises the material of the mid-fifteenth century *Craft of Dying*, often echoing his source, but toward different ends. While Erasmus agrees that death "is of mans lyfe the last part (as it were) of the playe, whereof hangeth eyther everlastynge blysse or man, or everlastynge damnation" (A2), the accessibility of this play to a mortal audience is unclear. In the place of the external rites of the deathbed, Erasmus concentrates on the spiritual processes experienced by the dying. As such, death's sacramental aspects become extraneous. While he admits that, "this surely is a Christen mans part, to wyshe, that he maye lacke none of the sacramentes," the rites are "great solacies and comfortes of the mynd, and helpynges of our beleve" (E5–E5v), rather than necessary preludes to salvation. Their absence does not threaten the health of the soul after death:

Surely I doubte not, but that many neyther assoyled of the prest, nor their maker receyved, nor ancyled, nor yet buryed, after the rytes of the churche, have gone to everlastynge joye and blys, where as some other, after all thes of the church solemnley done, and also buried in the churche next to the hyghe aultar, be caried downe to helle. (E5v)

Erasmus' emphasis on conscience rather than ritual, on the unseen struggle in the soul of the dying creature, informs the post-Reformation *ars moriendi* as it goes on to explore the troubled correspondence between internal state and outward signs in death. While Catholic *artes* continue to emphasize Satan's terrifying assaults (as Bellarmino describes it in one case, "the Divel appeared . . . in the forme of a blacke-More, from whose head and beard did drop downe hot and liquid pitch")[20] and the importance of ritual interventions to protect Moriens from temptation, reformers such as William Perkins argue that there is no scriptural basis for the sacraments to be received on the deathbed and no benefit to be derived from them.[21] Changes in beliefs concerning death's rituals, in turn, resulted in a reconfiguration of the deathbed scene and the roles of its actors and audience. "The drastic simplification of last rites administered by the clergy in the Reformation," Houlbrooke points out, "may have made the help given by members of the family more important."[22] And although that help included attending to both the spiritual and physical needs of the dying, reformers elevate the art of consolation, consistently associated with the masculine presence at the scene of death, while relegating to women – and thereby denigrating – the material concerns of the event. Conversely, male attendants, whose interests are coded as spiritual, are valued more highly (and noted more frequently in the literature) than their female counterparts.

As the reformed deathbed rethought the roles of the dying creature and his attendants, then, a renewed gendering of the scene of death emerged. From the beginning of the *ars moriendi* tradition, women played various parts, both actual and imagined, in the performance of the deathbed. The illustrations of the block book *Ars Moriendi* call attention to their roles. In the crowded deathbed scene of "The Temptation of Faith" (figure 15, p. 213), the Virgin intercedes for Moriens while, at the foot of the bed, a pagan queen (so identified by the scroll, "Fac sicut pagani," "Do not do as the pagans")[23] kneels to a female idol, a perverse alternative to the Virgin. In the foreground, a female figure of penance appears, much like Sirani's *Penitent Magdalene* (figure 1, p. 17), with rods in one hand and a scourge in the other. The woodcut describes the Virgin's function as mediatrix between Moriens and Christ as crucial to the medieval good death: thus *The Lamentacyon of the dyenge creature* also records "How the dyenge creature putteth his supplycacyon to the moder of mercy Mary replete with grace prynces of reuth / mercy & pyte to whome all synners resorteth whan they be soccourles."[24] Alongside the Virgin and the female saints and demons, virtues and vices, decorating the medieval deathbed, mortal women are also depicted, performing the necessary but admittedly unglamorous work of attending the body in death. In "The Temptation to Impatience" (figure 16), Moriens impatiently kicks aside his covers

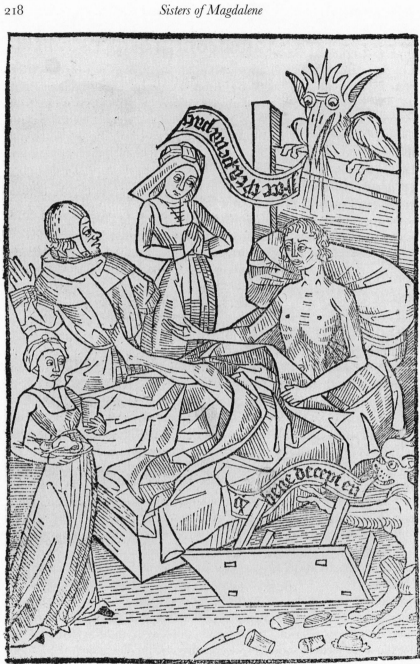

16 "The Temptation to Impatience." From *Ars Moriendi*.

as a female attendant (perhaps his wife) laments, "Ecce, quantam pe-
nam patitur" ("Lo, how much suffering he endures"). In the foreground,
a female servant enters with food and drink to find that the frustrated
Moriens has overturned the table. *The Craft of Dying* also notes, with a
touch of humor, women's work at the deathbed when it bemoans the
fact that many people deny death until the last possible moment, concluding thereby, "that religious people and women – for the honesty
of their estate – should not run but to a man that is a-dying and for
fire" (39).

While the woodcuts inscribe women's presence at the deathbed, post-
Reformation arts of dying circumscribe the significance of their attendance, literally masculinizing the deathbed scene as the exile of the Virgin
and female saints figuratively does so. To counter the temptation to
avarice (that is, the over-attachment to earthly possessions, including
one's wife and family), *The Craft of Dying* advises that, "When man is in
point of death, and hasteth fast to his end, then should no carnal friends,
nor wife, nor children, nor riches, nor no temporal goods, be reduced
unto his mind, neither be communed before him" (37).[25] On this point,
Catholic and Protestant writers agree. Thus Peter of Luca recommends
"the election or provision of two or of one faithful & wel-beloved companion or freind [*sic*], eyther seculer or religious, which in the end of thy
lyfe may be present with thee, and assist thee."[26] These friends are to
comfort and persuade Moriens to patience and constancy, and to ensure
"that none weep their [*sic*], that great sylence be kept, and that their be in
the chamber no great multitude of persons: they ought also to prohibite
that the sick person be too much molested with the visitings of his freindes
and kinsfolkes, and speciallie when his sicknes encreaseth, and that there
is no great hope of lyfe."[27] Calvinist Thomas Becon's *Sicke Mannes Salve*
also dramatizes the deathbed as a pseudo-Platonic dialogue in which
four male friends (Philemon, Eusebius, Theophile, Christopher) attend,
instruct, and comfort the dying Epaphroditus in the absence of his wife
and family who enter only to receive his final blessing.[28]

Increasingly, the deathbed scene is represented as one dominated by
male counselors, while women are imagined to be elsewhere, and mourning. As in the case of Katherine Brettergh's deathbed drama, numerous
clergy and laymen surround the dying to offer spiritual comfort and to
provide reliable witnesses of the events of the final illness, while women's
presence is discounted, noted but not elaborated. This movement is reflected in Samuel Clarke's commentary on Martin Luther's death: "He
lived chastely and holily in Wedlock above twenty years, and after his

death left three sons, and his Widdow, who lived seven years after him: who was much grieved that she was absent at his death, whereby she could not perform her last duty of love to him as she desired."[29] The high number of post-Reformation *artes moriendi* dedicated to women suggests the particular relevance of the subject to female attendants who, far too often, may have been called upon to "perform [their] last duty of love" to family members, even as the contents of these texts marginalize and remove their dedicatees from the actual scene of death.

Despite frequent representations of the deathbed as a forum for masculine consolation, early modern women's diaries make it clear that they attended the deaths of family members and neighbors, watching the dying and mourning their loss. Grace, Lady Mildmay records her resistance to the machinations of "plotters and workers of [an] unjust alteration" in her father's will as they dominated his deathbed: "I was brought to his chamber upon a sudden," she writes, and "as soon as I had done my duty to my father I was carried out of his presence into another room . . . I desired to watch with my father and to lie in the house, but I could not until they had effected the business in hand." She continues:

And when my father drew nearer and nearer towards the end, the pangs of death appearing on his face, and I kneeling down by his bedside weeping at the view thereof, he looked sternly upon me and shook me hard by the hand, saying 'Oh, Grace, Grace, Grace, I pray God bless thee. Thou shalt have much trouble with thy land, I tell thee, but I pray God you mayest well overcome it.' These were his last words to me, wherein, assuredly, the blessing of God was included.[30]

Alice Thornton's autobiography also describes her attendance, and that of female family members, on the dying. At her sister's death in 1645, Thornton herself "watch[ed] a whole week together," during which time clergymen (Mr. Siddall and Mr. Farrer) visited the dying woman and administered the Holy Sacrament. Thornton writes, "my griefe and sorrow was soe great for her, that I had brought myselfe into a very weake condition, in so much as my mother came to Thorpe with Dafeny Lightfoote, a cairefull servant, to help with my sister, and sent me home." Dafeny remained faithfully beside the sick woman for a full month, reporting her dying words and moments to Thornton.[31] Dafeny also attended the death of Thornton's mother in 1659, and Thornton's constant presence at her mother's deathbed is also evident in the careful detail with which she recounts the episode.[32] While, once again, a male counselor (Mr. Peter Samewaies) visits the sick woman to be-stow the sacrament of Communion, her female attendants are figured as offering comfort and support. Thornton reports that "all that Friday night, before she departed," her mother made "Dafeny to pray with her that praier of Dr. Smith made in his booke for a person at the point of death,"[33] while Thornton herself is the recipient rather than the bearer of consolation:

when she saw me weepe much, for this affliction of hers did indeed conserne me nearely, she said, 'Deare childe, why will you not be willing to part with me to God? Has he not lent me to be a comfort to you long enough?' . . . Certainly the words of a dieing freind prevailes much; and I doe believe the Lord had put words of perswasion into her mouth which prevailed more then all the world with me to moderate my excessive sorow.[34]

Presumably, alleviating her daughter's sorrow – however appropriate it might be to mark the passage of a parent – represents a spiritual victory for the dying mother as well.

The accounts of Mildmay and Thornton, like the visual record of the *Ars Moriendi*, point toward women's presence at the deathbed but, unlike their medieval predecessors, thematize the difficult status of women's mourning within that scene. Repeatedly, post-Reformation writers con-demn excessive mourning at the deathbed, frequently coding that im-moderation as feminine: thus Sutton's *Disce Mori* explains that "we blame not the affection it selfe, but the excess or want of moderation. We may not onely use moderate sorrow in the departure of others, but even in the departure of the godly and well disposed themselves."[35] Insofar as women were thought to be essentially given to immoderate mourning, their presence at the deathbed was troublesome at best. While male coun-selors, "eyther seculer or religious," can benefit the dying creature's soul through comfortable discourse and prayer, women can merely mourn. Surrounded by stoic male attendants – an improvement on the crowded supernatural scenes of the medieval *ars moriendi* – the classicized male Moriens faces his fate with a calm and confidence that devalues the mo-ment of death and views the event as the climax of life's prolonged act of dying.

Mary Sidney Herbert's translation of Philippe de Mornay's *Discours de la vie et la morte* is the best-known example of *ars moriendi* in a woman's hands, and typifies the period's interjection of classical Stoicism into the Christian consolatory tradition. Characteristically, the work closes with the familiar tag, "Die to live, Live to die."[36] While Edmund Molyneux's account of the good death of Herbert's mother gained wide readership in *Holinshed's Chronicles* and her brother's death was mourned in secular hagiographies, Herbert turned to De Mornay's philosophical treatise to gain an intellectual distance from the scene of death itself.[37] "In this decision," her editors conclude, "she followed the sixteenth-century shift in focus from depicting the deathbed scene like the original *Ars Moriendi* to instructing readers on the art of living as well as the art of dying."[38] The work must have had particular relevance to Herbert at the time, since she suffered the deaths of her three-year-old daughter Katherine, in 1584, and of her father, mother, and brother in 1586.[39] Thus the act of translation was also an act of self-consolation.

Published in 1592 in the same volume with Herbert's translation of Robert Garnier's *Marc Antonie*, the *Discourse* espouses a Stoic (specifically, Senecan) philosophy which is also reflected in the play.[40] Herbert's translation is almost unerringly faithful to De Mornay's original, so much so that it is virtually impossible to identify the woman's voice within the work. While the translation implicitly casts a woman as counselor, it is only through Herbert's ventriloquized performance of De Mornay's masculine counsel that she assumes this role. If the translation is virtually ungendered, though, the text's original language is not: in her fidelity to the French, Herbert translates the gender of her subject as well, with unsettling – and potentially revisionary – results. She writes:

Behold, now comes Death unto us: Behold her, whose approach we so much feare . . . Wee are afraide of her: but like little children of a vizarde, or of the Images of *Hecate*. Wee have her in horror: but because wee conceive her not such as she is, but ougly, terrible, and hideous: such as it pleaseth the Painters to represent unto us on a wall."[41]

While De Mornay's work conventionally argues that the fear of death is an inappropriate reaction to a theatrical and imagistic fraud, Herbert's translation startlingly refigures Sergeant Death as *La Morte*; an irresistible female force, as seductive as she is terrifying. The portrait of death as feminine is extremely unusual in early modern England, yet it appears twice in Herbert's corpus. In the period's most widely known example, Petrarch's *Triunfo della Morte*, Death appears as a woman "Black, and in black," as Herbert casts the image in her translation of the poem – despite the fact that the numerous visual renderings of the triumph, in woodcuts which popularized the work throughout Europe, routinely transform feminine Death into the more familiar "masculine" skeleton.[42]

Although Death's femininity in Herbert's works is arguably the unintentional by-product of diligent translation, it must certainly have struck contemporary readers of the *Discourse* and *Triumph of Death*, who may have associated the female translator with her feminized subject.

The figure of a feminine death at once departs from conventional renderings of death in the period and resonates with the treatment of Eve, as the mother of death, in the traditional *artes moriendi*. A block book *Ars Moriendi* now in the Columbina Library in Seville concludes with a diptych of woodcuts that remind its audience of both the female-authored origins of death and the female-born means of redemption.[43] In the first (figure 17), the Trinity affirms the masculinity of salvation in the enthroned figure of God the Father and the resurrected Christ who kneels before him to receive his crown of glory. In the second, though (figure 18), the work returns to Eden to recall the birth of death, depicting in the upper register the creation of Eve and, below Adam's recumbent form, the moment of the Fall itself. Together, the woodcuts associate the first Adam with the second, correcting the Fall in Eden with the Resurrection of Christ. As the final image of the *Ars Moriendi*, "The Creation of Eve and the Fall" calls to mind the crucial agency of women both in enabling death's assault on humankind and in alleviating its torments. The diptych argues that Eve's was a *felix culpa* permitting the Christian teleology of salvation to unfold and iconographically replacing fallen Eve with the Virgin who appears benevolently at Moriens' bedside in so many of the preceding images. Visually, literally, the *Ars Moriendi* enacts the meditative process described by Becon a century later: when Epaphroditus asks how he may avoid falling into despair on his deathbed, Philemon (a thinly-veiled Becon) responds, "Cast the eyes of your mind with strong faith on the Seed of the woman, which hath trodden down the serpent's head, and destroyed his power."[44]

In the face of the increasingly masculine scene of the Protestant deathbed and the Reformation exile of both the female saints and feminine mourning, Herbert's feminized figure of Death reminds us that implicit in death's genealogy is a maternal legacy. In the Virgin's absence, Becon's redemptive return to Genesis sanctifies Eve and justifies her crime as both the fateful origin of death and the means to Christian salvation. It is to this complex, polysemous female figure – at once the purveyor of death and the bearer of salvation – that Rachel Speght and Alice Sutcliffe turn to authorize their forays into the masculine discourse of consolation, creating and justifying the female-authored *ars moriendi* within and through the productive body of Eve.

17 "The Trinity." From *Ars Moriendi*.

18 "The Creation of Eve and the Fall of Man." From *Ars Moriendi*.

II

Joseph Swetnam's *Arraignment of Lewd, Idle, Froward, and Unconstant Women* opens with a grim portrait of Eve: "shee was no sooner made, but straightway, her mind was set upon mischiefe, for by her aspiring minde and wanton will, shee quickly procured mans fall, and therefore ever since they are and have beene a woe to man, and follow the line of their first leader."[45] *A Mouzell for Melastomus*, Rachel Speght's entry into the seventeenth-century pamphlet debate on women, offers a narrative of the Fall and a defense of Eve's role within it that parallel and prefigure Speght's treatment of Eden in her later work, *Mortalities Memorandum*. To refute the charge "that woman, though created good, yet by giving eare to Sathans temptations, brought death and misery upon all her posterity," she admits that Eve, "being the weaker vessel was with more facility to be seduced: Like as a Cristall glasse sooner receives a cracke then a strong stone pot."[46] The image of Eve as a crystal glass resonates with the literature of exemplarity (as suggested by its echo of Stubbes's title, *A Chrystal Glasse*) while, paradoxically, describing feminine weakness rather than virtue. This paradox begins the movement undertaken in *A Mouzell's* narrative of the Fall from an essentialist casting of sex in the Garden to a historicized, contingent notion of gender as manifested in culture. Eve, created good, is at once weak by nature and more attractive and refined than the strong stone pot that is man.[47] The double meaning of *glass* as both vessel and mirror invests Eve with significances that rest simultaneously in the material female body (a beautiful but imperfect container) and its social currency (a model of feminine behavior). Eve's troublesome exemplarity points to Speght's retrospective acculturation of the creation story itself and a reading of gender within that narrative that consistently overrides the original natures of the sexes toward affirming the social functions of gender as established by the Fall. Thus Speght argues that despite their different pre-lapsarian natures, man and woman commit "paralell" offenses (*Mouzell* 14): although woman sinned first, man's transgression was more serious since he, as the stronger vessel, "should have yeelded greatest obedience to God" (*Mouzell* 15). Thus joined in sin, both man and woman arrive at the same fate – although it is a fate enabled by woman: "by *Hevah's* blessed Seed (as Saint *Paul* affirmes) it is brought to passe, *that male and female are all one in Christ Jesus*" (*Mouzell* 16).

Speght's assertion of the equality of the sexes in Christ engages the familiar typology of the Fall as a *felix culpa* that both initiates and enables

Christian salvation. She exploits the gendering of that typology even as she describes its consequential eradication of gender. Grounded on the potentially radical restructuring of social hierarchies advocated by Galatians 3:28 ("There is neither Jew nor Greek, there is neither bond nor free, there is neither male nor female: for ye are all one in Christ Jesus"), Speght locates this merger of male and female within a chronology of the Fall that features woman in a complex central role as both cause and effect:

the first promise was made in Paradise, God makes to a woman, that by her Seede should the Serpents head be broken: whereupon *Adam* calles her *Hevah*, *life*, that as the woman had beene an occasion of his sinne, so should woman bring foorth the Saviour from sinne, which was in the fullnesse of time accomplished. (*Mouzell* 15–16)

This careful chronicle of events in Eden portrays the aftermath of the Fall as the founding moment not only of death, but of life as well – both intimately associated with Eve. Adam's calling of the woman by name, *Hevah* (in the Geneva Bible's rendering on which Speght, as a Calvinist, relied), inaugurates the redemptive march of Christian history. If the loss of Eden is a fall into death and mourning, it is also, Speght suggests, a fall into history, into culture, and the moment at which the pre-lapsarian sexes fall into gender.[48] Woman is the purveyor of death, but she is also *hevah* – the guarantor of life itself. Femininity finds its calling, as it were, in the consequences of events determined by the female.

Speght's defense of Eve by indicting Adam, while a strategy shared by other early modern women writers (not only those of the pamphlet debate, but Aemilia Lanyer as well), cannot be seen, in itself, as subversive of orthodoxy. The Church of England's *Certain Sermons or Homilies*, first published in 1562 and repeatedly reissued through the eighteenth century, instructed the faithful in its "Sermon of the State of Matrimonie" that "though a man had a companion in his fault, yet should he not thereby be without his fault . . . For Adam did lay the blame upon the woman, and she turned it unto the serpent: but yet neither of them was thus excused."[49] "The Second Homilie Concerning the death and Passion of our Saviour Christ" further explains:

When our great grandfather Adam had broken Gods commandement, in eating the apple forbidden him in Paradise, at the motion and suggestion of his wife, he purchased thereby, not onely to himselfe, but also to his posterity for ever, the just wrath and indignation of God, who according to his former sentence pronounced at the giving of the commandement, condemned both him and all his to everlasting death . . . [B]y this offence of onely *Adam*, death came upon all men to condemnation.[50]

Phillip Stubbes gives a similar interpretation to his wife in *A Chrsytal Glasse*, when Katherine confesses her belief that, "[man] had no sooner received the inestimable blessing of free will in innocency and integrity, but by hearkening to the poisoned suggestions of the wicked serpent, and by obeying his persuasions, he lost his free will, his integrity, and perfection" (B2). While Aughterson claims that Katherine's "rereading of the historical Fall in ungendered terms" carries "radical implications for women's power to speak and act in a religious field,"[51] Stubbes's elision of Eve, when read in light of these state-sanctioned Anglican sermons, seems less revisionary. And when we recall that this rereading is technically Phillip's rather than Katherine's, the exact location and quality of the woman's voice in this "radical" account is difficult to discern.[52] Yet a comparison of the passage with Speght's defense is nonetheless instructive, since *A Chrystal Glasse* suggests that both Stubbes's and Speght's textual performances of femininity (and perhaps Katherine Stubbes's non-textual deathbed performance) exploit common genderings of the Fall to exonerate Eve, on the one hand, and to authorize their female speakers, on the other.

Three times in her brief corpus of written works Speght treats the story of the Fall, each time inflecting it with gendered terms that resonate throughout her defense of women against Swetnam's arraignment, her autobiographical "Dreame," and the consolatory *Mortalities Memorandum*. Since original sin marks the birth of death, Speght's *ars moriendi* begins with a six-stanza rehearsal of the events in Eden that echoes the narrative's gendering in *A Mouzell*: "Thus eating both," Speght reaffirms, "they both did joyntly sinne, / And *Elohim* dishonoured by their act; / Doth ratifie, what he had earst decreed, That / *Death* must be the wages of their fact" (*MM* 61). Again she points toward the translation of Eve from woman to *life* and from sex to gender: while "In *Adam all men die*," she reminds us, "*Womans seede hath brooke the Serpents head*" (*MM* 61, 63). Finally, she associates the inaugural moment of mourning in the aftermath of the Fall with her own authorial project in *Mortalities Memorandum*:

> Considering then *Jehovahs* just decree,
> That man shall surely taste of *Death* through sinne,
> I much lament, when as I mete in mind,
> The dying state securely men live in;
> Excluding from their memories that day,
> When they from hence by *Death* must passe away.
>
> (*MM* 62)

As the epigraph which joins "A Dreame" to the *Memorandum* summarizes Speght's goal, "*Esto Memor Mortis*" (*MM* 60): the Fall into death prompts Speght's lament and her writing of the text as an exhortation to the Elect to "welcome *Death* with joy of heart" (*MM* 76).

In Speght's revision of Eden in "A Dreame," the uniquely gendered contours of her memorial project take shape and the characteristics of the female *ars moriendi* begin to emerge. In many ways, *Mortalities Memorandum* is a conventional entry in the consolatory literature of the period: Speght's handling of themes such as *contemptus mundi* (64, 66) and the good *versus* bad death (73–4, 76) and her imagery – life as a loan which God justly calls in (87), as a prison (64, 76), as a snake-filled garden (69) – are all consistent with the many Protestant arts of dying that appeared before and after her work (and, as we shall see, are all reiterated by Sutcliffe). Her avowed motives, too, are predictable and familiar: "from continuall thought of *Deaths* assault" – prompted by reading her book – "Doe sundry speciall benefits arise" (*MM* 85). Speght departs from convention, however, by prefacing *Mortalities Memorandum* with the autobiographical "Dreame," where we understand that this author has personal motives for composing a text which is at once an act of consolation *and* a work of mourning:

> But when I wak't, I found my dreame was true;
> For *Death* had ta'ne my mothers breath away,
> Though of her life it could not her bereave,
> Sith shee in glorie lives with Christ for aye;
> Which makes me glad, and thankefull for her blisse,
> Though still bewayle her absence, whom I misse.
>
> (*MM* 59–60)

Speght's lament for the post-lapsarian state of humankind here takes on the authenticity of direct experience. Valuing grief by experience, she unites the self-history recounted in "A Dreame" with the teleology of fall and redemption that opens *Mortalities Memorandum* and returns to Eden to anchor the feminine art of dying in the polysemous figure of Eve. Thus "A Dreame" rewrites Eden in the image of "*Eruditions* garden" (*MM* 51), a second paradise entered by way of *Experience* whose fruit, available to "both man and woman" (*MM* 53), is life-saving *Knowledge:* "'Tis life eternall God and Christ to *Know*" (*MM* 57).

Implicitly, Speght's defense of Eve as Hevah, *life,* exonerates women's desire for knowledge: thus "A Dreame" reverses the Fall by depicting her state of mind *prior* to her entry into Erudition's garden as "an irkesome griefe" (*MM* 51) that she later understands as Ignorance; a state of living–death (*MM* 55) which Thought "pitie[s] much and doe[s] bewayle" (*MM* 50) even as the speaker will "bewayle" the death of her mother at the poem's close (*MM* 60). Upon entering "the place / Where *Knowledge* growes," Speght like a second Eve is tempted by "the vertue of the plant" (*MM* 55) and learns that it is "a lawfull avarice, / To covet *Knowledge* daily more and more" (*MM* 57). Speght's rendering of knowledge as life – that is, knowledge of salvation through Christ as the guarantee of life after death – licenses her revisionary treatment of the woman in the garden and her reversal of the misogynistic censure of Eve's desire for knowledge. Insofar as the *ars moriendi* instructs Christians in the knowledge that remedies not only grief ("The onlie medicine for your maladie is *Knowledge*," *MM* 51) but also death ("'Tis life eternall, God and Christ to *Know*," *MM* 57), Speght's deployment of Eve as a figure for life-in-death or life-through-knowledge rationalizes the genre itself by constructing femininity at the fruitful juncture of these terms.

Speght portrays her education as the experience of a redeemed Eve in a second Eden that cures rather than kills. This portrayal informs the construction of the woman's voice in her work. Like Lanyer's clever defense of Eve's desire for knowledge in *Salve Deus Rex Judaeorum* ("Yet men will boast of Knowledge which he tooke / From *Eves* fair hand, as from a learned Booke," 85), Speght's defense of Eve is also an indictment of men's scholarly pretensions. Thus her second work implicitly continues the feminist critique of "masculinity . . . as a product of written language"[53] which is carried out explicitly in *A Mouzell for Melastomus*. "A Dreame" traces her educational history, including the unnamed "occurrence" (*MM* 57) that signaled the end of her studies, and records her foray into the pamphlet debate:

> But by the way I saw a full fed Beast
> Which roared like some monster, or a Devill.
> And on *Eves* sex he foamed filthie froth,
> As if that he had had the falling evil;
> To whom I went to free them from mishaps,
> And with a *Mouzell* sought to binde his chaps.
>
> (*MM* 58)

This quasi-heroic encounter with Swetnam suggests that misogyny is a monster best vanquished with learning. The studies of Speght's youth, although curtailed by the interruption that "made [her] rest content with that [she] had, / Which was but little, as effect doth show" (*MM* 57), are nonetheless adequate to enable her to defeat the vicious but untenable arguments of her opponent. The emphasis on experience as the source of knowledge in Speght's allegory of her education, as Simon Shepherd points out, opposes "the formal, received opinions of the 'authorities' and tradition,"[54] countering masculine authority with feminine experience as a defining feature of the woman's authorial voice. But the appearance of this secular beast is immediately followed in "A Dreame" by Speght's portrait of a second, more ferocious monster who is less easily tamed:

> Thus leaving them I passed on my way,
> But ere that I had little further gone,
> I saw a fierce insatiable foe,
> Depopulating Countries, sparing none;
> Without respect of age, sex, or degree,
> It did devoure, and could not daunted be.
>
> (*MM* 59)

The encounter with Death introduces a new level of experience into the poem and its author's autobiography ("with pearcing dart my mother deare it slew," *MM* 59) and the painful knowledge derived from that experience retroactively interprets and redirects Speght's literary career. Unlike her battle with Swetnam, for which she was prepared by years of learning grounded in youthful experience, her mother's death and the speaker's consequent mourning are a struggle for which she was entirely unprepared: "Her sodeine losse hath cut my feeble heart, / So deepe, that daily I indure the smart" (*MM* 60). The result is *Mortalities Memorandum* itself, an effort to "blaze the nature of this mortall foe" written both in response to Death's "cruell deed" and as a cure for the speaker's pain: "The profit may and will the paines requite" (*MM* 60). Speght's "paines" reveal her gendering of authority, since they are at once the conventional pains experienced by male and female writers alike in bringing forth the text as "off-spring" (*MM* 45) and the more personal pain of a mourning daughter for her absent mother. Again she turns to Eve, whose punishments for seeking knowledge – the fall into mourning and pain in childbirth – are simultaneously the results of death and its remedy. In acquiring direct knowledge of death in the loss of her mother, Speght stages in "A Dreame" the lesson of the *Memorandum* that follows: that mourning can only be overcome with the knowledge, enabled by Eve, that "by Christs *Death* grim *Mors* has lost his sting" (*MM* 75).

Mortalities Memorandum is dedicated to Speght's godmother, Marie Moundford, a figure whose presence in the text underscores the absence of Speght's recently deceased mother and counter-balances that of her father, invoked in an oft-quoted passage in the dedication: "I am now, as by a strong motive induced (for my rights sake) to produce and divulge this off-spring of my indevour, to prove them further futurely who have formerly deprived me of my due, imposing my abortive upon the father of me, but not of it" (*MM* 45). Speght's concern to locate her authorial presence at the fertile juncture of maternity and mourning – that is, in the figure of Eve – acknowledges both the paternal legacy of textual erudition which produced the "abortive" *Mouzell for Melastomus* and the maternal heritage of experience, associated with the female culture of mourning of which *Mortalities Memorandum* and its dedicatee are both products and *exempla*. Thus she assures Moundford, "I would not have any one falsely thinke that this *Memorandum* is presented to your person to implie in you defect of those duties which it requires; but sincerely to denote you as a paradigma to others; for what it shews to be done, shewes but what you have done" (*MM* 46). The language of duty with which Speght describes the lessons of her work, like the personal experience of loss that inflects her *ars moriendi*, energizes the material body of women's mourning in post-Reformation England and exploits the period's common association of women with the duties and rites attending the demise of the physical body. Herbert's trail-blazing translation of De Mornay's consolatory treatise, with its startling figure of feminized death, offers an important precedent for writers like Speght and Sutcliffe. But the deathbed performances of women such as Katherine Stubbes and Katherine Brettergh, and the good deaths of untold numbers of forgotten women in early modern England, provide persuasive, immediate models for women approaching the masculine discourse of consolation who find in feminine mourning – a recognized site of particularly volatile, powerful expression – fertile ground on which to establish their rights to public speech.

III

Like Speght's, Alice Sutcliffe's entry into the discourse of death takes place under the rubric of Experience: addressing her female dedicatees, Katherine and Susanna Villiers, widow and sister of the recently deceased George Villiers, Duke of Buckingham, Sutcliffe writes:

I have chosen a *Subject* not altogether *Pleasing*; but my ayme is, that it may prove *Profitable*, having observed in this short course of my *Pilgrimage*, how apt *Man* is, not to thinke of his *Mortalitie*, which stealeth upon him as a *Thiefe in the night*: *Experience* teacheth mee, that there is no *Action* wisely undertaken, whereof the *End* is not fore-called in the first place, howsoever it bee last put in execution. (A5–A5v)

This work born of observation and experience rather than textual erudition, again like Speght's, addresses itself to a surrogate mother: Sutcliffe says to Katherine Villiers, "you . . . have been more than a Mother to mee, I having onely from her received life, but next under God from your Grace, & your honorable *Sister* the being both of mee and mine" (A6v). She further cultivates the communal relationship between female mourners by pointing out that she as well as Buckingham's female family members, "In peerless woe . . . still lament [his] fate" (a1), casting herself and her patron as mother and daughter joined in grief. Finally, like *Mortalities Memorandum*, Sutcliffe's conventional *ars moriendi* is unconventional in its decision to append to the death manual proper a poem exploring the specifically feminine aspects of her subject in the figure of Eve: the eighty-eight-stanza "Of our losse by Adam, and our gayne by Christ" returns to Eden not only to rehearse the female-authored origins of death ("Wicked woman," she writes, "to cause thy husband dye," 144) but also to vindicate Eve as the enabler of the life-saving knowledge that her "Seed shall bruise the Serpents head" (150).

Meditations of Mans Mortalitie is similar to Speght's *Mortalities Memorandum* in tone and outlook. Sutcliffe also relies on the Geneva Bible and takes pains to distinguish between the "fearefull end of the Wicked" (1) and "the joyfull end of the godly" (57), who "feareth not Death, because through all [their] life [they] learned to dye" (62). Sutcliffe, like Speght, revisits the commonplaces of the *ars moriendi* throughout her work. Thus for Speght's "Life is but lent, we owe it to the Lord" (*MM* 87), Sutcliffe informs us that "after Death [man] must give account of his Stewardship, for [goods] are not his, but lent him of the Lord" (4). Speght compares life to "a Ship which swiftly slides the Sea" (*MM* 86), and Sutcliffe urges the Christian to "prove the Pilot of thy owne Ship, which now lyeth floating on the seas of this troublesome World" (12). While it is enticing to imagine that Sutcliffe may be directly imitating Speght, this supposition cannot be supported on the basis of these clichés. Rather, both works give us female authors, on the one hand, utilizing and mastering the masculine conventions of the genre and, on the other, supplementing them with textual gestures intended to define the specifically feminine characteristics of the *ars moriendi* in the woman's hands. In Sutcliffe's work, a series of commendatory verses by male poets and the closing poem, "Of our losse by Adam, and our gayne by Christ," constitute such gestures.

To counter-balance the female mourners assembled by Sutcliffe's dedication, a community of male literati is established within the *Meditations* by commendatory verses by Ben Jonson, Thomas May, George Wither, Peter Heywood, and Francis Lenton. Sutcliffe juxtaposes the female culture of mourning, grounded on women's common experience of loss, with the male culture of textual production and its values. While the text assumes that Sutcliffe is naturally included in the former group, her uneasy relationship to the latter is the primary subject of the commendatory verses. In fact, her relationship with these writers seems to have been virtually non-existent: both Lenton and Wither state in their poems that they never met Sutcliffe, and Wither's address of his poem "To Mr. John Sutcliffe Esq. upon the receipt of this Booke written by his Wife" suggests that she may have gained only indirect access to this circle of male writers through her husband's court connections:

> Sir, I receiv'd your Booke with acceptation,
> And thus returne a due congratulation,
> For that good Fortune, which hath blest your life
> By making you the *Spouse* of such a *Wife*.
> Although I never saw her, yet I see,
> The *Fruit*, and by the *Fruit* I judge the *Tree*.
>
> (n.p.)

Indeed, Wither's description of the book as John's announces Sutcliffe's exile from the community of male writers and ratifies her text only on the basis of her wifely obedience to a well-connected husband. The volume's title page, too, authorizes Sutcliffe's work by calling on her husband's presence and position: "Written, By Mrs. Alice Sutcliffe," it states, "Wife of John Sutcliffe Esquire, Groome of his Majesties most Honourable Privie Chamber" (A2).[55] Lenton's encomium agrees that it is Sutcliffe's identity as wife that most qualifies her as author: "Great Ladies that to vertue are inclin'd / See here the pious practice of a wife" (n.p.). As a group, the commendatory poems praise Sutcliffe and her text, but also definitively describe the learned woman as a rare exception rather than the rule. Wither condescendingly implies that women's writing can only be of value if it is manly, while hinting (in the act of denial) that men may, in fact, have written this extraordinary work and others like it:

> I am not of their mind, who if they see,
> Some *Female-Studies* fairely ripened be,
> (With Masculine successe) do peevishly,
> Their worths due honour unto them deny,
> By overstrictly censuring the same;
> Or doubting whether from themselves it came,
> For, well I know Dame *Pallas* and the *Muses*,
> Into that *Sexe*, their faculties infuses,
> As freely as to *Men*.
>
> (n.p.)

Heywood, too, admits, "It seems to me above thy Sex and State, / Some heavenly Sparke doth thee illuminate," but insists that Sutcliffe "Live still a praise, but no example to / Others, to hope, as thou hast done, to doe" (n.p.). Lenton concurs, "For she is Rara Avis in our *Nation*," and May encourages readers, "nor disdaine to take / that knowledge, which a Womans skill can bring. / All are not Syren-notes that women sing" (n.p.).

If the commendatory verses exclude Sutcliffe from engaging in the masculine literary and cultural economies that they exemplify and espouse, her treatment of the Fall in her closing poem deploys the figure of Eve to respond to their exclusionary poetics and to authorize her publication in the *ars moriendi* genre. In this respect, the inclusion of the poem in the volume parallels Speght's feminist scripting of Eve's central role in the Christian teleology of salvation, as the source of both death and life, and echoes her defense of women's education in "A Dreame." Like Speght, Sutcliffe describes the Fall as a lapse into gender, mourning, and history. She addresses Eve:

> Now seizes on your sicknesse Griefes and Feares,
> Which night and day with trouble will torment;
> Your sweet Delights, are turned all to teares,
> And now what you have done with woe repent!
> Nothing but Griefes and Feares and sad annoyes,
> You now possesse, in stead of endlesse Joyes.
>
> (148)

Sutcliffe's Eden shares with Speght's the notion that sex is translated into gender as a result of the Fall, when masculine and feminine social roles are assigned in the gender-specific punishments meted out by God:

> For as thou now conceives thy seed in sinne,
> So in great sorrow thou must bring it foorth,
> The gaine which thou by that same fruit didst winne,

Thou now dost find to be of little worth:
Obedience to thy Husband yeeld thou must,
And both must Dye and turned be to Dust.

(145–6)

While Speght's vindication of women's knowledge emphasizes the naming of Eve in Genesis 3:20, Sutcliffe turns to Genesis 3:16 to stress woman's great sorrow in childbirth and the imposition of the sentence of wifely obedience as concurrent with the appearance of death.[56] As Speght manipulates the figure of *Hevah* to support her authorial presence in *Mortalities Memorandum*, Sutcliffe's performance of wifely obedience in *Meditations of Mans Mortalitie* depends upon her affiliation with post-lapsarian Eve.

While Sutcliffe authorizes her textual performance throughout her "Glasse of . . . Mortality" (n.p.) by accepting a role much like Katherine Stubbes's as "a Mirrour of woman-hood" (A2v), she also stages an implicit challenge to the exclusionary masculine poetics of the volume's commendatory verses by tracing in Eve the origins of masculine erudition in feminine pride. May's assurance that "All are not Syren-notes that women sing" resonates ironically throughout the volume's frequent episodes of *contemptus mundi* where earthly temptations are compared to "the singing of Syrens" (82): as the closing poem states, Satan's "Mermaide Songs are onely sweet in sound, / Approach them not, lest Death thy life doth wound" (193). The misogynistic reading of Eve as an agent of satanic temptation, of course, lies behind May's assumption that some, if not all, of women's speech tempts men to sin. This conventional rendering of Eve's guilt is rehearsed by Sutcliffe as well, when she informs the Eve of her poem, "T'is [*sic*] not saying, the Serpent thee deceiv'd / That can excuse the fault thou didst commit" (145). Although Sutcliffe here seems to affirm Eve's guilt, her admonition echoes the Church of England's orthodox position ("Adam did lay the blame upon the woman, and she turned it unto the serpent: but yet neither of them was thus excused") and argues, as do the sermons quoted above, the mutual guilt of Adam and Eve. It is *Adam's* disobedience, she explains, rather than Eve's that signals the Fall:

> This onely sinne on all Mankinde did draw,
> Gods heavy wrath, for this, we suffer still.
> By ADAMS breaking Gods commanded Law;
> Sinne with a poysned dart our soules did kill:
> For through the breach thereof there entered death,
> For so 'twas sentenced by Gods owne breath.
>
> (167)

Moreover, the intimacy of Sutcliffe's direct address to Eve serves effectively to tell the story of the Fall from Eve's point of view, and emphasizes the relationship between the female author and her female protagonist as learned women; women experienced in death and knowledgeable of the means to life. Thus Sutcliffe presents the events in Eden, from mourning to joy, through Eve's eyes:

> No, you are in a laborinth of woe,
> And endlesse is the maze in which you goe.
> Yet courage, Woman, whose weake spirit's dead,
> GOD in his love a helpe for thee hath found,
> Bee sure thy Seed shall bruise the Serpent's head,
> CHRIST by his Death shall Sathan deadly wound.
>
> (150)

The *felix culpa* serves for Sutcliffe, as it does for Speght, to emphasize woman's centrality in redefining death as "a True guide to Eternall blisse" and "Portall to Heaven, by which we enter must" (177). As such, the poem ends by reminding the faithful of the benefits of death ("Now ends all sorrowes, now all griefes are done," 180), and offering the prayer that, "Unto this Happinesse and place of Joy, / In thy good time sweet Saviour Christ us bring" (199).

Sutcliffe's vindication of Eve's "syren-notes" takes one final turn that parallels Speght's indictments of masculine scholarly pretensions in her allegorical encounters with the "full fed Beast," Swetnam, and with the "insatiable foe," Death. As a result of the Fall, Sutcliffe explains, Satan's "Syren songs mans mortall Death intends; / And hee must Dye that thereto his eare lends" (162). More precisely, this state of affairs is a direct result of Eve's desire for knowledge: "'Twas Pride, made EVE desire still to excell; / When Sathan said, as Gods, you then shall be; / Incontinent, she tasted of that Tree" (160). She continues with an etiology of death that is also a history of human knowledge, tracing the origins of both to Eve's transgression:

> This Lep'rous sinne, infected so the bloud,
> That through her off-spring, it hath wholly runne;
> Before the child can know, the bad from good;
> It straight is proud, Nature, this hurt hath done.
> A female sinne, it counted was to be,
> But now Hermaphrodite, proved is shee.
>
> (161)

Sutcliffe's image of an Eve Hermaphrodite repeats in contemporary secular terms the implications of the parallel offenses of man and woman in original sin. Recalling Lanyer's comment, "Yet men will boast of Knowledge which he tooke / From *Eves* fair hand, as from a learned Booke," Eve Hermaphrodite makes Sutcliffe's case that masculinity, both as a cultural commodity and a biological fact, is figuratively constructed in and dependent upon a woman. As concurrent results of the Fall, Eve's maternity causes and cures death, while her transgressive desire for knowledge authors the "masculinity . . . as a product of written language" that the volume's commendatory poems so ably embody. Eve Hermaphrodite, finally, is a figure for Sutcliffe's own hermaphroditic authorial voice, which combines (in Wither's terms) "*Female-Studies*" with "Masculine successe." For Sutcliffe, as for Speght, the "full fed Beasts" (Sutcliffe 157) of sin that threaten to consume humankind can only be tamed with the life-saving knowledge enabled by Eve, that "[woman's] Seed shall bruise the Serpents head" (150). Thus Sutcliffe provides an image of the Christian's battle against Satan that recalls Speght's struggles with her own full-fed beasts:

> Who on this Panther skinne doth gazing stand,
> Had need beware who lyes in wayte to catch,
> Who holdes a Woolfe by th'eares but with one hand,
> Must with the other muzzell up his chaps:
> If better thou dost get leave not off so,
> But of all meanes to hurt, deprive thy Foe.
>
> (171–2)

It is the duty of "Eve's sex" (*MM* 58), Sutcliffe and Speght argue, to capture, tame, and anatomize the body of death in the female-authored *ars moriendi*, not only for the consolation of Christians but also in defense of women's rights to acquire and display knowledge in overcoming the "mortall foe[s]" (*MM* 60) that would silence them.

For Speght and Sutcliffe, women approaching the masculine *ars moriendi*, Eve offers a rich, productive figure for locating the woman's voice in the feminized merger of life, death, and knowledge that a feminist reading of the Fall affords. These women engage in the conventional, masculine discourse of consolation, but also suggest that they, *as* women, are uniquely qualified to treat the matter of death due to the cultural affiliation of early modern women with the physical body of death in the period's gendering of grief, and licensed by the legacy of Eve's fortunate fall into death, gender, and history in Eden. Their additions to the *ars moriendi* of poems that energize the female culture of mourning within the genre emphasize woman's experiential knowledge of death and her foundational role in Christian salvation. Speght and Sutcliffe thus open the genre to the woman's voice, rooted not in the physical bodies of these authors but in their fruitful constructions of femininity in the body of Eve; creations which allow them, in turn, to script their own performances of femininity as intimately tied to the mat(t)er of death.

IV

Over seventy years after the appearance of Alice Sutcliffe's *ars moriendi*, in the same year that Thomas Greenhill's *Nekrokedeia* claimed Mary Magdalene's art of embalming as the sole property of male surgeons, Lady Frances Norton published her *Memento Mori* (1705), where she, too, encourages the reader with the exemplary drama of death: "There is no Spectacle in the World so Profitable or more terrible, than to behold a Dying Man, who carries Heaven and Earth wrapp'd up in his Body; at which Time each Part returns Homeward."[57] At the dawn of the eighteenth century, Norton continues the legacy of her early modern predecessors, both male and female. In her work, the movements inaugurated in the post-Reformation *ars moriendi* reach their culmination. Thus her overall thesis states that "the Duty of Life is to Prepare for Death." She discounts entirely the agon of the deathbed as she recasts the art of dying as an art of living. Rather than describing the deathbed assaults of Satan's temptations, Norton condemns daily "Idleness, the Devil's Agent, which obstructs our Preparation for Death."[58] She argues vigorously against the possibility of eleventh-hour penance and salvation: "Death-bed Penitents, who have spent their Lives viciously, mean to mock God," she insists, "they would reap what they sowed not." Indeed, Norton points out that, "it were vain I should intend these ensuing Discourses to be read or studied by Sick or Dying Persons," since the infirmities of the final illness are likely to prevent the fruitful study of the text. On the contrary, care must be taken to die daily, well before the imposing arrival of Sergeant Death, since, "concerning Sinners really under the Arrest of Death, God hath made no Death-bed Covenant; the Scripture hath recorded no Promises, and given no Instructions for them."[59] Once Moriens is confined to the prison of the deathbed, the work's lessons come too late.

Norton's work is copious and inclusive in its recycling of the traditional wisdom of the Protestant *artes*. Her approach, not unlike Samuel Ward's in his catalogue of dying words, is to quote a variety of authorities on the subject at hand and tie together these quotations with her own prose. Her topics are conventional: good deaths and bad deaths compared; that grief must be moderate at the death of friends; that a well-spent life is always prepared for death; *contemptus mundi* revisited ("The Calamities of Life help to sweeten the bitter cup of Death").[60] Like Herbert, Norton is at ease with classical Stoicism, and quotes Seneca frequently to prove "The Happiness . . . of a Well-spent Life at the Hour of Death."[61] Throughout the treatise, the sex of its author is impossible to determine: Norton completely and successfully assumes the masculine voice of consolation, veiling her sex in the chorus of quotations that she employs.

The heritage of Speght's and Sutcliffe's female-authored *artes moriendi*, however, also informs Lady Norton's work. In the text's dedication, the material body of early modern women's communal culture of mourning once again appears to authorize her entry into the genre and to cast her work of comfort as also a work of mourning. Writing to Elizabeth Hambleton, Norton stresses the two women's shared sorrow at the loss of their daughters:

> Both your Ladyship and my Self have lately seen and felt such Sorrow for the Death and Departure of our Nearest and Dearest Friends . . . Death hath come so near to me as to fetch a Portion from my very Heart, that I cannot choose but dig my own Grave, and place my Coffin in my Eye, by these Reflecting Meditations of Death. In Scripture, where Sorrows are illustrated to the Height, God is pleased to have them compared to the Mother that mourneth for her Only Child. You can witness, Dear Madam, that She whom I have lost was not only my Only One, but in all Particulars an Extraordinary One. What Allowance must then be given for my Grief and yours; to lose Her whose Life was a Comfort, and whose Death (which signified a Fore-taste of that Glory) hath almost cost me mine!"[62]

Joined in mutual, empathetic mourning, Norton and her female dedicatee understand consolation as the difficult product of inconsolable grief: "Thus, as to a Dear Friend that hath often simpathiz'd with me in my Affliction," Norton concludes, "I hereby endeavour to suppress yours; since any Easement of your Trouble mitigates mine."[63]

Like her female predecessors, Norton insists upon the relevance of her intimate female experience of the body of death to her consolatory gestures, grounding her art of dying in her vivid and brutal memory of the physical body of death over which she has grieved. This insistence rewrites the post-Reformation scene of death, populating it once again with female mourners whose grief is revised and reinvested not only with emotive and affective power but also with the possibility of consolation based on a mutual sorrow derived from lived experience. Women such as Speght, Sutcliffe, and Norton cast themselves as sisters of Magdalene: like the mournful deathbed attendant of the medieval *ars moriendi* whose jar of balm offers a permanent reminder of the physical body of death and women's intimacy with it, these women take their place in the scene of death, performing the necessary and valuable functions of watching and mourning. Despite post-Reformation devaluations of women's works of mourning, these texts and the material practices from which they emerge and which they transmit bespeak a lasting, if overlooked, legacy whose meaning has only begun to be known.

Codicil: "a web of blacke"

When Isabella Whitney's "Lamentacion of a Gentilwoman upon the death of her late deceased frend William Gruffith Gent," appeared in Thomas Proctor's 1578 *Gorgeous Gallery of Gallant Inventions*, a prefatory verse promoted the poem as that of a woman but maintained the author's anonymity:

> A doubtfull, dying, dolefull, Dame,
> Not fearing death, nor forcing life:
> Nor caring ought for flitting fame,
> Emongst such sturdy stormes of strife:
> Here doth shee mourne and write her will,
> Upon her liked Lovers ende.[1]

The lament composed by a *dying* Dame with no pretensions to publicity artlessly but violently mourns, as (the period held) women tend to do. The author's impending death, a sorrowful response to Gruffith's, is a condition of her publication that responds to the early modern association of femininity with the physical body, including the body *in mortis*, and aligns the poem with mothers' legacies and Whitney's own "Will and Testament."[2]

Like the preface, the elegy that follows both veils and suggests the author's identity, while aggressively advertising her sex. The "Lamentacion" thoroughly understands itself as a public document and stages the possibility of a woman's publication as intimately associated with her experience and expression of grief. Whitney's bold and deliberate engagement with the post-Reformation gendering of grief earns the poem its place as a summary text with which to conclude this study. The elegy adopts and interrogates women's public rituals of lament, specifically the culturally sanctioned donning of mourning garments, finding points of contact between the female culture of mourning and women's access to print. The sartorial history of mourning in the period sought not to suppress

242

women's grief but to showcase it, demonstrating the persistence of the domestic and familial relationships that contained and defined early modern women. Whitney's elegy, accordingly, manipulates and troubles the gendering of grief to construct its speaker, to inflect the textual work of mourning with women's material responses to death, and to script her entry into print.

The "Lamentacion" explicitly meditates on Whitney's publication of her illicit grief (illicit, that is, because performed by Gruffith's lover, not his widow), and attempts to validate an unorthodox affect resulting from an unlawful union. Predictably, the speaker complains of her culture's insistence on moderate grief, commenting on the necessary work of women mourners and the contradictory restraints placed upon them:

> To bluntish blockes (I see) I doo complayne,
> And reape but onely sorrow for my share:
> For wel I know that Gods nor sprites can cure,
> The paynes that I for *Gruffith* doo endure.
>
> (117–20)[3]

The complaint indicts the celestial auditors (gods and sprites) who cannot console the speaker, and implies that more mundane readers may be equally unsympathetic, unwilling or unable to pity her careful state. While both meanings are fraught with challenges to the commonplaces of consolation, the latter directly questions the *place* of women's mourning, a debated locus that provides Whitney with a metaphor for female textual production. Evidence suggests that the "Lamentacion," in addition to appearing as an extra in Proctor's *Gorgeous Gallery*, was also issued as a broadside ballad, a genre which was a remarkably active forum for public lament and memorialization.[4] Whitney refers to this popular culture of mourning when she contrasts her poem with one posted for public readership at St. Paul's, where "elegies and ballads smeared the doors, windows, and advertising posts in and near the building:"[5]

> But *William* had a worldy freend in store,
> Who writ his end to small effect (God knowes)
> But *J.* and *H.* his name did show no more,
> Rime Ruffe it is, the common sentence goes,
> > It hangs at Pawles as every man goes by,
> > One ryme too low, an other rampes too hye.
>
> (37–42)

Whitney condemns J. H.'s elegy not only for its superficiality (as the product of a "worldly freend") but also for its over-exposure, its reduction of sentiment for Gruffith to the level of the common street where, "as every man goes by," sincere praise for his memory and grief at his passing are impossible. Instead of worldly praise, Whitney insists on her intimacy with Gruffith and, consequently, on the sincerity of her elegy's grief. The "Lamentacion" roots its poetics of sorrow in female mourner's material experience, promising to improve upon the male-authored elegy with natural expressions of grief proceeding from the woman writer's pen:

> Eche man doth mone, when faythfull freends bee dead,
> And paynt them out, as well as wit doo serve:
> But I, a Mayde, am forst to use my head,
> To wayle my freend (whose fayth) did prayse deserve:
> > Wit wants to will: alas? no skill I have,
> > Yet must I needes deplore my *Gruffithes* grave.
>
> > > > (7–12)

While Whitney's "forst" sorrow must be released, the "Lamentacion" continually refers to the hazards of women's public laments and the dangers attending their appearance in print. This indictment of cultural prohibitions on women's speech and mourning informs Whitney's mode of address (to "good Ladyes"), and her daring approaches to and pragmatic retreats from public expression:

> My mournfull Muse (good Ladyes) take in worth,
> And spare to speake the worst, but judge the best:
> For this is all, that I dare publish forth,
> The rest recorded is, within my brest:
> > And there is lodg'd, for ever to remayne,
> > Till God doth graunt (by death) to ease my payne.
>
> > > > (73–8)

Similarly, she closes the poem by vowing to "drinke up all, my sorrow secretly" (123). "And sith I dare not mourne, to open showe," she concludes, "With secret sighes and teares, my hart shall flow" (125–6).

Rooted firmly in the material culture of women's mourning, the "Lamentacion" stubbornly insists upon the value and importance of women's experiences and expressions of grief. Whitney's concern is, of course, to memorialize Gruffith: "for his prayse," she assures us, "my tristive tunes I send" (102). But the poem's main focus is on the female mourner rather than the male decedent, and Whitney devotes most of its space to recording the speaker's inconsolable sorrow and considering its implications for women's public speech. Her romantic history with Gruffith is recalled in a blazon anatomizing not the beloved corpse but the mourner's female body as defined by sartorial symbolism:

> For *William* white: for *Gruffith*, green: I wore,
> And red, longe since did serve to please my minde:
> Now, blacke, I weare, of mee, not us'd before,
> In liew of love, alas? this losse I find:
> > Now must I leave, both, White and Green, and Red,
> > And wayle my freend who is but lately dead.
>
> (13–18)

Because the speaker is merely Gruffith's lover and not his widow, her public expression of grief is illegitimate. This realization precipitates an affective crisis that figures both Whitney's desire to justify bringing the poem to print and the speaker's wish to claim the power of public mourning:

> Yet hurtfull eyes, doo bid me cast away,
> In open show, this carefull blacke attyre:
> Because it would, my secret love bewray,
> And pay my pate, with hatred for my hyre:
> > Though outwardly, I dare not wear the same,
> > Yet in my heart, a web of blacke I frame.
>
> (19–24)

The speaker's desire to wear black violates the function of early modern mourning attire, which was to guarantee the transfer of property by signaling the widow's continued submission to her husband's will.[6] Detailed restrictions on mourning enforced by the College of Arms both approved and limited women's public performances of grief, authorizing the moderate mourning of women firmly contained within the patriarchal household and outlawing the grief of those who mourned excessively, or ostentatiously, or who had no right to mourn if excluded from the decedent's immediate kin. Manipulating these restrictions on mourning, Whitney constructs the female author-as-mourner through her figurative encrypting of grief in an internalized "web of blacke." Although she denies that she is "*Minervaes* mate" (2)," it is under the aegis of Minerva, the goddess of weaving and writing, that she authorizes her elegy, playing upon women's association with weaving to justify her text and her grief. Removed from the social currency of public mourning and placed within the privacy of the speaker's breast, the web of black emblematizes the melancholic incorporation characteristic of early modern women's elegies, figures the textual work of mourning itself, and summarizes the female elegist's paradoxical approach to publication. By admitting that she "dare not mourn to open showe," Whitney advances her textual work of mourning and indicts the culture which finds no place for it.

This book has demonstrated how the gendering of rival styles of grief in post-Reformation England enabled constructions of male and female subjects in and through textual and cultural lamentational forms. Excessive mourning, condemned by reformers as effeminate, is defended by Whitney's improvisations on the essentialist view that intimately ties women's passions to their sexed bodies. Her framing of an internalized web of black effectively symbolizes the social creation of post-Reformation femininity within and by means of the work of mourning, revealing the performative aspects of the gendering of grief in textual and cultural forms. As a performative act, mourning engages gender-specific forms, gestures, and words to construct male and female subjects as essentially different. Mourning creates gender *as* natural: thus women appear to grieve artlessly and excessively by nature while manly sorrow is essentially stoic. Although nothing precludes the deployment of feminine gestures of mourning by the male writer, or vice versa, differences between male and female authors' interactions with conventional lamentational forms, established across a broad reading of representative early modern works, suggest different literary and cultural histories of men's and women's grief. Whitney's weaving into her poem of the semiotics of early modern death and its rituals sheds light on the distinctive features of women's writing as they have emerged throughout these chapters, and offers lessons in the need to historicize such complex and remarkable performances of affect and the critical language with which we treat the matter of death.

Notes

INTRODUCTION

1 William Shakespeare, *Henry V*, in G. Blakemore Evans (ed.), *The Riverside Shakespeare*, 2nd edn. (Boston: Houghton Mifflin, 1996), 2.3.3–6. Unless otherwise noted, all references to Shakespeare's plays are to this edition.

2 Sharon T. Strocchia, *Death and Ritual in Renaissance Florence* (Baltimore: Johns Hopkins University Press, 1992), p. 119.

3 See Otto Werdmuller, *A Most frutefull, pithye and learned Treatyse, how a Christen man ought to behave himself in the daunger of death*, trans. Miles Coverdale (London: E. Allde for William Blackwell, 1595?), p. 223. Unless otherwise noted, all subsequent citations are to this edition.

4 Abraham Darcie, *Funerall Teares (Fraunces, Duchess Dowager of Richmond and Lenox, Etc., her Funerall Teares)* (London: J. Beale for R. Field, 1624), n.p., lines 38–9.

5 Juliana Schiesari, *The Gendering of Melancholia: Feminism, Psychoanalysis, and the Symbolics of Loss in Renaissance Literature* (Ithaca: Cornell University Press, 1992), p. 18. See Steven Mullaney, "Mourning and Misogyny: *Hamlet, The Revenger's Tragedy* and the Final Progress of Queen Elizabeth I," *Shakespeare Quarterly* 45 (1994), 141, for an opposing view.

6 See Katharine Goodland, "'Why Should Calamity Be Full of Words?' The Representation of Women's Laments for the Dead in Medieval English and Shakespearean Drama" (PhD dissertation, Purdue University, 1999), pp. 43–157. I am grateful to Dr. Goodland for sharing her dissertation with me.

7 William Shakespeare, *1 Henry IV*, 5.3.59.

8 For a similar inverse pietà, see William Shakespeare, *King Lear*, 5.3.257.

9 I do not mean to imply that domestic space in the period is always feminine, or to overlook the well-documented hierarchy of gender that existed within the household. Rather, the domestic work associated with death was performed almost exclusively by women. On the gendering of domestic space, see Lorna Hutson, *The Usurer's Daughter: Male Friendships and Fiction of Women in Sixteenth-Century England* (New York and London: Routledge, 1994), and Lena Cowen Orlin, *Private Matters and Public Culture in Post-Reformation England* (Ithaca: Cornell University Press, 1994).

10 Shakespeare, *Henry V*, 2.3.10–26.

11 Werdmuller, *Most frutefull*, pp. 170–1.

12 Ibid., pp. 173–87.

13 David Cressy, *Birth, Marriage and Death: Ritual, Religion, and the Life-Cycle in Tudor and Stuart England* (Oxford University Press, 1997), p. 429.

14 F. G. Emmison, *Essex Wills (England) 1558–1565*, 2 vols. (Washington, DC: National Genealogical Society, 1982), vol. 1, pp. 184 and 244.

15 See Frances E. Dolan, *Whores of Babylon: Catholicism, Gender and Seventeenth-Century Print Culture* (Ithaca: Cornell University Press, 1999) and Catherine Belsey, *Shakespeare and the Loss of Eden* (New Brunswick: Rutgers University Press, 1999) for recent studies that share my methodology.

16 See Cressy, *Birth, Marriage and Death*; Christopher Daniell, *Death and Burial in Medieval England, 1066–1550* (New York and London: Routledge, 1997); Clare Gittings, *Death, Burial and the Individual in Early Modern England* (London: Croom Helm, 1984); Ralph A. Houlbrooke, *Death, Religion and the Family in England, 1480–1750* (Oxford: Clarendon Press, 1997); Bruce Gordon and Peter Marshall (eds.), *The Place of the Dead: Death and Remembrance in Late Medieval and Early Modern Europe* (Cambridge University Press, 2000); and Julian Litten, *The English Way of Death: The Common Funeral Since 1450* (London: R. Hale, 1991). The works of Philippe Ariès have had far-reaching influence: see *Western Attitudes Towards Death From the Middle Ages to the Present Time*, trans. Patricia Ranum (Baltimore: Johns Hopkins University Press, 1974); *The Hour of our Death*, trans. Helen Weaver (New York: Knopf, 1981); and *Images of Man and Death*, trans. Janet Lloyd (Cambridge, MA: Harvard University Press, 1985). Notable treatments of death in literary works include Nancy Lee Beaty, *The Craft of Dying: A Study of the Literary Tradition of the Ars Moriendi in England* (New Haven: Yale University Press, 1970); Lynn Enterline, *The Tears of Narcissus: Melancholia and Masculinity in Early Modern Writing* (Stanford University Press, 1995); Michael Neill, *Issues of Death: Mortality and Identity in English Renaissance Tragedy* (Oxford: Clarendon Press, 1997); and Schiesari, *Gendering of Melancholia*.

17 See Paul S. Fritz, "The Undertaking Trade in England: Its Origins and Early Development, 1660–1830," *Eighteenth-Century Studies* 28 (1994–5): 241–53.

18 See Diane Bornstein, "The Style of the Countess of Pembroke's Translation of Philippe de Mornay's *Discours de la vie et de la mort*," in Margaret Patterson Hannay (ed.), *Silent But For the Word: Tudor Women as Patrons, Translators, and Writers of Religious Works* (Kent State University Press, 1985), p. 127.

19 Wendy Wall, *The Imprint of Gender: Authorship and Publication in the English Renaissance* (Ithaca: Cornell University Press, 1993), pp. 296–310.

20 Sarah Tarlow, *Bereavement and Commemoration: An Archaeology of Mortality* (Oxford: Basil Blackwell, 1999), p. 32.

21 Quoted in Louise Schleiner, *Tudor and Stuart Women Writers* (Bloomington: Indiana University Press, 1994), pp. 209–10.

22 See Ramie Targoff, "The Performance of Prayer: Sincerity and Theatricality in Early Modern England," *Representations* 60 (1997), 49–65, for a related argument.

23 Tarlow, *Bereavement and Commemoration*, p. 24.

24 Schiesari, *Gendering of Melancholia*, p. 18.

25 Enterline, *Tears of Narcissus*, pp. 8–9.

26 See Mary Beth Rose, "Where are the Mothers in Shakespeare?" *Shakespeare Quarterly* 42 (1991), 291 and 295.

27 Judith Butler, *Gender Trouble: Feminist Theory and Psychoanalytic Discourse* (New York and London: Routledge, 1990), p. 7.

28 Thomas Laqueur, *Making Sex: Body and Gender from the Greeks to Freud* (Cambridge, MA: Harvard University Press, 1990), p. 24.

29 Butler, *Gender Trouble*, p. 7.

30 Ibid., p. 25.

31 Ibid., p. 146.

32 It is not my purpose to examine the fortunes of classical Stoicism in the early modern period: rather, I use the term throughout this book to describe the affective state which, for reformers, permits mourning in measure. The renewed humanist interest in classical Stoicism informs Werdmuller's treatise and others published in mid sixteenth-century London by Thomas Berthelet: see Desiderius Erasmus, *De Morto Declamatio*, published in English as *A treatyse perswading a man paciently to suffer the death of his freende* (London: Thomas Berthelet, 1531), Desiderius Erasmus, *Preparation to Deathe* (London: Thomas Berthelet, 1538), and Thomas Lupset, *A Compendius & Very Fruitful Treatyse Teachynge the Waye of Dyenge Well* (London: Thomas Berthelet, 1541). On classical Stoicism in the period, see Reid Barbour, *English Epicures and Stoics: Ancient Legacies in Early Stuart Culture* (Amherst: University of Massachusetts Press, 1998); Gordon Braden, *Renaissance Tragedy and the Senecan Tradition: Anger's Privilege* (New Haven: Yale University Press, 1985); and Andrew Shifflett, *Stoicism, Politics and Literature in the Age of Milton: War and Peace Reconciled* (Cambridge University Press, 1998).

33 See, most notably, Huston Diehl, *Staging Reform, Reforming the Stage: Protestantism and Popular Theater in Early Modern England* (Ithaca: Cornell University Press, 1997); Dolan, *Whores of Babylon*; Arthur F. Marotti, "Alienating Catholics in Early Modern England: Recusant Women, Jesuits, and Ideological Fantasies," in Arthur F. Marotti (ed.), *Catholicism and Anti-Catholicism in Early Modern English Texts* (New York: St. Martin's, 1999), pp. 1–34; and Alexandra Walsham, *Church Papists: Catholicism, Conformity and Confessional Polemic in Early Modern England* (Woodbridge, Suffolk: Royal Historical Society and Boydell Press, 1993).

34 See Peter Marshall, "The Map of God's Word: Geographies of the Afterlife in Tudor and Stuart England," in Gordon and Marshall (eds.), *Place of the Dead*, pp. 110–30.

35 Clive Burgess, "'Longing to be Prayed For': Death and Commemoration in an English Parish in the Late Middle Ages," in Gordon and Marshall (eds.), *Place of the Dead*, pp. 44–65.

36 Werdmuller, *Most frutefull*, p. 187.

37 Carlos M. N. Eire, *The War Against the Idols: The Reformation of Worship from Erasmus to Calvin* (Cambridge University Press, 1986), p. 315.

38 See Wall, *Imprint of Gender*; Karen Newman, *Fashioning Femininity and English Renaissance Drama* (University of Chicago Press, 1991); and Gail Kern Paster, *The Body Embarrassed: Drama and the Disciplines of Shame in Early Modern England* (Ithaca: Cornell University Press, 1993). The *locus classicus* of this idea in contemporary criticism is Suzanne W. Hull's *Chaste, Silent, and Obedient: English Books for Women, 1475–1640* (San Marino: Huntington Library, 1982).

39 Anne Clifford, *The Diaries of Lady Anne Clifford*, ed. D. J. H. Clifford (Wolfeboro Falls, NH: Alan Sutton, 1990), p. 21.

40 See Gittings, *Death, Burial and the Individual*, pp. 103–4.

41 Ariès, *Western Attitudes Towards Death*, pp. 11–12.

42 Margaret Hoby, *The Diary of Lady Margaret Hoby, 1599–1605*, ed. Dorothy M. Meads (London: Routledge, 1930), p. 182.

43 Strocchia, *Death and Ritual*, p. 173.

44 Ibid., p. 119.

45 Radford Mavericke, *The Mourning Weede*, in *Three Treatises Religiously Handled, and named according to the severall subjects of each Treatise: The Mourning Weede. The Mornings Joy. The Kings Rejoycing* (London: John Windet, 1603), c2v.

46 Erasmus, *A treatyse*, A2v–A3.

47 See William Gouge, *Of Domesticall Duties: Eight Treatises* (London: J. Haviland for W. Bladen, 1622), and John Milton, *Paradise Lost*, ed. Steve Ellredge (New York: W. W. Norton, 1975), 4: 440–93. See also Elizabeth V. Spelman, "Woman as Body: Ancient and Contemporary Views," *Feminist Studies* 8 (1982), 109–31.

48 Kate Lilley, "True State Within: Women's Elegy 1640–1740," in Isobel Grundy and Susan Wiseman (eds.), *Women, Writing, History 1640–1740* (Athens: University of Georgia Press, 1992), p. 72.

49 Ibid., p. 84.

50 See Mary Ellen Lamb, "The Cooke Sisters: Attitudes Towards Learned Women in the Renaissance," in Hannay (ed.), *Silent But For the Word*, p. 119.

I A MAP OF DEATH

1 St. John Chrysostom, *Commentary on St. John the Apostle and Evangelist*, trans. Sister Thomas Aquinas Goggin, 2 vols. (Washington, DC: Catholic University Press of America, 1960–9), vol. 2, p. 177.

2 Classical lament is antiphonal and antithetical, characteristics that Susan Letzer Cole, *The Absent One: Mourning, Ritual, Tragedy and the Performance of Ambivalence* (State College: Penn State University Press, 1985), pp. 2 and 56–7, argues persist into the sixteenth century. See also Margaret Alexiou, *Ritual Lament in Greek Tradition* (Cambridge University Press, 1974).

3 William Shakespeare, *Hamlet*, 1.2.93–4.

4 See, for example, Torquato Tasso, *Gerusalemme liberata*, ed. Marziano Guglielminetti (Milan: Garzanti, 1982), canto 8, lines 103–13.

5 Zachary Boyd, "The Queenes Lamentation for the Death of Her Sonne," in *The Last Battel of the Soule in Death*, 2 vols. (Edinburgh: Andro Hart, 1629), vol. 2, n.p. See Bettie Anne Doebler, *Rooted Sorrow: Dying in Early Modern England* (London and Toronto: Associated University Presses, 1994), pp. 230–41, for discussion.

6 See Ariès, *Western Attitudes*, p. 57, and *Images*, p. 198.

7 See Susan Haskins, *Mary Magdalen: Myth and Metaphor* (New York: Harper Collins, 1993), pp. 229–67.

8 Aemilia Lanyer, *The Poems of Aemilia Lanyer: Salve Deus Rex Judaeorum*, ed. Susanne Woods (Oxford University Press, 1993), p. 64. All further citations are to this edition and appear parenthetically.

9 Thomas Greenhill, *Nekrokedeia, or The Art of Embalming* (London: Thomas Greenhill, 1705), p. 117.

10 For instance, see Paul Lorrain, *Rites of Funerals Ancient and Modern* (London: R. Royston, 1683), pp. 249–50.

11 The anointing of Christ's head, also recorded in Matthew 26:12, is conflated throughout the period with Mary's anointing of Christ's feet in John 12:3–7.

12 Greenhill, *Nekrokedeia*, p. 112.

13 John Sweetnam, *S. Mary Magdalens Pilgrimage to Paradise* (St. Omer: English College Press, 1617), pp. 101 and 104–5.

14 Greenhill's rivals in the art of embalming are not women but members of the new profession "of the Undertakers or Burial-Men," p. 2.

15 Alexander Read, *Chirurgorum Comes: Or the Whole Practice of Chirurgery* (London: Edward Jones for Christopher Wilkinson, 1687), p. 708.

16 See Gittings, *Death, Burial and the Individual*, pp. 167–75; Claude Gaichard, *Funerailles, & diverses maineres d'enseuelir des Rommain, Grecs, & autres nations, tant anciennes que modernes* (Lyons: Jean de Tournes, 1581), pp. 523–33, and Roberto Bellarmino, *The Art of Dying Well*, trans. Edward Coffin (St. Omer: English College Press, 1622), pp. 361–2 and 389–90.

17 Philibert Guibert, *The Charitable Physitian*, trans. J. W. (London: Thomas Harper, 1639), pp. 143–4. See also Katharine Park, "The Criminal and the Saintly Body: Autopsy and Dissection in Renaissance Italy," *Renaissance Quarterly* 47 (1994), 6–7, on the identical techniques of embalming and autopsy, as opposed to dissection.

18 Ibid., p. 145. Read, *Chirurgorum Comes*, pp. 708–14, records similar methods of embalming.

19 Ibid., A2.

20 Ibid., A3v.

21 Fritz, "Undertaking Trade," 252, n. 21.

22 Gittings, *Death, Burial and the Individual*, p. 167. See also Read, *Chirurgorum Comes*, p. 710.

23 See John Dunton, *The Mourning-Ring* (London: John Dunton, 1682), p. 109, and Lorrain, *Rites of Funerals*, pp. 248–9.

24 In Thomas Becon's, *The Sicke Mannes Salve*, in *Prayers and Other Pieces of Thomas Becon*, ed. John Ayre (Cambridge University Press, 1846), p. 191,

male neighbors of the deceased "provide all things necessary for the comely furniture of the burial," while attendance on the corpse is ignored, implicitly falling to the widow and female neighbors. First published in 1561, the treatise went through eighteen editions by 1632.

25 Cressy, *Birth, Marriage and Death*, pp. 425–30.
26 See Gittings, *Death, Burial and the Individual*, pp. 112–14. See also Anonymous, *The Good-Wives Lamentation: Or, The Womens Complaint on the Account of Their Being to be Buried in Wollen* (London: L. C., 1678) and Anonymous, *The Good-Wives Vindication: Or An Answer to a Late Saucy Pamphlet Entitled The Womens Complaint* (London: L. C., 1678).
27 Quoted in Daniell, *Death and Burial*, p. 43.
28 Gittings, *Death, Burial and the Individual*, p. 108, notes that the related custom of the wake gradually faded in the seventeenth century.
29 See Emmison, *Essex Wills*, vol. 1, p. 27, and Phillis Cunnington and Catherine Lucas, *Costume for Births, Marriages and Deaths* (London: Adam and Charles Black, 1972), pp. 143–5. See also Walsham, *Church Papists*, p. 16, on the persistence of Catholic death rituals in Elizabeth's reign.
30 Henry Machyn, *The Diary of Henry Machyn*, ed. John Gough Nichols (London: Camden Society, 1848), p. 262, and Cressy, *Birth, Marriage and Death*, p. 436.
31 Ralph Josselin, *The Diary of Ralph Josselin, 1616–1683*, ed. Alan MacFarlane (Oxford University Press, 1976), p. 114.
32 Ibid., p. 203.
33 J. S. W. Helt, "Women, Memory and Will-Making in Elizabethan England," in Gordon and Marshall (eds.), *Place of the Dead*, p. 189.
34 Quoted in Cunnington and Lucas, *Costumes*, p. 185.
35 Mary Sidney Herbert, "The Dolefull Lay of Clorinda," in Margaret P. Hannay, Noel J. Kinnamon, and Michael G. Brennan (eds.), *The Collected Works of Mary Sidney Herbert, Countess of Pembroke*, 2 vols. (Oxford: Clarendon Press, 1998), vol. 1, pp. 119–35.
36 Hannay, et al. (eds.), *Collected Works*, vol. 1, p. 6.
37 Gittings, *Death, Burial and the Individual*, pp. 188–95. See Houlbrooke, *Death, Religion and the Family*, pp. 272–3, for an opposing view.
38 BL Add. MS 71131A, f. 1, "Sir Edward Coke-Lee Funeral (1605)."
39 William Cecil, "The order of mourners to be appointed. Mildred Cecille, 2nd wife died 1589," Salis Cal 3.462, Item 973, f. 1–2. Burghley is not listed among the mourners, but the order is written in his hand and suggests his participation.
40 See J. P. Earwaker (ed.), *Lancashire and Cheshire Wills and Inventories 1572–1696* (Manchester: Chetham Society, 1893), pp. 17–18.
41 Becon, *Sicke Mannes Salve*, p. 124.
42 Henry Petowe, *Elizabetha quasi vivens, Eliza's Funerall* (London: E. Allde for M. Lawe, 1603), B4. See also BL Hargrave MS 497, f. 26, "The Proceeding at Queen Elizabeth's Funeral from Whitehall to the Cathedral Church of Westminster on Thursday the 28th of April, AD 1603." Henry Chettle,

Englandes Mourning Garment (London: V. S. for Thomas Millington, 1603), F2, reports that 240 poor women participated.

43 Machyn, *Diary*, pp. 6 and 56.

44 Becon, *Sicke Mannes Salve*, p. 119.

45 On the *threnos*, see Alexiou, *Ritual Lament*.

46 William Birnie, *The Blame of Kirk-Buriall* (Edinburgh: Robert Charteris, 1606), CIv and C4–C4v.

47 Weever, *Ancient Funeral Monuments*, p. 15.

48 Anonymous, *Arden of Faversham* (New York: W. W. Norton, 1995), 14: 331–2.

49 See Giovanni Boccaccio, *Il Decamerone*, ed. Aldo Rossi (Bologna: L. Capelli, 1977), p. 24.

50 William Muggins, *London's Mourning Garment, or Funerall Teares: Worne and Shed for the Death of her Wealthy Citizens, and other her Inhabitants* (London: Ralph Blower, 1603), B3–C2v. All further citations are to this edition and appear parenthetically.

51 Mavericke, *Mourning Weede*, CI–CIv.

52 Boyd, "The Queenes Lamentation," n.p. Elizabeth Stuart's sorrows for the deaths of her brother, Prince Henry, in 1612 and her husband in 1632 were reportedly violent. See G. W. Pigman, *Grief and English Renaissance Elegy* (Cambridge University Press, 1985), pp. 80–1. Her reputation as an ideal mother is also relevant: see Valerie Wayne, "Advice for Women from Mothers and Patriarchs," in Helen Wilcox (ed.), *Women and Literature in Britain, 1500–1700* (Cambridge University Press, 1996), pp. 61–2.

53 Anonymous, *The Preparacyon to the Crosse with the Preparacyon to deeth* (London: Thomas Petyte, approx. 1545), N5v. Although this text shares its title with Erasmus' *Preparation*, published in English in 1538, it is not his work.

54 Ibid., N6–N6v.

55 Mavericke, *Mourning Weede*, C2v.

56 Chrysostom notes that the Lazarus episode corrects women's excessive mourning with Christ's measured grief: see Ernesto di Martino, *Morte e pianto rituale nel mondo antico: Dal lamento pagano al pianto di Maria* (Turin: Einaudi, 1958), p. 329. I am grateful to Randall Dodgen for helping me to obtain this work.

57 Greenhill, *Nekrokedeia*, pp. 79–80.

58 Boyd, "The Queenes Lamentation," n.p.

59 Ariès, *Hour of Our Death*, p. 361. See also R. C. Finucane, "Sacred Corpse, Profane Carrion: Social Ideals and Death Rituals in the Later Middle Ages," in Joachim Whaley (ed.), *Mirrors of Mortality: Studies in the Social History of Death* (London: Europa, 1981), pp. 45–7; and Park, "Criminal and Saintly Body," 10.

60 Gaichard, *Funerailles*, p. 472. See also Houlbrooke, *Death, Religion and the Family*, p. 225.

61 Darcie, *Funerall Teares*, n.p.

62 Ibid.

63 Ibid.

64 See Houlbrooke, *Death, Religion and the Family*, p. 260; Cunnington and Lucas, *Costumes*, pp. 128–36; and BL Add. MS 47713, f. 10v, "Establishment Lists after 1605."

65 Houlbrooke, *Death, Family and Religion*, pp. 248–9. See also Lou Taylor, *Mourning Dress: A Costume and Social History* (London: George Allen and Unwin, 1983), pp. 52–4.

66 Cunnington and Lucas, *Costumes*, p. 264.

67 Quoted in ibid., p. 154.

68 Lou Taylor, *Mourning Dress*, pp. 65–91.

69 Cunnington and Lucas, *Costumes*, p. 264. See also Clifford, *Diaries*, pp. 40–1.

70 Lou Taylor, *Mourning Dress*, pp. 66–70.

71 Houlbrooke, *Death, Religion and the Family*, p. 249.

72 Lou Taylor, *Mourning Dress*, pp. 73–99.

73 Clifford, *Diaries*, p. 74. Mourning garments for the aristocracy were governed by the College of Arms and their imitation by the lower social ranks influenced fashions for all classes. See Wilfrid Hooper, "The Tudor Sumptuary Laws," *English Historical Review* 30 (1915), 433–49.

74 See Roy Strong, *The Cult of Elizabeth: Elizabethan Portraiture and Pageantry* (London: Thames and Hudson, 1977), p. 106; Houlbrooke, *Death, Religion and the Family*, p. 249; and Cressy, *Birth, Marriage and Death*, p. 442.

75 Anonymous, *Englands Welcome to James, by the Grace of God, King of England, Scotland, France and Ireland, defender of the faith, &c.* (London: E. W. for C. K., 1603), n.p.

76 Quoted in Houlbrooke, *Death, Religion and the Family*, p. 272.

77 Weever, *Ancient Funeral Monuments*, p. 17.

78 On Robert Cecil's mourning, see Elizabeth Farber, "The Letters of Lady Elizabeth Russell (1540–1609)" (PhD dissertation, Columbia University, 1977), p. 190–3, and on Digby's, see Thomas Longueville, *The Life of Sir Kenelm Digby* (London: Longmans, 1896), pp. 216–17.

79 Dunton, *Mourning-Ring*, pp. 105–6. The passage lifted from Weever appears on p. 296.

80 Robert Southwell, *Triumphs Over Death* (London: V. S. for John Busbie, 1595), B2.

81 Michael MacDonald, *Mystical Bedlam: Madness, Anxiety and Healing in Seventeenth Century England* (Cambridge University Press, 1981), pp. 103–4.

82 Arthur Collins (ed.), *Letters and Memorials of State in the Reigns of Queen Mary, Queen Elizabeth, King James, King Charles the First, Part of the Reign of King Charles the Second and Oliver's Usurpation*, 2 vols. (London: T. Osborne, 1746), vol. 2, p. 142.

83 Ibid., vol. 2, p. 145.

84 Robert Persons, *A Discussion of the Answer of M. William Barlow* (St. Omer: English College Press, 1612), p. 214. On Persons, see Robert Corthell, "Robert Persons and the Writer's Mission," in Marotti (ed.), *Catholicism and Anti-Catholicism*, pp. 35–62.

85 See Richard Davey, *A History of Mourning* (London: McCorquodale and Co., 1890), pp. 46–8.

86 Jeremy Taylor, *The Rule and Exercises of Holy Dying* (London: R. R. for William Ballard, 1651), pp. 326–8.

87 Ibid., p. 329.

88 Anonymous, *Complaynte of the lover of Cryst saynt Mary Magdaleyn* (London: Wynkyn de Worde, 1520), B5. Further references are to this edition and appear parenthetically. The work appears in sixteenth-century editions of Chaucer's works as "The Lamentacion of Marie Magdaleine." See, for example, *The Works of Geoffrey Chaucer* (London: John Kyngston for John Wight, 1561), ff. 318–21v.

89 Gervase Markham, *Marie Magdalens Lamentations for the Losse of her Master Jesus* (London: Adam Islip for Edward White, 1601), C2. All further citations are to this edition and appear parenthetically.

90 J. C., *Saint Marie Magdalens Conversion* (Secret English Press, 1603), A1v.

91 The *Complaynte* went through at least nine editions between 1532 and 1602; Robert Southwell's *Saint Peter's Complaint and Saint Mary Magdalens Funerall Teares* (London: Society of Jesuits, 1620) also appeared in nine editions from 1591 to 1624. Only J. C. passes quickly over Mary's tears, devoting only four of 110 stanzas to them.

92 See also J. C., *Saint Marie Magdalens Conversion*, C2, and see Moshe Barasch, *Gestures of Despair in Medieval and Early Renaissance Art* (New York University Press, 1976).

93 See Sandro Sticca, *The Planctus Mariae in the Dramatic Tradition of the Middle Ages*, trans. Joseph R. Berrigan (Athens: University of Georgia Press, 1988), and Martino, *Morte e pianto*, pp. 334–44.

94 Quoted in Sticca, *Planctus Mariae*, p. 34.

95 Anonymous, *The Lamentacyon of the dyenge creature (Here Begynneth a lytell treatyse of the dyenge creature enfected with sykenes uncurable with many sorowfull complayntes)* (London: Wynkyn de Worde, 1507), A6v.

96 See also Sweetnam, *S. Mary Magdalens Pilgrimage*, p. 110.

97 See, for example, John Falconer, *The Mirrour of Created Perfection* (St. Omer: English College Press, 1632), p. 98.

98 Southwell, *Triumphs*, C2v.

99 See also Sweetnam, *S. Mary Magdalens Pilgrimage*, pp. 93–5.

100 Ibid., p. 142.

101 Ibid., p. 100.

102 Guibert, *Charitable Physitian*, p. 146. The preserved heart is a mainstay of medieval and early modern romance: see, for example, Boccaccio's tale of Ghismonda and Tancredi, *Decameron* 4.1.

103 Sweetnam, *S. Mary Magdalens Pilgrimage*, p. 104. He alludes to Ruth 1:20, "And she said unto them, Call me not Naomi, call me Mara: for the Lord hath dealt bitterly with me." In John 19:39, Nicodemus anoints Christ's body with "a mixture of myrrh and aloes," which were thought in the early modern period to be the ingredients of Mary's balm. See Greenhill, *Nekrokedeia*, p. 62.

104 Lewis Wager, *The Life of Marie Magdalene* (London: John Charlewood, 1566), A3.

105 Ibid., A4–A4v.
106 Ibid., B2v.
107 Ibid., C4v.
108 Ibid., H2–H2v.
109 J. C., *Saint Marie Magdalens Conversion*, C3v.
110 Sweetnam, *S. Mary Magdalens Pilgrimage*, p. 83.
111 See Barbara Kiefer Lewalski, *Writing Women of Jacobean England* (Cambridge, MA: Harvard University Press, 1993), pp. 212–41.
112 See also Lanyer, *Poems*, pp. 32, 33, 38, 80, and 107.
113 On the visual tradition of mourning angels, see Barasch, *Gestures of Despair*, pp. 96–102.
114 See Wall, *Imprint of Gender*, pp. 319–30.
115 See Lanyer, "A Description of Cooke-ham," in *Poems*, p. 138, for a similar gesture.
116 Woods (ed.), in Lanyer, *Poems*, p. 12.
117 See also William Leigh, *The Soules Solace Against Sorrow* (London: Felix Kingston, 1602), pp. 54–5: "Here is our gold, let him be crowned a King: here is our frankencense, let him be deified a God: here is our mirth, let him be buried like a man."
118 John Bradford, *A frutefull treatise and full of heavenly consolation against the feare of death* (London: William Powell, 1566–7), C4v–5.
119 Lanyer's emphasis on Christ's silence before his examiners further associates him with early modern women, whose chastity or promiscuity was often figured as analogous to their silence or speech.
120 Mavericke, *Mourning Weede*, C2v.
121 Ibid., C2v–C3.
122 Thomas Playfere, *The Meane in Mourning. A Sermon Preached at Saint Maries Spittle in London on Tuesday in Easter Weeke, 1595* (London: Felix Kyngston for Matthew Law, 1607). On the suburban area of the Spittal in Lanyer's lifetime, see Woods (ed.), in Lanyer, *Poems*, pp. xv–xviii.
123 Ibid., pp. 1–2.
124 Ibid., p. 3.
125 Ibid., pp. 84–5.
126 Ibid., pp. 2–3.
127 Ibid., pp. 10 and 5.
128 Ibid., p. 78.
129 Ibid., pp. 81–4.

DISPOSING OF THE BODY

1 Werdmuller, *Most frutefull*, A2v. This is STC 25254. An edition in the Folger dated 1555 (STC 25251) also reads on the spine, "Lady Jane Grey on Death."
2 Jane Grey, *Life, Death, and actions of the most chast, and religious lady Jane Grey* (London: G. Eld for John Wright, 1615), A2–A2v.

3 Thomas Hoby, "The Booke of the Travaile and lief of me, Thomas Hoby with diverse thinges woorth the notinge," BL Add. MS 2148, ff. 137–42.
4 On Feckenham, see Walsham, *Church Papists*, 24.
5 See Ruth Hughey, "A Ballad of Lady Jane Grey," *Times Literary Supplement*, December 7, 1933, 878, and John Foxe, *Acts and Monuments*, 7 vols. (New York: AMS Press, 1965), vol. 6, pp. 415–25. Paul Delaroche's nineteenth-century painting, *The Execution of Lady Jane Grey*, now in the National Gallery, London, is based on Foxe's account. On women's rhetorical power on the scaffold, see Catherine Belsey, *The Subject of Tragedy: Identity and Difference in Renaissance Drama* (New York: Methuen, 1985), pp. 190–1; Dolan, *Whores of Babylon*, pp. 157–210; Frances E. Dolan, "'Gentlemen, I have one thing more to say:' Women on Scaffolds in England, 1563–1680," *Modern Philology* 92 (1994), 157–78; and Newman, *Fashioning Femininity*, p. 69.

2 THE BODY OF HISTORY: EMBALMING AND HISTORIOGRAPHY IN SHAKESPEARE'S *HENRY VIII*

1 Quoted in Catherine Loomis, "Elizabeth Southwell's Manuscript Account of the Death of Queen Elizabeth [with text]," *English Literary Renaissance* 26 (1996), 486–7. See also Davey, *History of Mourning*, p. 43.
2 See Ariès, *Hour of our Death*, pp. 353–61.
3 Quoted in Loomis, "Elizabeth Southwell's Manuscript," 487.
4 Ibid., 482–509.
5 Persons, *Discussion*, pp. 216–28. He quotes Southwell anonymously on pp. 217–20. See also Loomis, "Elizabeth Southwell's Manuscript," 501–5, and John Watkins, "'Out of her Ashes May a Second Phoenix Rise': James I and the Legacy of Elizabethan Anti-Catholicism," in Marotti (ed.), *Catholicism and Anti-Catholicism*, pp. 122–6.
6 Loomis, "Elizabeth Southwell's Manuscript," 486 and 496. See also Francis Osborne, *Historical Memoirs of the Reigns of Queen Elizabeth and King James* (London: J. Grismond, 1658), pp. 61–2.
7 John Manningham, *Diary of John Manningham of the Middle Temple, 1602–1603*, ed. Robert Parker Sorlien (Hanover, NH: University Press of New England for University of Rhode Island Press, 1976), p. 223.
8 Quoted in Loomis, "Elizabeth Southwell's Manuscript," 487.
9 See Jonathan Sawday, *The Body Emblazoned: Dissection and the Human Body in Renaissance Culture* (New York and London: Routledge, 1995), pp. 213–29, for a similar discussion.
10 Finucane, "Sacred Corpse," p. 41.
11 Nigel Llewellyn, "The Royal Body: Monuments to the Dead for the Living," in Nigel Llewellyn and Lucy Gent (eds.), *Renaissance Bodies: The Human Figure in English Culture, 1540–1660* (London: Reaktion, 1990), p. 226. See also Julia M. Walker, "Reading the Tombs of Elizabeth I," *English Literary Renaissance* 26 (1996), 510–530, and Katherine Eggert, *Showing Like a Queen: Female Authority*

and Literary Experiment in Spenser, Milton and Shakespeare (Philadelphia: University of Pennsylvania Press, 2000), p. 137.

12 William Shakespeare, *The Famous History of The Life of King Henry VIII*, Epi., 10. All references are to this edition and appear parenthetically.

13 Quoted in Gittings, *Death, Burial and the Individual*, p. 190.

14 Piero Camporesi, *The Incorruptible Flesh: Bodily Mutation and Mortification in Religion and Folklore*, trans. Tania Croft-Murray (Cambridge University Press, 1988), p. 3. See also Park, "Criminal and Saintly Body," 1–3.

15 See, for example, Gaichard, *Funerailles*, p. 472, and Weever, *Ancient Funeral Monuments*, pp. 29–32.

16 John Mayer's *A Patterne for Women: Setting forth the most Christian life and most comfortable death of Mrs. Lucy, late wife to the worshipfull Roger Thornton, Esquire* (London: Edward Griffin for John Marriot, 1619), pp. 46–7, displays the difficulty in confirming that death had occurred. See also Park, "Criminal and Saintly Body," 3–4.

17 Elizabeth Russell, "Will," PRO PCC Dorset 56.

18 Ariès, *Hour of Our Death*, p. 362.

19 Clifford, *Diaries*, p. 37.

20 The burial is described in an inscription on Clifford's *Great Memorial Picture*. See George C. Williamson, *Lady Anne Clifford, Countess of Dorset, Pembroke & Montgomery, 1590–1676, Her Life, Letters and Work* (East Ardsley, Wakefield, Yorkshire: SR Publishers, Ltd., 1967), p. 490. The *Great Memorial Picture*, commissioned in 1646, is described on pp. 334–45 and 489–507.

21 Clifford, *Diaries*, p. 67.

22 Ibid., p. 242.

23 Ibid., p. 249.

24 Quoted in Williamson, *Lady Anne Clifford*, p. 465.

25 Clifford, *Diaries*, pp. 70 and 74.

26 See Llewellyn, "The Royal Body," pp. 218–40; Gittings, *Death, Burial and the Individual*, pp. 216–34; and Cunnington and Lucas, *Costumes*, pp. 201–40.

27 Read, *Chirurgorum Comes*, p. 711.

28 See Nigel Llewellyn, *Art of Death: Visual Culture in The English Death Ritual, c. 1500–1800* (London: Reaktion Books, 1991), pp. 94–100, and Lou Taylor, *Mourning Dress*, pp. 224–47, on memorial objects and jewelry.

29 See Cunnington and Lucas, *Costumes*, p. 243.

30 The painting shows affinities with post-Reformation tomb sculpture, which frequently includes effigies of husbands accompanied by more than one wife. A similar arrangement of figures is found in John Souch's *Sir Thomas Aston at the Deathbed of his Wife*. See Belsey, *Subject of Tragedy*, pp. 149–60, on both images.

31 Llewellyn, *Art of Death*, p. 32. See also Ariès, *Images of Man and Death*, pp. 198–200.

32 Quoted in Vittorio Gabrieli, *Sir Kenelm Digby: Un inglese italianato nell'eta della controriforma* (Rome: Edizioni di storia e letteratura, 1957), p. 246.

33 Gouge, *Of Domesticall Duties*, p. 476.

34 Camporesi, *Incorruptible Flesh*, pp. 181–2.
35 Pierre Chaunu, *La Mort à Paris: XVIe, XVIIe et XVIIIe siécles* (Paris: Fayard, 1978), pp. 259–60. See also Penny Roberts, "Contesting Sacred Space: Burial Disputes in Sixteenth-Century France," in Gordon and Marshall (eds.), *Place of the Dead*, p. 141.
36 Bellarmino, *Art of Dying*, p. 236.
37 Ibid., p. 251. See also Eamon Duffy, *The Stripping of the Altars: Traditional Religion in England, c. 1400–1580* (New Haven and London: Yale University Press, 1992), p. 313.
38 Ibid., pp. 245–6.
39 Peter of Luca, A *Dialogue of Dying Wel*, trans. R. Verstegan (Antwerp: A.C., 1603), E1.
40 Martin Luther, *The Pagan Servitude of the Church*, in John Dillenberger (ed.), *Martin Luther: Selections from his Writings* (New York: Anchor, 1961), pp. 355 and 279.
41 Houlbrooke, *Death, Religion and the Family*, pp. 154–5. See also Church of England, *The Book of Common Prayer, 1559: The Elizabethan Prayer Book*, ed. John E. Booty (Charlottesville: University of Virginia Press, 1976), pp. 300–6 and 20.
42 James Balmford, *A Short Dialogue Concerning the Plagues Infection* (London: Richard Boyle, 1603), p. 20.
43 Ibid., pp. 20–1.
44 George Hughes, *The Art of Embalming Dead Saints discovered in a Sermon preached at the Funerall of Master William Crompton, the later Reverend and Faithfull Pastor of the Church in Lanceston Cornwall, January the fifth, 1641* (London: A.N. for John Rothwell, 1642), p. 1.
45 Ibid., pp. 8–9.
46 Ibid., p. 51.
47 Abraham Cheare, "The Embalming of the Dead Cause, on Mark 14.8" in *Words in Season* (London: Nathan Brookes, 1668), pp. 113–14.
48 William Leigh, *Soules Solace*, p. 2.
49 Luther, *Pagan Servitude*, p. 260.
50 Ibid.
51 Church of England, *Book of Common Prayer*, p. 19.
52 Luther, *Pagan Servitude*, p. 268.
53 Gervase Markham, *The Teares of the Beloved, or The Lamentation of Saint John* (London: Simon Stafford for John Browne, 1602), B1. All further citations are to this edition and appear parenthetically.
54 Thomas Fuller, *The Holy State* (Cambridge: Roger Daniel for John Williams, 1642), pp. 52–3. I am grateful to Katharine Goodland for this citation.
55 William Shakespeare, *The Tragedy of King Richard II*, 3.2.54–5.
56 Ibid., 5.6.45–52.
57 See Shakespeare, *Henry IV, Part 1*, 5.4.24 and 5.3.25–8.
58 See Ariès, *Hour of Our Death*, p. 355.
59 Shakespeare, *Richard II*, 5.1.155–68.

60 Edward Coffin, "A True Relation of the Last Sickeness and Death of Cardinall Bellarmine who dyed in Rome the seavententh day of September 1621," in Bellarmino, *Art of Dying*, p. 329. See also Sawday, *Body Emblazoned*, pp. 85–140.

61 Ibid., p. 392.

62 Shakespeare, *Richard II*, 5.5.109–10.

63 Shakespeare, *Henry V*, 4.1.300–11.

64 See Maurice Hunt, "The Hybrid Reformations of Shakespeare's Second Henriad," *Comparative Drama* 32 (1998), 176–206.

65 Peter L. Rudnytsky, "*Henry VIII* and the Deconstruction of History," *Shakespeare Survey 43* (1991), 46.

66 See also Shakespeare, *Henry VIII*, 5.3.36–7, and see David Glimp, "Staging Government: Shakespeare's *Life of King Henry the Eighth* and the Government of Generations," *Criticism* 41 (1999), 41–66.

67 See Linda McJ. Micheli, "'Sit By Us': Visual Imagery and the Two Queens in *Henry VIII*," *Shakespeare Quarterly* 38 (1987), 463–4.

68 See Glimp, "Staging Government," 50, and Kim H. Noling, "Grubbing Up the Stock: Dramatizing Queens in *Henry VIII*," *Shakespeare Quarterly* 39 (1988), 291–306.

69 Rudnytsky, "*Henry VIII*," 48. See also Paul Dean, "Dramatic Mode and Historical Vision in *Henry VIII*," *Shakespeare Quarterly* 37 (1986), 177.

70 *Oxford English Dictionary, Compact Edition*. 2 vols. (Oxford University Press, 1971), vol. 1, p. 848.

71 Vanessa Harding, "Whose Body? A Study of Attitudes Towards the Dead Body in Early Modern Paris," in Gordon and Marshall (eds.), *Place of the Dead*, pp. 178–9.

72 See Noling, "Grubbing Up the Stock," 299–300, and Micheli, "'Sit By Us,'" 459–60.

73 See Micheli, "'Sit By Us,'" 459–66.

74 Noling, "Grubbing Up the Stock," 297 and 295.

75 Duffy, *Stripping of the Altars*, p. 389.

76 See Rudnytsky, "*Henry VIII*," p. 49, and Camille Wells Slights, "The Politics of Conscience in *All is True* (or *Henry VIII*)", *Shakespeare Studies* 43 (1991), 64.

77 Thomas Fuller, *The Church History of Britain: From the Birth of Jesus Christ until the Year M.C.D.XLVIII*, ed. J. S. Brewer (Oxford University Press, 1845), p. 258.

78 Walker, "Reading the Tombs," 522.

79 Ibid., 524.

3 HUMILITY AND STOUTNESS: THE LIVES AND DEATHS OF CHRISTIAN WOMEN

1 Phillip Stubbes, *A Chrystal Glasse for Christian Women* (London: Richard Jones, 1592), A1. All further citations are to this edition and appear parenthetically.

2 Kate Aughterson, *Renaissance Woman: A Source Book* (London and New York: Routledge, 1995), pp. 2–4.

3 See Hutson, *Usurer's Daughter*, pp. 1–51.
4 The three texts appear in William Harrison, *Deaths Advantage, Little Regarded, and the Soules Solace Against Sorrow. Preached in Two Funerall sermons at Childwal in Lancashire at the Buriall of Mistres Katherin Brettergh the third of June 1601. The one by William Harrison, one of the Preachers appointed by her Majestie for the Countie Palatine of Lancaster, the other by William Leygh, Bachelor of Divinitie and Pastor of Standish. Whereunto is annexed, the Christian life and godly death of the said Gentlewoman* (London: Felix Kyngston, 1602). All references to these three works are to this edition and appear parenthetically. For clarity's sake, I refer to the collected works as *Deaths Advantage* and to each text according to individual authors and titles on separate title pages in the volume: William Harrison, *Deaths Advantage, Little Regarded*; William Leigh's *Soules Solace*; and William Hinde, *A Brief Discourse of the Christian Life and Death of Mistris Katherin Brettergh* (London: Felix Kingston, 1601). Thomas King and F. R. Raines (eds.), *Lancashire Funeral Certificates* (Manchester: Chetham Society, 1869), p. 40, identify Hinde as the author of Brettergh's life.
5 Retha M. Warnicke and Bettie Anne Doebler (eds.), *Deaths Advantage Little Regarded* (Delmar, New York: Scholars' Facsimiles and Reprints, 1993), p. 5. Hinde's life was reprinted by Samuel Clarke, *The Second Part of the Marrow of Ecclesiastical History* (London: Thomas Sawbridge and William Birch, 1675), pp. 52–7.
6 Grey, *Life, Death, and Actions*, c2v–c3.
7 Becon, *Sicke Mannes Salve*, p. 119.
8 Emmison, *Essex Wills*, vol. 1, p. 18.
9 Balmford, *Short Dialogue*, p. 21.
10 Quoted in Frederic B. Tromly, "'According to sounde religion': The Elizabethan Controversy Over the Funeral Sermon," *JMRS* 13 (1983), 298.
11 Houlbrooke, *English Family*, p. 203.
12 Lancelot Langhorne, *Mary Sitting at Christs Feet, With the Christian Life and Comfortable Death of Mrs. Mary Swaine, for the encouraging of all Christian Gentlewomen, and other to walke in the steps of the religious Gentlewoman* (London: M. F. for Edward Wright, 1610), p. 4.
13 Tromly, "'Accordinge to sounde religion,'" 311. For a similar argument, see Larissa Juliet Taylor, "Funeral Sermons and Orations as Religious Propaganda in Sixteenth-Century France," in Gordon and Marshall (eds.), *Place of the Dead*, pp. 224–38.
14 Bettie Anne Doebler and Retha M. Warnicke, "Sex Discrimination After Death: A Seventeenth-Century English Study," *Omega* 17 (1986–7), 313–15.
15 J. Phillips, *An Epitaphe on the death of the right noble and most vertuous Lady Margarit Duglass good grace, Countesse of Linnox* (London: Edward White, 1578), lines 1–4 and 115–19.
16 Mayer, *A Patterne for Women*, A2v.
17 Robert Wolcomb, *The State of the Godly Both in this Life and in the Life to Come. Delivered in a Sermon at Chudleigh in Devon at the Funeralls of the right Worshipfull the Ladie Elizabeth Courtney, the 11 of November 1605, Whereunto is Annexed the Christian*

life and godly death of the sayd worshipfull Lady Elizabeth Courtney (London: Roger Jackson, 1606), pp. 71–81.

18 Humphrey Gunter, *A Profitable Memoriall of the Conversion, Life and Death of Mistris Mary Gunter, set up as a Monument to be looked upon, both by Protestants and Papists*, in Thomas Taylor, *The Pilgrims Profession, or a Sermon Preached at the Funerall of Mistris Mary Gunter by Mr. Thomas Taylor To Which (by his consent) also is added, A Short Relation of the Life and deth of the said Gentile-woman as a perpetuall Monument of her graces and vertues* (London J. D. for John Bartlett, 1622), pp. 121–92. On the work, see Retha M. Warnicke, "Eulogies for Women: Public Testimony of their Godly Example and Leadership," in Betty S. Travitsky and Adele F. Seeff (eds.), *Attending to Women in Early Modern England* (Newark: University of Delaware Press, 1994), p. 176.

19 Tromly, "'Accordinge to sounde religion,'" 303–9.

20 Langhorne, *Mary Sitting at Christs Feet*, p. 25.

21 Ibid., A1.

22 Henry Peacham, *Thestylis astrata: or, A Funerall Elegie upon the Death of the Right Honourable, most Religious and Noble Lady, Frances, Countess of Warwicke* (London: JH for Francis Constable, 1634), A2.

23 Henry Myddelmore, *The Translation of a letter written by a Frenche Gentilwoman to another Gentilwoman Straunger, her friend, upon the death of the most excellent and virtuous Ladye, Elenor of Koye, Princes of Conde, contayning her last wyll and Testament* (London: John Day for Humfrye Toye, 1564), C3v–C4.

24 See Margo Todd, "Humanists, Puritans, and the Spiritualized Household," *Church History* 49 (1989), 18–34.

25 Gunter, *A Profitable Memoriall*, pp. 151–5.

26 Ibid., p. 75.

27 Ibid., pp. 76–81.

28 Myddelmore, *A Translation*, A4–A5.

29 Langhorne, *Mary Sitting at Christs Feet*, p. 20.

30 Mayer, *A Patterne for Women*, p. 8.

31 Aughterson, *Renaissance Woman*, p. 4.

32 Doebler and Warnicke, "Sex Discrimination," 311–14.

33 Gunter, *A Profitable Memoriall*, pp. 185–6.

34 Myddelmore, *A Translation*, D4v–D5.

35 Phillip Stubbes, *The Anatomie of Abuses* (London: Richard Jones, 1583), A1v.

36 Ibid., B4v.

37 Ibid., n.p. On the jeremiad, see Alexandra Walsham, *Providence in Early Modern England* (Oxford University Press, 1999), pp. 281–325.

38 Ibid., D6–E7 and E7v–G4.

39 *The Anatomie of Abuses* is also presented in dialogue form, suggesting that Stubbes was practiced in deploying a variety of voices to articulate orthodox viewpoints.

40 Tromly, "'Accordinge to sounde religion,'" 296.

41 Warnicke and Doebler, *Deaths Advantage*, p. 7.

42 Tromly, "'Accordinge to sounde religion,'" 303.

43 Langhorne, *Mary Sitting at Christs Feet*, pp. 22–3. See also Gunter, *A Profitable Memoriall*, p. 125.

44 David Cressy, "Response: Private Lives, Public Performance, and Rites of Passage," in Travitsky and Seeff (eds.), *Attending to Women*, pp. 191–2. See also Houlbrooke, *Death, Religion and Family*, p. 163.

45 While Stubbes's and Gunter's biographies were written by husbands, most others were brought to press with husbands' help. See William Leigh, *Soules Solace*, G4–G4v.

46 Houlbrooke, *The English Family*, p. 222. See also Catherine Belsey, *Shakespeare*, pp. 90–101.

47 Gunter, *A Profitable Memoriall*, A4 and pp. 121–3. For Gunter's epitaph on his wife's tomb in Little Fawley, see Elias Ashmole, *Antiquities of Berkshire*, 3 vols. (London: E. Curll, 1719), vol. 2, p. 260.

48 Gunter, *A Profitable Memoriall*, pp. 163–74.

49 Ibid., p. 162.

50 Becon, *Sicke Mannes Salve*, p. 116.

51 Houlbrooke, *Death, Religion and the Family*, p. 189.

52 See also Gunter, *A Profitable Memoriall*, pp. 177–8.

53 See Anonymous, *The Craft of Dying*, in Francis M. M. Comper (ed.), *The Booke of the Craft of Dying and Other Early English Tracts Concerning Death* (New York: Arno Press, 1977), pp. 22–7. All further citations are to this edition and appear parenthetically.

54 Patricia Crawford, *Women and Religion in England, 1500–1720* (London and New York: Routledge, 1993), p. 97.

55 Gunter, *A Profitable Memoriall*, pp. 188–9. See also Langhorne, *Mary Sitting at Christs Feet*, p. 24.

56 On the Puritan *ars moriendi*, see Owen C. Watkins, *The Puritan Experience* (London and New York: Routledge, 1972), pp. 241–60. On the Bretterghs' Puritan leanings, see Roy G. Dottie, "The Recusant Riots at Childwall in May, 1600: A Reappraisal," in *Transactions of the Historic Society of Lancashire and Cheshire* 132 (1982), 1–28.

57 See Dottie, "Recusant Riots," 1–6, and Walsham, *Church Papists*, p. 76.

58 Warnicke and Doebler, *Deaths Advantage*, p. 17.

59 My account is indebted to Dottie, "Recusant Riots," 9–23.

60 Ibid., 9 and 26, n. 74.

61 F. R. Raines (ed.), *A Description of the State, Civil, and Ecclesiastical, of the County of Lancaster About the Year 1590* (Manchester: Chetham Society, 1875), pp. 5–6.

62 Dottie, "Recusant Riots," 9–10.

63 Ibid., 10–11.

64 Quoted ibid., 12.

65 Raines (ed.), *A Description*, p. 3.

66 Dottie, "Recusant Riots," 15–16.

67 Sutton, *Disce Mori*, pp. 273–4.

68 Raines (ed.), *A Description*, p. 6.
69 See Dolan, *Whores of Babylon*, pp. 45–94.
70 See John Walter, "Grain Riots and Popular Attitudes to the Law: Maldon and the Crisis of 1629," in John Brewer and John Styles (eds.), *An Ungovernable People: The English and their Law in the Seventeenth and Eighteenth Centuries* (New Brunswick: Rutgers University Press, 1980), pp. 62–3, and Natalie Zemon Davis, *Society and Culture in Early Modern France* (Stanford University Press, 1975), pp. 124–51.
71 Dottie, "Recusant Riots," 6–7 and 22.
72 Warnicke and Doebler, *Deaths Advantage*, pp. 16–17. On gender relations in Catholic households, see Walsham, *Church Papists*, pp. 78–80.
73 Ibid., p. 13.
74 Langhorne, *Mary Sitting at Christs Feet*, pp. 15–16.

4 LONDON'S MOURNING GARMENT: MATERNITY, MOURNING AND SUCCESSION IN SHAKESPEARE'S *RICHARD III*

1 Muggins, *Londons Mourning Garment*, E2, prints a bill of mortality that numbers the dead at 37,717. See also F. P. Wilson, *The Plague in Shakespeare's London* (Oxford University Press, 1927), pp. 88–115, and Paul Slack, *The Impact of the Plague in Tudor and Stuart London* (London: Routledge and Kegan Paul, 1985), pp. 173–92.
2 Thomas Byng, "Offering," in *Sorrowes Joy, or A Lamentation for our late deceased Soveraigne Elizabeth, with a triumph for the prosperous succession of our gratious King James, &c.* (Cambridge: John Legat, 1603), p. 10.
3 Thomas Dekker, *The Wonderfull yeare 1603: Wherein is shewed the picture of London, lying sicke of the Plague* (London: Thomas Creede, 1603), C3–C3v.
4 Thomas Brewer, *The Weeping Lady: Or, London Like Ninivie in Sack-Cloth* (London: B. A. and T. F. for Mathew Rhodes, 1629), B1v and A2v. See also Paul Slack, "Mirrors of Health and Treasures of Poor Men: The Uses of the Vernacular Medical Literature of Tudor England" in Charles Webster (ed.), *Health, Medicine and Mortality in the Sixteenth Century* (Cambridge University Press, 1979), pp. 165–236.
5 Patricia Crawford, "The Construction and Experience of Maternity in Seventeenth-Century England," in Valerie Fildes (ed.), *Women as Mothers in Pre-Industrial England: Essays in Memory of Dorothy McLaren* (London and New York: Routledge, 1990), p. 21. On childbed attendants, see Cressy, *Birth, Marriage and Death*, pp. 55–79.
6 Thomas Bentley, *Monument of Matrones: Containing Severall Lamps of Virginitie*, 8 vols. (London: Henry Denham, 1582), vol. 5, pp. 143–50. Donna J. Long, "'It is a lovely bonne I make to thee': Mary Carey's 'abortive Birth' as Recuperative Religious Lyric," in Jeff Johnson and Eugene Cunnar (eds.), *Discovering and Recovering the Seventeenth-Century Religious Lyric* (Pittsburgh: Dusquene University Press, forthcoming), notes that Bentley includes no prayers for child-loss, concluding that "women had to work through their

grief on their own." I am grateful to Dr. Long for sharing this work with me prior to publication.

7 Lucinda McCray Beier, "The Good Death in Seventeenth-Century England," in Houlbrooke (ed.), *Death, Ritual and Bereavement*, p. 44.

8 See Roger Schofield and E. A. Wrigley, "Infant and Child Mortality in England in the Late Tudor and Early Stuart Period," in Webster (ed.), *Health, Medicine and Mortality*, pp. 61–96; Lawrence Stone, *The Family, Sex and Marriage 1500–1800* (New York: Harper and Row, 1977), pp. 68–9; and Patricia Crawford, "From the Woman's Point of View: Pre-industrial England, in Patricia Crawford (ed.), *Exploring Women's Past: Essays in Social History* (Sydney: George Allen and Unwin, 1983), p. 71.

9 Thomas R. Forbes, "By What Disease or Casualty: The Changing Face of Death in London, in Webster (ed.), *Health, Medicine and Mortality*, p. 139.

10 Gouge, *Of Domesticall Duties*, p. 512.

11 See Houlbrooke, *Death, Religion and the Family*, p. 235.

12 See Rose, "Where are the Mothers," 300–3.

13 On breast feeding in the period, see Crawford, "Construction and Experience," in Fildes (ed.), *Women as Mothers*, pp. 22–7.

14 Richard Niccols, *Three Sister Teares at the Most Solemne Death of Henry Prince of Wales* (London: Richard Redmer, 1613), EI and EI v.

15 Jeremy Leech, *A Sermon Preached before the Lords of the Councel, in K. Henry the Seavenths Chapell, Sept. 23, 1607 At the Funerall of the most excellent & hopefull Princess, the Lady Marie's Grace* (London: H. L. for Samuel Macham, 1607), A3v–A4. On the sermon, see Warnicke, "Eulogies for Women," in Travitsky and Seeff (eds.), *Attending to Women*, pp. 178–80.

16 Ibid., p. 17. See also Shakespeare, *King Lear*, 4.6.182–3.

17 Andreas Hyperius, *Of Framing of Divine Sermons, or Popular Interpretation of the Scriptures (The Practice of Preaching)*, trans. John Ludham (London: Thomas East, 1577), z4 and z3–z3v.

18 Werdmuller, *Most frutefull*, pp. 197–9.

19 Erasmus, *A treatyse*, JIv–J2. Erasmus also praises the fortitude of "seely women" of his own day, who, to the shame of their male governors, "verraie moderately take in good woorth the death of their children."

20 Werdmuller, *Most frutefull*, p. 223.

21 Ibid., p. 235.

22 Peacham, *Thestylis astrata*, BIv.

23 Quoted in F. P. Wilson, *Plague in Shakespeare's London*, p. 88.

24 See Walsham, *Providence*, pp. 156–66.

25 Thomas Cogan, *The Haven of Health* (London: Henrie Midleton for William Norton, 1584), p. 262. See also Balmford, *Short Dialogue*, A3v–A4, and Henoch Clapham, *An Epistle Discoursing Upon the Present Pestilence* (London: T. C. for the Widow Newbery, 1603), B2.

26 Margaret Hoby, *Diary*, p. 207.

27 Ibid., p. 206. See F. P. Wilson, *Plague in Shakespeare's London*, pp. 3–6 and 99–103.

28 Brewer, *Weeping Lady*, A3.

29 Roger Fenton, *A Perfume Against the Noysome Pestilence, Prescribed by Moses Unto Aaron* (London: R. R. for William Aspley, 1603), A9–A10v.

30 Ibid., B5v.

31 Nathaniel Cannon, *Lachrimae: or Lamentations Over the Dead* (London: Felix Kyngston for William Welby, 1616), A2v. Dorothy White's *Lamentation Unto this Nation* (London: Robert Wilson, 1660) is a female-authored example of the genre.

32 See Walsham, *Providence*, pp. 310–15.

33 Thomas Nashe, *Christs Teares Over Jerusalem, Whereunto is annexed, a comparative admonition to London*, in Roland B. McKerrow (ed.), *The Works of Thomas Nashe*, 2 vols. (London: A. H. Bullen, 1904), vol. 2, p. 36. I am grateful to John Gibbs for drawing my attention to this work.

34 Ibid., p. 174.

35 Ibid., p. 71.

36 Ibid.

37 Ibid., pp. 71–4.

38 Ibid., p. 74.

39 Ibid., p. 76.

40 Ibid., pp. 76–7. Miriam's cannibalism exemplifies Freud's notion of melancholia in "Mourning and Melancholia," in James Strachey et al. (eds.), *The Standard Edition of the Complete Psychological Works*, 24 vols. (London: Hogarth Press, 1974), vol. 14, pp. 249–50. For discussion, see Julia Reinhard Lupton and Kenneth Reinhard, *After Oedipus: Shakespeare in Psychoanalysis* (Ithaca: Cornell University Press, 1993), pp. 19–26.

41 Nashe, *Christs Teares*, p. 76.

42 See Sawday, *Body Emblazoned*, pp. 221–3.

43 England and Wales, Sovereign (1603–25: James I), *Orders thought meete by his Majestie and his Privie Counsell, to be executed throughout the Counties of this Realme, in such Townes, Villages, and other places as are, or may be hereafter infected with the Plague, for the stay of further increase of the same* (London: Robert Barker, 1603), A4v.

44 F. P. Wilson, *Plague in Shakespeare's London*, p. 67.

45 England and Wales, Sovereign (1603–25: James), *Orders*, B2v.

46 Thomas Dekker, *English Villainies* (London: M. Parsons, 1638), K2.

47 Ibid., K2v–K3.

48 See Slack, *Impact of the Plague*, pp. 147 and 203, and Forbes, "By What Disease," in Webster (ed.), *Health, Medicine and Mortality*, pp. 120–1.

49 See England and Wales, Sovereign (1603–25: James I), *Orders*, A3v–A4.

50 Slack, *Impact of the Plague*, pp. 274–5.

51 Nathaniel Hodges, *Loimologia: Or An Historical Account of the Plague in London in 1665, with Precautionary Directions against the like Contagion* (London: E. Bell, 1720), pp. 8–9.

52 Nashe, *Christs Teares*, pp. 135, 140–1, and 144.

53 See Balmford, *Short Dialogue*, p. 71. For contradictory views as to whether flight can be justified, see Cogan, *Haven of Health*, p. 262 and Brewer, *Weeping Lady*, C1v.

54 On nursing fathers, see Debora Shuger, *Habits of Thought in the English Renaissance: Religion, Politics, and the Dominant Culture* (Berkeley: University of California Press, 1990), pp. 219–49.
55 Balmford, *Short Dialogue*, p. 6.
56 Werdmuller, *Most frutefull*, pp. 170–1. See also Becon, *Sicke Mannes Salve*, p. 93.
57 See Slack, *The Impact of the Plague*, pp. 197–244, and England and Wales, Sovereign (1603–25: James I), *Orders*, B4v. Clapham, *Epistle*, AIV–A2, states that the author "has been imprisoned for teaching, *That the plague was not infectious.*" See also Walsham, *Providence*, pp. 159–61.
58 Houlbrooke, *Death, Religion and the Family*, p. 192.
59 Dekker, *Wonderfull yeare*, CIV.
60 Clifford, *Diaries*, p. 21.
61 See Osborne, *Historical Memoirs*, p. 95.
62 Manningham, *Diary*, p. 209. See also Helen Hackett, *Virgin Mother, Maiden Queen: Elizabeth I and the Cult of the Virgin Mary* (New York and London: Macmillan, 1995), pp. 222–4; Christopher Haigh, *Elizabeth I* (New York: Longman, 1988), pp. 160–8; and Mullaney, "Mourning and Misogyny," 139.
63 Mavericke, *Mourning Weede*, C2v and B3v.
64 Ibid., CI.
65 See Genesis 35:16–20.
66 See Joseph Telushkin, *Jewish Literacy* (New York: William Morrow, 1991), pp. 32–3. I am indebted to Julia Reinhard Lupton for this source and insight into Rachel's significance.
67 Rachel figures mothers' immoderate grief at the Slaughter of the Innocents in medieval liturgical drama. See David Bevington, *Medieval Drama* (Boston: Houghton Mifflin, 1975), pp. 67–72.
68 Mavericke, *Mourning Weede*, C4v. See also Playfere, *Meane in Mourning*, pp. 50–1, who calls Christ both a "loving Rachell" and a "tender Pelican."
69 Richard Mulcaster, *The Translation of Certaine Latine Verses Written Uppon her Majesties Death, Called A Comforting Complaynt* (London: Edward Aggas, 1603), A2. See also John Watkins, "'Out of her Ashes,'" pp. 118–20.
70 Dekker, *Wonderfull yeare*, CIV.
71 Ibid., B2.
72 See Hackett, *Virgin Mother*, pp. 219–20.
73 Dennis Kay, *Melodious Tears: The English Funeral Elegy from Spenser to Milton* (Oxford: Clarendon Press, 1990), p. 82.
74 Petowe, *Elizabetha quasi vivens*, B3.
75 Anonymous, *A Mournefull Dittie, entitled Elizabeths losse, together with a welcome for King James* (London: Thomas Pavier, 1603), n.p.
76 Kay, *Melodious Tears*, pp. 78 and 90. Elegies for James were far fewer in number, but similarly employ the dismissive tactic of seasonal mourning: see, for example, Thomas Heywood, *A Funerall Elegie upon the Much Lamented Death of the Trespuissant and unmatchable King, King James* (London: Thomas Harper, 1625).
77 See Eggert, *Showing Like a Queen*, pp. 131–2.

78 Quoted in Kay, *Melodious Tears*, p. 78.

79 Diana Primrose, *A Chaine of Pearle, or A Memoriall of the peerles Graces, and Heroick Vertues of Queene Elizabeth, of Glorious Memory* (London: Thomas Paine by Philip Waterhouse 1630), CIV.

80 See Ian Frederick Moulton, "'A Monster Great Deformed': The Unruly Masculinity of Richard III," *Shakespeare Quarterly* 47 (1996), 253–4.

81 Linda Charnes, *Notorious Identity: Materializing the Subject in Shakespeare* (Cambridge, MA: Harvard University Press, 1993), p. 30.

82 William Shakespeare, *The Tragedy of Richard III*, 1.3.284–5. All further references appear parenthetically.

83 Phyllis Rackin, "*Richard III*," in Jean E. Howard and Phyllis Rackin, *Engendering a Nation: A Feminist Account of Shakespeare's English Histories* (New York and London: Routledge, 1997), p. 112.

84 Charnes, *Notorious Identity*, p. 55.

85 Moulton, "'A Monster Great Deformed,'" 254.

86 Howard and Rackin, *Engendering a Nation*, p. 148.

87 See Charnes, *Notorious Identity*, pp. 20–69.

88 Werdmuller, *Most frutefull*, pp. 193–5.

89 Southwell, *Triumphs*, BI. While the gendering of excessive grief as feminine is primarily a Protestant phenomenon, Southwell's treatise indicates that is also adopted by some Catholic authors.

90 Rackin, *Richard III*, in Howard and Rackin, *Engendering a Nation*, p. 101.

91 Philip Sidney, *A Defence of Poetry*, ed. J. A. van Dorsten (Oxford University Press, 1966), p. 45. See also Targoff, "Performance of Prayer," 61.

92 See Walsham, *Providence*, pp. 158–9.

93 Rackin, *Richard III*, in Howard and Rackin, *Engendering a Nation*, pp. 106–18.

94 Charnes, *Notorious Identity*, p. 27. See also Phyllis Rackin, *Stages of History: Shakespeare's English Chronicles* (Ithaca: Cornell University Press, 1990), pp. 27–8 and 61–71.

95 My discussion of *Richard III* is greatly indebted to Katharine Goodland, "'Why Should Calamity,'" pp. 210–33.

96 Davey, *History of Mourning*, p. 32.

97 Raines, *Description*, p. 5.

98 Ibid., p. 6. For discussion, see Cressy, *Birth, Marriage and Death*, pp. 400–1. Goodland, "'Why Should Calamity,'" pp. 210–11, makes the connection between the Lancashire disturbances and *Richard III*.

99 See Bevington, *Medieval Drama*, pp. 31–49 and 225–658, and Goodland, "'Why Should Calamity,'" pp. 53–157; Pamela Sheingorn, *The Easter Sepulcher in England* (Kalamazoo: Medieval Institute Publications, 1987); and Duffy, *Stripping of the Altars*, pp. 30–4. Charnes, *Notorious Identity*, p. 43, associates Anne's lamentation with the Corpus Christi cycles.

100 Quoted in Goodland, "'Why Should Calamity,'" pp. 186–7.

101 See Patrick Geary, *Living With the Dead in the Middle Ages* (Ithaca: Cornell University Press, 1994) and Brian Patrick McGuire, "Purgatory, the Communion of the Saints, and Medieval Change," *Viator* 20 (1989), 61–84.

102 See Bruce Gordon, "Malevolent Ghosts and Ministering Angels: Apparitions and Pastoral Care in the Swiss Reformation," in Gordon and Marshall (eds.), *Place of the Dead*, pp. 87–109.

103 See Charles Kightly, *The Customs and Ceremonies of Britain: An Encyclopaedia of Living Traditions* (New York: Thames and Hudson, 1986), p. 118.

104 See Houlbrooke, *Death, Religion and the Family*, pp. 269–70 and Llewellyn, *Art of Death*, pp. 95–6. Shakespeare's will, in Evans (ed.), *Riverside Shakespeare*, p. 1956, reads, "I gyve & bequeath to Mr. Hamlett Sadler xxvj s. viij d. to buy him A Ringe . . . & to my ffellowes John Hemynges Richard Burbage & Henry Cundell xxvj s. viij d A peece to buy them Ringes."

105 Neill, *Issues of Death*, pp. 292–301.

106 Charnes, *Notorious Identity*, pp. 44–5. See also Goodland, "'Why Should Calamity,'" pp. 214–15.

107 See Daniell, *Death and Burial*, pp. 1–29, and Duffy, *Stripping of the Altars*, pp. 368–76.

108 Kay, *Melodious Tears*, p. 2.

109 See Duffy, *Stripping of the Altars*, pp. 131–54.

110 See Nicole Loraux, *Mothers in Mourning*, trans. Corinne Pache (Ithaca: Cornell University Press, 1998), pp. 1–7.

111 See Patricia Demers, "The Seymour Sisters: Elegizing Female Attachment," *Sixteenth Century Journal* 30 (1999), 343–65, for a similar use of antiphonal, ritualized women's mourning.

112 The queens recall the tenth-century *quem quaeritis*, which presents the three Maries in stichomythic mourning for the loss of Christ's body. See Goodland, "'Why Should Calamity,'" pp. 224–5, and for an example, Bevington, *Medieval Drama*, pp. 39–44.

113 See Leah Marcus, *Puzzling Shakespeare: Local Reading and its Discontents* (Berkeley: University of California Press, 1988), pp. 51–105.

SISTERS OF MAGDALENE

1 Elizabeth Egerton, "True Coppie of certaine Loose Papers Left by the Right Honorable Elizabeth, Countess of Bridgewater, Collected and Transcribed together Here since Her Death Anno Domini 1663. Examined by Bridgewater," BL Egerton MS 607, ff. 119v–20 and 121v–22v.

5 "I MIGHT AGAINE HAVE BEEN THE SEPULCURE": MATERNAL MOURNING AND THE ENCRYPTED CORPSE

1 Vera Fortunati, *Lavinia Fontana of Bologna, 1552–1614* (Milan: Electa, 1998), p. 70. See also Angela Ghirardi, "Exempla per l'iconografia dell'Infanzia nel secondo Cinquecento padano," *Il Carrobbio* 21–22 (1993–4), 123–39.

2 See Barasch, *Gestures of Depair*, pp. 23–33.

3 See Adam White, "Westminster Abbey in the Early 17th Century: A Powerhouse of Ideas." *Church Monuments* 4 (1989), 29.

4 Warnicke, "Eulogies for Women," p. 179.

5 Alice Thornton, *The Autobiography of Mrs. Alice Thornton*, ed. Charles Jackson (Durham: Andrews & Company, 1875), pp. 94–5.

6 See Elspeth Graham, Hilary Hinds, Elaine Hobby, and Helen Wilcox (eds.), *Her Own Life: Autobiographical Writings by Seventeenth-Century Englishwomen* (London and New York: Routledge, 1989), pp. 148–9.

7 Wall, *Imprint of Gender*, pp. 296–310, argues that mother's legacies involve their authors' dissolution as a pre-condition for print. See also Rose, "Where are the Mothers," 311–13. For a provocative discussion of this gesture in maternal elegies, see Pamela Hammons, "Despised Creatures: The Illusion of Maternal Self-Effacement in Seventeenth-Century Child Loss Poetry," *ELH* 66 (1999), 25–49.

8 Dorothy Leigh, *The Mothers Blessing* (London: John Budge, 1618), p. 7. See also Elizabeth Grymeston, *Miscellanea, Meditations, Memoratives* (London: Felix Norton, 1604), A2, who explains, "there is no love so forcible as the love of an affectionate mother to her natural child."

9 Butler, *Gender Trouble*, p. 92.

10 See Jahan Ramazani, *The Poetry of Mourning: The Modern Elegy from Hardy to Heaney* (University of Chicago Press, 1994), pp. x–xi and 1–31.

11 Anne de Vere, "Foure Epytaphes, made by the Countes of Oxenford after the death of her young Sonne, the Lord Bulbeck," in John Soowthern, *Pandora* (New York: Columbia University Press, 1938), C4v. All further citations are to this edition and appear parenthetically.

12 Playfere, *Meane in Mourning*, p. 5.

13 Ibid., pp. 7–8.

14 Ibid., pp. 8–9, 26, and 44.

15 Playfere mentions the Virgin only indirectly, since her empathetic grief complicates Protestantism's view of moderate mourning. See Falconer, *Mirror*, for the persistence in Catholicism of the *planctus Mariae*, and see John Taylor, the Water Poet's *Life and Death of the Most Blessed among women, the Virgin Mary* (London: GE, 1620) for a Protestant example.

16 Edward Bury, *Death Improved, and Moderate Sorrow For Deceased Relations Reproved* (London: Thomas Parkhurst, 1693), pp. 3–4.

17 William Herbert, *Herberts Child-Bearing Woman From the Conception to the Weaning of the Child* (London: RA and JM, 1648), H7v–H8. I am indebted to Kathryn McPherson for bringing this source to my attention.

18 Crawford, "Construction and Experience," in Fildes (ed.), *Women as Mothers*, p. 16.

19 Clifford, *Diaries*, pp. 47–62.

20 Ibid., pp. 236–7 and 241.

21 D. J. H. Clifford, in ibid., p. 85. Clifford suffered the deaths of two more infant sons born prematurely by her second husband. See Williamson, *Lady Anne Clifford*, pp. 142 and 172.

22 Ibid., p. 246.

23 Ibid., p. 143. The *Great Memorial Picture*, commissioned by Clifford to record her ancestry, fulfills a similar function.

24 Ibid., pp. 176–9.
25 Thornton, *Autobiography*, pp. 126–7. For comment, see Mary Beth Rose, "Gender, Genre and History: Seventeenth Century Women and the Art of Autobiography," in Mary Beth Rose (ed.), *Women in the Middle Ages and the Renaissance* (New York: Columbia University Press, 1985), pp. 245–78.
26 Elspeth Graham, Hilary Hinds, Elaine Hobby, and Helen Wilcox, "'Pondering All These Things In Her Heart:' Aspects of Secrecy in the Autobiographical Writings of Seventeenth-Century Englishwomen," in Trev Lynn Broughton and Linda Anderson (eds.), *Women's Lives/Women's Times: New Essays on Auto/Biography* (Albany: SUNY Press, 1997), pp. 53–4.
27 Stone, *Family, Sex and Marriage*, p. 70. See also Philippe Ariès, *Centuries of Childhood: A Social History of Family Life*, trans. Robert Baldick (New York: Vintage Books, 1962), p. 39.
28 See, for example, Crawford, "From the Woman's Point of View," in Crawford (ed.), *Exploring Women's Past*, p. 62; Cressy, *Birth, Marriage and Death*, p. 393; Laurence, "Goodly Grief," in Houlbrooke (ed.), *Death, Ritual, and Bereavement*, pp. 62–76; Linda A. Pollock, *Forgotten Children: Parent-Child Relationships from 1500 to 1900* (Cambridge University Press, 1983); and Will Coster, "Tokens of Innocence: Infant Baptism and Burial in Early Modern England," in Gordon and Marshall (eds.), *Places of the Dead*, pp. 266–87.
29 Egerton, "True Coppie," f. 117v. For discussion, see Betty S. Travitsky, "His wife's prayers and meditations: MS Egerton 607," in Anne M. Haselkorn and Betty S. Travitsky (eds.), *The Renaissance Englishwoman in Print: Counterbalancing the Canon* (Amherst: University of Massachussets Press, 1990), pp. 241–60.
30 Ibid., ff. 119–119v.
31 Ibid., ff. 119v–21v.
32 Ibid., ff. 122v–23v.
33 Ibid., ff. 125–125v.
34 Ibid., ff. 126–126v.
35 See Butler, *Gender Trouble*, p. 70, and Nicholas Abraham and Maria Torok, "Introjection–Incorporation: Mourning *or* Melancholia," in Serge Lebovici and Daniel Widlocher (eds.), *Psychoanalysis in France* (New York: International University Press, 1980), pp. 3–16.
36 For recent attempts to refine the intersections between historical criticism and psychoanalysis, see Carla Mazzio and Douglas Trevor (eds.), *Historicism, Psychoanalysis and Early Modern Culture* (New York and London: Routledge, 2000) and Rose, "Where are the Mothers," 295.
37 Lupton and Reinhard, *After Oedipus*, p. 15.
38 Ibid., p. 19.
39 Clarke, *Marrow*, p. 250.
40 Francis Petrarch, "How a Ruler Ought to Govern His State" [*Seniles* 14:1], in Benjamin G. Kohl and Ronald G. Witt, *The Earthly Republic: Italian Humanists on Government and Society* (Philadelphia: University of Pennsylvania Press, 1978), pp. 77–8.

41 Clarke, *Marrow*, p. 250.

42 Josselin, *Diary*, p. 567. For similar accounts, see Henry Newcome, *The Autobiography of Henry Newcome, M.A.*, Richard Parkinson (ed.), 2 vols. (Manchester: Charles Simms and Co., 1852), vol. 2, pp. 252–4, and John Evelyn, *The Diary of John Evelyn*, E. S. de Beer (ed.), 3 vols. (Oxford: Clarendon Press, 1955), vol. 3, pp. 420–31.

43 Ibid., pp. 113–14.

44 Ibid., p. 114.

45 Ibid., pp. 114–15.

46 Ibid., p. 203.

47 Ibid., p. 568.

48 Ibid., p. 204.

49 Josselin's first diary entries, pp. 1–12, occur at the beginning of his career, recalling his life up to that point.

50 Anon., *Preparacyon*, N5. See Wayne, "Advice for Women," in Wilcox (ed.), *Women and Literature*, pp. 60–2, on Erasmus' emphasis on this *dictum* in *Puerpera (The New Mother)* and the colloquy's influence on early modern ideals of maternity.

51 Edward Vaughn, *A Divine Discoverie of Death* (London: William Jones for Richard Boyle, 1612), p. 184.

52 Dekker, *Wonderfull yeare*, C4v.

53 Ibid., C4v–D1.

54 Ibid., D1.

55 Ben Jonson, *Ben Jonson*, ed. C. H. Herford, Percy Simpson, and Evelyn Simpson, 11 vols. (Oxford University Press, 1925–52), vol. 8, p. 33, 1–4.

56 For similar views, see Playfere, *Meane in Mourning*, p. 84; Robert Southwell, *Triumphs*, B2; and Dorothy Leigh, *Mothers Blessing*, p. 193.

57 Pigman, *Grief and English Renaissance Elegy*, pp. 87–8.

58 Jonson, *Ben Jonson*, vol. 8, p. 41.

59 See Sawday, *Body Emblazoned*, p. 228, and Lilley, "'True State Within,'" p. 85.

60 See Pigman, *Grief and English Renaissance Elegy*, pp. 88–90.

61 Philippe de Mornay, *Philip Mornay, Lord of Plessis his Teares for the Death of his Sonne. Unto his Wife Charlotte Baliste*, trans. John Healey (London: G. Eld, 1609), A3v. All further citations are to this edition and appear parenthetically. De Mornay reportedly wrote the treatise in Latin and translated it into French "for the love of his wife" ("pour l'amour de sa femme"): see Charlotte d'Arbaleste de Mornay, *Histoire de la vie de Messire Phillippe de Mornay Seigneur du Plessis Marly, &c.* (Leyden: Bonaventure & Abraham Elsevier, 1647), p. 317.

62 Lucy Crump, *A Huguenot Family in the XVI Century: The Memoirs of Philippe de Mornay, Sieur de Plessis Marly Written by his Wife* (London: George Routledge, 1926), pp. 284–5.

63 Charlotte d'Arbaleste de Mornay, *Histoire*, pp. 318–19 and 322.

64 On early modern views of excessive grief as a fatal condition, see Cressy, *Birth, Marriage and Death*, p. 393; MacDonald, *Mystical Bedlam*, pp. 159–60; and

Laurence, "Goodly Grief," in Houlbrooke (ed.), *Death, Ritual and Bereavement*, pp. 75–6.

65 Freud, "Mourning and Melancholia," in Strachey, et al. (eds.), *Standard Edition* p. 253.

66 On De Vere's biography, see Schleiner, *Tudor and Stuart Women Writers*, pp. 85–6, and Ellen Moody, "Six Elegiac Poems, Possibly by Anne Cecil de Vere, Countess of Oxford," *English Literary Renaissance* 19 (1989), 158–60.

67 Moody, "Six Elegiac Poems," 161.

68 See Lilley, "'True State Within,'" p. 90, and Celeste Schenck, "Feminism and Deconstruction: Re-Constructing the Elegy," *Tulsa Studies in Women's Literature* 5 (1986), 16–20.

69 The image of the womb as sepulcher occurs in Becon's *Sicke Mannes Salve*, p. 93, figuring a desperate fear of death: "O that my mother had been my grave herself!"

70 See Laqueur, *Making Sex*, pp. 43–52.

71 This unorthodox resurrection employs "a nostalgia for maternal rather than paternal origins" which Schenck, "Feminism and Deconstruction," 23, sees as characteristic of women's elegies.

72 Kim Walker, *Women Writers of the English Renaissance* (New York: Twayne, 1996), pp. 61–2.

73 Freud, "Mourning and Melancholia," in Strachey, et al. (eds.), *Standard Edition*, p. 246.

74 See Abraham and Torok, "Introjection-Incorporation," in Lebovici and Widlocher (eds.), *Psychoanalysis in France*, p. 6.

75 Sawday, *Body Emblazoned*, p. 227.

76 Mary Carey, "Upon the Sight of my abortive Birth," in Germaine Greer, Susan Hastings, Jeslyn Medoff, and Melinda Sansone (eds.), *Kissing the Rod: An Anthology of Seventeenth-Century Women's Verse* (London: Virago Press, 1988), pp. 158–61, lines 28–9. All further citations are to this edition and appear parenthetically.

77 Josselin, *Diary*, p. 371.

78 Long, "'It is a lovely bonne,'" makes a similar point. A modern parallel is found in the film, *Alfie*, dir. Lewis Gilbert (Paramount Pictures, 1965), when the title character's sight of his child's fetus, whose abortion he has just procured, prompts a moral conversion from irresponsible womanizer to angst-ridden subject.

79 Gertrude Thimelby, "Upon a Command to Write on my Father," in *Tixall Poetry*, ed. Arthur Clifford (Edinburgh: James Ballantyne and Co., 1813), p. 92.

80 Grace, Lady Mildmay, *Autobiography*, in Randall Martin (ed.), *Women Writers of Renaissance England* (London and New York: Longman, 1997), p. 225.

81 Thomas Tuke, *A Discourse of Death* (London: William Stansbie for George Norton, 1613), pp. 46–7.

82 Quoted in Coster, "Tokens of Innocence," p. 271.

83 Helen Wilcox, "'My Soule in Silence'? Devotional Representations of Renaissance Englishwomen," in Claude J. Summers and Ted-Larry Pebworth (eds.), *Representing Women in Renaissance England* (Columbia: University of South Carolina Press, 1997), pp. 21–2.

84 Mary Carey, "Wretten by me att the same tyme; on the death of my 4th, & only Child, Robert Payler," in Greer, et al. (eds.), *Kissing the Rod*, p. 156.

85 See Moody, "Six Elegiac Poems;" Steven May, "The Countess of Oxford's Sonnets: A Caveat," *ELN* 29 (1992), 9–19; and Schleiner, *Tudor and Stuart Women Writers*, pp. 85–93.

86 Lilley, "'True State Within,'" p. 82.

87 Katherine Philips, "Epitaph: On her son H. P. at St. Syth's Church where her body also lies Interred," George Saintsbury (ed.), *Minor Poets of the Caroline Period*, 2 vols. (Oxford: Clarendon Press, 1905), vol. 1, p. 582, lines 11–14.

88 Ibid., lines 19–22.

89 Katherine Philips, "Orinda upon little Hector Philips," in Saintsbury (ed.), *Minor Poets*, vol. 1, pp. 590–1, lines 1–2 and 5–6.

90 Ibid., line 12.

91 Ibid., lines 13–20.

92 Katherine Philips, "In Memory of F. P. who died at Acton on the 24 of May, 1660, at Twelve and a Half of Age," in Saintsbury (ed.), *Minor Poets*, vol. 1, pp. 530–1, lines 79–80. For discussion, see Ellen Moody, "Orinda, Rosania, Lucasia, *et aliae*: Toward a New Edition of Katherine Philips," *Philological Quarterly* 66 (1987), 325–54.

93 Ibid., lines 1–2.

94 Ibid., lines 3–6.

95 Ibid., lines 15–16 and 65–6.

96 Ibid., lines 71–2.

97 Ibid., lines 75–8.

98 Ibid., lines 83–8.

99 Thomas Goad, "Approbation," in Elizabeth Jocelin, *The Mothers Legacie to her Unborne Childe* (London: F. K. for Robert Allot, 1635), A6v. On Jocelin's work and the other mother's legacies, see Elaine V. Beilin, *Redeeming Eve: Women Writers of the English Renaissance* (Princeton University Press, 1987), pp. 266–85.

100 Ibid., A3.

101 Ibid., A4v.

102 Ibid.

103 Jocelin, *Mother's Legacie*, A12v–B1.

104 Ibid., B1v.

105 See Wayne, "Advice for Women," in Wilcox (ed.), *Women and Literature*, p. 60.

106 Goad, "Approbation," A9v.

107 Ibid., A9v–10.

108 Ibid., A9v.

109 On the post-Reformation prayer closet and its relationship to subjectivity, see Richard Rambuss, *Closet Devotions* (Durham and London: Duke University Press, 1998), pp. 103–35.

110 Schenck, "Feminism and Deconstruction," 23.

6 "QUOD LICUIT FECI": ELIZABETH RUSSELL AND THE POWER
OF PUBLIC MOURNING

1 For clarity, I refer to Elizabeth Cooke Hoby Russell by the name of Russell throughout the chapter, despite the anachronism of that appellation prior to her marriage to John Russell in 1574.

2 David Nash Ford, "Beaten 'til the Blood Ran," http://www.britannia.com/ history/legend/bisham.html. This derogatory portrait of Russell is echoed in some criticism, particularly A. L. Rowse, "Bisham and the Hobies," in *Times, Persons, Places: Essays in Literature* (London: Macmillan, 1985), pp. 188–218.

3 On the Cooke sisters, see George Ballard, *Memoirs of Several Ladies of Great Britain*, ed. Ruth Perry (Detroit: Wayne State University Press, 1985), pp. 199–204; Beilin, *Redeeming Eve*, pp. 55–64; Farber, "Letters," pp. 14–30; Schleiner, *Tudor and Stuart Women Writers*, pp. 34–51; and Alan Stewart, "The Voices of Anne Cooke, Lady Anne and Lady Bacon," in Danielle Clarke and Elizabeth Clarke (eds.), *This Double Voice": Gendered Writing in Early Modern England*, (Houndsmills, Basingstoke, Hampshire: Macmillan, 2000), pp. 88–102.

4 William Camden, *Reges, Reginae, Nobiles, et allij in Ecclesia Collegiate B. Petri Westmonsterii Sepulti* (London: Melch. Bradwoodus, 1603), G1–G2. Later antiquarians also include Russell's epitaphs in textual tours of Westminster Abbey: see Edward Wedlake Brayley, *The History and Antiquities of the Abbey Church of St. Peter, Westminster*, 4 vols. (London: Hurt, Robinson and Co., 1823), vol. 2, pp. 157–9; Jodacus Crull, *The Antiquities of St. Peter's, or the Abbey-Church of Westminster*, 2 vols. (London: E. Bell, 1722), vol. 1, pp. 46–50; and John Dart, *Westmonasterium, or The History and Antiquities of The Abbey Church of St. Peters Westminster*, 2 vols. (London: James Cole, 1723), vol. 1, pp. 110–18.

5 Edward Phillips, *Theatrum Poetarum, or a Compleat Collection of all the Poets of all Ages* (London: Charles Smith, 1675), p. 156.

6 See Margaret J. M. Ezell, *The Patriarch's Wife: Literary Evidence and the History of the Family* (Chapel Hill: University of North Carolina Press, 1987), pp. 9–35, on early modern mothers' central roles in negotiating children's marriages.

7 See Farber, "Letters," pp. 45–6 and 96–109.

8 See Helen C. Gladstone, "Building an Identity: Two Noblewomen in England, 1566–1666," (PhD dissertation, Open University, 1989), pp. 66–84; Farber, "Letters," pp. 41–58, 110–38, and 276–86; Strong, *Cult of Elizabeth*, pp. 17–55; and Violet Wilson, *Society Women of Shakespeare's Time* (London: John Lane, 1924), pp. 23–40.

9 Series of monuments were commissioned in the period only by Russell and Anne Clifford, whose memorials are surveyed by Gladstone, "Building an Identity," pp. 120–208, and Williamson, *Lady Anne Clifford*, pp. 334–45, 386–92, and 404–14.

10 Schleiner, *Tudor and Stuart Women Writers*, p. 51.

11 The ghost story's origins appear to be in regional oral culture, since none of Russell's early biographers, who mostly rely on information from her epitaphs, report it.

12 Gladstone, "Building an Identity," p. 305.

13 Nigel Llewellyn, "Honour in Life, Death, and in the Memory: Funeral Monuments in Early Modern England," *Transactions of the Royal Historical Society* ser. 6, vol. 6 (1996), 180.

14 Elizabeth Russell, "Eulogy on Mrs. Robert Cecil," Salis MS 140.82. The poem is dated February, 1597.

15 Farber, "Letters," p. 210. The letter is one of three referring to Cecil's melancholy: see also pp. 190–201.

16 Ashmole, *Antiquities*, vol. 2, p. 469 and Schleiner, *Tudor and Stuart Women Writers*, p. 208. Ashmole, vol. 2, pp. 464–71, describes the Bisham tombs, and, following him, Schleiner, pp. 205–10, reprints and translates the inscriptions.

17 Camden, *Reges*, G2. Working from Camden, Schleiner, *Tudor and Stuart Women Writers*, pp. 47–50, reprints and translates the epitaphs.

18 Hoby's translation appeared in 1561. See Baldassare Castiglione, *The Book of the Courtier* (New York: AMS Press, 1967).

19 Schleiner, *Tudor and Stuart Women Writers*, p. 47, suggests that the tag means Russell had written more verse for the tombs than she could include, but no evidence of this survives.

20 Llewellyn, "Honour in Life," 192.

21 See Thomas Hoby, "Travels," ff. 177v–82, and Farber, "Letters," pp. 20–4.

22 Thomas Hoby, "Will," PRO PROB 11/48, f. 419.

23 Gladstone, "Building an Identity," p. 50.

24 BL Add. MS 18764, ff. 1–2, "A Bill of Traveling Expenses of his wife, to be allowed to the lady Hobye, wife to Sir Tho: Hobye, Knighte, his Queens Majesties Embassador in France."

25 BL Harley MS 7035, "T. Baker Collectanea Oxoniensia," f. 161.

26 Gladstone, "Building an Identity," pp. 252–65, describes the tomb.

27 College of Arms MS, 1.13, f. 77–8, "Description of the Funeral of Sir Thomas Hoby." See also BL Harley MS 7035, f. 161, "Description of the Funeral of Sir Thomas Hoby."

28 Ashmole, *Antiquities*, vol. 2, pp. 464–5. Unless otherwise noted, transcriptions are from the tombs, with citations to Ashmole's transcriptions, and Connie McQuillan's Latin translations in Schleiner.

29 Ashmole, *Antiquities*, vol. 2, pp. 465–6.

30 See Beier, "Good Death," in Houlbrooke (ed.), *Death, Ritual, and Bereavement*, pp. 55–6, and Houlbrooke, *Death, Religion and the Family*, pp. 191–2.

31 Ashmole, *Antiquities*, vol. 2, pp. 468–9; Schleiner, *Tudor and Stuart Women Writers*, pp. 207–8.

32 Ashmole, *Antiquities*, vol. 2, pp. 467–8; Schleiner, *Tudor and Stuart Women Writers*, pp. 206–7.

33 John Harington, *Ariosto's Orlando Furioso*, ed. Robert McNulty (Oxford: Clarendon Press, 1972), p. 434.

34 Julia M. Walker, "Reading the Tombs," 60. See also Lamb, "Cooke Sisters," p. 120.

35 Llewellyn, "Honor in Life," 197.

36 Adam White, "Westminster Abbey," 23 and 32, n. 21.

37 Gladstone, "Building an Identity," p. 260. For a different view, see Margaret Whinney, *Sculpture in Britain, 1530–1830* (London: Penguin Books, 1988), pp. 9 and 230, n. 30.

38 Ibid., pp. 52–3, 206, and 260–2. See also Peter J. Begent, *The Heraldry of the Hoby Memorials in the Parish Church of All Saints, Bisham, in the Royal County of Berkshire* (Maidenhead: Peter J. Begent, 1979), pp. 3 and 9.

39 Weever, *Ancient Funeral Monuments*, p. 10.

40 Because the tomb is badly damaged, the transcription is from Ashmole, *Antiquities*, vol. 2, pp. 470–1, and translation from Schleiner, *Tudor and Stuart Women Writers*, pp. 209–10. Gladstone, "Building an Identity," pp. 266–70, describes the tomb.

41 Jane Stevenson, "Female Authority and Authorization Strategies in Early Modern Europe," in Clarke and Clarke (eds.), *"This Double Voice,"* pp. 27 and 38, n. 51, sees the poem as an exception to her claim that early modern women Latinists could not articulate their experiences of motherhood in the limitations of their medium.

42 Ashmole, *Antiquities*, vol. 2, p. 470, records that in 1719 the gravestone was "lying before Sir Th. and Phil. Hoby's Monument," but it is now before Russell's.

43 Weever, *Ancient Funeral Monuments*, n.p.

44 Llewellyn, "Honour in Life," 179. On post-Reformation iconoclasm, see Diehl, *Staging Reform*, pp. 19–66, and Eire, *War Against the Idols*.

45 Weever, *Ancient Funeral Monuments*, p. 18, refutes this charge in defense of monuments' memorial function.

46 Ibid., p. 52. Weever reprints the proclamation in its entirety, pp. 52–4.

47 Llewellyn, *Art of Death*, p. 123.

48 Werdmuller, *Most frutefull*, p. 189.

49 Llewellyn, "Honour in Life," 190–1.

50 See Llewellyn, *Art of Death*, p. 106, and Tarlow, *Bereavement and Commemoration*, pp. 92–4 and 173.

51 Llewellyn, *Art of Death*, p. 104.

52 Margaret Hoby, *Diary*, p. 156, and Clifford, *Diaries*, pp. 29 and 75. See also Adam White, "Westminster Abbey," 15 and 43, n. 4 and 5.

53 Adam White, "Classical Learning and the Early Stuart Renaissance," *Church Monuments* 1 (1985), 20.

54 Houlbrooke, *Death, Religion and the Family*, p. 354, and *The English Family*, pp. 205–6.
55 Russell's brothers, Antony and Edward Cooke, died prior to 1555 and in 1566, respectively. See Begent, *Heraldry*, p. 54.
56 Farber, "Letters," p. 40.
57 *The Registers of Bisham, County Berkshire, 1560–1812*, transcribed by Edgar Powell (London: Parish Register Society, 1898), p. 19.
58 Gladstone, "Building an Identity," pp. 26, and 102–3.
59 Farber, "Letters," p. 121. From Blackfriars, Russell led a neighborhood movement in 1596 to prevent Shakespeare and Burbage from opening a "common playhouse" nearby. See Farber, "Letters," p. 55, and Rowse, "Bisham and the Hobies," p. 210.
60 Farber, "Letters," p. 137.
61 BL Hargrave MS 497, "Heraldic Collections, no. 24: The Christening of Elizabeth the first daughter of the Lord Russell Son and Heir to Francis Earl of Bedford and of Elizabeth his wife [Daughter of Sr. Anthony Cook, and widow of Sr. Thomas Hobby, Knight,] now Lady Russell Baptised in the Cathedral church of Westminster on Thursday 27. die Octob. 1575," f. 57. The account is published in J. H. Wiffen, *Memoirs of the House of Russell*, 3 vols. (London: Longman, 1833), vol. 1, pp. 502–5.
62 Ibid., ff. 57–8.
63 The wedding is described in Wiffen, *Memoirs*, vol. 2, pp. 57–8, and Collins, *Letters and Memorials*, vol. 2, pp. 195–203. For discussion, see Strong, *Cult of Elizabeth*, pp. 17–55.
64 Collins, *Letters and Memorials*, vol. 2, p. 195.
65 Farber, "Letters," pp. 284–5.
66 Collins, *Letters and Memorials*, vol. 2, p. 203. Whyte's account is the verbal equivalent of Robert Peake's *Queen Elizabeth Going in Procession to Blackfriars in 1600*. On the painting, see Strong, *Cult of Elizabeth*.
67 John Nichols, *The Progresses and Public Processions of Queen Elizabeth*, 3 vols. (London: John Nichols and Son, 1823), vol. 3, p. 132.
68 See BL Add. MS 2148, ff.. 183v–84v, "An Exhortation unto deth given to my Lord and Master the Lo: Russell when he laye upon his death bedd in London by Doctor Nowell deane of Paules, 1584." For Russell's funeral, see BL Stowe MS 586, "A Description of Funerals Served by Heralds, 1556–1594," f. 2v.
69 Gladstone, "Building an Identity," p. 64.
70 Adam White, "Westminster Abbey," 29–30, and John Webster, *The Duchess of Malfi*, ed. Elizabeth M. Brennan (New York: W.W. Norton, 1985), 4.2.153–6.
71 Gladstone, "Building an Identity," p. 204.
72 See Belsey, *Shakespeare*, pp. 114–16.
73 Gladstone, "Building an Identity," p. 272, suggests that the figures may represent Russell's daughters.
74 Camden, *Reges*, G1; Schleiner, *Tudor and Stuart Women Writers*, pp. 48–9. Camden prints the poems as they appear from top to bottom and left to

right on the monument, but Schleiner changes the order and titles them incorrectly. My transcriptions are from the monument, with reference to Camden, and McQuillan's Latin and Lynn E. Roller's Greek translations, both in Schleiner.

75 Lilley, "True State Within," pp. 78–9.
76 Camden, *Reges*, G1v.
77 Ibid., G1; Schleiner, *Tudor and Stuart Women Writers*, p. 48.
78 Ibid., See also Dart, *Westmonasterium*, vol.1, p. 117, for a vivid translation of the banqueting imagery.
79 Camden, *Reges*, G1v; Schleiner, *Tudor and Stuart Women Writers*, p. 49.
80 See also Edward Hoby, "Eulogy for John Russell," BL Add. MS 38223, f. 48.
81 Camden, *Reges*, G1v–G2; Schleiner, *Tudor and Stuart Women Writers*, pp. 49–50.
82 Camden, Reges, G2.
83 John Chamberlain, *The Letters of John Chamberlain to Mr.Carleton*, ed. Sarah Williams (London: Camden Society, 1861), p. 87.
84 Collins, *Letters and Memorials*, vol. 2, p. 204.
85 Gladstone, "Building an Identity," p. 83.
86 Farber, "Letters," p. 288.
87 See ibid., p. 311, and Collins, *Letters and Memorials*, vol. 2, pp. 142–3.
88 See Gladstone, "Building an Identity," p. 279, and Adam White, "Classical Learning," 22 and 32, n. 7 and 8.
89 See Dart, *Westmonasterium*, vol. 1, pp. 111–12, Crull, *Antiquities of St. Peter's*, vol. 1, pp. 49–50, and Brayley, *History and Antiquities*, vol. 2, p. 159, for descriptions of the monument, and Gladstone, "Building an Identity," pp. 284–96, and Adam White, "Classical Learning," for critical discussion.
90 Dart, *Westmonasterium*, vol. 1, p. 111. Adam White, "Classical Learning," 23, argues that Russell's depleted resources following Anne's marriage explains her daughter's financing of the monument.
91 See Adam White, "Classical Learning," 20, and "Westminster Abbey," 19.
92 Adam White, "Westminster Abbey," 19 and 43, n. 16.
93 Gladstone, "Building an Identity," pp. 83–4.
94 Crull, *Antiquities of St. Peter's*, vol. 1, p. 50. See also BL Add. MS 2148, f. 185, "Description of the Tomb of Bess Russell in Westminster Abbey." Both Brayley, *History and Antiquities*, vol. 2, p. 159 and Dart, *Westmonasterium*, vol. 1, p. 111, "positively reject" the story, but Schleiner, *Tudor and Stuart Women Writers*, p. 50, repeats it as fact.
95 See Strong, *Cult of Elizabeth*, pp. 26–7. Nan Russell wears a similar gown in Peake's *Procession Picture*.
96 Gladstone, "Building an Identity," p. 288.
97 Llewellyn, "Honour in Life," 184.
98 Weever, *Ancient Funeral Monuments*, pp. 11–12.
99 Russell had negotiated a marriage between Bess and Worcester's heir, William Somerset, in 1597, but on William's death, she married Nan to Somerset's younger brother Henry. See Farber, "Letters," pp. 59–60.

100 Farber, "Letters," p. 267.
101 Margaret Hoby, *Diary*, p. 203.
102 Elizabeth Russell, *A Way of Reconciliation, of a good and learned man* (London: R. Barker, 1605), A2v.
103 Farber, "Letters," p. 325.
104 Russell, *Way of Reconciliation*, A2v.
105 Ibid., A1.
106 Gladstone, "Building an Identity," p. 102.
107 Elizabeth Russell, "Letter to William Dethick," College of Arms MS Vin. 151, f. 325. See also Farber, "Letters," pp. 319–22.
108 Ibid., f. 326. See also Begent, *Heraldry*, pp. 11–12.
109 Russell, "Will," PRO PROB 11/113 – Dorset 56.
110 Gladstone, "Building an Identity," pp. 103 and 309, identifies the sculptor as William Cure II (d. 1632).
111 Ibid., p. 204.
112 Llewellyn, "Honour in Life," 191.
113 Ibid.
114 Russell commissioned a prepatory portrait for the effigy which still hangs in Bisham Abbey. There, too, the idealized portrait is represented in full mourning.
115 Rowse, "Bisham and the Hobies," pp. 93–4, argues that the coronet was added in response to ridicule, during Russell's appearance in a Star Chamber case, of her habitual self-appellation as "Dowager." On the case, see Felicity Heal, "Reputation and Honour in Court and Country: Lady Elizabeth Russell and Sir Thomas Hoby," *Transactions of the Royal Historical Society*, series 6, vol. 6, 161–78, and Farber, "Letters," pp. 330–2.
116 Gladstone, "Building an Identity," pp. 301–10; Begent, *Heraldry*, pp. 11–26; Ashmole, *Antiquities*, vol. 2, pp. 469–70; and *The Victoria History of the Counties of England: Berkshire*, ed. William Page, 3 vols. (London: University of London, 1972), vol. 3, pp. 149–51, describe the tomb.
117 Schleiner, *Tudor and Stuart Women Writers*, p. 209, for translation.
118 Gladstone, "Building an Identity," p. 306, transcribes the inscription. See Church of England, *Book of Common Prayer*, p. 309, for translation.
119 Begent, *Heraldry*, pp. 25–6. See also *Victoria History*, vol. 3, pp. 150–1.
120 For Russell's epitaphs for Katherine Killigrew's tomb, see Schleiner, *Tudor and Stuart Women Writers*, p. 210.
121 Weever, *Ancient Funeral Monuments*, p. 17.
122 Gladstone, "Building an Identity," pp. 29–30, notes that similar panels on Anne Clifford's tomb bear inscriptions by her grandchildren.

7 THE MAT(T)ER OF DEATH: THE DEFENSE OF EVE AND THE FEMALE *ARS MORIENDI*

1 Mavericke, *Mourning Weede*, C4v–D1.
2 Shakespeare, *Hamlet*, 5.2.336–7.

3 Anon., *Lamentacyon*, A2.

4 Doebler, *Rooted Sorrow*, p. 49.

5 Anon., *Lamentacyon*, A2.

6 Doebler, *Rooted Sorrow*, pp. 51–9, discusses the woodcuts in detail. See Beatty, *Craft of Dying*, p. 1–53, on the several texts that together comprise the medieval *ars moriendi*.

7 Warnicke, "Eulogies for Women," in Travitsky and Seeff (eds.), *Attending to Women*, p. 170.

8 Richard Whitford, *A Dayly Exercyse and Experyence of Death* (London: J. Waylande, 1537), C7–C7v.

9 Jeremy Taylor, *Rule and Exercises*, p. 94.

10 Eire, *War Against the Idols*, p. 315. For a fascinating discussion of Catholicism's "bewhored" female images and their impact upon representations of women, see Diehl, *Staging Reform*, pp. 156–81.

11 Dorothy White's *A Lamentation Unto this Nation* belongs more properly to the jeremiad tradition than to the *ars moriendi*. The only other female-authored art, Frances Norton's *Memento Mori*, is discussed below, as is Mary Sidney Herbert's translation of De Mornay's *Discours de la vie et la morte*.

12 Rachel Speght, *Mortalities Memorandum, with A Dreame Prefixed*, in Barbara Kiefer Lewalski (ed.), *The Polemics and Poems of Rachel Speght* (Oxford University Press, 1996), p. 74. All citations are to this edition and appear parenthetically.

13 Alice Sutcliffe, *Meditations of Mans Mortalitie*, ed. Patrick Cullen, in *The Early Modern Englishwoman: A Facsimile Library of Essential Works*, part 1, vol. 7 (Aldershot: Scolar Press, 1996), p. 20. All citations are to this edition and appear parenthetically. A first edition of Sutcliffe's work, entered in the Stationers' Register on January 30, 1633, is no longer extant.

14 Samuel Ward, *The Life of Faith in Death. Exemplified in the Living speeches of dying Christians* (London: Augustine Mathewes, for John Marriot and John Grismand, 1622), p. 9.

15 Ibid., pp. 23–4 and 39–40.

16 Peter of Luca, *Dialogue*, C2v.

17 Ward, *Life of Faith*, p. 50.

18 Ariès, *Hour of our Death*, pp. 297–315.

19 Houlbrooke, *Death, Religion and the Family*, pp. 218 and 147–8.

20 Bellarmino, *Art of Dying*, pp. 274–5.

21 William Perkins, *A Salve for a Sick Man* (Cambridge: John Legate, 1595), pp. 84–94.

22 Houlbrooke, *English Family*, p. 202.

23 I am grateful to Craig Kallendorf for his help in deciphering these Latin tags.

24 See Anon., *Lamentacyon*, B5v–C3.

25 In the medieval *ars moriendi* Moriens is always male. Later arts, influenced by funeral sermons, occasionally indicate their relevance to both sexes: see Lamb, *Gender and Authorship*, pp. 121–2.

26 Peter of Luca, *Dialogue*, E4v.

27 Ibid., E6–E6v.
28 Becon, *Salve*, pp. 130–4. The dying man's blessing of his family is a standard passage in the *ars moriendi*: see Peter of Luca, E8v–FI v, for a Catholic example.
29 Clarke, *Marrow*, p. 252.
30 Grace, Lady Mildmay, *Autobiography*, pp. 222–3.
31 Thornton, *Autobiography*, pp. 51–3.
32 Ibid., pp. 100–22. The account of her mother's life and death is the longest entry in the autobiography, suggesting its importance to Thornton's life.
33 Ibid., p. 109.
34 Ibid., p. 113.
35 Sutton, *Disce Mori*, p. 272.
36 Mary Sidney Herbert, *A Discourse of Life and Death*, in Hannay, et al. (eds.), *Collected Works*, vol. 1, p. 254.
37 Raphael Holinshed, *Chronicles of England, Scotland, and Ireland*, 6 vols. (New York: AMS Press, 1965), vol. 4, p. 879. For discussion, see Lamb, *Gender and Authorship*, pp. 122–3.
38 See Hannay, et al. (eds.), *Collected Works*, vol. 1, p. 211.
39 Bornstein, "Style," in Hannay (ed.), *Silent But For the Word*, p. 127.
40 See Lamb, *Gender and Authorship*, pp. 125–7.
41 Herbert, *Discourse*, in Hannay, *et al.* (eds.), *Collected Works*, vol. 1, p. 247.
42 Herbert, *Triumph of Death*, in Hannay, *et al.* (eds.), *Collected Works*, vol. 1, p. 274. The editors discuss the gendering of death in the visual tradition on p. 258. Edward Aggas' earlier translation of De Mornay's treatise, *The Defence of Death* (London: John Allde for Edward Aggas, 1576), D3–D3v, also retains the feminine gendering of death, as does Anna Hume's translation of Petrarch's triumph: see Greer, *et al.* (eds.), *Kissing the Rod*, pp. 101–106. Beyond this, I have found only one similar depiction: William Leigh, *Soules Solace*, p. 3, states "Death is the Lady and Empresse of all the world."
43 See Belsey, *Shakespeare*, pp. 152–5, on similar sixteenth-century images.
44 Becon, *Sicke Mannes Salve*, pp. 156–7.
45 Joseph Swetnam, *The Arraignment of Lewd, Froward, and Unconstant Women* (London: George Purslowe for Thomas Archer, 1615), BI.
46 Rachel Speght, *A Mouzell for Melastomus*, in Lewalski (ed.), *Polemics and Poems*, p. 13. All citations are to this edition and appear parenthetically.
47 The *querelle des femmes* commonly argues that Eve, created from Adam's rib rather than from dust, was "of a refined mould" (Speght, *Mouzell*, p. 18).
48 For related readings of the Fall, see Belsey, *Shakespeare*, pp. 85–127, and Amy Boesky, "Giving Time to Women: The Eternizing Project in Early Modern England," in Clarke and Clarke (eds.), *"This Double Voice,"* pp. 127–8.
49 Church of England, *Certain Sermons or Homilies Appointed to be Read in the Time of Queen Elizabeth I (1623)*, ed. Mary Ellen Rickey and Thomas B. Stroup (Gainesville: Scholar's Facsimiles and Reprints, 1968), p. 243. I am indebted to Ken A. Bugajski for this reference. The passage specifically admonishes wives to "bring not such excuses to me at this time: but apply all thy diligence to beare thine obedience to thine husband" (pp. 243–4). See Lanyer, *Poems*, pp. 84–7, for her defense of Eve.

50 Ibid., p. 181.

51 Aughterson, *Renaissance Woman*, p. 4.

52 Stubbes, *Anatomie*, c3v–c4, also exonerates Eve: "Adam, condescending to his wife her perswasions, or rather to the Serpent . . . tooke of the apple, & did eate, contrary to the expresse commandemant of his God."

53 Simon Shepherd (ed.), *The Women's Sharp Revenge: Five Women's Pamphlets from the Renaissance* (New York: St. Martin's, 1985), p. 15.

54 Ibid., p. 17

55 Sutcliffe's lack of direct connection with the male writers is affirmed by Jonson's poem which, as Greer, et al. (eds.), *Kissing the Rod*, p. 13, state, "is so contorted, being no more than a versification of her chapter headings, that we might suspect an element of parody."

56 See Belsey, *Shakespeare*, pp. 70–3.

57 Frances Norton, *Memento Mori* (London: John Graves, 1705), p. 57.

58 Ibid., pp. 56 and 83.

59 Ibid., pp. 6–7 and b2–b2v.

60 Ibid., pp. 16–25 ; 32–35; 46–8; 71–3; 91–4; 106.

61 Ibid., pp. 45–6. See also pp. 35–42 and 88.

62 Ibid., a2v–a3.

63 Ibid., a3v.

CODICIL: "A WEB OF BLACKE"

1 Thomas Proctor, *A Gorgeous Gallery of Gallant Inventions*, ed. Hyder Rollins (Cambridge, MA: Harvard University Press, 1926), p. 116. Rollins, p. 204, n. 11, attributes the prefatory poem to Proctor.

2 Isabella Whitney's "The Manner of her Will, or What She left to London," appeared in *A Sweet Nosgay* (London: Richard Jones, 1573), E2–E8v. For discussion, see Wall, *Imprint of Gender*, pp. 296–310, and Betty Travitsky, "The 'Wyll and Testament' of Isabella Whitney," *English Literary Renaissance* 10 (1980), 76–94. Proctor hints at Whitney's identity by alluding to the author's "will."

3 Isabella Whitney, "The Lamentacion of a Gentilwoman upon the death of her late deceased frend William Gruffith Gent," in Proctor, *Gorgeous Gallery*, pp. 116–20. All references to the poem are to this edition and appear parenthetically.

4 Rollins (ed.), in Proctor, *Gorgeous Gallery*, p. 204, n. 11, states that the poem was registered on December 20, 1577, six months after Proctor's book was licensed. Of eighty-eight ballads currently collected in *Britwell Ballads*, twenty-three are elegies, *memento moris*, or reports of notorious deaths.

5 Rollins (ed.), in Proctor, *Gorgeous Gallery*, p. 205, n. 36. He identifies the author as Jasper Heywood.

6 See Randall Martin, "Isabella Whitney's 'Lamentation upon the Death of William Gruffith,'" *Early Modern Literary Studies* 3:1 (1997): http://purl.oclc.org/emls/03–1/martwhit.html, para. 11, and Martin (ed.), *Women Writers*, pp. 303–10.

Bibliography

MANUSCRIPTS

BL Add. MS 2148, ff. 183v–84v. "An Exhortation unto deth given to my Lord and Master the Lo: Russell when he laye upon his death bedd in London by Doctor Nowell deane of Paules, 1584."

BL MS 2148, f. 185. "Description of the Tomb of Bess Russell in Westminster Abbey."

BL Add. MS 18764, ff. 1–2. "A Bill of Traveling Expenses of his wife, to be allowed to the lady Hobye, wife to Sir Tho: Hobye, Knighte, his Queens Majesties Embassador in France."

BL Add. MS 47713, f. 10v. "College of Arms Establishment Lists after 1605."

BL Add. MS 71131A, f. 1. "Sir Edward Coke-Lee Funeral (1605)."

BL Harley MS 7035, f. 161. "Description of the Funeral of Sir Thomas Hoby."

BL Hargrave MS 497, ff. 57–9. "Heraldic Collections, no. 24: The Christening of Elizabeth the first daughter of the Lord Russell Son and Heir to Francis Earl of Bedford and of Elizabeth his wife [Daughter of Sr. Anthony Cook, and widow of Sr. Thomas Hobby, Knight,] now Lady Russell Baptised in the Cathedral church of Westminster on Thursday 27. die Octob. 1575."

BL Stowe MS 586. "A Description of Funerals Served by Heralds, 1556–1594."

BL Add. MS 4244, f. 23. "Birch's Catalogue of Ladies famous for their Writings, or skill in the Learned Languages."

BL Harley MS 7035, f. 161. "T. Baker Collectanea Oxoniensia, A Letter from Elizabeth I to Elizabeth Hoby."

Camden, William. "Eulogy for John Russell." BL Add. MS 36294, f. 49b.

Cecil, William. "The order of mourners to be appointed Mildred Cecille, 2nd wife died 1589." Salis Cal 3.462, Item 973, ff. 1–2.

College of Arms MS, I. 13, ff. 77–8. "Description of the Funeral of Sir Thomas Hoby."

College of Arms MS 1586–1603, ff. 44–9 and ff. 215–19. "Description of the Funeral of John Russell."

Egerton, Elizabeth. "True Coppie of certain Loose Papers left by the Right Honorable Elizabeth, Countess of Bridgewater. Collected and Transcribed Together here since Her Death, Anno Domini 1663." BL Egerton MS 607.

Hoby, Edward. "Eulogy for John Russell." BL Add. MS 38223, f. 48.

Hoby, Thomas. "The Booke of the Travaile and lief of me, Thomas Hoby with diverse thiinge woorth the notinge." BL Add. MS. 2148, ff. 5–182.
"Will." PRO PROB 11/48, f. 419.
Lenox, Margaret, Countess of. "Will." PRO PROB 11/60/12.
Russell, Elizabeth. "Eulogy on Mrs. Robert Cecil." Salis. MS 140.82.
"Letter to William Dethick." College of Arms MS Vin. 151, f. 325.
"Will." PRO PCC Dorset 56.
Russell, John. "Letter to William Cecil." BL Lansdowne MS 20, f. 51.
Salis MS, Cecil Papers Maps, II, 14. "Proposed monument for Mildred and William Cecil."

PRIMARY SOURCES

Aggas, Edward. *The Defence of Death*. London: John Allde for Edward Aggas, 1576.
Alfie. Dir. Lewis Gilbert. Paramount Pictures, 1965.
Andreas Hyperius. *Of Framing of Divine Sermons, or Popular Interpretation of the Scriptures (The Practice of Preaching)*. Trans. John Ludham. London: Thomas East, 1577.
Anonymous. *Arden of Faversham* New York: W. W. Norton, 1995.
Ars Moriendi. Lyons: Engelhart Schultis? 1490?
Ars Moriendi. New York: De Vinne Press, 1902.
Complaynte of the lover of Cryst saynt Mary Magdaleyn. London: Wynkyn de Worde, 1520.
The Craft of Dying (c. 1450). In Comper (ed.), *Book of the Craft of Dying*, pp. 3–51.
Englands Welcome to James, by the Grace of God, King of England, Scotland, France and Ireland, defender of the faith, &c. London: E. W. for C. K., 1603.
The Good-Wives Lamentation: Or, The Womens Complaint on the Account of Their Being to be Buried in Wollen. London: L. C., 1678.
The Good-Wives Vindication: Or An Answer to a Late Saucy Pamphlet Entitled The Womens Complaint. London: L. C., 1678.
Here bygynneth a lytyll treatyse schortely compyled and called ars moriendi, that is to saye the craft for to dee for the healthe of mannes sowle (Westminster: William Caxton, 1491). In Comper (ed.), *Book of the Craft of Dying* pp. 91–102.
Here Begynneth a lytell treatyse of the dyenge creature enfected with sykenes uncurable with many sorowfull complayntes (The Lamentacyon of the dyenge creature). London: Wynkyn de Worde, 1507.
Here begynneth a lityll treatyse schort and abridged: speaking of the arte and crafte to know well to dee (Westminster: William Caxton, 1490). In Comper (ed.), *Book of the Craft of Dying*, pp. 55–90.
A Mournefull Dittie, entitled Elizabeths losse, together with a welcome for King James. London: Thomas Pavier, 1603.
The Preparacyon to the Crosse with the Preparacyon to deeth. London: Thomas Petyte, approx. 1545.

Sorrowes Joy, or A Lamentation for our late deceased Soveraigne Elizabeth, with a triumph for the prosperous succession of our gratious King James, &c. Cambridge: John Legat, 1603.

Ashmole, Elias. *Antiquities of Berkshire.* 3 vols. London: E. Curll, 1719.

Balmford, James. *A Short Dialogue Concerning the Plagues Infection.* London: Richard Boyle, 1603.

Baptista Mantuanus. *A Lamentable Complaynte of Baptista Mantuanus, an Italysh poete, wherein he famylyarly commonteth wyth hys owne myde, that Death is not to be feared.* London: John Daye, 1560.

Barlow, Thomas. *Pietas in Patrem, or a Few Teares upon the Death of His Father R. Barlow.* Oxford: William Turner, 1637.

Becon, Thomas. *The Sicke Mannes Salve.* In Ayre, John (ed.), *Prayers and Other Pieces of Thomas Becon,* pp. 88–191. Cambridge University Press, 1846.

Bellarmino, Roberto. *The Art of Dying Well.* Trans. Edward Coffin. St. Omer: English College Press, 1622.

Bentley, Thomas. *Monument of Matrones: Containing Severall Lamps of Virginitie.* London: Henry Denham, 1582.

Birnie, William. *The Blame of Kirk-Buriall.* Edinburgh: Robert Charteris, 1606.

Boccaccio, Giovanni. *Il Decamerone.* Ed. Aldo Rossi. Bologna: L. Cappelli, 1977.

Boyd, Zachary. "The Queenes Lamentation for the Death of Her Sonne." In *The Last Battel of the Soule in Death,* vol. 2, n. p. 2 vols. Edinburgh: Andro Hart, 1629.

Bradford, John. *A frutefull treatise and full of heavenly consolation against the feare of death.* London: William Powell, 1566–7.

Bradstreet, Anne. *The Works of Anne Bradstreet.* Ed. Jeannine Hensley. Cambridge: Harvard University Press, 1967.

Brewer, Thomas. *The Weeping Lady: Or, London Like Ninivie in Sack-Cloth.* London: B. A. and T. F. for Matthew Rhodes, 1629.

Bury, Edward. *Death Improved, and Moderate Sorrow For Deceased Relations Reproved.* London: Thomas Parkhurst, 1693.

Byng, Thomas. "Offering." In Anonymous, *Sorrowes Joy,* p. 10.

C., J. *Saint Marie Magdalens Conversion.* Secret English Press, 1603.

Camden, William. *Reges, Reginae, Nobiles, et allij in Ecclesia Collegiate B. Petri Westmonsterii Sepulti.* London: Melch. Bradwoodus, 1603.

Cannon, Nathaniel. *Lachrimae: or Lamentations Over the Dead.* London: Felix Kyngston for William Welby, 1616.

Carey, Mary. "Upon the Sight of my abortive Birth." Greer, et al. (eds.) *Kissing the Rod,* pp. 158–61.

"Wretten by me att the same tyme; on the death of my 4th, & only Child, Robert Payler." In Greer, et al. (eds.), *Kissing the Rod,* pp. 156–7.

Castiglione, Baldassare. *The Book of the Courtier.* Trans. Thomas Hoby. New York: AMS Press, 1967.

Chamberlain, John. *The Letters of John Chamberlain to Mr. Carleton.* Ed. Sarah Williams. London: Camden Society, 1861.

Chaucer, Geoffrey. *The Works of Geoffrey Chaucer.* London: John Kyngston for John Wight, 1561.

Cheare, Abraham. "The Embalming of the Dead Cause, on Mark 14.8." In *Words in Season*, pp. 107–73. London: Nathan Brookes, 1668.

Chettle, Henry. *Englandes Mourning Garment.* London: V. S. for Thomas Millington, 1603.

Chrysostom, St. John. *Commentary on St. John the Apostle and Evangelist.* Trans. Sister Thomas Aquinas Goggin. 2 vols. Washington, DC: Catholic University Press of America, 1960–69.

Church of England. *The Book of Common Prayer, 1559: The Elizabethan Prayer Book.* Charlottesville: Folger Shakespeare Library and University of Virginia Press, 1976.

Book of Common Prayer. With the Psalter or Psalmes of David. Of that Translation which is appointed to be used in Churches. London: Robert Barker, 1616.

Certain Sermons or Homilies Appointed to be Read in the Time of Queen Elizabeth I (1623). Ed. Mary Ellen Rickey and Thomas B. Stroup. Gainesville: Scholar's Facsimiles and Reprints, 1968.

Clapham, Henoch. *An Epistle Discoursing Upon the Present Pestilence.* London: T. C. for the Widow Newbery, 1603.

Clarke, Samuel. *The Marrow of Ecclesiastical History.* London: Robert White for William Roybould, 1654.

The Second Part of the Marrow of Ecclesiastical History. London: Thomas Sawbridge and William Birch, 1675.

Clifford, Anne. *The Diaries of Lady Anne Clifford.* Ed. D. J. H. Clifford. Wolfeboro Falls, NH: Alan Sutton, 1990.

Coffin, Edward. "A True Relation of the Last Sickeness and Death of Cardinall Bellarmine who dyed in Rome the seavententh day of September 1621. And of such things as happened in, or since his Buriall." In Bellarmino, *Art of Dying*, pp. 329–416.

Cogan, Thomas. *The Haven of Health.* London: Henrie Middleton for William Norton, 1584.

Collins, Arthur, ed. *Letters and Memorials of State in the Reigns of Queen Mary, Queen Elizabeth, King James, King Charles the First, Part of the Reign of King Charles the Second and Oliver's Usurpation.* 2 vols. London: T. Osborne, 1746.

Comper, Francis M. M. (ed.). *The Book of the Craft of Dying and Other Early English Tracts Concerning Death.* New York: Arno Press, 1977.

Darcie, Abraham. *Funerall Tears. (Fraunces, Duchess Dowager of Richmond and Lenox, Etc., her Funerall Teares).* London: J. Beale for R. Field, 1624.

Dekker, Thomas. *English Villanies.* London: M. Parsons, 1638.

The Wonderfull yeare 1603: Wherein is shewed the picture of London, lying sicke of the Plague. London: Thomas Creede, 1603.

De Mornay, Charlotte d'Arbaleste. *Histoire de la vie de Messire Phillippe de Mornay Seigneur du Plessis Marly, &c.* Leyden: Bonaventure & Abraham Elsevier, 1647.

De Mornay, Philippe. *Philip Mornay, Lord of Plessis his Teares for the Death of his Sonne. Unto his Wife Charlotte Baliste.* Trans. John Healey. London: G. Eld, 1609.
Philippi Mornai Lachrima. Paris, 1606.

De Vere, Anne. "Foure Epytaphes, made by the Countes of Oxenford after the death of her young Sonne, the Lord Bulbeck." In John Soowthern, *Pandora*, C3v–C4v. New York: Columbia University Press, 1938.

Dunton, John. *The Mourning-Ring.* London: John Dunton, 1682.

England and Wales, Sovereign (1603–25: James I). *Orders thought meete by his Majestie and his Privie Counsell, to be executed throughout the Counties of this Realme, in such Townes, Villages, and other places as are, or may be hereafter infected with the Plague, for the stay of furher increase of the same.* London: Robert Barker, 1603.

Erasmus, Desiderius. "The Funeral." In *Ten Colloquies.* Trans. Craig R. Thompson, pp. 92–112. Indianapolis: Bobbs-Merrill, 1957.
The Preparation to Deathe. London: Thomas Berthelet, 1538.
A treatyse perswading a man paciently to suffer the death of his freende (De morto declamatio). London: Thomas Berthelet, 1531.

Evelyn, John. *The Diary of John Evelyn.* Ed. E. S. de Beer. 3 vols. Oxford: Clarendon Press, 1955.

Falconer, John. *The Mirrour of Created Perfection.* St. Omer: English College Press, 1632.

Fenton, Roger. *A Perfume Against the Noysome Pestilence, Prescribed by Moses Unto Aaron.* London: R. R. for William Aspley, 1603.

Fuller, Thomas. *The Church History of Britain: From the Birth of Jesus Christ until the Year M. C. D. XLVIII.* Ed. J. S. Brewer. Oxford University Press, 1845.
The Holy State. Cambridge: Roger Daniel for John Williams, 1642.

Gaichard, Claude. *Funerailles, & diverses maineres d'enseuelir des Rommain, Grecs, & autres nations, tant anciennes que modernes.* Lyons: Jean de Tournes, 1581.

Goad, Thomas. "Approbation." In Jocelin, *Mothers Legacie*, A3–A10v.

Gouge, William. *Of Domesticall Duties: Eight Treatises.* London: J. Haviland for W. Bladen, 1622.

Greenhill, Thomas. *Nekrokedeia, or The Art of Embalming.* London: Thomas Greenhill, 1705.

Grey, Lady Jane. *Life, Death, and Actions of the Most Chast, learned and Religious Lady Jane Grey, Daughter to the Duke of Suffolke.* London: G. Eld for John Wright, 1615.

Grymeston, Elizabeth. *Miscellanea, Meditations, Memoratives.* London: Felix Norton, 1604.

Guibert, Philibert. *The Charitable Physitian.* Trans. J. W. London: Thomas Harper, 1639.

Gunter, Humphrey. *A Profitable Memoriall of the Conversion, Life and Death of Mistris Mary Gunter, set up as a Monument to be looked upon, both by Protestants and Papists.* In Thomas Taylor, *Pilgrims Profession*, pp. 121–92.

Hall, Joseph. *The King's Prophecie, or Weeping Joy.* London, 1603.

Har, W. *Epicedium: A Funerall Song Upon Lady Helen Branch.* London: Thomas Creede, 1594.

Harington, John. *Ariosto's Orlando Furioso*. Ed. Robert McNulty. Oxford: Clarendon Press, 1972.

Harrison, William. *Deaths Advantage, Little Regarded, and the Soules Solace Against Sorrow. Preached in Two Funerall sermons at Childwal in Lancashire at the Buriall of Mistres Katherin Brettergh the third of June 1601. The one by William Harrison, one of the Preachers appointed by her Majestie for the Countie Palatine of Lancaster, the other by William Leygh, Bachelor of Divinitie and Pastor of Standish. Whereunto is annexed, the Christian life and godly death of the said Gentlewoman*. London: Felix Kyngston, 1602.

Herbert, Mary Sidney. *The Collected Works of Mary Sidney Herbert, Countess of Pembroke*, Ed. Margaret P. Hannay, Noel J. Kinnamon, and Michael G. Brennan. 2 vols. Oxford: Clarendon Press, 1998.

A Discourse of Life and Death and Marcus Antonius. London: William Ponosby, 1592.

A Discourse of Life and Death. In Hannay, et al. (eds.), *Collected Works*, vol. 1, pp. 229–54.

"The Dolefull Lay of Clorinda." In Hannay, et al. (eds.), *Collected Works*, vol. 1, pp. 119–35.

Herbert, William. *Herberts Child-Bearing Woman From the Conception to the Weaning of the Child*. London: R. A. and J. M, 1648.

Heywood, Thomas. *A Funerall Elegie upon the Much Lamented Death of the Trespuissant and unmatchable King, King James*. London: Thomas Harper, 1625.

Hinde, William. *A Brief Discourse of the Christian Life and Death of Mistris Katherin Brettergh, the late wife of Master William Brettergh of Bretterghoult in the Countie of Lancaster, who departed this world the last of May, 1601*. London: Felix Kyngston, 1601.

Hoby, Margaret. *Diary of Lady Margaret Hoby, 1599–1605*. Ed. Dorothy M. Meads. London: Routledge, 1930.

Hoby, Thomas. *The Travels and Life of Sir Thomas Hoby, Knight, of Bisham Abbey, Written by Himself, 1547–1564*. Ed. Edgar Powell. London: Royal Historical Society, 1902.

Hodges, Nathaniel. *Loimologia: Or An Historical Account of the Plague in London in 1665*. London: E. Bell, 1720.

Holinshed, Raphael. *Chronicles of England, Scotland, and Ireland*. 6 vols. New York: AMS Press, 1965.

Hughes, George. *The Art of Embalming Dead Saints discovered in a Sermon preached at the Funerall of Master William Crompton, the later Reverend and Faithfull Pastor of the Church in Lanceston Cornwall, January the fifth, 1641*. London: A. N. for John Rothwell, 1642.

Jocelin, Elizabeth. *The Mothers Legacie to her Unborne Childe*. London: F. K. for Robert Allot, 1635.

Johnson, Richard. *Anglorum Lacrimae: In a sad passion complayning the death of our late Souveraigne Lady Queene Elizabeth: Yet Comforted againe by the vertuous hopes of our most Royall and Renowned King James: whose Majestie God long Continue*. London: Thomas Pavier, 1603.

Jonson, Ben. *Ben Jonson*. Ed. C. H. Herford, Percy Simpson and Evelyn Simpson. 11 vols. Oxford University Press, 1925–52.

Josselin, Ralph. *The Diary of Ralph Josselin, 1616–1683*. Ed. Alan MacFarlane. Oxford University Press, 1976.

King Thomas, and Raines, F. R., eds. *Lancashire Funeral Certificates*. Manchester: Chetham Society, 1869.

Langhorne, Lancelot. *Mary Sitting at Christs Feet, With the Christian Life and Comfortable Death of Mrs. Mary Swaine, for the encouraging of all Christian Gentlewomen, and other to walke in the steps of the religious Gentlewoman.* London: M. F. for Edward Wright, 1610.

Lanyer, Aemilia. *The Poems of Aemilia Lanyer: Salve Deus Rex Judaeorum*. Ed. Susanne Woods. Oxford University Press, 1993.

Leech, Jeremy. *A Sermon Preached before the Lords of the Councel, in K. Henry the Seavenths Chapell, Sept. 23, 1607 At the Funerrall of the most excellent & hopefull Princes, the Lady Marie's Grace*. London: H. L. for Samuel Macham, 1607.

Leigh, Dorothy. *The Mothers Blessing: Or, The Godly Counsaile of a Gentle-woman, Not Long Since Deceased, Left Behind for her Children*. London: John Budge, 1618.

Leigh, William. *The Soules Solace Against Sorrow*. London: Felix Kingston, 1602.

Lorrain, Paul. *Rites of Funeral Ancient and Modern, in Use Through the Known World*. London: R. Royston, 1683.

Lupset, Thomas. *A Compendius & Very Fruitful Treatyse Teachynge the Waye of Dyenge Well*. London: Thomas Berthelet, 1541.

Luther, Martin. *The Pagan Servitude of the Church*. In Dillenberger, John (ed.), *Martin Luther: Selections from his Writings*, pp. 249–361. New York: Anchor, 1961.

Machyn, Henry. *The Diary of Henry Machyn*. Ed. John Gough Nichols. London: Camden Society, 1848.

Maningham, John. *The Diary of John Manningham of the Middle Temple, 1602–1603*. Ed. Robert Parker Sorlien. Hanover, NH: University Press of New England for the University of Rhode Island Press, 1976.

Markham, Gervase. *Marie Magdalens Lamentations for the Losse of her Master Jesus*. London: Adam Islip for Edward White, 1601.

   The Teares of the Beloved, or The Lamentation of Saint John. London: Simon Stafford for John Browne, 1602.

Mavericke, Radford. *The Mourning Weede*. In *Three Treatises Religiously Handled, and named according to the severall subjects of each Treatise: The Mourning Weede. The Mornings Joy. The Kings Rejoycing*. London: John Windet, 1603.

Mayer, John. *A Patterne for Women: Setting forth the most Christian life and most comfortable death of Mrs. Lucy, late wife to the worshipfull Roger Thornton, Esquire*. London: Edward Griffin for John Marriot, 1619.

Mildmay, Grace, Lady. *Autobiography*. In Martin, Randall (ed.), *Women Writers of Renaissance England*, pp. 211–31. London and New York: Longman, 1997.

Milton, John. *Paradise Lost*. Ed. Steve Ellredge. New York: W. W. Norton, 1975.

Muggins, William. *London's Mourning Garment, or Funerall Teares: Worne and Shed for the Death of her Wealthy Citizens, and other her Inhabitants*. London: Ralph Blower, 1603.

Mulcaster, Richard. *The Translation of Certaine Latine Verses Written Uppon her Majesties Death, Called A Comforting Complaynt.* London: Edward Aggas, 1603.

Myddelmore, Henry. *The Translation of a letter written by a Frenche Gentilwoman to another Gentilwoman Straunger, her friend, upon the death of the most excellent and virtuous Ladye, Elenor of Koye, Princes of Conde, contayning her last wyll and Testament.* London: John Day for Humfrye Toye, 1564.

Nashe, Thomas. *Christs Teares Over Jerusalem, Whereunto is annexed, a comparative admonition to London.* In McKerrow, Ronald B. (ed.), *The Works of Thomas Nashe*, vol. 2, pp. 1–186. 2 vols. London: A. H. Bullen, 1904.

Newcome, Henry. *The Autobiography of Henry Newcome, M. A.* Ed. Richard Parkinson. 2 vols. Manchester: Charles Simms and Co., 1852.

Newton, Thomas. *Atropoion Delion, or, The Death of Delia: With the Teares of her Funerall. A Poeticall Excusive Discourse of our late Eliza.* London: W. Johnes, 1603.

An Epitaphe upon the worthy and honorable Lady, the Lady Knowles. London: William How for Richard Jones, n. d.

Niccols, Richard. *Epicedium. A Funeral Oration upon the death of the late deceased Princesse of famous memorye, Elizabeth by the grace of God, Queen of England, France and Ireland.* London: E. White, 1603.

Three Sister Teares at the Most Solemne Death of Henry Prince of Wales. London: Richard Redmer, 1613.

Norton, Lady Frances. *Memento Mori; or Meditations on Death.* London: John Graves, 1705.

Osborne, Francis. *Historical Memoirs of the Reigns of Queen Elizabeth and King James.* London: J. Grismond, 1658.

Oxford English Dictionary. Compact Edition. 2 vols. Oxford University Press, 1971.

Peacham, Henry. *Thestylis astrata: or, A Funerall Elegie upon the Death of the Right Honourable, most Religious and Noble Lady, Frances, Countess of Warwicke.* London: J. H. for Francis Constable, 1634.

Perkins, William. *A Salve for a Sick Man.* Cambridge: John Legate, 1595.

Persons, Robert. *A Discussion of the Answer of M. William Barlow.* St. Omer: English College Press, 1612.

Peter of Luca. *A Dialogue of Dying Wel.* Trans. R. Verstegan. Antwerp: A. C., 1603.

Petowe, Henry. *Elizabetha quasi vivens, Eliza's Funerall.* London: E. Allde for M. Lawe, 1603.

Petrarch, Francis. "How a Ruler Ought to Govern His State" [*Seniles* 14:1]. In Kohl, Benjamin G. and Witt, Ronald G. (eds.), *The Earthly Republic: Italian Humanists on Government and Society*, pp. 77–9. Philadelphia: University of Pennsylvania Press, 1978.

Philips, Katherine. "Epitaph: On her son H. P. at St. Syth's Church where her body also lies Interred." In Saintsbury, George (ed.), *Minor Poets of the Caroline Period*, vol. 1, p. 582. 2 vols. Oxford: Clarendon Press, 1905.

"In Memory of F. P. who died at Acton on the 24 of May, 1660, at Twelve and a Half of Age." In Saintsbury (ed.), *Minor Poets*, vol. 1, pp. 530–1.

"Orinda upon little Hector Philips." In Saintsbury (ed.), *Minor Poets*, vol. 1, p. 590.

"On the death of my first and dearest childe, Hector Philips, borne the 23rd of Aprill, and dy'd the 2d of May 1655. set by Mr Lawes." In Greer, et al. (eds.), *Kissing the Rod*, pp. 196–7.

Phillips, Edward. *Theatrum Poetarum, or a Compleat Collection of all the Poets of all Ages*. London: Charles Smith, 1675.

Phillips, J. *An Epitaphe on the death of the right noble and most vertuous Lady Margarit Duglass good grace, Countesse of Linnox*. London: Edward White, 1578.

Playfere, Thomas. *The Meane in Mourning. A Sermon Preached at Saint Maries Spittle in London on Tuesday in Easter Weeke, 1595*. London: Felix Kyngston for Matthew Law, 1607.

Ponet, John. *Diallacticon viri boni et literati, de veritate corporis Christi in Eucharista*. Strasburg: R. Rihel, 1557.

Powell, Thomas. *Vertues Due: or, A True Modell of the Life of the Right Honorable Katherine Howard, Late Countess of Nottingham*. London: Simon Stafford, 1603.

Primrose, Diana. *A Chaine of Pearle, or A Memoriall of the peerles Graces, and Heroick Vertues of Queene Elizabeth, of Glorious Memory*. London: Thomas Paine by Philip Waterhouse, 1630.

Proctor, Thomas. *A Gorgeous Gallery of Gallant Inventions*. Ed. Hyder Rollins. Cambridge, MA: Harvard University Press, 1926.

Raines, F. R., ed. *A Description of the State, Civil, and Ecclesiastical, of the County of Lancaster About the Year 1590*. Manchester: Chetham Society, 1875.

Read, Alexander. *Chirurgorum Comes: Or the Whole Practice of Chirurgery*. London: Edward Jones for Christopher Wilkinson, 1687.

Rogers, Thomas. *Celestiall Elegies of the Goddesses and the Muses, Deploring the Death of the Right Honourable and Vertuous Ladie, the Ladie Fraunces Countesse of Hertford, late wife unto the right honourable Edward Seymor, Viscount Beauchamp and Earle of Hertford*. London: Richard Bradocke, for J. B., 1598.

Russell, Elizabeth. *A Way of Reconciliation, of a good and learned man, touching the Truth, Nature, and Substance of the Body and Blood of Christ in the Sacrament*. London: R. Barker, 1605.

S., H. *Queen Elizabeths Losse and King James his Welcome*. London: T. C. for John Sythicke, 1603.

Shakespeare, William. *The Riverside Shakespeare*. Ed. G. Blakemore Evans, et al. 2nd edn. Boston: Houghton Mifflin, 1996.

Sidney, Philip. *A Defence of Poetry*. Ed. J. A. Van Dorsten. Oxford University Press, 1966.

Soowthern, John. *Pandora*. Ed. George Parks. New York: Columbia University Press, 1938.

Southwell, Robert. *Saint Peter's Complaint and Saint Mary Magdalens Funerall Teares*. London: Society of Jesuits, 1620.

The Triumphs Over Death. London: V. S. for John Busbie, 1595.

Speght, Rachel. *Mortalities Memorandum, with A Dreame Prefixed.* In Lewalski, Barbara Kiefer (ed.), *The Polemics and Poems of Rachel Speght,* pp. 43–90. Oxford University Press, 1996.

A Mouzell for Melastomus. In Lewalski (ed.), *Polemics and Poems,* pp. 1–28.

Spenser, Edmund. *Daphnaida. An Elegie Upon the Death of the Noble and Vertuous Douglas Howard.* London: William Ponsonby, 1591.

Stubbes, Phillip. *The Anatomie of Abuses.* London: Richard Jones, 1583.

A Chrystal Glasse for Christian Women. London: Richard Jones, 1592.

Sutcliffe, Alice. *Meditations of Mans Mortalitie.* Ed. Patrick Cullen. In *The Early Modern Englishwoman: A Facsimile Library of Essential Works,* Part 1, vol 7. Aldershot: Scolar Press, 1996.

Sutton, Christopher. *Disce Mori: Learne to Die.* London: John Wolfe, 1600.

Sweetnam, John. *S. Mary Magdalens Pilgrimage to Paradise.* St Omer: English College Press, 1617.

Swetnam, Joseph. *Arraignment of Lewd, Idle, Froward and Unconstant Women.* London: George Purslowe for Thomas Archer, 1615.

Tasso, Torquato. *Gerusalemme liberata.* Ed. Marziano Guglielminetti. Milan: Garzanti, 1982.

Taylor, Jeremy. *The Rule and Exercises of Holy Dying.* London: R. R. for William Ballard, 1651.

Taylor, John, the Water Poet. *Life and Death of the Most Blessed among women, the Virgin Mary.* London: George Eld, 1620.

Taylor Thomas. *The Pilgrims Profession, or a Sermon Preached at the Funerall of Mistris Mary Gunter by Mr. Thomas Taylor To Which (by his consent) also is added, A Short Relation of the Life and deth of the said Gentile-woman as a perpetuall Monument of her graces and vertues.* London J. D. for John Bartlett, 1622.

Thimelby, Gertrude. "Upon a Command to Write on my Father." In Clifford, Arthur (ed.), *Tixall Poetry,* p. 92. Edinburgh: James Ballantyne and Co., 1813.

Thornton, Alice. *The Autobiography of Mrs. Alice Thornton.* Durham: Andrews & Company, 1875.

Tuke, Thomas. *A Discourse of Death, Bodily, Ghostly, And Eternall, Nor unfit for Souldiers Warring, Seamen sayling, Strangers traveling, Women Bearing, nor any other living that thinkes of Dying.* London: William Stansbie for George Norton, 1613.

Vaughn, Edward. *A Divine Discoverie of Death.* London: William Jones for Richard Boyle, 1612.

W., T. *The Lamentation of Melpomene for the death of Belphoebe our Late Queene.* London: W. W. for C. K., 1603.

Wager, Lewis. *The Life of Marie Magdalene.* London: John Charlewood, 1566.

Ward, Samuel. *The Life of Faith in Death. Exemplified in the Living speeches of dying Christians.* London: Augustine Mathewes, for John Marriot and John Grismand, 1622.

Webster, John. *The Duchess of Malfi.* Ed. Elizabeth M. Brennan. New York: W. W. Norton, 1985.

Weever, John. *Ancient Funeral Monuments.* London: Thomas Harper, 1631.

Werdmuller, Otto. *A Most frutefull, pithye and learned Treatyse, how a Christen man ought to behave himself in the daunger of death.* Trans. Miles Coverdale. London: William Blackwell, 1590.

White, Dorothy. *A Lamentation Unto this Nation.* London: Robert Wilson, 1660.

Whitford, Richard. *A Dayly Exercyse and Experyence of Death.* London: J. Waylande, 1537.

Whitney, Isabella. "The Manner of her Will, or What She left to London." In *A Sweet Nosgay*, E2–E8v. London: Richard Jones, 1573.

"The Lamentacion of a Gentilwoman upon the death of her late deceased frend William Gruffith Gent." In Proctor, *Gorgeous Gallery*, pp. 116–20.

Wolcomb, Robert. *The State of the Godly Both in this Life and in the Life to Come. Delivered in a Sermon at Chudleigh in Devon at the Funeralls of the right Worshipfull the Ladie Elizabeth Courtney, the 11 of November 1605, Whereunto is Annexed the Christian life and godly death of the sayd worshipfull Lady Elizabeth Courtney.* London: Roger Jackson, 1606.

SECONDARY SOURCES

Abraham, Nicholas, and Torok, Maria. "Introjection–Incorporation: Mourning *or* Melancholia." In Lebovici, Serge, and Widlocher, Daniel (eds.), *Psychoanalysis in France*, pp. 3–16. New York: International University Press, 1980.

Alexiou, Margaret. *Ritual Lament in Greek Tradition.* Cambridge University Press, 1974.

Ariès, Philippe. *Centuries of Childhood: A Social History of Family Life.* Trans. Robert Baldick. New York: Vintage Books, 1962.

The Hour of Our Death. Trans. Helen Weaver. New York: Knopf, 1981.

Images of Man and Death. Trans. Janet Lloyd. Cambridge, MA: Harvard University Press, 1985.

Western Attitudes Towards Death: From the Middle Ages to the Present Time. Trans. Patricia Ranum. Baltimore: Johns Hopkins University Press, 1974.

Aughterson, Kate, ed. *Renaissance Woman: A Source Book. Constructions of Femininity in England.* London and New York: Routledge, 1995.

Ballard, George. *Memoirs of Several Ladies of Great Britain: Who Have Been Celebrated for Their Writings or Skill in the Learned Languages, Arts, and Sciences.* Ed. Ruth Perry. Detroit: Wayne State University Press, 1985.

Barasch, Moshe. *Gestures of Despair in Medieval and Early Renaissance Art.* New York University Press, 1976.

Barbour, Reid. *English Epicures and Stoics: Ancient Legacies in Early Stuart Culture.* Amherst: University of Massachusetts Press, 1998.

Beaty, Nancy Lee. *The Craft of Dying: A Study of the Literary Tradition of the Ars Moriendi in England.* New Haven: Yale University Press, 1970.

Begent, Peter J. *The Heraldry of the Hoby Memorials in the Parish Church of All Saints, Bisham, in the Royal County of Berkshire.* Maidenhead: Peter J. Begent, 1979.

Beier, Lucinda McCray. "The Good Death in Seventeenth-Century England." In Houlbrooke (ed.), *Death, Ritual, and Bereavement*, pp. 43–61.

Beilin, Elaine V. *Redeeming Eve: Women Writers of the English Renaissance*. Princeton University Press, 1987.

Belsey, Catherine. *Shakespeare and the Loss of Eden*. New Brunswick: Rutgers University Press, 1999.

The Subject of Tragedy: Identity and Difference in Renaissance Drama. New York: Methuen, 1985.

Bevington, David. *Medieval Drama*. Boston: Houghton Mifflin, 1975.

Boesky, Amy. "Giving Time to Women: The Eternizing Project in Early Modern England." In Clarke and Clarke (eds.), *"This Double Voice,"* pp. 123–41.

Bornstein, Diane. "The Style of the Countess of Pembroke's Translation of Philippe de Mornay's *Discours du la vie et de la mort*." In Hannay (ed.), *Silent But for the Word*, pp. 126–48.

Braden, Gordon. *Renaissance Tragedy and the Senecan Tradition: Anger's Privilege*. New Haven: Yale University Press, 1985.

Brayley, Edward Wedlake. *The History and Antiquities of the Abbey Church of St. Peter, Westminster*. 2 vols. London: Hurt, Robinson and Co., 1823.

Burgess, Clive. "'Longing to be Prayed For': Death and Commemoration in an English Parish in the Later Middle Ages," in Gordon and Marshall (eds.), *Place of the Dead*, pp. 44–65.

Butler, Judith. *Gender Trouble: Feminism and the Subversion of Identity*. New York and London: Routledge, 1990.

Camporesi, Piero. *The Incorruptible Flesh: Bodily Mutation and Mortification in Religion and Folklore*. Trans. Tania Corft-Murray. Cambridge University Press, 1988.

Charnes, Linda. *Notorious Identity: Materializing the Subject in Shakespeare*. Cambridge, MA: Harvard University Press, 1993.

Chaunu, Pierre. *La Mort à Paris: XVIe, XVIIe et XVIIIe siècles*. Paris: Fayard, 1978.

Clarke, Danielle and Clarke, Elizabeth (eds.). *"This Double Voice": Gendered Writing in Early Modern England*. Houndsmills, Basingstoke, Hampshire: Macmillan, 2000.

Cole, Susan Letzer. *The Absent One: Mourning, Ritual, Tragedy and the Performance of Ambivalence*. State College: Penn State University Press, 1985.

Corthell, Robert. "Robert Persons and the Writer's Mission." In Marotti (ed.), *Catholicism and Anti-Catholicism*, pp. 35–62.

Coster, Will. "Tokens of Innocence: Infant Baptism and Burial in Early Modern England." In Gordon and Marshall (eds.), *Place of the Dead*, pp. 266–87.

Crawford, Patricia. "The Construction and Experience of Maternity in Seventeenth-century England." In Fildes, Valerie (ed.), *Women as Mothers in Pre-Industrial England: Essays in Memory of Dorothy McLarne*, pp. 3–38. London and New York: Routledge, 1990.

"From a Woman's View: Pre-Industrial England, 1500–1750." In Crawford, Patricia (ed.), *Exploring Women's Past: Essays in Social History*, pp. 49–86. Sydney: George Allen and Unwin, 1983.

Women and Religion in England, 1500–1720. London and New York: Routledge, 1993.

Cressy, David. *Birth, Marriage and Death: Ritual, Religion, and the Life-Cycle in Tudor and Stuart England*. Oxford University Press, 1997.

"Response: Private Lives, Public Performance, and Rites of Passage." In Travitsky and Seeff (eds.), *Attending to Women*, pp. 187–97.

Crull, Jodacus. *The Antiquities of St. Peter's, or the Abbey-Church of Westminster*. 2 vols. London: E. Bell, 1722.

Crump, Lucy. *A Huguenot Family in the XVI Century: The Memoirs of Philippe de Mornay, Sieur de Plessis Marly Written by his Wife*. London: George Routledge, 1926.

Cunnington, Phillis and Lucas, Catherine. *Costume for Births, Marriages and Deaths*. London: Adam and Charles Black, 1972.

Daniell, Christopher. *Death and Burial in Medieval England, 1066–1550*. London and New York: Routledge, 1997.

Dart, John. *Westmonasterium, or The History and Antiquities of The Abbey Church of St. Peters Westminster*. 2 vols. London: James Cole, 1723.

Davey, Richard. *A History of Mourning*. London: McCorquodale and Co., 1890.

Davis, Natalie Zemon. *Society and Culture in Early Modern France*. Stanford University Press, 1975.

Dean, Paul. "Dramatic Mode and Historical Vision in Henry VIII." *Shakespeare Quarterly* 37 (1986): 176–89.

Demers, Patricia. "The Seymour Sisters: Elegizing Female Attachment." *Sixteenth Century Journal* 30 (1999): 343–365.

Diehl, Huston. *Staging Reform, Reforming the Stage: Protestantism and Popular Theater in Early Modern England*. Ithaca: Cornell University Press, 1997.

Doebler, Bettie Anne. *Rooted Sorrow: Dying in Early Modern England*. London and Toronto: Associated University Presses, 1994.

Doebler, Bettie Anne and Warnicke, Retha M. "Sex Discrimination After Death: A Seventeenth-Century English Study." *Omega* 17 (1986–7): 309–19.

Dolan, Frances E. "'Gentlemen, I have one thing more to say': Women on Scaffolds in England, 1563–1680." *Modern Philology* 92 (1994): 157–78.

Whores of Babylon: Catholicism, Gender and Seventeenth-Century Print Culture. Ithaca: Cornell University Press, 1999.

Dottie, Roy G. "The Recusant Riots at Childwall in May, 1600: A Reappraisal." *Transactions of the Historic Society of Lancashire and Cheshire* 132 (1982): 1–28.

Duffy, Eamon. *The Stripping of the Altars: Traditional Religion in England, c. 1400–1580*. New Haven and London: Yale University Press, 1992.

Earwaker, J. P. (ed.). *Lancashire and Cheshire Wills and Inventories 1572–1696*. Manchester: Chetham Society, 1893.

Eggert, Katherine. *Showing Like a Queen: Female Authority and Literary Experiment in Spenser, Milton and Shakespeare*. Philadelphia: University of Pennsylvania Press, 2000.

Eire, Carlos M. N. *The War Against the Idols: The Reformation of Worship from Erasmus to Calvin*. Cambridge University Press, 1986.

Emmison, F. G. *Essex Wills (England) 1558–1565*. 2 vols. Washington, DC: National Genealogical Society, 1982.

Engel, William G. *Mapping Mortality: The Persistence of Memory and Melancholy in Early Modern England*. Amherst: University of Massachusetts Press, 1995.

Enterline, Lynn. *Tears of Narcissus: Melancholia and Masculinity in Early Modern Writing*. Stanford University Press, 1995.

Ezell, Margaret J. M. *The Patriarch's Wife: Literary Evidence and the History of the Family*. Chapel Hill: University of North Carolina Press, 1987.

Farber, Elizabeth. "The Letters of Lady Elizabeth Russell (1540–1609)." PhD dissertation, Columbia University, 1977.

Finucane, R. C. "Sacred Corpse, Profane Carrion: Social Ideals and Death Rituals in the Later Middle Ages." In Whaley, Joachim (ed.), *Mirrors of Mortality: Studies in the Social History of Death*, pp. 49–60. London: Europa, 1981.

Forbes, Thomas R. "By What Disease or Casualty: The Changing Face of Death in London." In Webster (ed.), *Health, Medicine and Mortality*, pp. 117–39.

Ford, David Nash. "Beaten 'til the Blood Ran." http://www.britannia.com/history/legend/bisham.html.

Fortunati, Vera. *Lavinia Fontana of Bologna, 1552–1614*. Milan: Electa, 1998.

Freud, Sigmund. "Mourning and Melancholia." In Strachey, James, et al. (eds.), *The Standard Edition of the Complete Psychological Works*, vol. 14, pp. 243–58. 24 vols. London: The Hogarth Press, 1974.

Fritz, Paul S. "The Undertaking Trade in England: Its Origins and Early Development, 1660–1830." *Eighteenth-Century Studies* 28:2 (1994–5): 241–53.

Gabrieli, Vittorio. *Sir Kenelm Digby: Un inglese italianato nell'eta della controriforma*. Rome: Edizioni di storia e letteratura, 1957.

Geary, Patrick. *Living With the Dead in the Middle Ages*. Ithaca: Cornell University Press, 1994.

Ghirardi, Angela. "Exempla per l'iconografia dell'Infanzia nel secondo Cinquecento padano." *Il Carrobbio* 21–22 (1993–4): 123–39.

Gittings, Clare. *Death, Burial and the Individual in Early Modern England*. London: Croom Helm, 1984.

Gladstone, Helen C. "Building an Identity: Two Noblewomen in England, 1566–1666." PhD dissertation, Open University, 1989.

Glimp, David. "Staging Government: Shakespeare's *Life of King Henry the Eighth* and the Government of Generations." *Criticism* 41 (1999): 41–66.

Goodland, Katharine. "'Why Should Calamity Be Full of Words?' The Representation of Women's Laments for the Dead in Medieval England and Shakespearean Drama." PhD dissertation, Purdue University, 1999.

Gordon, Bruce. "Malevolent Ghosts and Ministering Angels: Apparitions and Pastoral Care in the Swiss Reformation." In Gordon and Marshall (eds.), *Place of the Dead*, pp. 87–109.

Gordon, Bruce and Marshall, Peter (eds.). *The Place of the Dead: Death and Remembrance in Late Medieval and Early Modern Europe*. Cambridge University Press, 2000.

Graham, Elspeth, Hinds, Hilary, Hobby, Elaine, and Wilcox, Helen (eds.). *Her Own Life: Autobiographical Writings by Seventeenth-Century Englishwomen.* London and New York: Routledge, 1989.

"'Pondering All These Things In Her Heart:' Aspects of Secrecy in the Autobiographical Writings of Seventeeth-Century Englishwomen." In Broughton, Trev Lynn and Anderson, Linda (eds.), *Women's Lives / Women's Times: New Essays on Auto/Biography*, pp. 51–72. Albany: State University of New York Press, 1997.

Greer, Germaine, Hasting, Susan, Medoff, Jeslyn, and Sansone, Melinda (eds.). *Kissing the Rod: An Anthology of Seventeenth-Century Women's Verse.* London: Virago, 1988.

Hackett, Helen. *Virgin Mother, Maiden Queen: Elizabeth I and the Cult of the Virgin Mary.* New York and London: Macmillan, 1995.

Haigh, Christoper. *Elizabeth I.* New York: Longman, 1988.

Hammons, Pamela. "Despised Creatures: The Illusion of Maternal Self-Effacement in Seventeenth-Century Child Loss Poetry." *ELH* 66 (1999): 25–49.

Hannay, Margaret Patterson. *Silent But For the Word: Tudor Women as Patrons, Translators, and Writers of Religious Works.* Kent State University Press, 1985.

Harding, Vanessa. "Whose Body? A Study of Attitudes Towards the Dead Body in Early Modern Paris." In Gordon and Marshall (eds.), *Place of the Dead*, pp. 170–87.

Haskins, Susan. *Mary Magdalen: Myth and Metaphor.* New York: Harper Collins, 1993.

Heal, Felicity. "Reputation and Honour in Court and Country: Lady Elizabeth Russell and Sir Thomas Hoby." *Transactions of the Royal Historical Society*, series 6, vol. 6: 161–78.

Helt, J. S. W. "Women, Memory and Will-Making in Elizabethan England." In Gordon and Marshall (eds.), *Place of the Dead*, pp. 188–205.

Hobby, Elaine. "Orinda and Female Intimacy." In Pacheco, Anita (ed.). *Early Women Writers: 1600–1720*, pp. 73–88. New York: Longman, 1998.

Hooper, Wilfrid. "The Tudor Sumptuary Laws." *English Historical Review* 30 (1915): 433–49.

Houlbrooke, Ralph A. *The English Family, 1450–1700.* London and New York: Longman, 1984.

Death, Religion and the Family in England, 1480–1750. Oxford: Clarendon Press, 1997.

(ed.). *Death, Ritual, and Bereavement.* London and New York: Routledge, 1989.

Howard, Jean E. and Rackin, Phyllis. *Engendering a Nation: A Feminist Account of Shakespeare's English Histories.* New York and London: Routledge, 1997.

Hughey, Ruth. "A Ballad of Lady Jane Grey." *Times Literary Supplement*, Dec. 7, 1988: 878.

Hull, Suzanne F. *Chaste, Silent, and Obedient: English Books for Women, 1475–1640.* San Marino: Huntington Library, 1982.

Hunt, Maurice. "The Hybrid Reformations of Shakespeare's Second Henriad." *Comparative Drama* 32 (1998): 176–206.

Hutson, Lorna. *The Usurer's Daughter: Male Friendships and Fiction of Women in Sixteenth-Century England.* London and New York: Routledge, 1994.

Kay, Dennis. *Melodious Tears: The English Funeral Elegy from Spenser to Milton.* Oxford: Clarendon, 1990.

Kightly, Charles. *The Customs and Ceremonies of Britain: An Encyclopaedia of Living Traditions.* New York: Thames and Hudson, 1986.

Lamb, Mary Ellen. "The Cooke Sisters: Attitudes Towards Learned Women in the Renaissance." In Hannay (ed.), *Silent But For the Word*, pp. 107–25.

Gender and Authorship in the Sidney Circle. Madison: University of Wisconsin Press, 1990.

Laqueur, Thomas. *Making Sex: Body and Gender from the Greeks to Freud.* Cambridge, MA: Harvard University Press, 1990.

Laurence, Anne. "Goodly Grief: Individual Responses to Death in Seventeenth Century Britain." In Houlbrooke (ed.), *Death, Ritual, and Bereavement*, pp. 62–76.

Levin, Carole. "Lady Jane Grey: Protestant Queen and Martyr." In Hannay (ed.), *Silent But For the Word*, pp. 92–106.

Lewalski, Barbara Keifer. *Writing Women of Jacobean England.* Cambridge, MA: Harvard University Press, 1993.

Lilley, Kate. "True State Within: Women's Elegy 1640–1740." In Grundy, Isobel and Wiseman, Susan (eds.), *Women, Writing, History 1640–1740*, pp. 72–92. Athens: University of Georgia Press, 1992.

Litten, Julian. *The English Way of Death: The Common Funeral Since 1450.* London: R. Hale, 1991.

Llewellyn, Nigel. *The Art of Death: Visual Culture in The English Death Ritual, c. 1500–1800.* London: Reaktion Books, 1991.

"Honour in Life, Death, and in the Memory: Funeral Monuments in Early Modern England." *Transactions of the Royal Historical Society* ser. 6, vol. 6 (1996): 179–200.

"The Royal Body: Monuments to the Dead for the Living." In Gent, Lucy and Llewellyn, Nigel (eds.), *Renaissance Bodies: The Human Figure in English Culture, 1540–1660*, pp. 218–40. London: Reaktion Books, 1990.

Long, Donna J. " 'It is a lovely bonne I make to thee': Mary Carey's 'abortive Birth' as Recuperative Religious Lyric." In Johnson, Jeff and Cunnar, Eugene (eds.), *Discovering and Recovering the Seventeenth-Century Religious Lyric.* Pittsburgh: Duquesne University Press, forthcoming.

Longueville, Thomas. *The Life of Sir Kenelm Digby.* London: Longmans, 1896.

Loomis, Catherine. "Elizabeth Southwell's Manuscript Account of the Death of Queen Elizabeth [with text]." *English Literary Renaissance* 26 (1996): 482–509.

Loraux, Nicole. *Mothers in Mourning.* Trans. Corinne Pache. Ithaca: Cornell University Press, 1998.

Lupton, Julia Reinhard and Reinhard, Kenneth. *After Oedipus: Shakespeare in Psychoanalysis.* Ithaca: Cornell University Press, 1993.

MacDonald, Michael. *Mystical Bedlam: Madness, Anxiety and Healing in Seventeenth Century England.* Cambridge University Press, 1981.

McGuire, Brian Patrick. "Purgatory, the Communion of the Saints, and Medieval Change." *Viator* 20 (1989): 61–84.

McPherson, Kathryn. "Great-Bellied Women: Religion and Maternity in Seventeenth-Century England." PhD dissertation, Emory University, 1998.

Marcus, Leah. *Puzzling Shakespeare: Local Reading and its Discontents.* Berkeley: University of California Press, 1988.

Marotti, Arthur F. "Alienating Catholics in Early Modern England: Recusant Women, Jesuits, and Ideological Fantasies." In Marotti (ed.), *Catholicism and Anti-Catholicism*, pp. 1–34.

   (ed.). *Catholicism and Anti-Catholicism in Early Modern English Texts.* New York: St. Martin's, 1999.

Marshall, Peter. "'The Map of God's Word': Geographies of the Afterlife in Tudor and Stuart England." In Gordon and Marshall (eds.), *Place of the Dead*, pp. 110–30.

Martin, Randall. "Isabella Whitney's 'Lamentation upon the Death of William Gruffith.'" *Early Modern Literary Studies* 3 (1997): http://purl.oclc.org/emls/03-1/martwhit.html.

   (ed.). *Women Writers of the Renaissance.* New York: Longman, 1998.

Martino, Ernesto di. *Morte e pianto rituale nel mondo antico: Dal lamento pagano al pianto di Maria.* Turin: Einaudi, 1958.

May, Steven. "The Countess of Oxford's Sonnets: A Caveat." *ELN* 29 (1992): 9–19.

Mazzio, Carla and Trevor, Douglas, eds. *Historicism, Psychoanalysis and Early Modern Culture.* New York and London: Routledge, 2000.

Micheli, Linda McJ. "'Sit By Us': Visual Imagery and the Two Queens in *Henry VIII.*" *Shakespeare Quarterly* 38 (1987): 452–66.

Moody, Ellen. "Orinda, Rosania, Lucasia, *et aliae*: Toward a New Edition of Katherine Philips." *Philological Quarterly* 66 (1987): 325–54.

   "Six Elegiac Poems, Possibly by Anne Cecil de Vere, Countess of Oxford." *English Literary Renaissance* 19 (1989): 152–70.

Moulton, Ian Frederick. "'A Monster Great Deformed': The Unruly Masculinity of Richard III." *Shakespeare Quarterly* 47 (1996): 251–68.

Mullaney, Steven. "Mourning and Misogyny: *Hamlet, The Revenger's Tragedy* and the Final Progress of Elizabeth I." *Shakespeare Quarterly* 45 (1994): 139–62.

Murdin, William. *A Collection of State Papers Relating to Affairs in the Reign of Queen Elizabeth from the Year 1571 to 1596.* London: William Bowyer, 1759.

Neill, Michael. *Issues of Death: Mortality and Identity in English Renaissance Tragedy.* Oxford: Clarendon Press, 1997.

Newman, Karen. *Fashioning Femininity and English Renaissance Drama.* University of Chicago Press, 1991.

Nichols, John. *The Progresses and Public Processions of Queen Elizabeth.* 3 vols. London: John Nichols and Son, 1823.

Noling, Kim H. "Grubbing Up the Stock: Dramatizing Queens in *Henry VIII*." *Shakespeare Quarterly* 39 (1988): 291–306.

Orlin, Lena Cowen. *Private Matters and Public Culture in Post-Reformation England.* Ithaca: Cornell University Press, 1994.

Park, Katharine. "The Criminal and the Saintly Body: Autopsy and Dissection in Renaissance Italy." *Renaissance Quarterly* 47 (1994): 1–34.

Paster, Gail Kern. *The Body Embarrassed: Drama and the Disciplines of Shame in Early Modern England.* Ithaca: Cornell University Press, 1993.

Pigman, G. W., III. *Grief and English Renaissance Elegy.* Cambridge University Press, 1985.

Rambuss, Richard. *Closet Devotions.* Durham and London: Duke University Press, 1998.

Rackin, Phyllis. "*Richard III*." In Howard and Rackin, *Engendering a Nation,* pp. 100–18.

Stages of History: Shakespeare's English Chronicles. Ithaca: Cornell University Press, 1990.

Ramazani, Jahan. *The Poetry of Mourning: The Modern Elegy from Hardy to Heaney.* University of Chicago Press, 1994.

Registers of Bisham, County Berkshire, 1560–1812. Transcribed by Edgar Powell. London: Parish Register Society, 1898.

Roberts, Penny. "Contesting Sacred Space: Burial Disputes in Sixteenth-Century France." In Gordon and Marshall (eds.), *Place of the Dead,* pp. 131–48.

Rose, Mary Beth. "Gender, Genre and History: Seventeenth Century Women and the Art of Autobiography." In Rose, Mary Beth (ed.), *Women in the Middle Ages and the Renaissance,* pp. 245–78. New York: Columbia University Press, 1985.

"Where are the Mothers in Shakespeare? Options for Gender Representation in the English Renaissance." *Shakespeare Quarterly* 42 (1991): 291–314.

Rowse, A. L. "Bisham and the Hobies." In *Times, Persons, Places: Essays in Literature,* pp. 188–218. London: Macmillan, 1965.

Rudnytsky, Peter L. "*Henry VIII* and the Deconstruction of History." *Shakespeare Survey 43* (1991), pp. 43–57.

Sawday, Jonathan. *The Body Emblazoned: Dissection and the Human Body in Renaissance Culture.* New York and London: Routledge, 1995.

Schenck, Celeste. "Feminism and Deconstruction: Re-Constructing the Elegy." *Tulsa Studies in Women's Literature* 5 (1986): 13–27.

Schiesari, Juliana. *The Gendering of Melancholia: Feminism, Psychoanalysis, and the Symbolics of Loss in Renaissance Literature.* Ithaca: Cornell University Press, 1992.

Schleiner, Louise. *Tudor and Stuart Women Writers.* Bloomington: Indiana University Press, 1994.

Schofield, Roger and Wrigley, E. A. "Infant and Child Mortality in England in the Late Tudor and Early Stuart Period." In Webster (ed.), *Health, Medicine and Mortality,* pp. 61–96.

Sheingorn, Pamela. *The Easter Sepulcher in England.* Kalamazoo: Medieval Institute Publications, 1987.

Shepherd, Simon, ed. *The Women's Sharp Revenge: Five Women's Pamphlets from the Renaissance.* New York: St. Martin's Press, 1985.

Shifflett, Andrew. *Stoicism, Politics and Literature in the Age of Milton: War and Peace Reconciled.* Cambridge University Press, 1998.

Shuger, Debora. *Habits of Thought in the English Renaissance: Religion, Politics, and the Dominant Culture.* Berkeley: University of California Press, 1990.

Slack, Paul. *The Impact of the Plague in Tudor and Stuart London.* London: Routledge and Kegan Paul, 1985.

"Mirrors of Health and Treasures of Poor Men: The Uses of the Vernacular Medical Literature of Tudor England." In Webster (ed.), *Health, Medicine and Mortality*, pp. 65–236.

Slights, Camille Wells. "The Politics of Conscience in *All is True* (or *Henry VIII*)." *Shakespeare Studies* 43 (1991): 59–68.

Spelman, Elizabeth V. "Woman as Body: Ancient and Contemporary Views." *Feminist Studies* 8 (1982): 109–31.

Stevenson, Jane. "Female Authority and Authorization Strategies in Early Modern Europe." In Clarke and Clarke (eds.), *"This Double Voice,"* pp. 16–41.

Stewart, Alan. "The Voices of Anne Cooke, Lady Anne and Lady Bacon." In Clarke and Clarke, (eds.), *"This Double Voice,"* pp. 88–102.

Sticca, Sandro. *The Planctus Mariae in the Dramatic Tradition of the Middle Ages.* Trans. Joseph R. Berrigan. Athens: University of Georgia Press, 1988.

Stone, Lawrence. *The Family, Sex and Marriage 1500–1800.* New York: Harper and Row, 1977.

Strocchia, Sharon T. *Death and Ritual in Renaissance Florence.* Baltimore: Johns Hopkins University Press, 1992.

Strong, Roy. *The Cult of Elizabeth: Elizabethan Portraiture and Pageantry.* London: Thames and Hudson, 1977.

Targoff, Ramie. "The Performance of Prayer: Sincerity and Theatricality in Early Modern England." *Representations* 60 (1997): 49–65.

Tarlow, Sarah. *Bereavement and Commemoration: An Archaeology of Mortality.* Oxford: Basil Blackwell, 1999.

Taylor, Larissa Juliet. "Funeral Sermons and Orations as Religious Propaganda in Sixteenth-Century France." In Gordon and Marshall (eds.), *Place of the Dead*, pp. 224–38.

Taylor, Lou. *Mourning Dress: A Costume and Social History.* London: George Allen and Unwin, 1983.

Telushkin, Joseph. *Jewish Literacy.* New York: William Morrow, 1991.

Todd, Margo. "Humanists, Puritans, and the Spiritualized Household." *Church History* 49 (1989): 18–34.

Travis, Peter. "The Social Body of the Dramatic Christ in Medieval England." *Early Drama to 1600, Acta* 13 (1985): 17–36.

Travitsky, Betty S. "His Wife's prayers and meditations: MS Egerton 607." In Haselkorn, Anne M. and Travitsky, Betty S. (eds.), *The Renaissance English-woman in Print: Counterbalancng the Canon*, pp. 241–60. Amherst: University of Massachusetts, 1990.

"The 'Wyll and Testament' of Isabella Whitney." *English Literary Renaissance* 10 (1980): 76–94.

Travitsky, Betty S. and Seeff, Adele F. (eds.). *Attending to Women in Early Modern England*. Newark: University of Delaware Press, 1994.

Tromly, Fredric B. "'Accordinge to sounde religion': The Elizabethan Controversy Over the Funeral Sermon." *JMRS* 13 (1983): 293–312.

The Victoria History of the Counties of England: Berkshire. Ed. William Page. 3 vols. London: University of London, 1972.

Walker, Julia M. "Reading the Tombs of Elizabeth I." *English Literary Renaissance* 26 (1996): 510–30.

Walker, Kim. *Women Writers of the English Renaissance*. New York: Twayne, 1996.

Wall, Wendy. *The Imprint of Gender: Authorship and Publication in the English Renaissance*. Ithaca: Cornell University Press, 1993.

Walsham, Alexandra. *Church Papists: Catholicism, Conformity and Confessional Polemic in Early Modern England*. Woodbridge, Suffolk: Royal Historical Society and Boydell Press, 1993.

Providence in Early Modern England. Oxford University Press, 1999.

Walter, John. "Grain Riots and Popular Attitudes to the Law: Maldon and the Crisis of 1629." In Brewer, John and Styles, John (eds.), *An Ungovernable People: The English and their Law in the Seventeenth and Eighteenth Centuries*, pp. 47–84. New Brunswick: Rutgers University Press, 1980.

Warnicke, Retha M. "Lady Mildmay's Journal: A Study in Autobiography and Meditation in Reformation England." *Sixteenth Century Journal* 20 (1989): 55–68.

"Eulogies for Women: Public Testimony of their Godly Example and Leadership." In Travitsky and Seeff (eds.), *Attending to Women*, pp. 168–86.

Warnicke, Retha M. and Doebler, Bettie Anne (eds.). *Deaths Advantage Little Regarded*. Delmar, New York: Scholars' Facsimiles and Reprints, 1993.

Watkins, John. "'Out of her Ashes May a Second Phoenix Rise': James I and the Legacy of Elizabethan Anti-Catholicism." In Marotti (ed.), *Catholicism and Anti-Catholicism*, pp. 116–36.

Watkins, Owen C. *The Puritan Experience*. London and New York: Routledge, 1972.

Wayne, Valerie. "Advice for Women from Mothers and Patriarchs." In Wilcox, Helen (ed.), *Women and Literature in Britain, 1500–1700*, pp. 56–79. Cambridge University Press, 1996.

Webster, Charles, ed. *Health, Medicine and Mortality in the Sixteenth Century*. Cambridge University Press, 1979.

Westminster Abbey Record Series. *Act of the Dean & Chapter of Westminster, 1543–1609*. Ed. C. S. Knighton. 2 vols. Woodbridge: Boydell Press, 1999.

Whinney, Margaret. *Sculpture in Britain, 1530–1830.* London: Penguin Books, 1988.

White, Adam. "Classical Learning and the Early Stuart Renaissance." *Church Monuments* 1 (1985): 20–33.

"Westminster Abbey in the Early 17th Century: A Powerhouse of Ideas." *Church Monuments* 4 (1989): 15–53.

Wiffen, J. H. *Memoirs of the House of Russell.* 3 vols. London: Longman, 1833.

Wilcox, Helen. "My Soule in Silence? Devotional Representations of Renaissance Englishwomen." In Summers, Claude J. and Pebworth, Ted-Larry (eds.), *Representing Women in Renaissance England,* pp. 9–23. Columbia: University of Missouri Press, 1997.

Williamson, George C. *Lady Anne Clifford, Countess of Dorset, Pembroke & Montgomery, 1590–1676, Her Life, Letters and Work.* East Ardsley, Wakefield, Yorkshire: S. R. Publishers, Ltd., 1967.

Wilson, F. P. *The Plague in Shakespeare's London.* Oxford University Press, 1927.

Wilson, Violet. *Society Women of Shakespeare's Time.* London: John Lane, 1924.

Index